MICROSOFT OFFICE 2000

NO EXPERIENCE REQUIRED

MICROSOFT® OFFICE 2000
NO EXPERIENCE REQUIRED™

Gini Courter
Annette Marquis

SYBEX®

San Francisco • Paris • Düsseldorf • Soest• London

Associate Publisher: Amy Romanoff
Contracts and Licensing Manager: Kristine O'Callaghan
Acquisitions & Developmental Editor: Sherry Bonelli
Editor: Anamary Ehlen
Project Editor: Malka Geffen
Technical Editor: B.K. DeLong
Book Designers: Patrick Dintino, Catalin Dulfu, Maureen Forys
Graphic Illustrator: Tony Jonick
Electronic Publishing Specialist: Nila Nichols
Production Coordinators: Julie Sakaue and Charles Mathews
Indexer: Matthew Spence
Cover Designer: Design Site
Cover Illustrator/Photographer: Jack D. Myers

Library of Congress Card Number: 99-60014
ISBN: 0-7821-2293-0

Manufactured in the United States of America

10 9 8 7 6 5 4 3 2 1

Contents at a Glance

skills

Table of Contents

Introduction

Office 2000: No Experience Required is designed to help you understand and master the essential skills required to get the most out of Microsoft Office 2000. You might have "No Experience" in Office 2000, but we assume that you know more than a small amount about PCs: that you can find your way around floppy disks and hard drives and can use a mouse (or can figure it out on your own), and understand basic concepts like the difference between saving and opening files. So we won't bore you with long explanations of entry-level topics. Instead, we'll help you learn about program features that will make a difference in the way you work with each of the products in the Office 2000 Professional Suite. Prepare yourself for a marvelous adventure: this version of Office Pro really hums!

About This Book

This book has three sections. The first section, Skill 1, is a warm-up that gets you ready to work with the user interface common to the various programs in Office 2000. The second section, Skills 2–10, features the applications themselves: six in all, and each incredibly dynamic. The third section, Skills 11–13, focuses on more advanced topics, like macros and Web publishing, that are used in more than one Office 2000 program. To master any of the Office 2000 applications, you'll need to hit all three sections to get a good start, a thorough grounding in application-specific topics, and a real workout in the advanced features.

Each skill begins with a Featuring list that highlights the contents of the skill. Throughout the skill, you'll find lists of the steps (see below) to follow to complete a task: construct a form, sort a list, create a new style. If you need a refresher or have to get something done in a hurry, you can go directly to the list. Skills are divided into sections—1.1, 1.2, and so on—that cover one or more topics.

CREATING A STYLE

1. Select cells that are the same as, or similar to, the style you want to create.
2. Choose Format ➤ Style from the menu bar.
3. Enter a new name for the style.
4. Use the check boxes to disable formatting features that should not be included in the style.
5. Click the Modify button and change any format options you wish in the Format Cells dialog box. Click OK to close the dialog box.
6. Click the Add button to add the new style. Click Close to close the dialog box, or click OK to apply the style to the current selection and close the Style dialog box.

Your knowledge of computer applications, like any true skill, will increase with hands-on practice. Beginning with Skill 2, each section ends with Hands On exercises that you can use to practice what you've learned in the section. Each skill ends with *Are You Experienced?*: a list of topics that you can use to inventory your personal proficiency in the techniques and concepts you've just acquired.

If, like many users, you've learned many of your computer skills under pressure, rushing to meet a deadline, you've probably had to be satisfied with discovering one method that got the job done. Most of us hang on to that single method and use it from that point forward. But in Windows programs, there's always more than one way to accomplish a task, and in some situations, one method may be clearly superior to the others. This is a good time to increase your skills portfolio by learning the *best*, most *efficient* ways to work in the Office 2000 programs. Watch for Tips, like the one shown below, which provide shortcuts or additional information so you can work more efficiently with the software.

TIP TIP TIP TIP TIP TIP TIP TIP TIP TIP TIP TIP TIP TIP TIP TIP TIP TIP TIP TIP TIP TIP TIP

You can also enter notes directly from Slide Show view. Right-click on a slide to open the shortcut menu, and select Speakers Notes to open the Notes dialog box for that slide. Enter your note, then choose OK to return to the Slide Show.

All Office 2000 applications have an Undo button to reverse the latest action. But some actions can't be undone, or can only be undone if you notice the problem immediately. Throughout this book, warnings like the one shown below are provided when actions are irreversible, or when the integrity of your completed document could be compromised by an error that's relatively easy to make, like assuming that a formula will recalculate when the underlying numbers change.

WARNING WARNING WARNING WARNING WARNING WARNING WARNING WARNING

If you change any of the numbers in cells included in the formula, you must select the cell with the results and click AutoSum again. Word's AutoSum does not recalculate on its own.

Text that needs to be entered literally is set in a different type style. For example, you might be instructed to enter the name Johnson in an Outlook item, or =Hours * Rate as a formula in Excel.

A Quick Tour of the Book

Skill 1, "Working in Office 2000," is a quick survey of terms, features, and techniques common to all the Office 2000 applications. If you're moving to Office 2000 from DOS or mainframe applications, this chapter will help you get used to the 32-bit Office environment. If you've used previous Windows versions of Office or other Windows applications, skim through the skill to find out what's new in Office 2000 and to make sure you're prepared to move on to the applications.

Skills 2–10 cover the Office 2000 Professional applications. Skills 2, 3, and 4 cover Word 2000 word-processing software from beginning to end. Skills 5 and 6 focus on Excel, the number-crunching data analysis and charting program. Skill 7 covers PowerPoint, from planning an electronic presentation to delivering it on the Internet. In Skill 8, you'll learn how to create an Access database from scratch. Skill 9 will get you up and running in Outlook 2000, the newest version of the desktop information manager that's become the new corporate standard. And in Skill 10, you'll create and publish documents ranging from brochures to newsletters to Web pages using Publisher 2000, the newest addition to Office Professional. Skills 2 through 10 don't assume that you've learned one application before another, so you can begin with any of the Office 2000 programs.

Skills 11, 12, and 13 turn to advanced topics that are relevant to more than one Office 2000 application. Skill 11 addresses object linking and embedding (OLE), and shows you how to use Office applications as OLE clients and servers to display data from one program in another. Skill 12 focuses on creating Web-based documents for Internet and intranet use. In Skill 13, you'll learn the basics of macro creation for Office 2000 products.

Where to Go from Here

Begin with Skill 1 for an introduction to the common features of the Office 2000 products. Then, focus on a particular application and develop your skills in that area. If you're new to Office 2000, it's a good idea to start with Word, Skills 2–4. You probably are familiar with the concepts behind word processing, and you'll find it easiest to build on your text-based knowledge there. If you already have some Windows experience, you can head right to one of the other applications if you prefer. With the exception of Publisher, skills for each application are not dependent on each other, so you can work through applications in the order that makes the most sense to you. Skill 10 assumes a working knowledge of the Word information in Skills 2 and 3.

Skill 11 covers graphics and object linking and embedding. To get the most from OLE, you need proficiency with at least two Office 2000 applications. Skill 12, "Internet Publishing with Office 2000," shows you how to create Web-ready documents in Word, Excel, PowerPoint, Outlook, Publisher, and Access. When you've completed the skill(s) for any of these applications, you can jump to Skill 12 and learn how to publish your creations as HTML documents. Skill 13, "Creating and Using Macros in Office 2000," assumes that you are proficient with Word, Excel, or PowerPoint and ready to create macros to automate tasks in those applications.

We hope this book does what it is intended to do, and that the skills you learn will help you exceed your expectations and extend your personal goals. Let us know; we enjoy hearing from our readers.

Annette Marquis and Gini Courter
Sybex, Inc.
1151 Marina Village Parkway
Alameda, CA 94501

e-mail: authors@triadconsulting.com

SKILL 1

Working in Office 2000

- → **Using features of application windows**
- → **Working with files**
- → **Entering and editing text**
- → **Selecting, moving, and copying text**
- → **Enhancing text with fonts and colors**

Today's software tools provide many challenges, but they also provide even greater opportunities to show off your skills, impress your boss and your customers, and earn the respect–and envy–of your co-workers. Microsoft Office 2000 is a toolkit jam-packed with powerful tools. Whether you work for a multinational corporation or run your own small business, Office 2000's top-of-the-line tools will help you upgrade your existing skills so you can work smarter and more efficiently. With Office 2000 you can manage your busy calendar, track important contacts, make sound financial projections, produce impressive proposals, create dynamite presentations, and establish and maintain a sensational presence on the World Wide Web.

This skill will familiarize you with the shared features in Office 2000. If you've used Office 95 or Office 97, a lot of this will be old territory, but you should still quickly work through the skill, particularly to see the new and enhanced features in Office 2000. So whatever your prior experience, we recommend that you skim "Working in Office 2000;" you're sure to pick up one or two new concepts that you'll use over and over.

1.1: Mastering Office Pro

Microsoft Office Professional 2000 features some of the most popular and powerful software programs around. The suite includes the latest, most powerful versions of Microsoft's award-winning office productivity tools:

- Word: word processor
- Excel: spreadsheet
- Access: database
- PowerPoint: presentation software
- Outlook: desktop information manager
- Publisher: design and layout software

If you have worked with prior releases of these products, you'll just need to learn some new and improved techniques for the Office 2000 version. Office 2000 programs support better integration than ever before: between applications, between yourself and other users, and with the Internet and intranets. The Office 2000 suite now includes Microsoft Publisher, to help you design and lay out all kinds of printed materials from newsletters to letterhead to invitations.

Office Professional 2000 also includes a number of smaller tools:

- Microsoft Graph: a program to create line, bar, and pie charts for use in Office applications

- WordArt: a text-graphics program

- The Clip Gallery: an archive of clip art, sounds, and video

All the applications include the Office Assistant, an active Help feature that offers timesaving advice to help you work more efficiently.

1.2: Exploring Common Features in Office

One of the best things about Office 2000 software is that each application has several useful features in common. If you want to save a letter in Word, a database in Access, or a spreadsheet in Excel, the Save button not only looks the same but you can locate it in approximately the same place. This section explores some of Office's universal, commonly used features to give you a general introduction. You'll get more detailed, application-specific information in upcoming skills on each Office component.

Launching the Shortcut Bar and New Office Documents

Typical of Windows applications, you have more than one way to get the job done. You can start using Office 2000 three ways: clicking a New Document button on the Office Shortcut Bar, using the Start menu to open a New Office Document, or navigating through the Programs menu to open the actual Office application. The Microsoft Office Shortcut Bar does not automatically appear the first time you use Office 2000 after installation. To open it, click the Start button and choose Programs ➤ Microsoft Office Tools ➤ Microsoft Office Shortcut Bar. You'll be asked if you want it to open automatically when you launch Windows, and then the Shortcut Bar will appear in its default position along the right side of the screen:

NOTE NOTE NOTE NOTE NOTE NOTE NOTE NOTE NOTE NOTE NOTE NOTE NOTE NOTE NOTE
The Office Shortcut Bar opens vertically by default. You can click and drag it against any edge of the screen, or drag it out to make it a free-floating palette.

The Shortcut Bar is, obviously, the easiest way to launch any of the Office 2000 applications, and it even has a button for Publisher. If you elect not to show the Shortcut Bar on your desktop, try one of these other two ways to open a new document or an Office application. Click the Windows Start button to open the Start menu:

Choose New Office Document or Open Office Document from the top of the Start menu. For brand-new, blank documents, Office 2000 presents you with a host of choices via the New Office Document dialog box—everything from memos and legal briefs to spreadsheets and Web pages are represented there. If you prefer to launch the application and then open a document, choose Programs from the Start menu. The Office 2000 programs appear as individual choices on the Programs menu. Click any program to launch it.

Using the Office 2000 Interface

The Office 2000 applications share a common user interface. This means, for example, that once you're familiar with the *application window* in Excel (see Figure 1.1), getting around in the application window in Word will be a piece of cake. Likewise, you'll notice a lot of other similarities between the applications. Working in Windows applications is like déjà vu; you will see certain features and tools again and again.

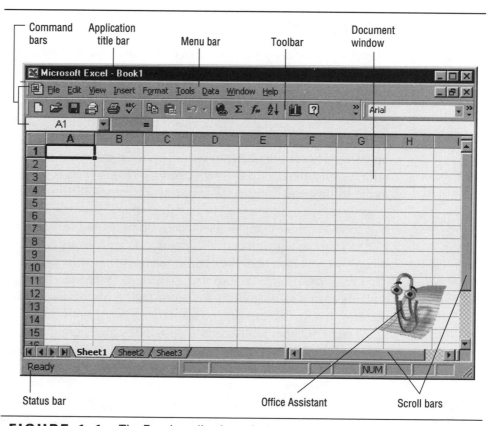

FIGURE 1.1: The Excel application window

At the top of each application window is a *title bar* that contains three buttons: Minimize, Maximize or Restore, and Close. Use these buttons to change the size of your window or to close the window itself. When you're working in an application, you'll usually want to maximize it. Before you switch to something else, minimizing the first application will free up system resources, making more memory available to the active application. When a window is maximized, the Restore button is displayed; when it is restored, the Maximize button is displayed. Even with the application window maximized, the Windows Taskbar shows all open applications, so you can easily switch between open Office 2000 applications by clicking an application's Taskbar button. Clicking the Close button on the title bar closes the application, returning you to the Windows desktop or to another open application.

The Document Window

In each application, your work area is known as the *document window*. Here you're surrounded by the tools you need to get the job done: *scroll bars* to move the display, a status bar to keep you informed of an operation's progress, and the *command bars* at the top of the screen to access all the program's features. You'll use two types of command bars: menu bars and toolbars. The menu bar organizes the features into categories: File, Edit, Help, etc. Clicking on any of the categories opens up a list of related features for you to choose from. Many of the menu bar options open dialog boxes which allow you to set several options at once related to the feature you choose—all the print options, all the font settings, etc.

Toolbars are the command bars with graphical buttons located below the menu bar. Toolbars make many of the most commonly used features only one click away. Use toolbars when you want a shortcut to a common feature and the menu bar when you want to see *all* the options related to a feature.

In Office 2000, Personal toolbars, comprised of the Standard and Formatting toolbars of previous versions, share one row to conserve space in the document window. If a toolbar button you want to use is not available, click the down arrow to the right of either toolbar and choose the button from the list. This button will replace a less frequently used button from your toolbar. Use toolbars when you want a shortcut to a common feature and the menu bar when you want to see *all* the options related to a feature.

Office 2000 menus are also personalized to the features you use most commonly. If a pull-down menu has more than a handful of commands, Microsoft has "folded" up less commonly used features. When you see a set of small, double arrows at the bottom of a pull-down menu, select them to reveal all the menu commands, or wait a few seconds, and the menu will "unfold"—you don't even need to click the mouse (see Figure 1.2).

FIGURE 1.2: The Word Edit menu with all the available commands showing

NOTE NOTE NOTE NOTE NOTE NOTE NOTE NOTE NOTE NOTE NOTE NOTE NOTE NOTE NOTE

If the Personal toolbars option does not suit you, you can display full menus and view the complete Standard and Formatting toolbars on separate rows by choosing View ➣ Toolbars ➣ Customize and clearing the first three check boxes on the Options tab.

Accessing Commands

If toolbars and menu bars aren't enough, you can execute commands from one of the many context-sensitive shortcut menus or by using shortcut keys. For example, to copy selected text in any application, you can:

- Click the Copy button on the Standard toolbar.

- Choose Edit ➢ Copy from the menu bar.

- Right-click on the selected text; then choose Copy from the free-floating shortcut menu.

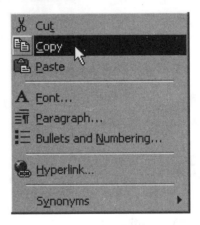

- Hold Ctrl and press C.

Notice that the Copy button and the keyboard shortcut are both shown on the Copy menu selection, so you can use the menu bar to help you identify quicker ways to access features you commonly use. *ScreenTips* provide additional help with commands. If you're uncertain which toolbar button to use, point to the button and hover for a moment; a ScreenTip will appear, showing the button's name.

The Office Assistant

The *Office Assistant* is Microsoft's social help interface for Office 2000. The Office Assistant (see Figure 1.3) crosses all applications and provides help for specific features of each application. You can choose from several Assistants by selecting

Choose Assistant from the shortcut menu. Each has its own "personality," including Rocky the power puppy, Mother Nature symbolized as a globe, and an animated Genius with a definite resemblance to Albert Einstein.

FIGURE 1.3: Office Assistant Clippit offering help

The new, improved Office Assistant is free to move around within the application window and displays tips that guide you to better ways to complete a task. The Assistant will offer help the first time you work with a feature or if you have difficulty with a task. Sometimes the offer is subtle—Clippit will blink, Rocky wags his tail, or the Genius produces a light bulb. Sometimes the Assistant can be entertaining; in Office 2000 the Assistant icon changes shape during certain basic tasks like saving or running SpellCheck. Offers of help can also be a bit more direct. If, for example, you open a Wizard, the Office Assistant pops up to ask if you'd like help with the feature.

After you've worked with Office 2000 for a few days, you might decide that you'd like a little less help from your eager Assistant. To change the Assistant's options, right-click on the Assistant, and then choose Options from the shortcut menu to open the Office Assistant dialog box. Click the Options tab to display the Options page, shown in Figure 1.4.

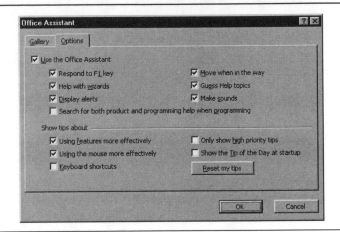

FIGURE 1.4: The Office Assistant dialog box

The Office Assistant is shared by all the Office 2000 programs. Any options you change affect the Assistant in all the Office programs, so if you need an increased level of assistance with Excel, you get the same increased level of assistance with Word.

When you're ready to go it alone, you can close the Assistant window to return it to the Standard toolbar. If you start to get lonely, just click the Office Assistant button to invite the Assistant back into your office.

TIP TIP TIP TIP TIP TIP TIP TIP TIP TIP TIP TIP TIP TIP TIP TIP TIP TIP TIP TIP TIP TIP

For help with any dialog box in Office 2000, click the dialog box Help button (with the question mark), then click on the dialog box control you want help with.

1.3: Working with Files

One of the great things about Office 2000 is that the dialog boxes used for common file functions are similar in all the applications. In this section, we'll look at the common features of the dialog boxes; features specific to an application are covered in the skills for that application.

Creating Something New

You can easily create new documents from the Windows Start menu. Selecting New Office Document opens the New Office Document dialog box, shown in Figure 1.5. Each tab contains *templates* for a number of similar documents. Some of the templates (for example, the Fax templates) include text, graphics, or other content. Blank document templates for all the applications—a blank template for an Access database, Word document, Excel worksheet, and PowerPoint presentation—are found on the General page of the New Office Document dialog box.

TIP TIP TIP TIP TIP TIP TIP TIP TIP TIP TIP TIP TIP TIP TIP TIP TIP TIP TIP TIP TIP TIP TIP

Binders are collections of other documents. You use binders to hold all the documents for one project so you can switch between the documents quickly or print them all at once.

To open an application, simply double-click any document in the dialog box.

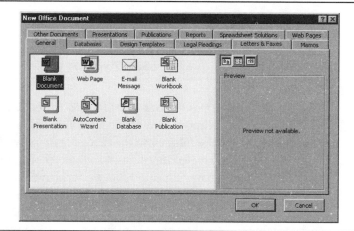

FIGURE 1.5: The New Office Document dialog box

If you're already in an application, you have two ways to create a new document. Click the New button on the Standard toolbar to open a new, blank document in the active application. If you want a new template instead of a blank document, choose File ➤ New from the menu bar to open the New Office Document dialog box with templates appropriate for the active application.

Saving a File

When you're finished working with a document or have completed a sizable amount of work and want to store it before continuing, choose File ➤ Save from the menu bar, or click the Save button on the Standard toolbar to open the Save As dialog box, shown in Figure 1.6.

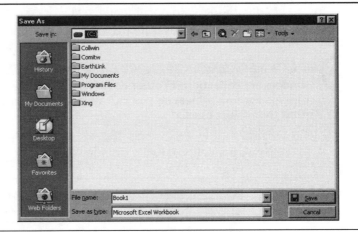

FIGURE 1.6:   The Excel Save As dialog box

The dialog box opens to your default *folder* (directory), but clicking in the Save In text box opens a drop-down list of accessible drives, as shown in Figure 1.7. Select a drive, and the folders on the drive are displayed in the pane below the list.

Double-clicking any folder opens it so that you can view the files and folders it contains. When you have located the proper drive and folder, enter a filename in the File Name text box at the bottom of the dialog box. With Windows 95/98, filenames can be up to 256 characters long, use uppercase and lowercase letters, and contain spaces. They can't contain punctuation other than underscores, hyphens, and exclamation points. And unlike filenames on the Macintosh, they are not case-sensitive: *MY FILE* and *My File* are the same filename. Make sure the name of the current drive or folder appears in the Save In text box, then click the Save button to save the file.

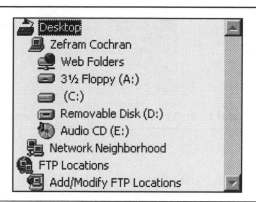

FIGURE 1.7: Save In drop-down list

 WARNING WARNING WARNING WARNING WARNING WARNING WARNING WARNING

All the Office 2000 program dialog boxes locate documents based on file *extension*—the three characters following a period in a filename. For example, Word documents have the .doc extension. Don't create your own extensions or change the extensions of existing documents. If you do, the Office 2000 applications will have trouble finding your files—and that means so will you!

Using Save As

After you've saved a file once, clicking Save saves the file without opening the dialog box. If you want to save a previously saved file with a new name or save it in another location, choose File ➢ Save As from the menu bar to open the Save As dialog box. The Save As feature is particularly useful if you are using an existing document to create a new document and you want to keep both the original *and* the revised document.

If you share files with people using other programs, or older versions of Office programs, they may not be able to open your Office 2000 files. You can, however, save your file in a format they can open. In the Save As dialog box, scroll through the Save As Type drop-down list and select an appropriate file format. The Save As Type drop-down list from Word is shown in Figure 1.8.

FIGURE 1.8: Save As Type drop-down list

Closing a File

To remove a document from the document window, choose File ➤ Close. If you close a document that has been changed since it was last saved, you will be prompted to save your changes.

Sending Files Using E-mail

Every Office 2000 application—Word, Excel, PowerPoint, Outlook, Access, and Publisher—has two new standard features to help you send files via e-mail. You can either send your file as an e-mail message, or you can attach it to an existing e-mail message, by simply choosing one File menu option.

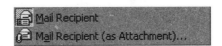

To send a document as an e-mail message, open it in the appropriate Office application and choose File ➤ Send To ➤ Mail Recipient. A space appears at the top of the document where you can fill in the e-mail address(es) and send it on its way.

If you prefer to send the document as an attachment, choose File ➤ Send To ➤ Mail Recipient (As Attachment). A separate e-mail window appears, showing the document as an icon in a window at the bottom, with space for you to type a message before you send it out.

Opening an Existing File

You can open an existing Office 2000 document in three ways. If the document was created recently, click the Windows Start button and open the Documents menu. If the document appears there, you're in luck—you can open it directly from the menu.

If the document doesn't appear on the Documents menu, choose Open Office Document from the Start menu, and Office opens an Open Office Document dialog box. Use the Look In drop-down list to locate the folder that contains the file.

If you're already working in PowerPoint, for example, and want to open an existing presentation, click the Open button on the Standard toolbar to open the Open dialog box, shown in Figure 1.9.

FIGURE 1.9:   PowerPoint's Open dialog box

This Open dialog box is just like the Open Existing Document dialog box, but it is filtered to only show PowerPoint files. Use the Look In drop-down list to locate the proper folder and file.

Converting Files from Other Formats

Office 2000 applications will open files created in other applications and earlier versions of Office. However, Access and Publisher use different file formats than those used in previous versions, so the application has to create a converted copy of the file before it can be opened. For instance, Access 2000 will open a database created in Access 2 or Access 97, but it tells you to convert the database, as shown in Figure 1.10. If you choose not to convert the database, you won't be able to change the database's structure, but you will still be able to use the database.

NOTE NOTE NOTE NOTE NOTE NOTE NOTE NOTE NOTE NOTE NOTE NOTE NOTE NOTE NOTE

Word, Excel, and PowerPoint documents created in Office 2000 do need to be converted before they can be opened in Office 97. You may lose a little special formatting that is only available in Office 2000, but you will still be able to work with the Office 2000 document using Office 97.

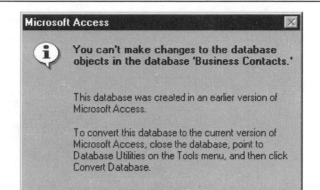

FIGURE 1.10: Access conversion prompt

Print Preview and Printing

Every Office 2000 application except PowerPoint and Publisher allows you to preview a document before printing. Click the Print Preview button on the Standard toolbar to open the preview window. The preview windows themselves vary in each application.

To print a document, choose File ➢ Print from the menu bar to open the Print dialog box, shown in Figure 1.11. While each application's Print dialog box is slightly different, all allow you to select a printer, choose a number of copies, and specify what should be printed. Clicking the Options button at the bottom of the dialog box opens an Options page where you select print quality and other settings. Application-specific Print settings are discussed in the skills for each program.

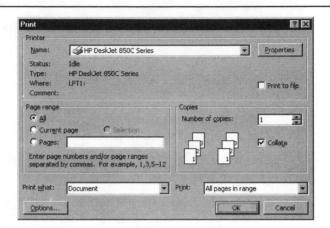

FIGURE 1.11: Word's Print dialog box

   To immediately send a document to the printer using the default print options (and without opening a dialog box), click the Print button on the Standard toolbar. This can be convenient in most of the applications, but is problematic in Power-Point, where the default print settings are full-page pictures of each slide in a presentation. What a way to tie up a printer!

1.4: Editing in Office 2000

Many editing features are shared among Office 2000 applications. Each application may have a quicker or easier way of editing in particular circumstances, but in this section, you'll learn those features that work no matter where you are or what you're doing.

The Insertion Point

The insertion point, or cursor, is the flashing vertical bar that shows where the next character you type will appear. You'll see the blinking insertion point, shown in Figure 1.12, as soon as you open a document or form. The only exception is Excel, where the insertion point only appears after you begin typing.

> All the applications include an Office Assistant, an active help
> feature that constantly monitors your actions and offers time saving advice
> to help you work more efficiently.|

FIGURE 1.12: The insertion point moves to the right as new text is added.

When you move the mouse pointer into an area where you can enter or edit text, the pointer changes to an I-beam. To edit existing text, move the insertion point by moving the I-beam to the text you want to edit. Click, and the insertion point will jump to the new position. Then you can type new text, or delete existing text, at the insertion point.

Correcting Mistakes

Helping you to correct mistakes is one of the many things Office 2000 does exceptionally well. In its simplest form, Office will let you erase existing text manually. At its most powerful, Office can automatically correct the words you most commonly misspell.

Backspace and Delete

Most people are familiar with using the Backspace and Delete keys on the keyboard to delete text, but you're not alone if you confuse when to use which one:

- Backspace (represented by a left-pointed arrow on the keyboard) erases one character to the *left* of the insertion point.

- Delete erases one character to the *right* of the insertion point.

Use whichever is more convenient, based on where your insertion point is.

Undo and Redo

Office 2000 is exceptionally forgiving. The Undo button on the Standard toolbar lets you reverse an action or a whole series of actions you have taken. The Undo button will dim when you have reached the last action you can undo. Click the drop-down arrow next to the Undo button and scroll down the history to reverse multiple actions in one step:

If you change your mind again, clicking the Redo button reverses the last Undo. In Office 2000, you can still use the Undo and Redo histories to reverse multiple actions in all the applications. Each application, though, has its own rules about how far you can undo, so it's a good idea to review that information in the specific application's skills.

Overtype and Insert Modes

The default editing mode in Office 2000 is Insert: if you enter new text in the middle of existing text, the original text will move to the right to accommodate it. Overtype mode replaces existing text with the newly entered text. To toggle between Insert and Overtype modes, press the Insert key on the keyboard.

A Quick Look at Spelling

No matter how many spelling tests you may have failed in elementary school, you can still produce documents that are free of spelling errors. The Spelling feature is available in all Office 2000 applications, including e-mail created in Outlook. Word and PowerPoint will flag misspelled words as you type by placing a wavy red line underneath possible misspellings.

mispelled

All you have to do is right-click on a flagged word to open the Spell It pop-up menu, which lists suggestions for the proper spelling. Click on the correct spelling, choose to Ignore the word, or have Office Add the spelling to your custom dictionary—a good idea with names you use a lot. That way Spell It won't flag the name the next time you use it.

In the other applications, you'll have to ask Office to check your spelling by clicking the Spelling button on the Standard toolbar. Office reviews your document, flags possible misspelled words, and opens the Spelling and Grammar dialog box:

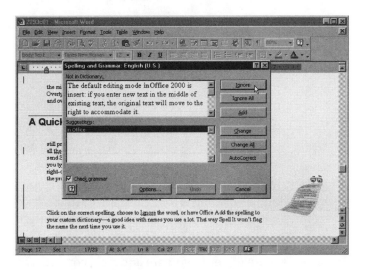

The Spelling and Grammar dialog box gives you all the same options as the Spell It pop-up menu and a few additional ones. Here you can choose to Ignore All occurrences of the word or to Change All occurrences to the correct spelling. You can also enter the correct spelling. All the Office applications share a custom dictionary, so words you add in one application aren't flagged in others.

Automatic Fixes for Common Errors

Most Office 2000 applications access a shared feature called AutoCorrect. With AutoCorrect you can build your own list of common misspellings. When Office encounters one of those words, it automatically fixes it for you. Some words, such as "adn" and "teh," are already in the list. As you correct misspelled words, you can add them to the AutoCorrect list. AutoCorrect is one of the options in both the Spell It pop-up menu and the Spelling and Grammar dialog box. You can also access it from Tools ➤ AutoCorrect.

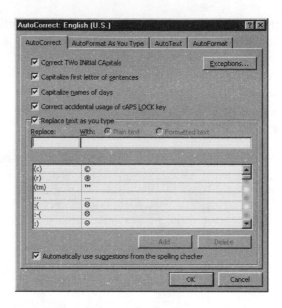

Once you add a word to the AutoCorrect list, you never have to worry about correcting the spelling error again. Also, AutoCorrect can recognize and replace common combinations of symbols like the copyright symbol (c) and the "smilicon :)" now popular online. A couple of words of caution, though:

- Be sure to verify you are adding a correctly spelled word to the Auto-Correct list.

- Don't add words that mean something else when you spell them differently. For example, if you commonly reverse the "r" and the "o" in "from," don't add this error to the AutoCorrect list, or every time you want to type "form" AutoCorrect will automatically change the word to "from."

AutoCorrect also gives you a number of options that you can leave on or turn off based on your personal preferences, such as correcting two initial capitals and capitalizing the names of days. Choose Tools ➤ AutoCorrect to open the Auto-Correct dialog box. If you want to turn AutoCorrect off entirely, click to remove the check mark in front of Replace Text As You Type. The Exceptions button provides you with two options. You can add abbreviations that you type regularly, so that AutoCorrect doesn't automatically capitalize the next word. You can also add words that require two initial caps, so it doesn't automatically change them.

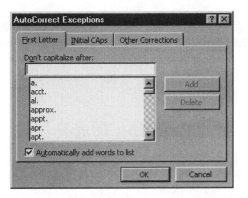

Although AutoCorrect is designed to prevent typing and spelling errors, it is also valuable as a shortcut tool. You can enter words that you type regularly into your AutoCorrect list to save yourself time and keystrokes—long company names, for example, or legal or medical terminology. Just enter a code that you will recognize, such as USA, and AutoCorrect will expand it for you into United States of America. However, if you think you will ever want to use the abbreviation without expanding it, enter a slash (/) or some other character in front of the abbreviation (/USA). Then you can choose whether to have AutoCorrect supply the long form (by typing /USA) or use the abbreviation (by typing USA without the slash).

1.5: Selecting, Moving, and Copying

Whether you are correcting mistakes or shuffling your whole document around, the first step is knowing how to select text. Once text is selected, it can be moved, copied, deleted, aligned, or resized.

Selecting Text

Each application has its own shortcuts to selecting. However, no matter where you are, you can always drag to select—even in a dialog box. To select by dragging, move the insertion point to the beginning or the end of the desired text string, hold down the mouse button, and move in the desired direction. Selected text changes to reverse video—the opposite color from the rest of the text. To unselect text, click anywhere in the document.

Selected text is automatically deleted if you press any key on the keyboard. If you accidentally delete text in a document, click Undo. Undo won't work in dialog boxes.

Moving and Copying Text

Now that you can select text, you can move and copy text in any of the Office applications; for example, you would move text to rearrange sentences in a Word document or topics in a PowerPoint presentation. When you *move* a selection, the original is deleted and placed in the new location. *Copying* text leaves the original in place, and creates a copy in the new location.

You can move text by cutting it from its current location and pasting it in a new location. When you cut a block of text, it is deleted from your document and copied to the *Clipboard*. Copying text moves a copy of the text to the Clipboard without deleting the original. The Clipboard is part of the computer's memory set aside and managed by Windows. The Clipboard can hold only one piece of information at a time, but that piece of information can be text, a graphic, or even a video clip.

MOVING OR COPYING TEXT

1. Select the text you want to move or copy.

2. Click the Cut or Copy button on the Standard toolbar.

3. Move the insertion point to where you want the text to appear.

4. Click the Paste button.

All the moving and copying techniques work with pictures or other objects just as they do with text. For more information on working with objects, see Skill 11.

TIP TIP TIP TIP TIP TIP TIP TIP TIP TIP TIP TIP TIP TIP TIP TIP TIP TIP TIP TIP TIP TIP TIP TIP

Cut, Copy, and Paste are standard Windows functions, and as a result they have corresponding shortcut keys that you can use even if menu and toolbar options are not available. Select the text or object and press Ctrl+X to cut, Ctrl+C to copy, or Ctrl+V to paste.

Pasting Multiple Items

A new feature of Office 2000 is Collect and Paste, which lets you copy up to 12 items and save them to a temporary Clipboard where you can select and paste them all at once. This makes it easier to move several items from one place to another, without forcing you to scroll up and down or split the screen.

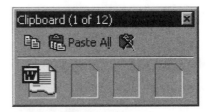

To select items for collecting and pasting, choose your items in order by pressing Edit ➤ Copy or Edit ➤ Cut, and the Clipboard toolbar appears. After you move to the new location in the document where you want to paste the items, insert them one by one by clicking them and clicking the Paste button, or clicking the Paste All button on the Clipboard toolbar.

1.6: Adding Pizzazz

One of the primary benefits of using Windows applications is the ease with which you can give your documents a professional appearance. The right combination of fonts, font styles, sizes, and attributes can make your words or numbers jump right off the page.

Fonts and Font Styles

Selecting the right font can be the difference between a professional-looking document and an amateur effort that's tedious to read. Fonts are managed by Windows, which means that a font available in one application is available in all Windows applications. You can access fonts and many of their font attributes right from the Formatting toolbar. Word's Formatting toolbar is shown in Figure 1.13.

FIGURE 1.13: Word's Formatting toolbar

To change the font, click the drop-down arrow next to the font name. Either Times New Roman or Arial is the default font, depending on the application. All Windows True Type fonts (designated by the TT in front of them) are scaleable, which means that you can make them any size by entering the desired size in the Font Size text box. Of course, you can also select from the sizes listed in the drop-down list.

To turn on Bold, Italics, or Underline, click the corresponding button on the toolbar. Remember that you must select existing text before you can change the font or font style.

For all of the available font options, choose Format ➤ Font, or in Excel choose Format ➤ Cells, and click the Font tab to open the Font dialog box:

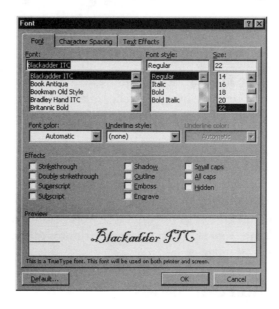

Here you can see what the fonts look like in the Preview window. You can also choose from several underline options, although the options differ depending on the application. For example, you can choose a Wave underline style in Word and a Double Accounting underline style in Excel. You can also apply a number of different effects to your text such as Strikethrough, Superscript, and Subscript. Word and PowerPoint also have effects such as Shadow and Emboss.

With all the color printers around today, being able to add colors to text is an important feature. Font Color is available from most toolbars as well as from the Font dialog box. There are also many new fancy, decorative fonts available in Office 2000, a few of which are shown in Figure 1.14.

This is Blackadder ITC.

THIS IS CASTELLAR.

This is Jokerman.

This is Lucida Calligraphy.

This is Ravie.

FIGURE 1.14: Some new decorative fonts shown in Word

Copying Existing Formats

Once you have formatted text just the way you like it, there is no need to recreate it for other text that you want formatted the same way. You can easily copy that format to other text in your document using the Format Painter.

Select the text with the format you want to copy and click the Format Painter button on the Standard toolbar. Your mouse pointer changes shape to an I-beam with a paintbrush next to it.

Drag the Format Painter I-beam over some existing text, and it will be reformatted to look just like the text you copied. Once you've applied the format, the Format Painter will turn off automatically. If you need to copy the formatting more than once, select the text you want to copy and double-click (instead of single-clicking)

the Format Painter button. When you are finished, click the Format Painter button again to turn it off.

The Format Painter not only copies fonts and font attributes but other formatting such as line spacing, bullets and numbering, borders and shading, and indents.

Are You Experienced?

Now you can...

- ☑ Use scroll bars, command bars, and other application features
- ☑ Create new documents, open existing documents, and save documents where you want in the format you choose
- ☑ Enter text and correct mistakes
- ☑ Revise text with Move and Copy
- ☑ Add formatting to text

Mastering the Basics of Word

- Creating a document
- Applying editing techniques
- Applying special formatting
- Automatically numbering or bulleting lists
- Finding text and spelling errors
- Printing your documents

Whether you are a new or seasoned Word user, in Word 2000 you will find all the features you need to create professionally designed documents. This new version of Word is loaded with helpful, timesaving features that will allow you to focus on the content of your documents rather than on how to use the software. If you're new to Microsoft Office 2000, you might want to look at Skill 1, "Working in Office 2000" and then return to this skill.

2.1: Creating Word Documents

In this section, we'll review the basics of entering and editing text in Word. If you've used other word processors, this section will introduce you to the fundamentals you need to create great-looking documents in Word 2000. If you're an experienced user of other versions of Word, this will introduce you to a number of features that are new in Word 2000.

The Word Window

Although the Word application window is similar to the other Office 2000 application windows, you're going to want to know about a few things. The document window, contained within the application window, includes a ruler bar that you'll use to set tabs and columns. You'll find View buttons at the left end of the horizontal scroll bar and Browse buttons at the bottom of the vertical scroll bar. Figure 2.1 identifies features of the Word application window that differ from those in the other Office 2000 applications.

Ruler bar   Document window

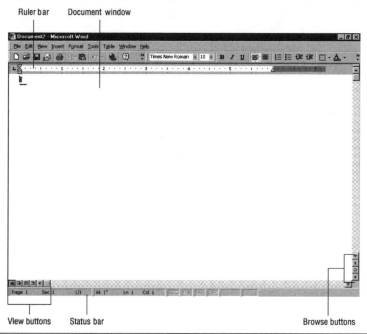

View buttons   Status bar   Browse buttons

FIGURE 2.1: Word application and document windows

Getting Around

You probably already know how to use scroll bars to move around in a document. You'll be happy to know that Word 2000 has a number of other tools that make it easy to navigate documents of any length. Rather than using the vertical scroll bar arrows, you can drag the scroll box to display a ScrollTip that shows the page number you are scrolling past. If the document has headings, the heading also appears in the tip:

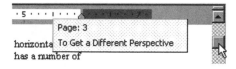

Another way to get around in your document is by browsing. On the bottom of the vertical scroll bar is a set of Browse buttons: Previous Page, Select Browse Object, and Next Page.

Click the Select Browse Object button to open a menu, and then select the object type you'd like to browse:

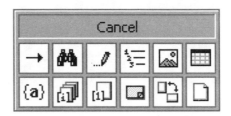

To Get a Different Perspective

Word 2000 gives you several ways to view documents, depending on whether you are outlining, writing, preparing to print, or just reading a document. To the left of the horizontal scroll bar are the View buttons:

 Normal   Best used for entering, editing, and formatting text. Headers, footers, graphics, and columns are not visible in this view.

 Web Layout   In this view, Word displays your document just as it will appear in your Web browser. Because of the new Web capabilities of Office 2000, a document appears almost exactly the same in Web Layout view and Normal or Print Layout view. You can see this in Figure 2.2. The same document is displayed in both windows, with the top window displaying in Normal view and the bottom window displaying in Web Layout view.

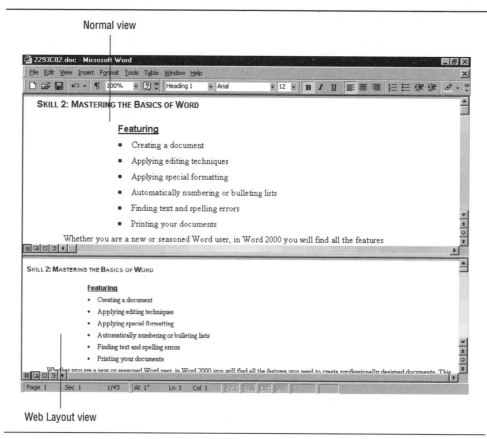

Normal view

Web Layout view

FIGURE 2.2: The same document displayed in both Normal and Web Layout views

Print Layout   Allows you to work with your document exactly as it will look when it is printed.

Outline   Useful when you are developing a document's structure and content and want to create a preliminary outline or review the outline while developing a document.

This is a good time to open any Word document and spend a few moments examining any features described above that are unfamiliar. If you don't have a Word 2000 document, open any WordPerfect or Word document and Word 2000 will convert it.

Entering Text

Word 2000 tries to make your life easier right from the first letter you type by watching what you're doing and figuring out how it can be most helpful. As you enter text, Word does several things behind the scenes unless you've told Word not to do so (see Figure 2.3):

- The Office Assistant evaluates what you are doing to see if it has any suggestions.

- The AutoCorrect feature automatically corrects misspelled words that are in its dictionary, such as "teh" and "adn."

- The Spelling and Grammar feature (also called Spell It) reviews your text to determine if there are other possible misspellings or grammatical errors.

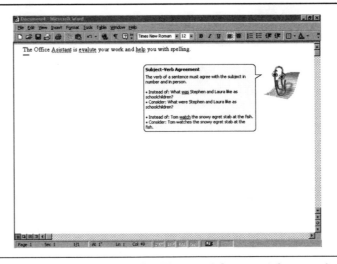

FIGURE 2.3: Office Assistant, Spelling, and Grammar features in action

 TIP TIP TIP TIP TIP TIP TIP TIP TIP TIP TIP TIP TIP TIP TIP TIP TIP TIP TIP TIP TIP TIP TIP
If you find the Office Assistant annoying, choose Help ➢ Hide Office Assistant.

To enter text in Word, begin typing in the document window. Text you type is entered at the flashing insertion point. The insertion point will move over to accommodate the new text. If you want to overtype existing text, turn on Overtype mode. To toggle between Insert and Overtype modes, press the Insert key on the keyboard or double-click the control on the status bar labeled OVR. OVR will turn black, indicating that Overtype mode is active:

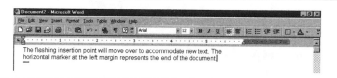

Text will automatically wrap to the next line when you reach the right margin. Within a paragraph, just let text wrap automatically to the next line. Pressing Enter at the end of a line inserts a *hard return* to create a new paragraph or a blank line.

In Normal view, you will see a black horizontal line at the left margin. This represents the end of your document. In Normal view, you cannot move the insertion point or insert text or objects below the marker until you claim the space by entering text or by pressing the Enter key. Figure 2.4 shows the insertion point and the End of Document marker.

FIGURE 2.4: Insertion point and End of Document marker

In Print Layout and Web Layout views, you can double-click anywhere on the page and then type text where you clicked. This new feature of Word 2000 is called Click and Type. Here's how it works:

- If you double-click the right side of the page, text is right-aligned.

- If you double-click the left side of the page, text is left-aligned.

- If you double-click the center of the page, text is centered.

See the section "Aligning and Formatting" later in this chapter for information about aligning text.

Moving the Insertion Point

Word provides several ways to move the insertion point using the keyboard. You can use the arrow keys to move the cursor up a line, down a line, and one character to the left or right, or you can use the special keys listed in Table 2.1.

TABLE 2.1: Navigation Keys

Key	Action
Home	The beginning of the current line
End	The end of the current line
Ctrl+Home	The beginning of the document
Ctrl+End	The end of the document
Page Up	Up one screen
Page Down	Down one screen
Ctrl+Page Up	The top of the screen
Ctrl+Page Down	The bottom of the screen
Ctrl+Left Arrow	One word to the left
Ctrl+Right Arrow	One word to the right

Correcting Mistakes

To correct mistakes that you make while typing, use the Backspace or Delete key, or click the Undo button on the Standard toolbar. Press Ctrl+Backspace and Ctrl+Del to delete whole words at a time.

Hands On

1. Open a new Word document. Enter two or three lines of text. Intentionally misspell a word and notice that it is marked with a wavy red underline. Enter a grammatically incorrect sentence (like "People is crazy.") and notice that it is marked with a green line. Use the shortcut keys listed in Table 2.1 to move around the document. Move the insertion point to the beginning of the document, and use Ctrl+Delete to delete each word in the first sentence.

NOTE NOTE NOTE NOTE NOTE NOTE NOTE NOTE NOTE NOTE NOTE NOTE NOTE NOTE NOTE

The Word 2000 grammar-checking feature takes advantage of "down-time" to review your completed sentences. If you intentionally make a grammatical error, you may have to move on to the next sentence or next paragraph before it will catch up with you and mark it as questionable.

2.2: Editing Document Text

You can tell that a person is a Word power user because they use very few steps to complete a task. They're not just proficient: they're efficient, particularly with skills that are used frequently in Word. Knowing several ways to select and replace text will let you streamline many of the other tasks you'll be doing with your documents.

SKILL
2

Selecting Text

Although you can always drag to select text, Word offers you a number of other options. You can use any of these methods, but some methods are easier in certain situations. For example, if you've ever tried to drag to select text over multiple pages, you have already experienced the wonders of an out-of-control accelerated mouse pointer. On the other hand, if you choose another method to select such as Shift-select (see Table 2.2 below), you can select text smoothly without creating a single gray hair.

TABLE 2.2: Selecting Text

To select:	Do this:
A word	Double-click anywhere in the word.
A sentence	Hold Ctrl and click anywhere in the sentence.
A paragraph	Triple-click anywhere in the paragraph.
Single line	Move the pointer into the left margin. When the pointer changes to a right-pointing arrow, point to the desired line and click.
Entire document	Choose Edit ➤ Select All from the menu bar, or hold Ctrl and click in the left margin.
Multiple lines	Move the pointer to the left margin. With the right-pointing arrow, point to the first desired line and click. Without releasing the mouse button, drag to select additional lines.
Multiple words, lines, or sentences	Move the I-beam into the first word, hold the mouse button, drag to the last word, and release.
Multiple words, lines, or sentences using Shift-select	Click the first word, move to the last word (with mouse button released), hold Shift and click. Everything between the two clicks is selected.

TIP TIP TIP TIP TIP TIP TIP TIP TIP TIP TIP TIP TIP TIP TIP TIP TIP TIP TIP TIP TIP TIP TIP TIP TIP

If you begin entering text when other text is selected, the selected text will be deleted and the text you enter will replace it. This is an easy way to replace one word or phrase with another. It also works when you don't want it to—for example, when you forget you still have text selected from a previous action. When you are finished working with selected text, remember to click somewhere in the document to remove the selection.

Copying and Moving Text

You already know how to move and copy text using the toolbar and menu bar. You'll find it easy to move and copy text short distances using a method called *drag-and-drop*. Drag-and-drop works best when you can see both the *source*, the location of original text, and the *destination*, the place you want the moved or copied text to appear.

MOVING TEXT USING DRAG-AND-DROP

1. Identify the text you want to move and its destination.
2. Select the text and drag it to its new location while holding down the right mouse button. Drop the selection into position by releasing the mouse button.
3. Select Move Here from the shortcut menu.
4. If you split the screen, drag the Resize control to remove the split.

Use the same techniques to copy text from one location to another in a single document and move or copy text between documents. If you want to work with more than one document, open both documents, and choose Window ➢ Arrange All to see both documents. (When you want to work on just one of the documents again, click the Maximize button on the document's title bar.)

COPYING TEXT USING DRAG-AND-DROP

1. Identify the text you want to copy and its destination.
2. Select the text and drag it to its new location while holding down the right mouse button. Drop the text into position.
3. Select Copy Here from the shortcut menu.

You can also use the left mouse button to drag and drop text, but you don't get the shortcut menu. Instead, the text is moved to the new location with no questions asked. If you want to copy text with the left mouse button, you must hold down the Ctrl key while dropping the text. It's easy to forget to hold down Ctrl or accidentally release Ctrl before the text is dropped, so it is good to get in the habit of dragging with the right mouse button. All the drag-and-drop techniques work with other Office 2000 and Windows applications such as the Windows Explorer.

Hands On

1. Enter two paragraphs of at least three sentences each in a new document. Experiment with each of the techniques described in Table 2.2 several times until you feel comfortable using them.

2.3: Applying Text Enhancements

All the fonts used by Windows programs are managed by Windows, so fonts available in one Office 2000 application are available in all the others. Skill 1 provides a general overview of how to apply fonts and font styles to text. In this section, we'll focus on the font features that are specific to Word.

Applying Fonts and Font Styles in Word

Unless you need unique formatting such as a double underline, you'll be able to make most of your font formatting changes using the Formatting toolbar. The toolbar includes buttons and drop-down menus that let you choose a font, font size, effects (such as bold, italics, and underline), and font color. If you need font options that are not available on the toolbar, open the Font dialog box by choosing Format ➤ Font:

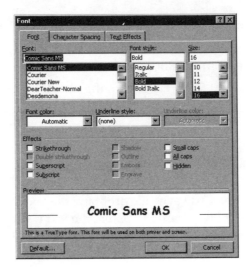

Word's Font dialog box has three page tabs: Font, Character Spacing, and Text Effects. On the Font page you can select font attributes and see how a font will look by noting the changes in the preview as you apply desired Styles, Sizes, Font Colors, Underline Style and Colors, and Effects.

Word 2000 provides numerous underline options. Click the drop-down arrow to take a look at them.

Special Text Effects

There are eleven effects that you can apply from the Font tab in the Font dialog box. You can use Strikethrough and Double-strikethrough to show proposed deletions in a contract or bylaws. Use Superscript and Subscript to place special characters in formulas (H_2O) and footnotes (as in Miller[1]). Shadow, Outline, Emboss, and Engrave stylize the text so that it stands out, as shown in Figure 2.5.

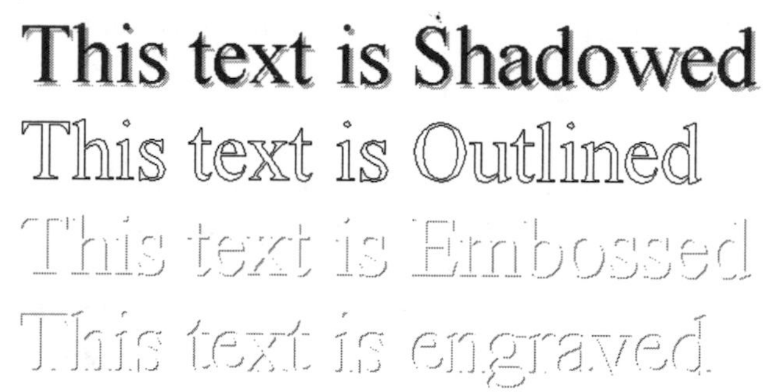

This text is Shadowed
This text is Outlined
This text is Embossed
This text is engraved

FIGURE 2.5: Text effects in Word

Small Caps and All Caps are typically used in stylized documents such as letter-heads or business cards. The Small Caps effect converts lowercase letters to smaller versions of the capital letters. To use Small Caps, enter all the text in lowercase and then apply the Small Caps effect.

Hidden text doesn't print and can only be seen when Show/Hide is enabled. This effect was much more commonly applied when there weren't other, more effective ways such as Comments (see Skill 4) to include nonprinting, invisible document notes.

TIP TIP TIP TIP TIP TIP TIP TIP TIP TIP TIP TIP TIP TIP TIP TIP TIP TIP TIP TIP TIP TIP TIP

Rather than manually marking revised text with Strikethrough, you can use Word 2000's powerful Track Changes feature. Word also has an automatic foot-noting system. Both features are discussed in Skill 4.

Character Spacing

Use character spacing to adjust the distance between characters. For example, you can spread a title such as *Memorandum* across a page without having to space two or three times between characters:

M E M O R A N D U M

Character spacing is commonly used in advanced desktop publishing when you want to size and scale characters precisely.

Text Effects

On the Text Effects tab there are six options designed for documents that will be read on-screen. They cause your text to blink, sparkle, or shimmer: Blinking Background, Las Vegas Lights, Marching Black Ants, Marching Red Ants, Shimmer, and Sparkle Text. To apply one of these special effects, select the text you want to animate, choose Format „ Font „ Text Effects, and select one of the six options. To turn the special effect off, select the text again and select None from the list of options. A word of advice: if you're going to apply animation, use it sparingly and don't apply it until you are done editing document text. Overdone, it is annoying, and animated documents use more computer resources, slowing down your system.

Highlighting Text for a Distinct Look

If you are creating a document and want to call someone's attention to a particular part of your text, you can *highlight* it so that it stands out for review. This is the computer equivalent of using a highlighter pen on the printout: if you have a color printer, the text will appear highlighted when printed. (Don't overlook the value of highlighting sections of text as a self-reminder.)

Select the text you want to highlight and click the drop-down arrow next to the Highlight button to choose and apply a highlight color. The button will save the last chosen pen color, so if you want to use the same color again, just click directly on the Highlight button. To turn highlighting off, select the highlighted text and choose None from the Highlight button drop-down list.

If you prefer, you can choose a color to apply and highlight several sections of text. With no text selected, choose a highlight color. Drag the pen over the text you want to highlight. The highlight pointer will remain active until you click the Highlight button again to turn it off.

APPLYING TEXT ENHANCEMENTS

1. Select the text you want to enhance.
2. Change font, font size, bold, italics, underline, and text color from the Formatting toolbar.
3. Choose Format ➤ Font to open the Font dialog box for more advanced features.
4. Click any of the effects to turn them on, or clear the check box to turn them off.
5. Click the Character Spacing tab to adjust the settings to expand or condense the characters.
6. Click the Text Effects tab to select from the list of animation options.
7. To highlight text, click the Highlight button and drag it over the text you want to highlight.

SKILL
2

Hands On

1. Enter several lines of text. Apply at least three different fonts and font styles. Highlight a sentence; remove the hightlight.

2. Enter your name. Change it to a 24-point font of your choice. Copy your name five times. Apply a different special effect to each copy. Underline two of the copies, using a different underline style for each.

2.4: Aligning and Formatting

In addition to formatting text or characters, skilled Word users must know how to format lines and paragraphs of text. In this section, you'll learn how to use indents and tabs and to control how text flows on the page.

Aligning Text

Word provides four options, shown in Figure 2.6, for aligning paragraph text: left, center, right, and full (justify).

This paragraph is **left-aligned**. Left-alignment is the most common alignment. It means that text lines up with the left margin and leaves a ragged edge at the right margin. Left-aligned text is the easiest to read.

This paragraph is **centered**. Centering is generally used for headings and desktop publishing creations. Centered text is equally positioned between the left and right margins.

This paragraph is **right-aligned**. Right alignment is used in headers and footers and other text that you intend to be put off to the side. It means that text lines up with the right margin and leaves a ragged edge at the left margin. Right-aligned text is the hardest to read.

This paragraph is **justified** or fully aligned. Justified text appears formal because text lines up evenly with the left and right margins. It is often used in documents with columns of text. Sometimes the paragraph looks unbalanced because too many spaces have to be inserted between characters.

FIGURE 2.6: Aligning paragraph text

To align text, position the insertion point anywhere in the paragraph and click one of the alignment buttons on the Formatting toolbar:

Using Indentation Options

Word 2000 offers three ways to access the paragraph-indenting features: the Formatting toolbar, the ruler, and the Paragraph dialog box.

You'll find the easiest method to change indents on the Formatting toolbar. Click anywhere in the paragraph you want to indent or select multiple paragraphs, and click the Decrease Indent button to reduce the left indent by ½ inch. Click the Increase Indent button to extend the indent by ½ inch.

Creating Indents Using the Ruler

The second method of indenting paragraphs—using the ruler—can take a little work to master but is a very visual way to set left, right, hanging, and dual indents. You can use the ruler to set tabs as well as indents and left and right margins in Page Layout view.

If you prefer to do most of your work without the ruler, turn the ruler off by choosing View ➢ Ruler to remove the check. To make the ruler temporarily visible, point to the narrow gray line under the command bars and the ruler will reappear. As soon as the pointer moves back to your document, the ruler will slide back under the command bars.

There are four indent markers on the ruler, shown in Figure 2.7:

- A *first line indent* works the same as pressing Tab on the keyboard.

- A *hanging indent* (sometimes called an outdent) "hangs" the remaining lines in a paragraph to the right of the first line when this marker is positioned to the right of the first line indent marker.

- A *left indent* sets a paragraph off from the rest of the text by moving all lines in from the left margin.

- A *right indent* moves text in from the right margin and is typically combined with a left indent to make a *dual indent*. Dual indents are used most commonly to set off block quotations.

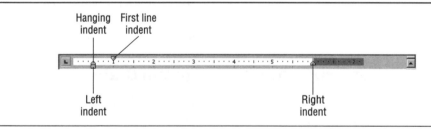

FIGURE 2.7: Indent markers on the ruler

To change the indents for existing text, select the paragraph or paragraphs you want to indent and drag the indent marker on the ruler to the desired location. Moving the first line or the hanging indent marker indents or outdents the first line of each paragraph. Moving the left or right indent marker indents all lines of each paragraph.

If you forget which marker is which, point to any of them for a moment and view the ScreenTip. You can use the ruler to set indents before entering text. Position the insertion point where you plan to enter the new text. The indents will apply to all newly entered text until you change the indent settings.

INDENTING USING THE TOOLBAR AND RULER

1. Click in the paragraph you want to indent, and click the Increase Indent button or the Decrease Indent button on the Formatting toolbar.
2. To use the ruler: change to Normal view and turn the ruler on if it is not already visible (choose View ➤ Ruler).
3. Select the text you want to indent.
4. Drag the First Line Indent marker to the right to indent the first line in a paragraph.
5. Drag the Hanging Indent marker to the right to indent all but the first line in a paragraph.
6. Drag the Left Indent marker to indent all the selected text.
7. Drag the Right Indent marker to indent the selected text from the right margin.

If you select paragraphs that do not share the same indent settings, one or all of the indent markers on the ruler will be dimmed. Click the dimmed marker(s) to make the indent settings the same for all the selected paragraphs.

Indenting Using the Paragraph Dialog Box

The third way to set indents is by using the Paragraph dialog box, shown in Figure 2.8. To access the dialog box, choose Format ➤ Paragraph or right-click and choose Paragraph from the shortcut menu.

On the Indents and Spacing page, click the up and down arrows next to the Left and Right text boxes (called *spin boxes* because you can "spin" through the options), or enter decimal numbers directly in the text boxes. In the Special control, you can select First Line or Hanging to indent or outdent the first line of the paragraphs by ½ inch. If you want the indent to be more or less than 0.5 inch, enter the special indent value in the By control.

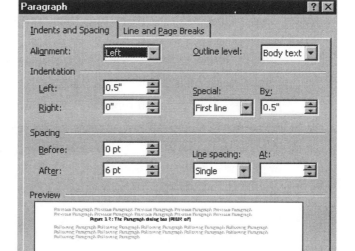

FIGURE 2.8: The Paragraph dialog box

INDENTING USING THE PARAGRAPH DIALOG BOX

1. Select the text you want to indent and open the Paragraph dialog box (choose Format ➢ Paragraph or right-click and choose Paragraph).

2. Use the spin box controls to change the Left and Right indent settings.

3. Click the Special drop-down arrow to select First Line or Hanging indent.

4. Click OK to close the Paragraph dialog box and see your changes.

Setting Line Spacing Options

Word 2000 provides six options for adjusting *line spacing*, the vertical distance between lines of text:

Single Enough room to comfortably display the largest character on a line

1.5 lines One-and-a-half single lines

Double Twice as much room as single spacing

At Least A minimum line spacing for the selection

Exactly Makes all lines evenly spaced regardless of the size of the fonts or graphics included in those lines

Multiple Used to enter line spacing other than single, 1.5, and double

To change the line spacing for existing text, select the paragraphs you want to change. Open the Paragraph dialog box (choose Format ➢ Paragraph or right-click and select Paragraph from the shortcut menu), and click the drop-down list to select from the line-spacing options:

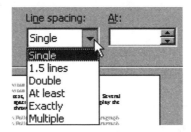

At Least and Exactly require you to enter a point size in the At text box. Multiple requires you to enter the amount by which to multiply. For example, you can triple-space selected paragraphs by choosing Multiple and then entering 3 in the At control.

SETTING LINE SPACING

1. Select the text whose line spacing you want to change.
2. Choose Format ➢ Paragraph to open the Paragraph dialog box. Click the Indents and Spacing tab if the page is not visible.

continued

3. Click the Line Spacing drop-down list to select the desired line spacing.

4. If you are choosing At Least, Exactly, or Multiple, enter a number in the At control.

5. Click OK to return to the document and review the changes.

To see all the formatting that is applied to a paragraph, choose Help ➣ What's This? and click the paragraph. You'll get an information box, such as the one shown in Figure 2.9, that displays paragraph and font formatting related to the paragraph. Choose Help ➣ What's This? again to turn it off.

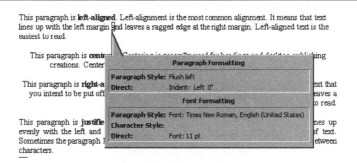

FIGURE 2.9: Using What's This? to view formatting

Using Tabs

Tab stops are markers set by default at half-inch intervals across the width of the document. Pressing the Tab key moves the cursor from one tab stop to the next. One of the most common uses of a tab is to indent the first line of a paragraph.

Tabs are also used to create *parallel columns*, vertically aligning text within a document. You can change the tab-stop settings by using the ruler or the Tabs dialog box. Setting the stops includes choosing the alignment type and location for each tab stop you want to use. Figure 2.10 shows four of the five basic types of tab stops:

Left　The default type. Text appears to the right of the tab stop.

Center　Text is automatically adjusted to the left and the right of the tab stop until it is centered under the tab stop.

Right   Text appears to the left of the tab stop.

Decimal   Used for numeric entries. Text lines up with the decimal point.

Bar   Inserts a vertical line in your document at the tab stop. In earlier versions of Word, the Bar tab was used to create a vertical separator for columns. With Word 2000, you can do this automatically when you set up columns.

TUESDAY'S SCHEDULE			
Employee	**Shift Responsibility**	**Shift Hours**	**Rate**
Jeff Morse	stock shelves	7:30 a.m. – 2:30 p.m.	$7.50
Jessica Beecham	next weeks' schedule	10:00 a.m. – 5:30 p.m.	$8.25
Sean Callan	purchasing	12:00 p.m. – 9:30 p.m.	$10.00
Seneca Sojourn	order shipping	5:00 p.m. – 1:30 a.m.	$8.50

FIGURE 2.10: Four of the five types of tab stops were used to align these columns.

Setting Tab Stops Using the Ruler

At the left end of the ruler in Print Layout view is a Tab Selection button that allows you to select the type of tab you want to set. By default it is set on Left Tab. Click the button to toggle through the five tab choices.

Once you have chosen the type of tab you want to set, click the ruler to set a tab. The tab-stop marker appears, and all the tabs to the left of the marker are deleted. If you want to move the tab stop, click on the marker and drag it to a new location on the ruler.

If you want the tab stops to apply to existing text, be sure to select the text first—before clicking the ruler. Unless you select the entire document or the last paragraph in the document, the tab stops will only apply to the selected paragraph(s). You can, however, set the tab stops for a blank document before you start entering text, and then the tab stops can be used throughout the document. To clear a tab stop, point to the tab stop and simply drag it off the ruler.

SETTING TABS USING THE RULER

1. Click the Tab button at the left end of the ruler to toggle through the five tab choices.

2. Click the ruler to set the tab stops—all the default tab stops to the left of the new tabs are deleted.

3. Drag the tab-stop marker on the ruler to change the tab position.

4. Drag the tab-stop marker off the ruler to remove the tab stop.

TIP TIP TIP TIP TIP TIP TIP TIP TIP TIP TIP TIP TIP TIP TIP TIP TIP TIP TIP TIP TIP TIP TIP TIP

In most situations, it is easier to create parallel columns using Word's Tables feature than it is to use tabs. If you're using tabs to create parallel columns, you're not using the most efficient tool. See Skill 3.3 for information regarding tables.

Setting Tab Stops and Leaders Using the Tabs Dialog Box

You can also create tab stops using the Tabs dialog box. Make sure the insertion point is located where you want the new tab stops to begin. (If the text you want to format is already entered, select it.) Access the Tabs dialog box, shown in Figure 2.11, by choosing Format ➤ Tabs.

In the Tab Stop Position text box, type the location for the tab stop you want to create. In the Alignment control, choose how you want text to align at the tab stop. The Leader control lets you select a *leader* to lead the reader's eye across the text. The leader (see Figure 2.12) precedes the tabbed text.

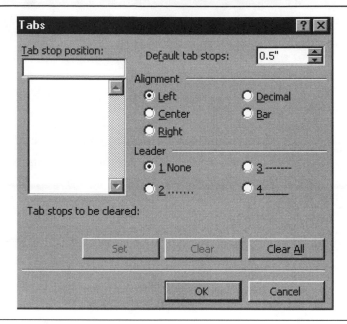

FIGURE 2.11: The Tabs dialog box

Telephone List

Rianne Anderson	517-555-9999
Charlotte Cowtan	810-555-3333
Tisha Deeghan	810-555-8897
Bonnie John-Murray	517-555-4466
Maya Campbell	810-555-9898
Helen Marquis	501-555-5555
Jarrett and Jeanne Marquis	804-555-2345
Seneca Jean Sojourn	517-555-0123
Lyrica Anne Sojourn	517-555-2345

FIGURE 2.12: Tab stops and leaders

When you have set the position, type, and leader (if you wish) for the tab stop, click the Set button. The new tab stop will be added to the tab-stop list. Repeat these steps to set any other tab stops.

You can also use the dialog box to change an existing tab stop. Select the tab stop from the list below the Tab Stop Position control. Change the Alignment and Leader options; then click Set. To remove an existing tab stop, select it from the list and click the Clear button. Clicking Clear All removes all the tab stops you added, reverting to the default tab settings. When you are done setting tab stops, click OK to close the Tabs dialog box.

SETTING TABS AND LEADERS USING THE TABS DIALOG BOX

1. Open the Tabs dialog box by choosing Format ➤ Tabs.

2. Type a decimal value in the Tab Stop Position text box.

3. Select an alignment style and, optionally, a leader style.

4. Click OK.

5. Enter text, pressing Tab between each column.

To see where tabs have been typed in existing text, click the Show/Hide Paragraph Marks button on the Standard toolbar. You'll see a right-pointed arrow to indicate a tab:

```
TUESDAY'S·SCHEDULE¶
¶
·Employee        →     Shift·Responsibility   →     Shift·Hours          →         Rate¶
¶
Jeff·Morse       →        stock·shelves    →     7:30·a.m.–2:30·p.m.    →       $7.50¶
Jessica·Beecham  →    next·weeks'·schedule  →   10:00·a.m.–5:30·p.m.    →       $8.25¶
Sean·Callan      →         purchasing      →    12:00·p.m.–9:30·p.m.    →      $10.00¶
Seneca·Sojoum    →       order·shipping    →     5:00·p.m.–1:30·a.m.    →       $8.50¶
```

Hands On

1. In a new document, set tabs to enter the text below in parallel columns. Set a right tab for the times and center the number of weeks. Save the document as *Class Schedule*.

Class	Day	Time	Weeks
Access	Monday	1 p.m.–3 p.m.	10
Excel	Tuesday	11 a.m.–2 p.m.	7
Publisher	Friday	8 a.m.–4 p.m.	2
PowerPoint	Monday	5 p.m.–7 p.m.	4
Outlook	Saturday	9 a.m.–5 p.m.	1
Word	Thursday	7 a.m.–10 a.m.	7

2. In a new document, enter the following text and format each paragraph as described in the paragraph.

```
    A first line indent works the same as pressing the Tab key on
the keyboard. Single-line spacing provides enough room to comfort-
ably display the largest character on a line.
    A hanging indent (sometimes called an outdent) "hangs" the first
line of a paragraph to the left of the remaining lines. Double
spacing provides twice as much room between lines of text as single
spacing.
    A left indent sets a paragraph off from the rest of the text by
moving all lines in from the left margin. Line spacing of 1.5
leaves one-and-a-half single lines between each line of text.
    A right indent moves text in from the right margin and is typi-
cally combined with a left indent to make a dual indent. Dual
indents, like the dual indent used in this paragraph, are used
most commonly to set off block quotations. Multiple line spacing
is used to specify the number of lines: in this paragraph, 3 lines.
```

3. In a new document, set a left tab at .5, a center tab at 2, a right tab at 4.25, and decimal tab at 5, and then enter the text shown in Figure 2.10 or similar text of your own. Select the line of column headings and change the tab stop for Shift Hours to a Center tab and the tab stop for Rate to a Right tab. Move both tabs so that the headings line up appropriately with the columns.

2.5: Adding Lists, Numbers, Symbols, and the Date and Time

When you know how to use some of Word's special formatting features, you can easily create bulleted and numbered lists that have a professional look. Using the Symbol dialog box, you can insert everything from a happy face to the sign for infinity, and you can use Word's date and time features to add the date to a document even if, at the moment, you don't know what month it is.

SKILL 2

Numbering and Bullets

We live in a world of list makers (even if you ignore late-night talk show hosts), and Word 2000 makes it easy to create bulleted and numbered lists. If you begin a list with a number, Word will number following paragraphs when you press Enter. Begin with an asterisk, and Word will bullet each paragraph.

  To apply numbers to existing text, select the paragraphs and click the Numbering button on the Formatting toolbar. Use the Bullets button to bullet existing paragraphs of text.

CREATING A NUMBERED OR BULLETED LIST

1. If the text you want to number is already entered, highlight the paragraphs to be numbered, and click the Numbering or Bullets button to number or bullet each paragraph.

   –OR–

1. To automatically number text as you type, type the number 1 and a period, space once, then enter your text for item 1. For bullets, begin with an asterisk and a space.

2. Press Enter. Word will automatically number the next item 2 and press the Numbering button on the Formatting toolbar, or bullet the next item and press the Bullets button.

continued ▶

---

3. Continue entering text and pressing the Enter key to create numbered or bulleted points.

4. When you are finished creating the list, press Enter twice to turn automatic numbering or bullets off.

You can also begin numbering by clicking the Numbering button before you type your first paragraph. If you want to use letters rather than numbers in automatic numbering, type "A." rather than "1." to begin. Word will number the second and succeeding paragraphs B, C, D, and so on. If you number your first paragraph "I.", Word will use Roman numerals to number your paragraphs.

TIP TIP TIP TIP TIP TIP TIP TIP TIP TIP TIP TIP TIP TIP TIP TIP TIP TIP TIP TIP TIP TIP TIP TIP TIP

If automatic numbering or bullets do not work when you follow the steps above, choose Tools ➢ AutoCorrect to open the AutoCorrect dialog box. Make sure that Automatic Bulleted Lists is checked under AutoFormat and Automatic Bulleted Lists and Automatic Numbered Lists are checked under AutoFormat As You Type.

Modifying the Bullet or Number Format

When you use the Bullets and Numbering features, Word supplies a standard, round bullet and leaves a default amount of space between the bullet or number and the text that follows. You can choose a different bullet character, number format, or spacing before entering your list, or you can modify the format of an existing list. If the bulleted or numbered list has already been entered, select the paragraphs you want to change. To change formats, choose Format ➢ Bullets and Numbering to open the Bullets and Numbering dialog box, shown in Figure 2.13.

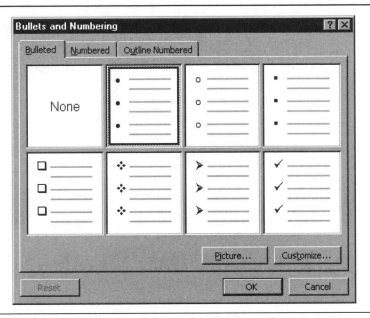

FIGURE 2.13: The Bullets and Numbering dialog box

Click the Bulleted, Numbered, or Outline Numbered tab. The dialog box displays seven styles for bulleted text, seven styles for numbered lists, and seven styles for outline numbering. You can simply select any of the styles shown.

TIP TIP TIP TIP TIP TIP TIP TIP TIP TIP TIP TIP TIP TIP TIP TIP TIP TIP TIP TIP TIP TIP TIP TIP TIP
See Skill 3 for information about outlines and outline numbering.

But you aren't limited to the styles shown in the samples. Select the Bulleted tab, and click the Customize button to open the Customize Bulleted List dialog box, as shown in Figure 2.14. (The Customize button will be dimmed if None is selected.)

SKILL
2

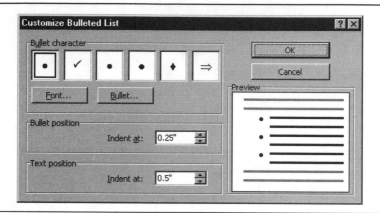

FIGURE 2.14: The Customize Bulleted List dialog box

Here you can change the bullet's font by clicking the Font button to open the Font dialog box. You can replace any of the bullet characters that appear here to create your own list of favorites. Click one of the bullet characters you don't want to use at this time to select it for replacement. Click the Bullet button to open the Symbol dialog box, shown in Figure 2.15.

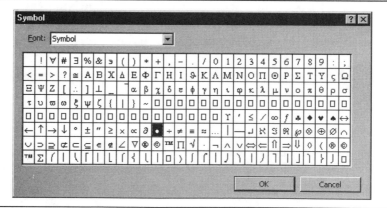

FIGURE 2.15: The Symbol dialog box

The Symbol Font drop-down list contains symbol and display fonts. Choose a font or symbol set from the list, and the characters in the symbol set will be displayed in the *character map* below the drop-down. Any of the individual characters shown can be used as a bullet character. Click any character, and then click OK to replace the selected bullet character with the symbol you've chosen. You will then be able to select the new symbol from the Bullet Character samples.

TIP TIP TIP TIP TIP TIP TIP TIP TIP TIP TIP TIP TIP TIP TIP TIP TIP TIP TIP TIP TIP TIP TIP

If you share documents with others, be sure to select bullets from fonts or symbol sets that also appear on their computers, or bullets will be changed when they open your documents. Monotype Sorts and Wingdings are common to most computers.

The *Bullet Position* control lets you change the position of the bullet relative to the left margin. The *Text Position* control adjusts the position of text relative to the bullet. As you modify the Bullet and Text Position settings, the Preview will change to reflect your modifications.

If you want to use a picture instead of a symbol or character, click the Picture button in the Bullets and Numbering dialog box to open the Insert Picture dialog box, and make a selection.

The Customize Numbered List dialog box, shown in Figure 2.16, works much the same as Customized Bulleted List but there are a few important differences. Here, you can enter a number format such as "Chapter 1", "Section 1", or even "_____ 1" to create a check-off list. Choose a style from the Number Style drop-down list. You can also have the numbering start at a number other than 1. To change the alignment of the number in the area before the text, click the Number Position drop-down list and choose between Left, Center, and Right.

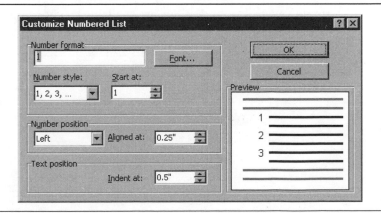

FIGURE 2.16: The Customize Numbered List dialog box

CUSTOMIZING NUMBER AND BULLET FORMATS

1. Select the list whose numbering or bullet style you want to change.
2. Choose Format ➤ Bullets and Numbering.
3. Make sure the tab you want (Numbered or Bulleted) is displayed.
4. Click a number, letter, or bullet format. To choose a different format, click Customize.
5. Enter a number format, or choose to change the bullet character by clicking the Bullet button. If numbering, enter the starting number if it is other than 1.
6. Adjust the Bullet or Number Position and the Text Position as desired.
7. Click OK to save your changes and return to your document.

To remove numbers and bullets from text, select the bulleted or numbered list and then click the Bullets or Numbering button on the toolbar to turn bullets or numbering off.

Creating Special Characters

Many symbols used regularly in business documents aren't on the standard keyboard. Word 2000 makes many of these common symbols available to you with simple keystrokes, and others are available by choosing Insert ➤ Symbol.

Choose Insert ➤ Symbol and select the Symbols tab to open the symbol character map, shown in Figure 2.15 earlier in this chapter. Select the Special Characters tab, shown in Figure 2.17.

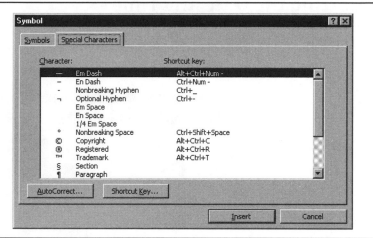

FIGURE 2.17: The Special Characters page

Choose from the symbol font sets or special characters shown and then click the Insert button to insert the symbol into your document. If you need the symbol more than once, copy and paste it to the other locations. The AutoCorrect method suggested for abbreviations in Skill 1.4 can also be applied to create special characters and symbols such as ©, ™, and →. To add a symbol to the AutoCorrect list, select the symbol and click the AutoCorrect button or choose Tools ➢ AutoCorrect. Enter a character string that will automatically be replaced with the desired symbol—enter (p) for ¶, for example. Make sure it is a character string you don't use in other situations, or you will find it replaced with the symbol every time you type it.

USING SPECIAL CHARACTERS

1. Choose Insert ➢ Symbol.
2. Choose a symbol from the font symbol sets shown in the character map on the Symbol page or from the list on the Special Characters page.
3. Add regularly used symbols to the AutoCorrect list by clicking Auto-Correct and entering a text string in the Replace text box.

Inserting the Date and Time

Word 2000 provides 17 formats you can use when inserting the current date and/or time, so the format you want is probably among them. Choose Insert ➤ Date and Time to open the Date and Time dialog box:

Select a format from the list. If you would like to automatically update the field to the current date and time every time you open the document, click the Update Automatically check box. This inserts date and time as a field rather than as text. A *field* serves as a placeholder which is replaced with current data. (Be careful not to use this option when the date on a document is important to mark a paper trail.) A Date and Time field is most useful when a document is in draft form and you want to know when it was last worked on, or when a memo or notice is regularly printed and mailed and should always have the current date. The Date and Time field is only updated when you print the document or right-click the field and choose Update Field. Go to Print Preview to see the changed date and time. When you return to the document, the date and time will be updated.

INSERTING THE DATE AND TIME

1. Choose Insert ➤ Date and Time.
2. Select the desired Date and Time format.
3. Click the Update Automatically check box if you want to insert Date and Time as a field.
4. Click OK to insert the date and time into your document.

Hands On

1. Enter a list of at least 10 things you have to do this week.

   a) Select the list and turn on Numbering. Select the list again and turn on Bullets.

   b) Change the bullet characters to some other symbol, such as a right-pointed arrow.

2. Type a new list below the To Do list that includes things you need to buy or errands you need to run. Start by entering the number 1, a period, and a space. When you press Enter after the first item, the number 2 should appear and a tab should be automatically inserted after each of the two numbers. If Automatic Numbering is not turned on, go to Format ➤ Auto-Format to open the AutoFormat dialog box. Click Options to open the Auto-Correct dialog box, click the AutoFormat As You Type tab, and make sure Automatic Bulleted Lists and Automatic Numbered Lists are checked.

3. On a new blank line, choose Insert ➤ Symbols and insert a symbol or special character that you might use often. Add it to the AutoCorrect list so you can type a few characters and have them replaced with the symbol. After you have entered it, type the characters and see if AutoCorrect changes them to your symbol.

4. In the same document:

   a) Use Ctrl+Home to move to the top of your document. Choose Insert ➤ Date and Time to add the date and time to your document in a format that includes the time. Enable Update Automatically.

   b) Below the Date and Time field, choose Insert ➤ Date and Time again but do not enable Update Automatically. Save and close the document. Wait a couple of minutes and reopen the document. Switch to Print Preview and zoom in on the date and time. The first time will reflect the current time, and the second time should still reflect the time the field was originally entered.

2.6: Replacing and Checking Text

As you create documents in Word, you may want to use the same text in another document or correct an error that occurs several times. Word 2000 offers several features to help you replace and check text—including grammar—efficiently. There's even a thesaurus to help you find that perfectly descriptive word or phrase.

Creating and Applying Frequently Used Text

Word has two features that let you easily insert frequently used text and graphics. The first option—AutoCorrect—is included in Skill 1 because it is common to all Office 2000 applications. The second feature, *AutoText*, is particular to Word and allows you to store formatted text or graphics, even entire paragraphs, and then recall them with a couple of keystrokes.

To create an AutoText entry, select the text you want to store as AutoText. To include the text's format such as font and font style, before selecting, click the Show/Hide Paragraph Marks button on the Standard toolbar and make sure you include the paragraph mark in the selection. Choose Insert ➤ AutoText ➤ New to create the entry (see Figure 2.18). You will be prompted to give the entry a name—make it short and easy to remember. To insert the AutoText in a document, type the name you assigned to the entry and press the F3 key.

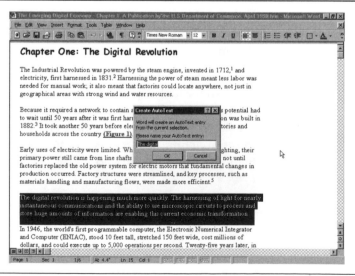

FIGURE 2.18: Creating AutoText

Word provides a number of canned AutoText entries that you can access from the Insert ➤ AutoText menu:

Just choose a category, and then select the entry you want to insert into your document.

TIP TIP TIP TIP TIP TIP TIP TIP TIP TIP TIP TIP TIP TIP TIP TIP TIP TIP TIP TIP TIP TIP TIP TIP TIP

If you're inserting a lot of AutoText into a document, you can turn on the Auto-Text toolbar by choosing View ➤ Toolbars ➤ AutoText. The toolbar's All Entries drop-down menu is the same as the menu bar's AutoText menu.

Delete AutoText entries in the AutoCorrect dialog box (choose Insert ➤ AutoText ➤ AutoText) by selecting the entry you want to delete and clicking the Delete button:

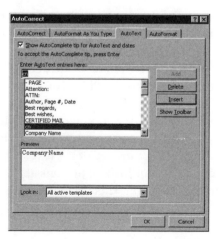

CREATING, INSERTING, AND DELETING AUTOTEXT

1. Select the text to include in the AutoText. To include formatting, click the Show/Hide Paragraph Marks button and select the text, including the paragraph mark.

2. Choose Insert ➣ AutoText ➣ New and name the AutoText.

3. To insert the AutoText in a document, type the entry's name and press the F3 key.

4. To delete an AutoText entry, click the AutoText button on the toolbar to open the AutoText dialog box. Select the AutoText entry and click the Delete button.

Finding and Replacing Text

When you are working with a long document, one of the fastest ways to make repetitive changes to a document is through Find and Replace. *Find* helps you locate a *text string*, and *Replace* substitutes new text for the existing string.

Using Find

To locate a word or phrase, click the Select Browse Object button and choose Find. Click the More button to see all the available options in the Find and Replace dialog box, shown in Figure 2.19.

Enter the text you want to locate in the Find What text box. You can have Word search the entire document (All), or for faster searching, just choose to search above (Up) or below (Down) the insertion point. You can also search for words that are in the same case as you entered (Match Case).

When you have entered your Search options, click the Find Next button to identify the first occurrence of the text string. You can then close the Find dialog box and use the blue browse buttons at the bottom of the vertical scroll bar to move to previous or next occurrences of the string.

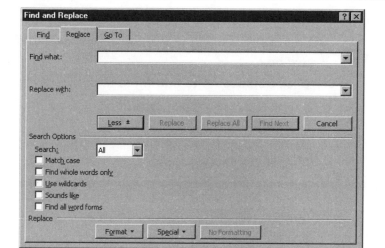

FIGURE 2.19: Find and Replace dialog box

Using Replace

Replace allows you to replace one or all occurrences of a word or phrase with different text.

FINDING AND REPLACING TEXT

1. Click Select Browse Object button and the Find button to open the Find dialog box.

2. Enter the characters you want to search for in the Find What text box. Click Find Next.

3. Close the Find dialog box and click the Next Find/Go To button at the bottom of the vertical scroll bar. Browse through each of the occurrences of the text string.

4. To replace text, open the Find dialog box again and click the Replace tab.

continued

5. Enter the text string you want to search for in the Find What text box and the characters you want to replace it with in the Replace With text box.

6. Click Replace All to complete the replace operation in one step. If you want to review each replacement, choose Replace. Click Find Next to locate the next occurrence. You may need to reposition the dialog box to see the text. Click Replace until you have made all the replacements.

More about Spelling and Grammar

Spell-checking software has been around for a long time, but Word 2000 adds some nice touches. A wavy red line appears under any suspected misspelled word. Right-click the word to choose from a list of possible corrections:

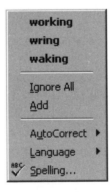

Click the correct word in the list, or correct the misspelling manually. For more information about using the Spelling feature, see Skill 1.4.

Grammar

Grammar Checker uses natural language processing to evaluate sentence structure and word usage to determine if you may be making grammatical errors. Word 2000 not only identifies possible errors on the fly but will actually make suggestions about how to rewrite the text to make it grammatically correct. In Figure 2.20,

Grammar Checker identifies a sentence written in passive voice and makes a suggestion about how the sentence could be reworded to give it more punch.

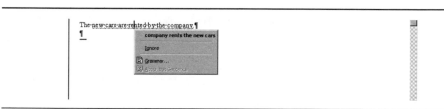

FIGURE 2.20: Grammar Checker

To use Grammar Checker, right-click any word or phrase that has a wavy green line under it. Grammar Checker gives you four options:

- Make one or more suggested corrections

- Leave the text alone

- Open the Grammar dialog box

- Get some additional information about this grammar issue

Click the About This Sentence button to receive some reference information about this particular grammar problem:

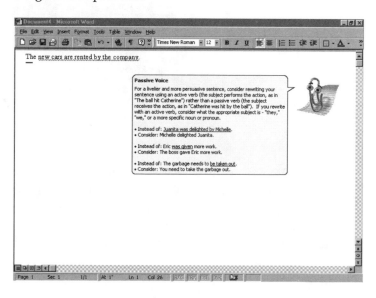

CHECKING SPELLING AND GRAMMAR ON THE FLY

1. Right-click any words that have a wavy line underneath them and choose the correct word or grammar correction from the list.
2. Add words to the Spelling dictionary by clicking the Add button.
3. To see why text was flagged for a grammatical error, click the About This Sentence button.

If you would prefer to wait until you have finished entering and editing text to check the spelling and grammar, you can turn off the Automatic Spelling and Grammar option. Choose Tools ➤ Options ➤ Spelling and Grammar, and click the Check Spelling As You Type and the Check Grammar As You Type check boxes:

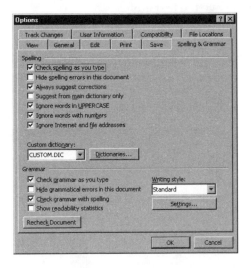

When you are ready to check your document, click the Spelling and Grammar button on the Standard toolbar. Word will review the entire document and stop at any misspelled words or grammar questions. You can choose to accept or ignore the suggestions. Click Next Sentence to resume the process. If you would prefer not to check the grammar, clear the Check Grammar check box.

WARNING WARNING WARNING WARNING WARNING WARNING WARNING WARNING
Although Word's Grammar Checker is a dramatic step forward in electronic proofreading, it regularly makes recommendations to fix text that is already correct or misses sentences that are obviously wrong. If you are uncertain, check another grammar reference.

CHECKING SPELLING AND GRAMMAR USING THE TOOLBAR

1. Click the Spelling and Grammar button on the Standard toolbar.

2. Accept or ignore any suggested corrections.

3. Click Next Sentence to resume checking.

4. Click Add to add the word to the dictionary.

5. Click Change All or Ignore All to change or ignore all occurrences in the current document.

6. Click the Check Grammar check box to turn off grammar checking.

NOTE NOTE NOTE NOTE NOTE NOTE NOTE NOTE NOTE NOTE NOTE NOTE NOTE NOTE NOTE
When you open a document or enter text, Word 2000 can automatically detect the language and use the appropriate spelling and grammar dictionaries. Word supports more than 80 languages. To use this feature, you need to install the languages you want to use from the Office 2000 Language Pack and install the correct keyboard layout from the Windows control panel.

Using the Thesaurus Command

Rather than highlighting errors that you may have made, the thesaurus offers help only when called upon. It's there to help you find more descriptive, entertaining, or precise words to liven up your text.

USING THE THESAURUS

1. Click the word you want to look up and choose Tools ➢ Language ➢ Thesaurus to open the Thesaurus dialog box, shown in Figure 2.21.

2. Click words in the Meanings column that best represent your context to see synonyms for them. Double-click to get a list of words that have the same or similar meaning.

3. Enter a new word to look up in the Replace with Synonym text box.

4. To review previously looked up words, select from the drop-down list under Looked Up.

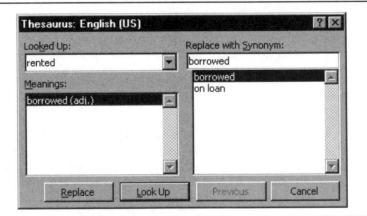

FIGURE 2.21: The Thesaurus dialog box

TIP TIP TIP TIP TIP TIP TIP TIP TIP TIP TIP TIP TIP TIP TIP TIP TIP TIP TIP TIP TIP TIP TIP TIP TIP

To quickly find a synonym, right-click a word in your document, choose Synonyms from the shortcut menu, and then select a synonym from the list.

Hands On

1. Create and store an AutoText entry for your return address, including formatting, to be used on personal correspondence.

2. If you created Doc 1 at the end of Skill 2.2, open it. Use the Replace All option in Find and Replace to replace each instance of `Doc 1` with `Document One`.

3. Check the spelling and grammar in an existing document.

4. Enter the following text, and then use the Thesaurus (and a bit of humor if you wish) to improve it:

    ```
    Wanted: Fun companion for good times. Any age over 18 is fine.
    Must be interesting. Should be cute. Big or small, give me a call
    at 800-555-0000 or send a good picture to Nice Person, 555 Pining
    Away Lane, Seattle, WA.
    ```

5. Open a document that contains misspellings. If you don't have any Word 2000 documents with errors (or if you want to pretend that you don't), you can enter the text below in a new document.

    ```
    Every year, several employes are given a specail bonus at holiday
    time. Employees who have done exceptoinal jobs are given cars to
    drive for the next year. The new cars are rented by the company.
    The current years cars have to be returned and are sold to other
    employees at a discounted rate. The holiday program coresponds to
    the annual awards banquet where many employees are given awards
    for there performance.
    ```

2.7: Getting into Print

Although we are transmitting more and more documents electronically these days, we still print a lot of documents. In this section, we'll look at your printing options and also discuss how to print envelopes and labels, a handy feature for home and office work.

Using Print Preview

Previewing your document before printing it gives you the chance to see how the pages break and whether there are any layout problems that will make the document look less than its best.

To open the Print Preview dialog box, click the Print Preview button on the Standard toolbar or choose File ➤ Print Preview:

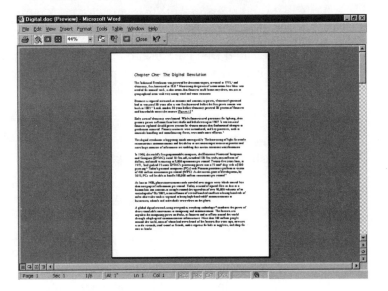

Table 2.3 shows the options available in Print Preview.

TABLE 2.3: Options in Print Preview

Button	Button Name	What It Does
	Print	Prints the document.
	Magnify	When pressed, click on the document to zoom in or out. Inactivate to edit the document.
	One Page	Shows only one page of the document.
	Multiple Page	Shows a maximum of six pages at one time.
31%	Zoom	Changes the magnification level.

TABLE 2.3: Options in Print Preview *(continued)*

Button	Button Name	What It Does
	View Ruler	Turns the vertical and horizontal rulers on and off.
	Shrink to Fit	Reduces the document by one page to prevent spill-over.
	Full Screen	Turns full screen mode on.
Close	Close	Closes Print Preview.
	Context-Sensitive Help	Click and then click on any button to activate Help about that button.

Inserting Page Breaks

Word paginates documents automatically—when text exceeds the length of a page, Word moves to the next page by inserting a soft page break. After you've previewed your document, you might decide you want a page to break earlier: at the end of a cover page, or just before a new topic. To insert a *hard page break* that forces the page to break at the insertion point's current location, press Ctrl+Enter.

Changing Page Orientation and Paper Size

If you think that your document would look better in *landscape* orientation (11 x 8.5) than *portrait* (8.5 x 11), you can change the orientation in Page Setup. Choose File ➤ Page Setup ➤ Paper Size, or double-click the gray frame at the top of the ruler bar to open the dialog box.

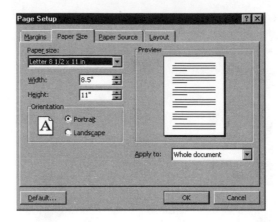

You can also change to another paper size entirely, including a custom size for nonstandard forms such as note cards or half-sheets. If you choose custom size, enter the dimensions for height and width. If you want to apply a page-size change to only part of your document, position the insertion point at the beginning of the page you want to change, go to Page Setup, change the page size, and choose This Point Forward in the Apply To control. To apply the change to a single page and not all the pages that follow it, move the insertion point to the end of the last page with this formatting, select This Point Forward, and change back to the original paper size.

CHANGING PAGE ORIENTATION AND PAPER SIZE

1. To change page orientation for the entire document, choose File ➤ Page Setup ➤ Paper Size.

2. Click the Portrait or Landscape Orientation option.

3. To change paper size, click the Paper size drop-down list and select an option. If you choose Custom, enter the dimensions of the paper in the Height and Width text boxes.

4. To change page orientation for only part of a document, choose This Point Forward in the Apply To text box.

Aligning Text Vertically

After you have the page orientation and paper size set, you may want to create a title page for your document. One easy way to do this is to enter the text you want on the title page and then center text vertically on the page between the top and bottom margins. To activate this feature, position the insertion point on the page you want to align. Choose File ➤ Page Setup and click the Layout tab. Under Vertical Alignment, you will find four options:

Top   The default setting where text lines up with the top margin.

Center   Text on the page is centered between the top and bottom margins.

Justified   Text is spread out so that each line is the same distance apart with the top line at the top margin and the bottom line at the bottom margin.

Bottom   Text lines up with the bottom margin.

ALIGNING TEXT VERTICALLY

1. Click the page that contains the text you want to align.
2. Choose File ➤ Page Setup ➤ Layout and choose Top, Center, Justified, or Bottom from the Vertical Alignment drop-down list. Click OK.

Setting Margins

Word's default *margins*, the white space between text and the edge of the paper the text will be printed on, are 1 inch on the top and bottom and 1.25 inches on the left and right sides of the page. To change margins, use the Margins page of the Page Setup dialog box, shown in Figure 2.22, and set the following options:

- Top, Bottom, Left, and Right spin box controls set the amount of white space on the four edges of the document.
- The *gutter margin* is used to add additional space to a document that will be bound.
- The *mirror margin* feature helps you format margins for back-to-back printing.

The default for the Apply To control is Whole Document. You can, however, change margins from the insertion point forward for the rest of a document by choosing This Point Forward from the Apply To drop-down list.

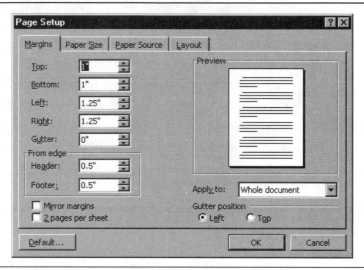

FIGURE 2.22: The Page Setup dialog box

CHANGING DOCUMENT MARGINS

1. Position the insertion point where you want the margin changes to take effect.

2. Choose File ➢ Page Setup to open the Page Setup dialog box, and click the Margins tab.

3. Click the Mirror margins check box to activate mirror margins, if desired.

4. Use the spin box arrows or type in the text boxes to increase or decrease the margins.

5. Click OK to return to the document.

If you prefer, you can change margins using the vertical and horizontal rulers in Print Preview or in Print Layout view. Point to the margin line on the ruler and the pointer changes to a double-headed arrow. When you hold down the mouse button, a dotted line extends through the document, showing the location of the margin. Drag the dotted line in the desired direction to adjust the margin.

NOTE NOTE NOTE NOTE NOTE NOTE NOTE NOTE NOTE NOTE NOTE NOTE NOTE NOTE NOTE

You can also print 2, 4, 6, 8, or 16 pages to a sheet. In the Zoom section of the Print dialog box, select the number of pages from the Pages per Sheet drop-down list, and select the paper size from the Scale to Paper Size drop-down list.

Printing Options

If you click the Print button on the Standard toolbar, Word uses the current print options. By default, one copy of the document is sent to the Windows default printer. If you want to change the print settings, choose File ➤ Print to open the Print dialog box:

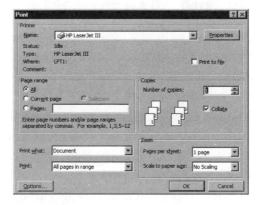

In the Print dialog box you can:

- Choose another printer

- Print only designated pages of a document, including current page, a range of pages, or selected text

- Choose to print the document properties (who created it, when it was created, how many words, characters, and so on) or other lists such as Auto-Text entries

- Indicate in the Print text box whether to print just even pages, just odd pages, or both

- Specify the number of copies and have them collated (pages 1, 2, 3 for each copy rather than all copies of page 1, then all copies of page 2, etc.)

- Print to a file so that someone without Word 2000 can print your document

Set the print options the way you want them and click Print to send the document to the printer.

Creating and Printing Envelopes and Labels

One of the time-saving features of Office 2000 is its ability to maintain address books that are shared among the applications. (See Skill 9 for information about Outlook address books.) Combine that with Word's Envelopes and Labels feature, and it has never been easier to prepare documents for mailing.

CREATING AND PRINTING AN ENVELOPE

1. If you are writing a letter, enter the name and address you want on the envelope as the inside address in the letter.

2. Choose Tools ➤ Envelopes and Labels and choose the Envelopes tab, shown in Figure 2.23.

3. The Name and Address you entered should appear in the Delivery Address box. If it does not, close the dialog box, copy the name and address, reopen the dialog box, and use Ctrl+V or Shift+Ins to paste it.

4. Choose to enter or omit a return address.

5. Click the Options button to open the Envelope Options dialog box.

6. Click the Envelopes Options tab to set envelope options such as envelope size, delivery point bar code, and fonts.

7. Click the Printing Options tab to set printing options such as feed method and the printer tray that contains the envelope, and click OK.

8. Click the Print button to send the envelope to the printer.

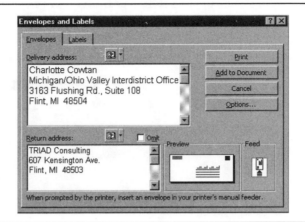

FIGURE 2.23: The Envelopes page of the Envelopes and Labels dialog box

TIP TIP TIP TIP TIP TIP TIP TIP TIP TIP TIP TIP TIP TIP TIP TIP TIP TIP TIP TIP TIP TIP TIP

If you want your return address to appear as the default in the Envelopes and Labels dialog box, choose Tools ➤ Options ➤ User Information and enter your mailing address.

The Labels feature gives you the option to print one label or a full page of the same label. (See Skill 4 for information about creating individualized labels for different people.) Click the Labels tab of the Envelopes and Labels dialog box (choose Tools ➤ Envelopes and Labels):

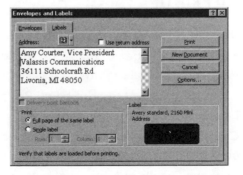

Choose whether you would like a full page of the same label or a single label. You can even specify which row and column to print on so you can use up those

partial sheets of labels left over from other printing jobs. If you want to print a full page of return address labels, click the Use Return Address check box.

The default label is Avery standard, 2160 Mini Address. If this is not the kind of label you use, click the Options buttons to select a different label:

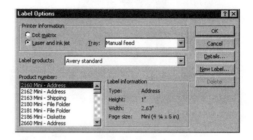

Choose the product and product number you want to use from the list provided. Click the Details button to see the actual measurements and layout of the labels you have selected or the New Label button to design custom labels. Click OK to close either page and OK again to return to the Envelopes and Labels dialog box.

You can now print the labels. If you are creating return address labels or labels that you want to save, click the New Document button to paste the labels into a new document. Save the document before sending the labels to the printer. In the future, to print more of the same labels, you can open the label document and print it without having to recreate the labels.

CREATING AND PRINTING LABELS

1. Choose Tools ➢ Envelopes and Labels ➢ Labels.
2. Enter any changes to the Address box. Click Use Return Address if you want to create return address labels.
3. Check if you want to print a Full Page of the Same Label or a Single Label.
4. Click the Options button to select a different label product or to change the printer information.
5. Click the Details or New Label buttons to adjust the dimensions of the labels selected.

continued

6. Close the New Label or Details pages and the Labels Options pages by clicking OK or Cancel.

7. Click the Print button to send the labels to the printer or the New Document button to create a label document that can be saved for re-use.

SKILL
2

Hands On

1. Create and print an envelope that includes your return address.

2. Create a full page of return labels for yourself. Create and save a new document containing the labels.

3. Type a letter and create an envelope for it that you add to your document. Preview it in Print Preview before printing it.

Are You Experienced?

Now you can...

- ☑ Create a document in Word
- ☑ Apply fonts and special formatting, including special effects
- ☑ Indent and align text
- ☑ Automatically add bullets or numbers to a list
- ☑ Use Find and Replace to replace existing text or find text in a document
- ☑ Check your spelling and grammar
- ☑ Use the Thesaurus to find synonyms
- ☑ Set print options
- ☑ Change page layout settings

Applying Advanced Formatting Techniques

- ➔ Formatting pages and setting text flow options
- ➔ Working with newspaper columns
- ➔ Constructing high-quality tables
- ➔ Using styles, templates, and shortcuts
- ➔ Creating and modifying outlines

3.1: Formatting Pages

Page numbers—or headers and footers—make a lengthy document easier to follow. Word 2000 can help you with everything from automatically numbering the pages to inserting different headers and footers on odd and even pages. You can also adjust hyphenation and other text flow options to make sure your final document looks its best.

Formatting Sections

Word 2000 organizes the formatting for documents in sections. A *section* is a part of a document that has a specified number of columns and that uses a common set of margins, page orientation, headers and footers, and sequence of page numbers. Word automatically inserts section breaks when you:

- Format text as columns (see Skill 3.2)

- Change Page Setup options and indicate that you want the changes to apply to This Point Forward

You will want to manually insert a section break to apply different page size or header and footer formatting within a document.

Section breaks can be viewed in Normal and appear as double-dotted lines with the words Section Break and the type of break in them. Breaks can be seen in any of the other views by turning on Show/Hide.

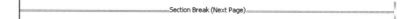

INSERTING AND DELETING SECTION BREAKS

1. Move the insertion point to where you'd like the break and choose Insert ➤ Break.
2. Choose where you'd like the next section to begin by selecting one of the four section options in the Break dialog box.
3. Switch to Normal view to see the section breaks in your document.
4. To delete a section break, select it and press the Delete key.

Creating and Modifying Page Numbers

Whether or not you have inserted section breaks, you may want a simple way to automatically number the pages. Nothing could be more effortless than Word's Page Numbering feature. Choose Insert ➤ Page Numbers to open the Page Numbers dialog box, shown in Figure 3.1.

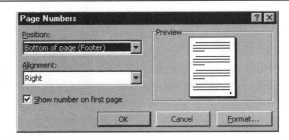

FIGURE 3.1: The Page Numbers dialog box

You have four options:

Position   Bottom of Page or Top of Page

Alignment   Left, Center, Right, Inside, or Outside (use Inside or Outside when you have turned on mirror margins in Page Setup)

Show Number on First Page

Format   Opens the Page Number Format dialog box:

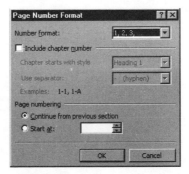

The Page Number Format dialog box allows you to choose a numbering style such as "A, B, C" or "1, 2, 3" and to include a chapter number, if you desire. You could, for example, click the Include Chapter Number check box to show 1–1 as the chapter and page number. If you would like to start your page numbering at a number other than 1, enter a number in the Start At text box. Once you have made your formatting choices, click OK to return to the Page Numbers dialog box and OK again to insert the page numbers. To view the page numbers, switch to Print Layout view or Print Preview.

If your document has more than one section, you can set up different page numbering for each section. Position the insertion point on the first page of the document (which is the beginning of the first section) and add page numbering. Then move the insertion point to the first page of the *second* section, and choose Insert ➢ Page Numbers again. Click Format to set up the formatting for this section's numbering. If you want the page numbering to continue from the first section, choose that option in the Page Number Format dialog box. Repeat the process for any additional sections. If you want to remove page numbers, you need to edit the header or footer where the page number appears.

Creating Headers and Footers

Page numbers are certainly useful, but you'll probably also want to include other information on each page: all rights reserved, your name, or the name of your company, for example. For this type of information, use the Header and Footer feature. Headers and footers are placed in the top and bottom margins. To insert a header or footer, choose View ➢ Header and Footer. The existing document text is immediately dimmed and the Header text box at the top of your document opens. A floating Header and Footer toolbar, like the one shown in Figure 3.2, also opens.

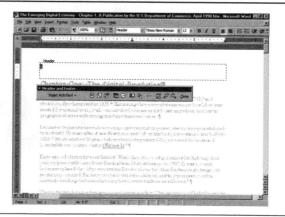

FIGURE 3.2: Header and Footer view

Enter the text you want to appear in the Header text box. Use the toolbar buttons to create and modify the headers and footers:

TABLE 3.1: Header and Footer toolbar buttons

Button	Button Name	What It Does
Insert AutoText ▾	Insert AutoText	Provides drop-down list of AutoText entries
	Insert Page Number	Inserts page number placeholder
	Insert Number of Pages	Inserts placeholder for total number of pages
	Format Page Number	Opens Page Number Format dialog box
	Insert Date	Inserts placeholder for date
	Insert Time	Inserts placeholder for time
	Page Setup	Opens the Layout page of Page Setup dialog box
	Show/Hide Document Text	Makes document text visible or invisible while working with background
	Same As Previous	Makes header or footer the same as in the previous section
	Switch between Header and Footer	Changes view between header and footer text box
	Show Previous	Moves to previous section's header
	Show Next	Moves to next section's header
Close	Close Header and Footer	Closes Header and Footer view

Whether you are creating headers, footers, or both, the process is the same. Just move to the header or footer you want to add or edit. Use the Switch between Header and Footer and Show Previous/Show Next buttons to navigate between the headers and footers in each section of your document.

TIP TIP TIP TIP TIP TIP TIP TIP TIP TIP TIP TIP TIP TIP TIP TIP TIP TIP TIP TIP TIP TIP TIP
To suppress the header or footer on the first page, choose the Different First Page option from the Layout tab of the Page Setup dialog box and leave the header or footer blank.

Taking Care of Loose Ends

Before you print the final version of a document, you should clean up dangling words, bad line and page breaks, and extra spaces that detract from the appearance of your document. You can clean up these loose ends in three ways:

- Are there spaces at the ends of lines because long words wrap to the beginning of the next line? If so, use Hyphenation.

- Does the document have text strings that should be kept together but are broken over two lines? If so, use nonbreaking spaces.

- Are there paragraphs or lines of paragraphs that should be kept together but currently break across two pages? If so, use Text Flow Options.

Make sure you have done all your editing and formatting before attempting any of this final cleanup. When you add, delete, or reformat text, you have to clean up the document all over again.

Handling Line Breaks

Word 2000 includes options for automatically and manually hyphenating your documents. To have Word automatically hyphenate your document, choose Tools ➢ Language ➢ Hyphenation and click the Automatically Hyphenate Document check box:

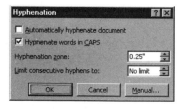

TIP TIP TIP TIP TIP TIP TIP TIP TIP TIP TIP TIP TIP TIP TIP TIP TIP TIP TIP TIP TIP TIP TIP

If you want to prevent a word or phrase that contains a hyphen (such as a phone number) from breaking at the end of a line, you can insert a *nonbreaking hyphen* by holding down Ctrl+Shift when you enter the hyphen. To enter an *optional hyphen*, a hyphen that breaks a word or a phrase at the designated place if it occurs at the end of a line, hold down Ctrl when you enter the hyphen.

Nonbreaking Spaces   Occasionally, you might have a text string, such as an address, that should not be separated at the end of a line. You can protect this string by inserting nonbreaking spaces instead of regular spaces within the text string. Similar to a nonbreaking hyphen, text connected with *nonbreaking spaces* will move to the next line rather then breaking between lines. To insert a non-breaking space, hold Ctrl and Shift when you press the spacebar.

Handling Page Breaks

Word 2000 offers a number of other ways to keep text together. One of these options, with the tacky name *Widow/Orphan Control*, is on by default. This feature prevents the first line of a paragraph from being left alone at the bottom of the page (an orphan) or the last line of a paragraph from appearing by itself at the top of a new page (a widow). You can turn Widow/Orphan Control off in the Line and Page Breaks tab of the Paragraph dialog box (choose Format ➢ Paragraph ➢ Line and Page Breaks):

If you want to keep specific lines or paragraphs of text together, first select the text and then open the dialog box.

ADJUSTING LINE AND PAGE BREAKS

1. Choose Format ➤ Paragraph ➤ Line and Page Breaks to turn text flow options—Widow/Orphan Control, Keep Lines Together, Keep with Next, and Page Break Before—on or off.
2. Press Ctrl+Shift+hyphen to insert a nonbreaking hyphen.
3. Press Ctrl+hyphen to insert an optional hyphen.
4. Press Ctrl+Shift+spacebar to insert a nonbreaking space.

Hands On

1. Open an existing document, or create a new document that is at least three pages long. Save the document before proceeding.

   a) Add a header that contains the name of the document and the date to all but the first page.

   b) Insert a centered page number. Do not number the first page.

   c) Save the document under a different name and then print it.

2. Manually hyphenate an existing document.

3. Create a footer for the odd pages and a different footer for the even pages of a document.

3.2: Working with Columns

Some kinds of information are most effectively presented in tabular or newspaper columns. Tabular parallel columns, discussed in Skill 2.4 and Skill 3.3, display corresponding text in columns (like a phone book). With *newspaper columns*, text flows from the bottom of one column to the top of the next. If you create newsletters, flyers, reports, announcements, or other types of publications, you'll probably use Word's newspaper columns feature quite a bit.

Working with Newspaper Columns

Working with columns requires a little advance design work. You'll find that it is often easier to enter document text into a single column and then convert the text into multiple columns. Because of the space between the columns, one page of text takes up more than a page when poured into two or more columns. As a result, you may have to go back and edit text to get it to fit on a prescribed number of pages. However, by first focusing on your writing and then switching your attention to the design issues, you'll very likely end up with a higher quality product in the long run.

SKILL
3

Entering and Editing Text in Columns

To work with columns, switch to Print Layout view so you can actually see the columns as they will appear on the page.

CREATING COLUMNS

1. Switch to Print Layout view. Select the text you want to change to columns.
2. Click the Columns button on the Standard toolbar and drag to select the number of columns you want.
3. To make equal columns, like those in Figure 3.3, move the insertion point to the end of the text and insert a continuous section break (choose Insert ➢ Break ➢ Continuous.
4. To enter a title that spans the columns, enter the title at the beginning of the first column. Select the title, click the Columns button, and drag to select one column.

FIGURE 3.3: Text in columns

Revising Column Structure

Word provides you with several options for changing the number of columns in your document, the column width, and the white space in the gutter between columns.

RESTRUCTURING COLUMNS

1. To add or delete columns, click in the columns section of your document and click the Columns button. Drag to select the desired number of columns.

2. Drag the Move Columns marker on the ruler to change column width and to move columns left or right.

3. Drag the Left or Right Margin markers on the ruler to change the white space between columns.

5. Open the Columns dialog box (choose Format ➤ Columns), shown in Figure 3.4, to create as many as 10 columns, to lock columns so they are of equal width, to insert a line between columns, or to enter exact measurements for column widths and spacing.

6. To move text into the next column, move the insertion point in front of the text you want to move. Open the Columns dialog box and choose This Point Forward in the Apply To control. Click the Start New Column check box to move the text to the next column.

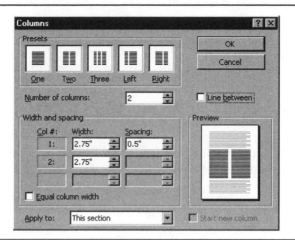

FIGURE 3.4: Columns dialog box

Hands On

1. Open an existing document, or create a new document that contains several paragraphs of text.

   a) Select the text and convert it to two columns. Balance the column length by inserting a continuous section break.

   b) Use the ruler to change the column widths, making the first column wider than the second.

   c) Add a line between the columns.

   d) Add a title that spans both columns. Save the document as *Working with Columns*.

   e) Move the last sentence that begins in the first column to the second column by using Keeping Text Together options.

2. In the same document:

   a) Change *Working with Columns*, or another document with columns, back to a single column. (You may have to delete additional section breaks—switch to Normal view to see them.)

b)   Use the Presets in the Columns dialog box to change the text to three columns of equal width.

c)   Balance the columns' length.

d)   Add another paragraph of text to the end of the section.

3.3: Constructing High-Quality Tables

Although you can use tabs to present information in parallel columns, it is far easier to use Word's powerful Tables features. With tables, every block of text can be easily formatted, edited, deleted, and moved around without affecting the remainder of the text. Tables are one of the most versatile tools in the Word 2000 toolkit.

Creating and Revising Tables

You create tables in Word 2000 in three ways: using the Insert Table button, using the Insert Table dialog box, and using the Draw Table button.

To use the Insert Table button, click the button and drag the number of columns and rows you want in your table.

When you release the mouse button, a blank table appears in your document.

To create a table using the Insert Table dialog box, choose Table ➤ Insert Table. Enter the number of rows, columns, and column widths in the appropriate controls. When you create a table, it's easiest if you determine the number of columns you're going to need before you start. You can always add columns later, but it may mean changing the widths of the other columns to accommodate them. Adding rows, on the other hand, is as simple as pressing Tab at the end of a row. To create a table that is as wide as your page, leave the Fixed Column Width setting on Auto. When you've entered all the settings, click OK to create the table.

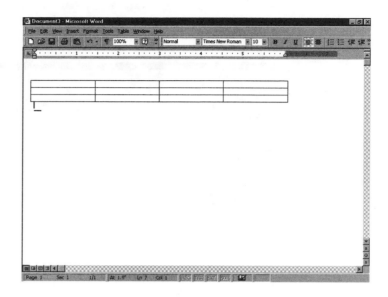

You can also draw a table exactly the way you want it to appear.

 Clicking the Tables and Borders button on the Standard toolbar opens the Tables and Borders toolbar; the mouse pointer will change to a pencil. Drag the pencil to create a rectangle about the size of the table you want:

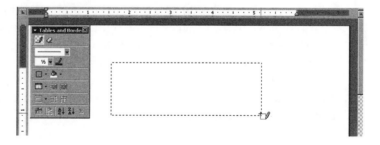

When you release the mouse button, the outside border of the table appears in your document. Use the pencil again to draw in column and row borders:

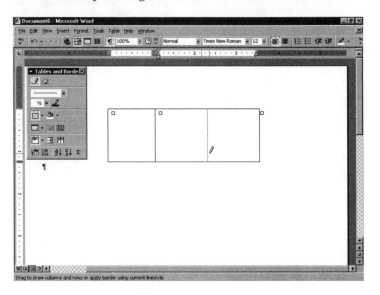

Entering and Editing Text

Once you have created a table, you enter text by clicking in any *cell* (the intersection of a column and row). Use the Tab key or the Right Arrow key on the keyboard to move to the next cell to the right. Shift+Tab or the Left Arrow key will move one cell to the left. The Up and Down Arrow keys will move the insertion point to the cell below or above the current cell.

If you created your table by drawing it, click the Draw Table button on the Tables and Borders toolbar or close the toolbar to change the pointer back from a pencil to that old familiar I-beam so you can begin typing.

Table 3.2 shows how to select portions of a table:

TABLE 3.2: Selecting in Tables

To Select	Action
A cell	Triple-click in cell.
A row	Move mouse to left margin, point to the row, and click.
Multiple rows	Select first row, hold down mouse button, and drag down the desired number of rows.
A column	Move mouse to above column. It will change to a downward pointed arrow. Click. –OR– Hold down Alt key and click in column.
Multiple columns	Select first column, hold down mouse button, and drag the desired number of columns. –OR– For contiguous columns, select first column (any method) and then hold down Shift and select last column (any method).
Entire table	Choose Table ➤ Select Table. –OR– Hold down Alt key and double-click.

Formatting Text in Tables

Each table cell can be formatted separately. Whatever you can do to a paragraph, you can do to the text within a cell. Use the Formatting toolbar or the Format menu to apply fonts, font effects, alignment, bullets and numbering, and indents and spacing to the text in a table.

The Tables and Borders toolbar also provides some additional formatting options unique to tables.

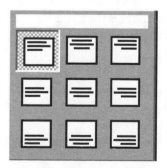

Click one of the nine alignment options to place text exactly where you want it in a cell.

Rotating Text in Tables

When you really want to draw attention to your text, rotate it so that it is no longer running in the traditional direction across the page. With Word's Text Direction feature, you can rotate text in a table so that it runs vertically, facing either right or left. Select the cell or group of cells that contain the text you want to rotate. Then click the Change Text Direction button on the Tables and Borders toolbar. The button is a toggle button, which means that the first click rotates the text so that it is facing left, the second click flips it so it faces right, and the third click returns it to the tried-and-true horizontal.

As the text rotates, so do some of the buttons on the Formatting and Tables and Borders toolbars. The alignment buttons, Numbering, Bullets, and Text Direction all change to match the rotation of the text:

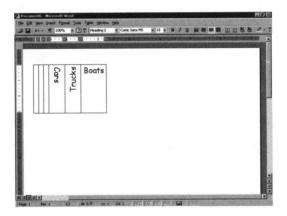

Even the I-beam and insertion point rotate, so editing can be a little disconcerting at first, but it's technically no different from horizontal editing. The main thing to remember is that you have to drag the mouse vertically to select text. Once you've gotten the hang of that, you're all set.

ENTERING, EDITING, AND POSITIONING TEXT IN TABLES

1. Click in any cell and begin typing. Use the Tab key to move one cell to the right, Shift+Tab to move to the left, and arrow keys to move up and down or left and right.

2. Apply any character or paragraph formatting options to the text. Each cell is treated as a paragraph.

3. Click one of the alignment buttons on the Tables and Borders toolbar to reposition text within a cell.

4. Click the Change Text Direction button on the Tables and Borders toolbar to rotate text vertically.

SKILL 3

Modifying Table Structure

You can easily modify tables. You can add or delete rows and columns, change column and row widths, and merge and split cells without upsetting the rest of the table text.

Adding and Deleting Rows and Columns

To add a row at the end of a table, simply move to the last cell in the table and press Tab. If you want to insert rows in the middle of the table, select the number of rows you want to insert and choose Table ➤ Insert Rows Above or Table ➤ Insert Rows Below, or right-click and choose Insert Rows from the shortcut menu. Word will insert the rows ahead of the first selected row.

To delete rows, select the rows you want to delete. Choose Table ➤ Delete ➤ Rows, or right-click and choose Delete Rows from the shortcut menu. If you select a cell rather than an entire row, choose Table ➤ Delete ➤ Cells, which opens the Delete Cells dialog box:

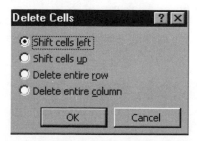

You can choose to delete the current cell and shift the remaining cells left or up. If you want to delete a whole row or column, choose Delete Entire Row or Delete Entire Column.

Inserting columns works the same way as inserting rows. New rows and new columns are the same width as the ones you select to create them, so you may have to adjust the widths of newly inserted columns if they no longer fit the width of the page.

TIP TIP TIP TIP TIP TIP TIP TIP TIP TIP TIP TIP TIP TIP TIP TIP TIP TIP TIP TIP TIP TIP TIP TIP TIP

To insert a column at the end of a table, click in the last column and then choose Table ➤ Insert ➤ Columns to the Right. To insert a column at the beginning of the table, click in the first column and then choose Table ➤ Insert ➤ Columns to the Left.

Changing Column and Cell Widths

The easiest way to adjust a column or a row is to move the insertion point to the border between the row or column. The insertion point will change to a double-headed arrow, allowing you to drag the border in either direction:

1	2	3	4	5
A	B	C	D	E
F	G	H	I	J
K	L	M	O	P
Q	R	S	T	U
V	W	X	Y	Z

If you drag with a cell selected, you're only changing the width for that cell. To be certain, you can, of course, select the entire column or row before dragging.

At times you may want to make all the columns the same width or all rows the same height (for example, when creating a calendar). Select the columns or rows you want to be the same width or height and choose Table ➤ AutoFit ➤ Distribute Columns Evenly or Table ➤ AutoFit ➤ Distribute Rows Evenly, and Word will do the work for you. The Tables and Borders toolbar also has buttons to distribute rows and columns evenly.

You can make another quick adjustment after you enter all the text in your table. Select the columns you want to adjust and choose Table ≻ AutoFit ≻ AutoFit to Contents to automatically adjust the width of the columns to the widest entry.

You can also enter exact height and width measurements for columns and rows. Choose Table ≻ Table Properties to open the Table Properties dialog box. To adjust the width of a column, select the Column tab, as shown in Figure 3.5, and change the measurement in the Preferred Width spin box. Click the Previous Column or Next Column button to adjust the measurement of the previous or next column.

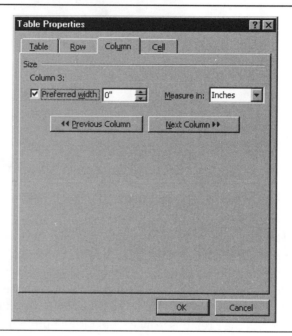

FIGURE 3.5: The Table Properties dialog box, with the Column tab selected

To adjust the height of a row, select the Row tab in the Table Properties dialog box, as shown in Figure 3.6, and change the measurement in the Specify Height spin box.

SKILL
3

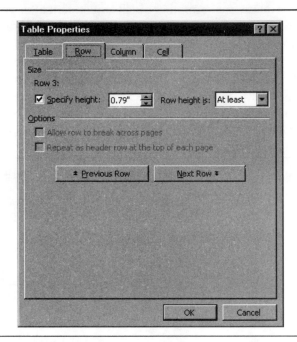

FIGURE 3.6: The Table Properties dialog box, with the Row tab selected

The Row tab offers some other important options. In the Row Height Is box, select At Least if you want the rows to maintain a minimum height regardless of what is in them. Select Exactly when you want to designate a row height that doesn't change. This is useful when you are creating calendars, for example, and you want the row height to stay the same regardless of the contents.

Click the Previous Row or Next Row button to adjust the height and other characteristics of the previous or next row.

Merging and Splitting Cells

It doesn't take much work with tables to discover that you don't want the same number of cells in every row or column. You might want to put a title in a single cell that spans the top of the table. Or you might be creating a form, such as the order form shown in Figure 3.7, and want fewer columns for the totals. When you want to make one cell from two or more cells, you *merge* the cells. *Split* cells to separate a single cell into multiple cells.

Order Form			
Item	Price	Quantity	Total
Subtotal			
		Sales Tax	
		Total	

FIGURE 3.7: An order form with merged cells

To merge cells, simply select the cells you want to merge and Choose Tables ➢ Merge Cells, or click the Merge Cells button on the Tables and Borders toolbar.

If you prefer the visual approach, you can use the Eraser on the Tables and Borders toolbar to erase the border between cells you want to merge. Drag the Eraser horizontally to merge rows or vertically to merge columns.

Use the Draw Table pencil from the Tables and Borders toolbar to draw cell borders where you need them to split cells, or choose Table ➢ Split Cells, or click the Split Cells button, to open the Split Cells dialog box:

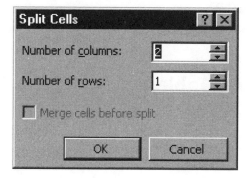

Use the dialog box's spin box controls to enter the number of columns and rows you would like to divide the selected cell(s) into.

MODIFYING TABLE STRUCTURE

1. Insert rows at the end of a table by clicking in the last cell and pressing Tab. Insert rows in the middle of the table by selecting the number of rows you want to insert and choosing Table ➢ Insert ➢ Rows Above or Table ➢ Insert ➢ Rows Below.

2. Delete rows by selecting the rows you want to delete and choosing Table ➢ Delete ➢ Rows.

3. Insert columns by selecting the number of columns you want to insert and selecting Table ➢ Insert ➢ Columns to the Left or Table ➢ Insert ➢ Columns to the Right.

4. Change the width of columns by pointing to the cell border and dragging the border with the double-headed arrow pointer.

5. Merge cells by selecting the cells you want to merge and choosing Table ➢ Merge Cells or by clicking the Merge Cells button.

6. Split cells by using the Draw Table button on the Tables and Borders toolbar.

Formatting Tables

Before you print your table, you might want to put some finishing touches on it to give it that polished, professional look. Word 2000 offers both automatic and manual table formatting options to add and remove borders, change border types, and add colors and shading.

Using AutoFormat

AutoFormat provides you with a number of formats that you can apply in one easy step. Click anywhere in your table and choose Table ➢ Table AutoFormat to open the Table AutoFormat dialog box shown in Figure 3.8.

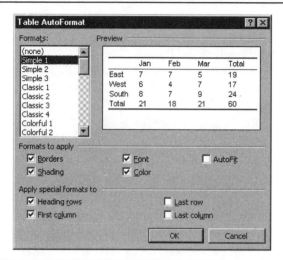

FIGURE 3.8: Table AutoFormat dialog box

AutoFormat applies borders, shading, fonts, and colors. Most of the formats include special formatting for the header row, last row, and first and last columns since these often contain titles or summary information. Turn check marks on or off to indicate which formatting options you want to apply. Choosing any of the formats will give you a preview of the format. Click OK when you want to apply the selected format to your table. If you're not satisfied, click Undo, or choose Table AutoFormat again and select a different format.

Adding Your Own Borders and Shading

You don't have to settle for the predesigned AutoFormats. You can adjust Auto-Formats manually or start from scratch, whichever you prefer. Either way, you'll want to turn on the Tables and Borders toolbar before you begin formatting.

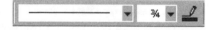

The Line Style, Line Weight, and Border Color buttons all relate to the cell borders. Click the drop-down arrow next to Line Style or Line Weight to select from the list of choices available. Clicking the Border Color button opens a color menu. Select a color, and use the pencil pointer to draw over borders that you want to color. Make sure you draw over the entire length of the border, or the color will not be applied. All three buttons are dynamic, which means that your most recent choice appears on the button to make it easy to reapply.

To apply a border, select the cells you want to apply a border to, select the Line Style, Line Weight, and Border Color you want to apply, and click the Borders button to open a drop-down menu. Click the type of border you want to apply.

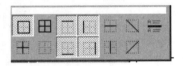

 Click the Shading Color button drop-down to open a menu of shading colors, including various shades of gray. If you are applying a lot of different borders and shading to your table, you can pull the menus off the toolbar so they float on the surface of your document:

You can then apply as many borders or shades as you want without having to open the menus each time. To float the menus, click the drop-down arrow to open the menu. Point to the gray bar at the top of the menu, and the bar will turn the same color as your Windows title bars. Drag the menu into the document. When you're finished with the menu, just click its Close button.

TIP TIP TIP TIP TIP TIP TIP TIP TIP TIP TIP TIP TIP TIP TIP TIP TIP TIP TIP TIP TIP TIP

Borders and Shading are not limited to use in tables. You can apply the same skills you just learned to any paragraph of text. Just select one or more paragraphs and click the Tables and Borders button or choose Format ➢ Borders and Shading.

Centering Tables Horizontally

If you've adjusted the column widths in your table, it may no longer extend across the entire width of the page. In Word 2000, you can center the table between the left and right margins by selecting the entire table and clicking the Center button on the Formatting toolbar.

TIP TIP TIP TIP TIP TIP TIP TIP TIP TIP TIP TIP TIP TIP TIP TIP TIP TIP TIP TIP TIP TIP TIP TIP

It is possible to include calculations in Word tables. However, the Word Help file on formulas suggests that if you know how to use Excel, embedding all or part of a worksheet is often easier than using formulas in a Word table. We certainly agree. To learn more about embedding Excel worksheets into Word, see Skill 11.

Hands On

1. Open a new document:

   a) Change the Page Orientation to Landscape. Using the Draw Table feature, insert a seven-column, six-row table to create a calendar for the current month.

   b) Select the columns and click Distribute Columns Evenly. Enter the names of the days of the week in the first row of the table. Center the day names horizontally and vertically. Change the font and font size as appropriate.

   c) Insert a new row at the top of the table. Merge the cells in the row and enter the current month and the year using a large font size. Center the text vertically and horizontally. Shade the row.

   d) Enter and right-align dates for the month in the appropriate cells of the table.

   e) Drag the last row so it is just above the bottom margin. Select the date rows and choose Distribute Rows Evenly to make them all the same size.

   f) Change the outside border to a thicker, more decorative border. Change the bottom border under the title to a different border type.

     g)   Identify two important dates in the month and shade them.

     h)   Insert a document title and an introductory paragraph of text *above* the table. (Press Ctrl+Home to move to the top of the document and press Enter to create blank lines above the table.) Insert a border around the title and apply shading to it.

2. Create a table that shows information related to a project you are working on. Use Borders and Shading to make the table attractive. Use all the table features you know to improve the table's appearance.

3.4: Working Smarter with Word

One of the things that computers are supposed to prevent is repeating the same tasks over and over again, and Word 2000 does its share of prevention. Learning to use styles and templates may take a bit of practice, but once they become part of your routine, you'll wonder how you lived without them.

You've Got Style, Baby!

Word's *Styles* feature lets you save existing formats and apply them to other text. Styles can include fonts, sizes, font attributes, alignment, character spacing, paragraph spacing, bullets and numbering, borders, indenting, and just about any other formatting you can think of. Once you've created a style, all you have to do to apply the style is select it from a list. But the major benefit of styles is that if you change a style, all the text using that style is automatically changed, too—much easier than adjusting the font size on 25 subheadings.

APPLYING STYLES

1. Click the Styles drop-down arrow on the Formatting toolbar and choose a style from the list.
2. To apply a style to existing text, select the text and then choose the style.

Getting to Know the Styles

When you open a new Word document, you'll find a list of default styles available for your use:

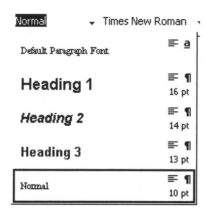

To use any of the default styles, click the drop-down arrow next to Normal and select the style you want to apply. You can apply a style before entering text, or you can apply it to selected text. You'll notice that the items on the list are formatted to show the style.

A Style All Your Own

Once you start working with styles, it won't be long before you're dissatisfied with the basic selection and want to create your own styles. Not a problem. Simply format a paragraph the way you would like the style to appear, and click in the Style text box. Type the name of your style and press Enter. The newly created style in Figure 3.9 is 26-point bold, italic, Comic Sans MS, centered, with a shadow border.

FIGURE 3.9: A newly created style

Now when you look at the drop-down list, the new style appears on the list and illustrates what it looks like:

To apply the style to other text, select the text and select the style from the list.

Redefining Styles

After you've created and applied a style, you may decide that you don't like the font or you need some extra spacing between paragraphs. It's in situations like this that styles really shine. You can redefine the style, and it will automatically change all the text formatted in that style throughout the entire document. To change a style, select a paragraph that uses the style and make the desired changes. While the paragraph is still selected, click in the Styles text box, and rather than typing in a new name, just press Enter. The Modify Style dialog box appears, which gives you two choices: Do you want to update the style to reflect the changes you made to this selection, or do you want to cancel the changes you made and reapply the prior formatting?

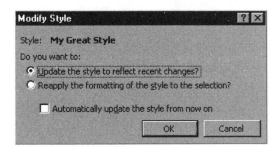

This dialog box also allows you to automatically update the style if you make future changes to text where the style is applied. It's safer to ignore this check box because you're not warned when your formatting changes will affect a style.

Some styles include spacing before or after a paragraph. If you want to change the amount of spacing included in a style, select a sample paragraph, choose Format ➤ Paragraph, and on the Indents and Spacing page, adjust Spacing Before and After. When you've made the changes, redefine the style.

CREATING AND REDEFINING STYLES

SKILL 3

1. Format a paragraph with the options you would like contained in the style.

2. Click in the Style text box and type a name for the new style; press Enter.

3. Select another paragraph and choose the new style from the drop-down list.

4. To redefine a style, select a paragraph and change the formatting. Click in the Style text box and press Enter.

5. Choose Update the Style to Reflect Recent Changes.

If you create a style that you would like to have available whenever you create documents, you can assign the style to the Normal template, which opens every time you create a new blank document. Choose Format ➤ Style, select the style from the list, and choose Modify. Click the Add to Template check box. Now every time you create a new blank document, your style will be available.

To delete a style from the Normal template, choose Format ➤ Style, select the style from the list and choose Organizer to open the Style Organizer. Choose the style or styles in the To NORMAL.DOT list and click the Delete button, then choose Yes; to delete several selected styles without further prompting, click Yes to All. Click Close to close the Style Organizer. Remember, though, that any and all documents based on the style will be reformatted to another style, so you should never delete a style that has been used in existing documents.

NOTE NOTE NOTE NOTE NOTE NOTE NOTE NOTE NOTE NOTE NOTE NOTE NOTE NOTE
You cannot delete any of Word's built-in styles.

TIP TIP TIP TIP TIP TIP TIP TIP TIP TIP TIP TIP TIP TIP TIP TIP TIP TIP TIP TIP TIP TIP TIP TIP

To automatically apply heading styles 1 through 9 as you are creating a document, choose Tools > AutoCorrect to open the AutoCorrect dialog box. Click the AutoFormat As You Type tab, and in the Apply As You Type section, click the Headings check box. To automatically apply heading styles 1 through 9 when AutoFormatting a document, click the AutoFormat tab in the AutoCorrect dialog box, and in the Apply section, click the Headings check box.

Hands On

1. Open an existing document that contains a title and several subheadings. If you'd prefer to create a new document, enter a title at the top of the document, enter a heading, and type a paragraph.

    a) Enter at least two more paragraphs, including headings above each one.

    b) Select the title and apply the Heading 1 style to it.

    c) Select the first heading and apply the Heading 2 style. Use the Format Painter to apply the Heading 2 style to other similar headings (see Skill 1.6 for information about the Format Painter).

    d) If you have subheadings, apply the Heading 3 style to them.

    e) Redefine the Heading 2 style, using a different font and other formatting options and update the style to reflect these changes.

    f) Create a new paragraph style for the body text of your document.

    g) Apply the new style to each of the body text paragraphs.

3.5: Creating Outlines in Word

You may remember outlining as that horrible thing you had to do in school before your teacher would accept an assigned paper. Just trying to figure out which Roman numeral came next could be enough to spoil a good topic. You'll be happy to know that's not the kind of outlining we're talking about here. In Word 2000, you can use heading styles (see Skill 3.4) to view the major topics covered in your document—without having to scroll through pages and pages of text. You can collapse and expand heading levels to see more or less of your document at one time, making it a lot easier to ensure you've covered the essential subject matter. You can even print a collapsed outline of your completed document to use as a summary.

TIP TIP TIP TIP TIP TIP TIP TIP TIP TIP TIP TIP TIP TIP TIP TIP TIP TIP TIP TIP TIP TIP TIP

If you want to re-establish a relationship with those Roman numerals for old times' sake, go to Format ➤ Bullets and Numbering and click the Outline Numbered tab.

SKILL
3

Creating an Outline

When you create an outline in Word 2000, you create the document's headings and subheadings in Outline view. After the outline is finished, you enter body text in Normal, Print Layout, or Web Layout view. If you're starting a new document, click the Outline View button on the horizontal scroll bar. If you are using the Personal toolbar, the Outlining toolbar appears below it. If you are using the Standard and Formatting toolbars on two lines, the Outlining toolbar appears below the Formatting toolbar. The default style is set to Heading 1. To begin the outline, enter your first heading and press Enter. You can choose to enter all your first-level headings and then go back and enter lower level headings, or you can switch back and forth between them. Heading 1 does not actually refer to the first heading but to the first *level* of headings. You can have several level-1 headings in your document. To move down a level to Heading 2, press Tab. There are nine outlining levels you can use, as shown in Figure 3.10. If you want to change to a higher heading level, press Shift+Tab.

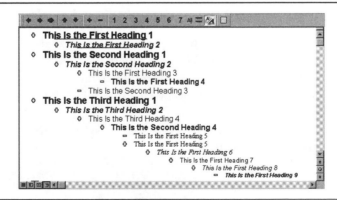

FIGURE 3.10: Outlining heading levels

Promoting and Demoting Headings

When you want to change the level of an existing heading, you *promote* or *demote* it to move it to a higher or lower level. Select the heading as you would select a line. If you'd like to promote or demote a heading and any subheadings underneath it, point to the *outline symbol* (plus, minus, or square) in front of the heading, and click using the four-headed arrow (a plus means a heading has subheadings; a minus means that it does not) to select the entire section. With the text selected, click the Promote or Demote button on the Outlining toolbar.

You can demote headings to body text by clicking the Demote to Body Text button.

CREATING AN OUTLINE

1. Click the Outline View button to switch to Outline view.
2. Enter a level-one heading (Heading 1). Press Enter.
3. Press Tab to move to a lower heading level; press Shift+Tab to return to a higher level.
4. Select a single heading by clicking in the left margin; select a whole section by clicking the plus or minus sign in front of the section.
5. To promote and demote selected text, click the Promote and Demote buttons.

Viewing and Printing Selected Levels

Once you have entered your outline, you can display as many levels as you would like at one time. Click any of the seven Show Heading buttons on the Outlining toolbar to *collapse* the outline which, in effect, hides all lower levels. For example, if you click Show Heading 3, Headings 4 and above and body text will not be displayed.

When some outline levels aren't displayed, the squiggly line tells you that there are hidden levels:

Click the All button to *expand* the outline and see all levels again.

If you want to focus on a particular point, you can collapse lower levels and then expand just the one you want to see. Click the Show Heading 1 button to collapse the outline. Move the mouse pointer to the left margin and select the heading you want to expand.

Click the Expand button to expand one level at a time, or double-click the plus sign next to the heading to expand all levels in the section.

Click the Collapse button to collapse one level at a time.

One of the great things about Outline view is that you can print the entire outline or any portion of it. Collapse or expand the outline so it shows just what you want to print, and then click the Print button. Print Preview will still show the entire outline. Don't worry about it. Only the expanded sections and headings will actually print.

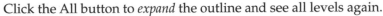

TIP TIP TIP TIP TIP TIP TIP TIP TIP TIP TIP TIP TIP TIP TIP TIP TIP TIP TIP TIP TIP TIP TIP TIP TIP

Heading styles are directly supported in Outline view. Even if you didn't origi-nally create a document in Outline view, as long as you used heading styles you can use the outlining features.

After you've created your outline, switch to Normal, Web Layout, or Print Layout view and enter body text under each heading, as shown in Figure 3.11. Just click to the right of the heading you want to write about, press Enter, and type the text. If you decide you are not satisfied with the outline, you can switch back to Outline view at any time and rearrange it.

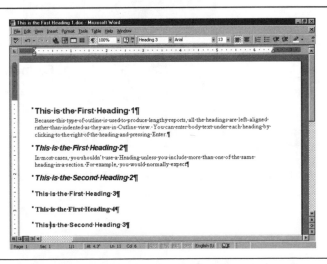

FIGURE 3.11: Entering body text in Print Layout view

VIEWING AND PRINTING SELECTED PORTIONS OF AN OUTLINE

1. Click any of the Show Heading buttons to hide headings below that level.
2. Click Show All to see the entire document.
3. Double-click the outline symbol to expand or collapse a section.
4. To print an outline, expand or collapse as desired and click Print.

Navigating with the Document Map

You can use the Document Map feature to navigate through a long document with relative ease, no matter what view you are in. Choose View ➤ Document Map in any view to open a frame, like the one shown in Figure 3.12, which contains all the headings. Just click a heading to move to that section.

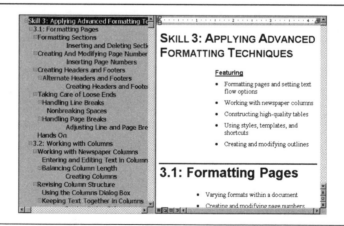

FIGURE 3.12:   Navigating with the Document Map

Unlike Outlining, the Document Map doesn't affect printing, so you can't use it to print parts of the document.

Modifying an Outline

Not only can you collapse and expand an outline, you can select a section of the outline and move it to another location. In Outline view, click the plus sign in front of the section, then drag it toward its new location. A horizontal line will appear. Drag and drop the line to move the section.

 You can use the Move Up and Move Down buttons on the Outlining toolbar, but make sure you click the button enough times to drop the section into the right spot. It's easy to rearrange your document in ways that you didn't anticipate— another reason that it's always a good idea to save before major rearranging.

MODIFYING AN OUTLINE

1. Select the section you want to move by clicking its outline symbol.
2. Drag the section to its new location and drop it when the horizontal line is where you want the text.

Using Templates

Every document is based on a template. A *template* is a collection of document formatting options and content that is available when you create a new document. (The Normal, or standard, template also includes your AutoText entries, macros, toolbars, custom menu settings, and shortcut keys.) To help make your work easier, Word 2000 includes additional templates for preformatted documents and template *Wizards* that walk you through a series of steps to customize a preformatted document.

When you choose File ➤ New from within Word or New Office Document from the Windows Start menu, you are presented with a choice of templates. Figure 3.13 shows the Letters & Faxes page of the New dialog box within Word. The available templates list depends on how Word was installed and whether any new templates have been created on your computer.

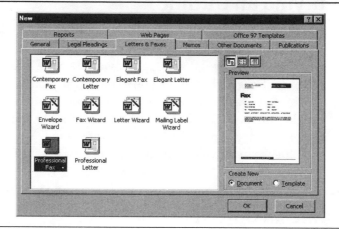

FIGURE 3.13: New dialog box

Any file with a `.dot` extension is a document template. Selections with `.wiz` are template Wizards. Select any template to see a preview in the Preview window. (Templates created by other users often can't be previewed.) When you have selected a template you want to use, click OK.

Templates include placeholders where you can insert your text. They also generally include instructions to help you use the template. In the template shown in Figure 3.14, you can insert personalized text and then resave the template, so you can use it again without re-entering your company or personal information.

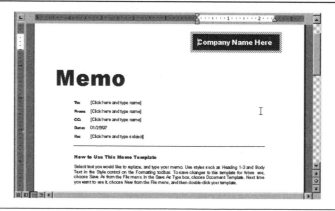

FIGURE 3.14: Professional Memo template

When you save a document created from a template, you must give it a name just like any other new document. If you want to re-use the revised document as a template for future documents, or if you've created a document from scratch that you want to use as a template, click the Save As Type drop-down arrow in the Save As dialog box and choose Document Template (*.dot):

```
Word Document (*.doc)
Web Page (*.htm; *.html)
Document Template (*.dot)
Rich Text Format (*.rtf)
Text Only (*.txt)
Text Only with Line Breaks (*.txt)
```

Selecting Document Template opens the Templates folder. If you wish, you can save your template in one of the folders in the Places bar. Enter a descriptive name for your template in the File Name control and save the template. Your template will now appear in the File ➢ New dialog box under the appropriate category or the General tab.

WARNING WARNING WARNING WARNING WARNING WARNING WARNING WARNING

If you are saving a regular document and the Save As dialog box forces you to save the document as a template, you may have a version of a Word macro virus on your system. You should immediately run a virus scan using virus protection software that can detect the Word Concept and other macro viruses. Visit the Microsoft Web site at http://www.microsoft.com **for more information about macro viruses.**

Hands On

1. Create an outline on any topic with several heading levels similar to the one shown in Figure 3.10, or open a document that includes heading levels.

   a. Collapse the outline to show only Heading 1.

   b. Double-click an outline symbol to expand the subordinate text.

   c. Demote two headings on the outline. Promote them back again or promote two other headings.

   d. Expand the entire outline.

   e. Switch to Normal view and enter body text under at least two of the headings.

    f. Turn on the Document Map and navigate through your document.

    g. Switch back to Outline view and move one heading and its subordinate text to another location.

Are You Experienced?

Now you can...

- ☑ **Insert section breaks and content for headers and footers**
- ☑ **Determine where pages and lines should break**
- ☑ **Create and modify newspaper columns**
- ☑ **Build and format tables to display information**
- ☑ **Use existing styles and create your own**
- ☑ **Create and work with outlines**

Working with Complex Documents

- ⊕ **Creating and manipulating data sources**
- ⊕ **Creating personalized merge documents**
- ⊕ **Building online documents**
- ⊕ **Working with references and authorities**
- ⊕ **Editing in workgroups and protecting files**

Increasing your Word 2000 expertise is a sure way to know you're making the best use of your precious time and resources. Effectively using advanced features such as mail merge, table of contents, and workgroup editing will set you apart from the crowd and give you a storehouse of tools to organize even the most unmanageable project.

4.1: Managing Data in Word

Word is more than just a word processor; it is a tool for managing information. Using Word, you can enter, sort, and search through lists of data: names, addresses, and items in an inventory. You can merge data lists with other Word documents and print labels, envelopes, and form letters. In this skill, you will learn to create and sort lists. You'll learn how to produce form letters, labels, and other merged documents in Skill 4.2.

Understanding Mail Merge

The ability to store lists—of personal or business contacts, members of groups or clubs, or videotapes, CDs, or books—puts extra power in your hands. Using Word, you can access data stored:

- In a file created using Word

- In a file created with other Microsoft Office products

- In an external file created using other software

The file that contains a list of information is called a *data source*. (The term *database* also refers to this kind of file.) You can easily sort the information in the data source or use the data source to create labels or envelopes. Create a *main document* that refers to the information in the data source, and you can *merge* the main document with the data source to create personalized letters, labels, or other documents.

Creating a New Data Source in Word

The Mail Merge Helper (which works like a Wizard) helps you create data sources and produce merged documents. To create a new data source using the Mail

Merge Helper, choose Tools ➣ Mail Merge. Begin by clicking the Create button (see Figure 4.1) under Main Document and selecting the type of document you will create using your data source. Although Word asks you to specify a type of document, your choice at this point doesn't preclude creating another type of main document later.

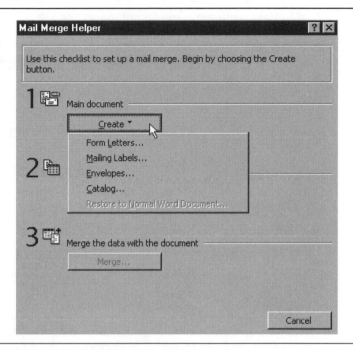

FIGURE 4.1: The Mail Merge Helper

After you select the type of main document you want to create, Word asks if you want to use the active (open) document or a new document for your main document:

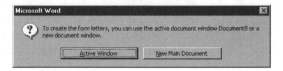

Choose Active Window if the open document is blank or if you've already opened a previously saved document to modify it for use with this merge; if you have any other document open, choose New Main Document.

Click the Get Data button, and then choose Create Data Source from the drop-down list. The Create Data Source dialog box, shown in Figure 4.2, comes with a list of *field names* (categories of data) commonly used in mail merges. Scroll the list to find field names you may want to use.

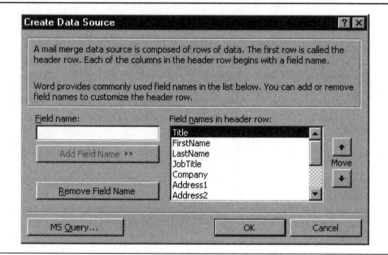

FIGURE 4.2: Create Data Source dialog box

Field names must be less than 40 characters, must not contain spaces, and must begin with a letter rather than a number. Field names cannot contain any characters that you can't put in filenames—such as periods, commas, colons, semicolons, slashes, and backslashes—and no two fields in a data source can have the same name.

TIP TIP TIP TIP TIP TIP TIP TIP TIP TIP TIP TIP TIP TIP TIP TIP TIP TIP TIP TIP TIP TIP TIP TIP TIP

If you are creating several data source files, it's helpful to use the same field names in each data source. For example, if you use FirstName in one data source, don't use FNAME or First in other source files. If you use the same field names, you'll often be able to use the same main documents with different data source files, rather than creating new main documents.

By default, all the field names in the list are included in the data source. To remove a field name from the list, select it, then click the Remove Field Name button. To add a field name to the list, type the name in the Field Name control, and click the Add Field Name button. If you enter an illegal field name (for example, a name that contains a space or that already appears on the list), the Add Field Name button will be disabled to prevent you from adding the illegal name.

After you enter and arrange all the field names, click OK. You will be prompted to save the data source file. When you save the file, Word will remind you that the file contains no records and will ask whether you want to edit the data source or edit the main document. At this point, you can begin entering information in the data source file by choosing Edit the Data Source.

TIP TIP TIP TIP TIP TIP TIP TIP TIP TIP TIP TIP TIP TIP TIP TIP TIP TIP TIP TIP TIP TIP TIP TIP

When you save a data source file, it's a good idea to name the document so that it is easily identifiable as a data source file. You might want to begin all your data source filenames with Data, for example, Data - Employees.

Entering Records

Click the Edit Data Source button to open the Data Form dialog box, shown in Figure 4.3. Enter the information for each field in your first record. When you are ready to enter another record, click the Add New button. You can add other records any time you need to, so you don't have to enter all 10,000 employees right now.

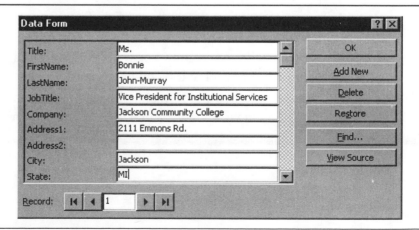

FIGURE 4.3: The Data Form dialog box to enter records

When you are finished, you can view all the records by clicking the View Source button. If you have 31 or fewer field names, Word places your document in a table. With 32 or more field names, the data source is displayed in columnar form.

CREATING AND ENTERING RECORDS IN A DATA SOURCE FILE

1. Choose Tools ≻ Mail Merge.
2. Choose Create and select a type of main document.
3. Indicate whether you want to use the active window as the main document or to create a new document.
4. Choose Get Data, and then choose Create Data Source.
5. Review the list of suggested field names in the Create Data Source dialog box; delete field names that you don't want.
6. Add new field names by entering them in the Field Name text box and clicking Add Field Name.
7. Use the Move arrows to put your fields in the desired order.
8. Click OK when you are finished entering field names and are ready to save the file.
9. Enter a filename for the data source file in the Save As dialog box. Click Save.
10. To begin entering data, choose Edit Data Source when the Option dialog box is presented.
11. Enter records in the Data Form dialog box, pressing Tab between each field and Enter at the end of a record.
12. Click OK when you are finished entering records to go to the Main Document, or click View Source to go directly to the data table.

Editing Records and Managing Fields

When the active file is a data source file, Word automatically displays a Database toolbar:

From the toolbar, you can conveniently access tools you will use to manage the data source. You can enter new records, edit, or delete records in the data source just as you would in any table.

To add a new record to the end of your data source, click the Add New Record button on the Database toolbar.

To delete a record, move the insertion point within the record you want to delete; then click the Delete Record button on the Database toolbar. Be careful not to delete the first row that contains the field names. If you do, you will have to re-create it to use this file as a data source. Save the data source file again to save the records.

To add, remove, or rename fields in your data source, click the Manage Fields button to open the Manage Fields dialog box:

If you prefer to enter or view records using the data form, click the Data Form button on the toolbar to reopen the Data Form dialog box.

TIP TIP TIP TIP TIP TIP TIP TIP TIP TIP TIP TIP TIP TIP TIP TIP TIP TIP TIP TIP TIP TIP TIP TIP
You can convert an existing table to a data source by deleting text that precedes the table in the document, deleting any blank rows in the table itself, and renaming column headers so that they follow field name conventions. Word 2000 will recognize a document that meets these requirements as a data source. To use other database options with your table, choose View ➢ Toolbars to turn on the Database toolbar.

Sorting It Out

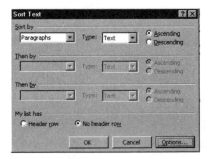

You can organize your data source by sorting it on any field: last name, zip code, or any other field that you find useful. Records can be sorted in *ascending order* (A to Z, or 0 to 9) or in *descending order* (Z to A, or 9 to 0). To sort the records in the data source, place the insertion point anywhere in the column you want to sort by. Click the Sort Ascending or Sort Descending button on the Database toolbar to sort the records in the order you specified.

SORTING A DATA SOURCE

1.   Open a data source document in Data Source view.
2.   Move the insertion point to the column that you want to sort by.
3.   Click the Sort Ascending or Sort Descending button on the Database toolbar.

Sorting Lists, Paragraphs, and Tables

You can sort any list in Word, whether or not it's a data source. You can sort regular tables, bulleted lists, and even ordinary paragraphs. First, select what you want to sort. Choose Table ➤ Sort from the menu bar to open the Sort dialog box:

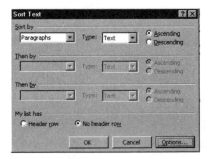

If you've clicked in a table or data source, the Sort By drop-down list shows you a list of field names based on the header row of the table. If you've selected a bulleted list or several paragraphs of text, the Sort By list gives you only two options: Paragraphs and Field 1. Choose Paragraphs to sort by the first word in each paragraph, or Field 1 to sort by the first field or tabular column. Choose whether the type of data you want to sort is text, numbers, or dates, and select ascending or descending order. If you are sorting data in a table or data source, you can indicate up to three sort levels. If your table has a header row, mark the Header Row button. When you have entered all the sort criteria, click OK to process the sort.

 WARNING WARNING WARNING WARNING WARNING WARNING WARNING WARNING

It's a good idea to save your document before you sort, and always check your data immediately after a sort to make sure it sorted correctly. If it did not, click Undo, or close the document without saving and reopen your saved copy.

SKILL 4

SORTING LISTS, TABLES, AND PARAGRAPHS

1. Select the data you want to sort.
2. Choose Table ➤ Sort.
3. Enter what you want to sort by, the type of data you are sorting, and the sort order (ascending or descending).
4. If you're sorting a table, enter additional sort levels, if desired, and indicate if there is a header row.
5. Click OK to process the sort.

Hands On

1. Create a data source file that contains information about your friends and family:

    a) Include fields that will give maximum flexibility in retrieving the data. The file should contain the following information: name, address, phone number, birth date, spouse/significant other's name, other.

    b) Enter at least 10 records. Leave fields blank if you do not have the information.

    c) Sort alphabetically by last name.

2. Open a document that contains a table:

    a) Convert the table to a data source. Resave the document under a different name.

    b) Switch to the Data Form dialog box (choose View ➤ Toolbars ➤ Database and click the Data Form button) and enter at least five new records.

    c) Sort the records alphabetically.

3. Open a document with a bulleted list and sort the list in descending order. Sort it again in ascending order.

4.2: Creating Customized Merge Documents

After you create a Word data source or identify a data source created in Excel, Access, or as a delimited text file in some other application, open the Mail Merge Helper (choose Tools ➤ Mail Merge) to create a main document. You have four choices of main documents:

Form Letters   Letters or reports you want to personalize

Mailing Labels   Address labels or any other kind of label, such as name tags, video tape or disk labels, file folder labels

Envelopes   Envelopes fed directly into your printer

Catalogs   Lists of data such as phone lists or membership directories

Word will ask if you want to use the current document or begin in a new document window. If the current window is empty, you can choose either option. Otherwise, you should begin in a new window. Word again displays the Mail Merge Helper. Click the Get Data button, and choose Open Data Source. In the

Open Data Source dialog box, select the data source to use with the main document you are creating. After the data source is confirmed, Word will return to the main document and open a dialog box to remind you that the main document has no merge fields, so you cannot merge the main document and data source yet. Choose Edit Main Document to open the Mail Merge toolbar and begin creating the main document:

A main document contains two kinds of text: regular and variable. *Regular text* will be the same in each version of the merged document—like the body text in a letter. *Variable text* is represented by a merge field. *Merge fields* take the place of text that will be different in each merged document—for example, the recipient's name and address.

In the main document, enter, edit, and format regular text as you would in any Word document. Insert a merge field where you want text from the data source to appear in your final, merged document. Place the insertion point where you want the merge field to appear, then click the Insert Merge Field button on the database toolbar to display the list of field names from the data source:

Choose the field name from the list, and Word inserts the merge field, as shown in Figure 4.4.

August 29, 1999

«Title» «FirstName» «LastName»
«JobTitle»
«Company»
«Address1»
«Address2»
«City», «State» «PostalCode»

Dear «Title» «LastName»:

We are excited about the prospect of working with you on the Web-based economic development program in your region. We believe that the use of an intranet to communicate with businesses in your communities is a critical part of your overall strategy and are looking forward to developing an attractive, easy-to-navigate Web site full of valuable information for all those involved. Int*net technology is moving so fast that every day there are new tools available to make your visions a reality. We will be submitting a proposal to you by the end of next week, and we can then meet to discuss the project in more detail.

Again, thanks for the opportunity , and we'll look forward to hearing from you.

Sincerely,

Annette Marquis   Gini Courter

FIGURE 4.4: Main document with merge codes

As soon as you've set up the main document the way you want it, you'll want to save it for use in future merges. When you use an existing main document, open the main document before you start the Mail Merge Helper. When you are prompted by the Helper to use the active document or to create a new main document, choose the active document.

TIP TIP TIP TIP TIP TIP TIP TIP TIP TIP TIP TIP TIP TIP TIP TIP TIP TIP TIP TIP TIP TIP TIP TIP

When you save a merge document, it's a good idea to indicate the type of document somewhere in the filename. We suggest that you begin main documents with the word Main and when appropriate, the name of the data source it is linked to (Main – Acknowledgment Letter to Clients), so that you can identify your main documents easily.

CREATING A MAIN DOCUMENT

1. Choose Tools ➢ Mail Merge from the menu bar.
2. Choose Create and then select the type of main document that you want to create.

continued▶

3. Indicate whether you want to use the document in the active window or to create a new main document.

4. Choose Get Data under Data Source to open an existing data source file or to create a new data source.

5. Click Edit Main Document to enter the regular text in the main document.

6. Move the insertion point to the position where you want data from the data source to appear. Click Insert Merge Field and select field names from the list to insert merge fields at the desired positions.

7. Save the main document.

Previewing the Merged Document

You've almost done it! When the main document and data source are merged, Word will generate a separate document or listing (if you are setting up a catalog) for each record in the data source, based on the layout of the main document.

To see what the first merge document will look like, click the View Merged Data button on the Mail Merge toolbar. The toolbar includes a set of *navigation buttons* that you can use to preview all the merged documents.

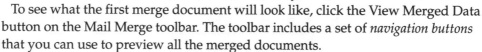

Click again on the View Merged Data button to return to the main document.

Merging Documents

You have created a main document and specified a data source. If everything looked OK when you previewed the merge results, you are ready for the actual merge. If the main document is not active, activate the main document window. The Mail Merge toolbar gives you a number of options, depending on how confident you are that everything is set the way you want it. The most daring choice is

Merge to Printer. Choose this option *only* if you have previewed your merge and everything is in perfect order (check that nobody has left purple and green paper in the printer!).

A much more conservative choice is Merge to New Document. Word will conduct the merge and create a new document with the results. Once the merge is printed, there is no reason to save the merge results. If you need to print it again at a later date, you'll want to do the merge again, in case you've updated any of the records in the data source.

Your final option is to open the Merge dialog box, shown in Figure 4.5. To do so, click the Merge button.

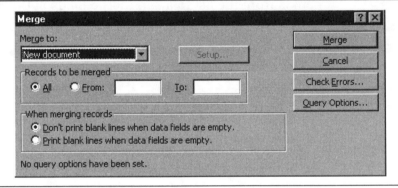

FIGURE 4.5: Merge dialog box

Here, you can choose to merge to a new document, a printer, an e-mail, or a fax, and you can specify only a portion of the records to merge. If you want Word to ignore blank fields (like Address2), indicate that by checking the appropriate box.

MERGING A MAIN DOCUMENT WITH A DATA SOURCE

1. Create the main document and data source.
2. Click the Merge, the Merge to New Document, or the Merge to Printer button on the Mail Merge toolbar.
3. Preview the merge results (unless you sent the document directly to the printer).
4. Print the merge document when you are satisfied.
5. Close the merge document without saving changes.

Specifying Records to Merge

Suppose you have a list of names and addresses and only want to send letters to people in a certain zip code or state. You can *filter* records based on criteria that you establish. After you select your data source and main document, click the Merge button to open the Merge dialog box. In the database world, a *query* is a tool used to select a group of records that meet specific criteria. Click the Query Options button to open the Filter Records page of the Query Options dialog box, shown in Figure 4.6.

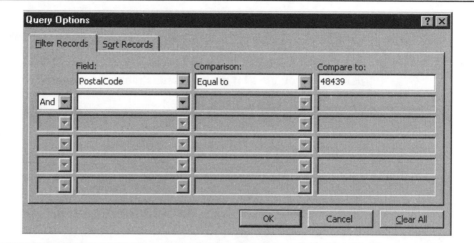

FIGURE 4.6: Query Options dialog box

In the Field drop-down list, select the field you want to use to select records. If, for example, you want to merge records with zip code 48439, choose the Postal-Code field. To send letters to all the customers whose last name is Jones, choose LastName. In the Compare To control (at the far right of the dialog box), enter the text string you are looking for in the selected field: **48439** or **Jones**. The comparison box lets you determine how the records in the data source are compared to the text string.

Using And and Or

Once you enter a Compare To text string, the word *And* appears in the drop-down box to the left of the second row of the Query Options dialog box. You can enter multiple query criteria and select, for example, the records for people in California where the data source doesn't list a zip code. The single most confusing thing about writing queries is knowing when to use And and when to use Or. If you can master this, you qualify as an expert query writer!

Choosing And means both comparisons must be true for a match. If you enter the Field, Comparison, and Compare To information in the example given above, choosing And will select all records where the State is California *and* the Postal-Code field in the data source is blank.

Use Or when you want to select two possible values for the same field. If you select records where State is equal to California *and* State is equal to Nevada, no records will be selected (since no single record includes both states). Choosing Or will select records for both states.

TIP TIP TIP TIP TIP TIP TIP TIP TIP TIP TIP TIP TIP TIP TIP TIP TIP TIP TIP TIP TIP TIP TIP TIP

Here's a general rule for troubleshooting queries: if you expected some records to be selected but none were, you probably used And when you should have used Or. If you got a lot more records than you expected, you probably used Or when you should have used And.

Sorting Records

After you select your merge criteria, you can also choose how you want your data sorted by clicking the Sort Records tab in the Query Options dialog box. See Skill 4.1 for more information about sorting. When you've set your query options, click OK, and you're ready to merge.

SELECTING AND SORTING RECORDS TO MERGE

1. Choose the Merge button from the Mail Merge toolbar.
2. Click Query Options to open the Query Options dialog box.
3. Select the field you want to use to select records.
4. Choose a comparison criterion.
5. Enter the text string you are looking for in the Compare To control.
6. Enter other desired query criteria by selecting And or Or and then selecting the criteria.
7. Click the Sort tab to sort the resulting merged document.

continued ▶

8. Select the desired sort fields and indicate whether you want the records to be sorted in ascending or descending order.

9. Choose OK to return to the Merge dialog box.

10. Click Merge to begin the merge.

Creating Catalogs and Lists

A *catalog* main document is used to create lists; each record is listed directly under the previous record on the same page. Word doesn't shine its brightest with catalogs. However, if you know how to work around the awkwardness of Word's catalog merge, it's still the most convenient way to present a list of the records in a data source.

When you choose Catalog as the main document type from the Mail Merge Helper, in the main document, you can either create a table to hold the merge field codes or use tabs to separate the codes. We encourage you to use a table; it produces consistent results with the least amount of hassle. Enter any text you want to appear with each *record* of the data source, but don't include other surrounding text. If, for example, you want a heading to appear above the records in the list, *don't* enter it now, or your merged document will include a heading, a record, another heading, another record, and so forth.

You can click the View Merged Data button to see each individual record as it will appear in the merged document, but you have to actually do the merge to see them all together. You can sort or select records before merging.

After you merge the data source and main document, you can add titles, column headings, and any other information to the merged document, as shown in Figure 4.7, before you print it. Merged catalogs are the exception to the suggestion that you not save merge results. If you have to add a lot of heading and title information after the merge, you may want to save it for future reference.

Client List
August 15, 1999

Client	Company	Phone Number
Amy Courter	Valassis Communications, Inc	(313) 555-7639
Charlotte Cowan	Unitarian Universalist Association	(810) 555-3456
Bonnie John-Murray	Jackson Community College	(517) 555-6786
Jarrett Marquis	Marquis Computer Instruction	(757) 555-9897
Gail Parker	Parkwood Professionals, Inc.	(810) 555-2375

FIGURE 4.7: Catalog merge document with headings

CREATING A MERGED LIST

1. Choose Tools ➣ Mail Merge.

2. Create or open a main document and a data source. Select Catalog as the main document type.

3. Edit the main document to include any text you want to appear with each record and insert the field codes in the desired positions.

4. Preview the merge, using View Merged Data to see individual records in the merge.

5. Run the merge, setting query options to select and sort records as desired.

6. Add any additional text, headings, or titles to complete the document before printing.

7. Save the merge results document.

Creating Envelopes and Labels

Labels and envelopes are two other types of main documents. To create labels, begin by choosing Mailing Labels from the Create Main Document drop-down list. After you select a data source, a dialog box appears. Click the Set Up Main

Document button. The Label Options dialog box opens (see Figure 4.8), offering you a choice of label sizes. You can select Avery and Maco labels by the number printed on the box. You have to set the dimensions for other brands of labels, but some other brands have the corresponding Avery number printed somewhere on the box.

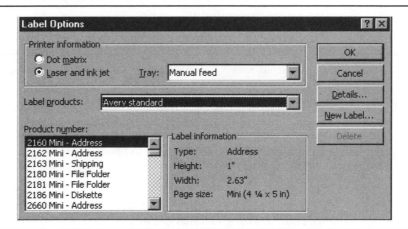

FIGURE 4.8: Label Options dialog box

After you select a label, click the OK button to open the Create Labels dialog box, shown in Figure 4.9.

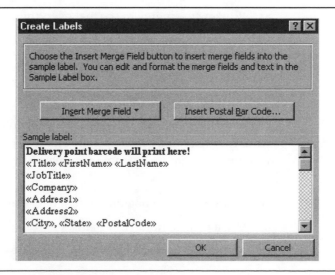

FIGURE 4.9: Create Labels dialog box

The Sample Label pane is like the main document window. Click the Insert Merge Field button to insert merge code fields in the label. Enter any other text from the keyboard. If you want to print a delivery point barcode to help out the post office, click Insert Postal Bar Code and identify which field holds the zip code and which is your main address field. Preview your labels before printing them. If you can't see all the needed text, it's easier to re-create the labels from scratch rather than editing them.

If you want to save the label document, you can close the Mail Merge Helper and save the document, or you can wait until after you have merged the labels. Include the word *Labels* (instead of *Main*) at the beginning of the filename.

Creating Envelopes

To create envelopes, choose Envelope rather than Label. Select the Envelope Size from the list provided. Choose OK to proceed to the Envelope Address dialog box. Insert Merge Field names just as you did in the Create Labels dialog box which looks and behaves just like the dialog box described for building labels. When you close the Envelope Address dialog box, Word will open the Mail Merge Helper so you can merge envelopes.

Hands On

1. Create a form letter with field codes to represent data in an existing data source file.

    a) Preview the merge to see that everything is correct.

    b) Merge to a new document.

    c) Be sure to save your data source file (if you made any changes to it) and your main document. Discard the merge document without saving changes.

2. Create mailing labels to a select group of people from an existing data source file. Select only those people on the list who meet certain criteria (from the same zip code, from the same city, name begins with the same letter, and so on).

3. Create a catalog main document for a data source file:

    a) Use a table to hold your fields.

    b) Merge the main document with the data source.

    c)   Add a title to the document and header rows to the columns.

    d)   Format the table to improve its appearance.

    e)   Print the table.

4.3: Publishing Online Forms

As more people have computers on their desktops and more computers are networked together, the paperless office is becoming a reality. One way that's happening is through the creation and use of online forms. If you need to create a vacation request form, why go to the trouble of creating the form, printing it, making copies, and distributing them? With an online form, the employee opens the form online, fills it out and sends it by e-mail to the boss, who approves (or disapproves) it and returns the e-mail. It's all over in a matter of minutes—no copies, no lost forms, no missed vacations.

Designing a Form

Because you'll want to use the online form over and over again, you need to create your form as a template. Choose File ➤ New, choose Blank Document from the General tab, click the Create New Template option button, and then click OK:

The new template will open as `Template1`. It's not a bad idea to save it now so you can quickly save changes as you create the form. Since you've identified this as a template, the Save As dialog box opens to the Templates folder and shows the file type as Document Template. Save the template in one of the existing template folders, or create a new folder for online forms. Now the template will be available in the Templates folder for users to select when they create a new document.

    Before you start creating your form, sketch it on paper or use an existing hardcopy form as a model. This will give your online form a better ultimate design and will save you the time and frustration of trying to design the form while you're creating it. Once you have decided on a design, right-click on any toolbar and activate the Forms toolbar.

The Forms toolbar includes buttons to insert form fields, to create tables and frames to position questions and prompts on the page, to turn form-field shading on or off, and to protect the form so that users can only enter data where you have placed fields.

The easiest way to lay out the form is by using a table. Tables allow you to place text on different parts of the screen without worrying about user-entered text wrapping to a new line.

 Click the Draw Table or Insert Table buttons on the Forms toolbar to create a table. Figure 4.10 shows an example of an online form that was created using tables. The gridlines and borders have been turned off except for the bottom borders, which form the lines for users' responses.

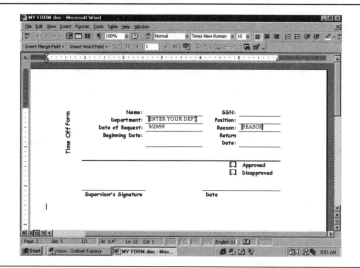

FIGURE 4.10: Online form created using tables

Figure 4.11 shows the same form with table gridlines turned on. As you can see, rows and columns aren't evenly distributed, and extra cells have been inserted to provide the appropriate spacing for items on the form.

FIGURE 4.11: Online form showing gridlines

After you enter field names and prompts in the table, you can split cells, merge cells, change borders, and adjust column and row widths as needed. Since the form is to be viewed online, don't forget to add colors, shading, and graphics to really make an impression. For more information about working with tables, see Skill 3.3; for graphics, see Skill 11. See "Adding Field Controls" later in this skill for more detail on adding fields.

Using Frames and Text Boxes

The Forms toolbar has an option for frames, which allow you to place an item precisely at any position on a form. You may want to frame small tables so that you can position them easily on the page.

Click the Insert Frame button, drag a rectangle the approximate size of your table, and then insert a table into the frame. You can resize a frame by dragging one of the black handles around its borders (the mouse pointer changes to a double-headed arrow when you can drag the handle). To reposition the frame, click on the frame to select it, and with the four-headed arrow mouse pointer, drag the frame to a new position.

If it's text you want to position, however, Word's text box feature, found on the Drawing toolbar, is a much more flexible option. With text boxes, you can apply 3-D effects, shadows, fills, and background, and in addition to changing the orientation of the text, you can flip and rotate the boxes themselves. For more information about text boxes, see Skill 10.

DESIGNING A FORM

1. Open the New dialog box, choose Blank Document, and click Template in the Create New option. Click OK to create a blank template.
2. Choose File ≻ Save As to save the template in the most appropriate template folder. Give the template a descriptive name.
3. Display the Forms toolbar by right-clicking on any toolbar and choosing Forms from the list.
4. Design the form using a table for the body of the form and bottom borders to provide user-response lines.
5. Save the template.

Adding Field Controls

Once your form is laid out, you must add *fields* or placeholders to your form that other people can use to submit their information. You can access three types of fields from buttons on the Forms toolbar:

 Text fields   Open fields of any length where users can enter text.

 Check Box fields   Users can check or clear these boxes to indicate answers.

 Drop-Down fields   Users choose a response from a list of choices you provide.

When your form is completed and you turn on protection, users will only be able to enter text or choices in the fields. The rest of the document will be off-limits to them.

To insert a field, position your cursor where you would like the field to appear, and then click one of the three form field buttons found on the left end of the toolbar—Text, Check Box, or Drop-Down.

It's helpful to have the Form Field Shading button turned on while you are creating the form so that you can see where the fields are.

After you enter a field, specify the options you want to apply to the field. Double-click the field to open the appropriate Form Field Options dialog box. The options for text form fields, shown in Figure 4.12, include:

Type   Regular text, number, date, current date, current time, or calculation.

Default Text   If there is a response that users would most commonly give, making it the default means they will only have to enter responses that differ from the default.

Maximum Length   Unlimited or a specified number of characters, which limits the length of user entries.

Text Format   Uppercase, Lowercase, First Capital, or Title Case to format user entries.

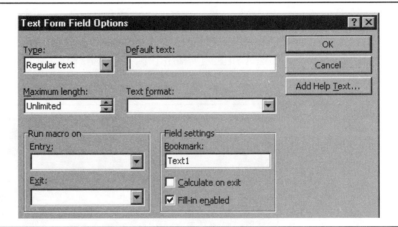

FIGURE 4.12: The Text Form Field Options dialog box

You can also run macros on entry into and exit from a field (see Skill 13 for more information about macros), set bookmarks, or have Word calculate the field on exit. If you want to restrict user access to a field, you can clear the Fill-in Enabled check box.

The Add Help Text option will endear you forever to your users:

Use this option to add text to the status bar and provide even more detailed instructions when users press the F1 key. Just click Type Your Own and enter whatever text you would like to have appear when the user moves into the field.

The unique options for check box form fields, shown in Figure 4.13, include:

Check Box Size   Either Auto, which makes your check box the size of the text, or Exactly, which lets you designate how large the box will be.

Default Value   Determines whether the box is checked when the form opens.

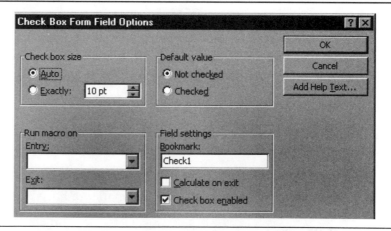

FIGURE 4.13: The Check Box Form Field Options dialog box

The only unique option for drop-down form fields, shown in Figure 4.14, is the list of drop-down items, which you must supply. Enter the text in the Drop-Down Item text box and click the Add button. After you create your list, you can use the

Move buttons to rearrange the items. Select an item and click Remove to delete or edit an item from the list. Unfortunately, the first item always shows up on the form as if it is the default. The only way around this is to enter a blank item (press the spacebar a few times before you press Add) or to make the first item instructional: `Select your department`. However, if you provide either of these options, you cannot prevent users from selecting these as their choice, so think carefully about this before deciding which way you want to go.

When your form is ready to distribute, you may want to turn off Form Field Shading (click the Form Field Shading button). This is purely optional, but because the shading does not correspond to the actual length of the field, it can give users the wrong impression about how much they should enter in a field.

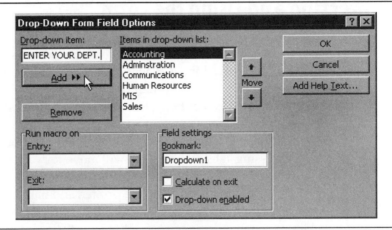

FIGURE 4.14: Drop-Down Form Field Options dialog box

ADDING FORM FIELDS

1. Click in the space where you want the field to appear. Click the Text Form Field, Check Box Form Field, or Drop-Down Form Field buttons on the Forms toolbar to insert the field.

2. Double-click on the field to edit the form field options.

3. Enter text, check box, and drop-down list options, as appropriate.

continued ▶

4. Click the Add Help Text button to insert your own status bar and F1 Help key instructions into the form.

5. Click OK to save the help instructions and OK again to return to your form.

6. When you are finished setting options in all the fields, you can click the Form Field Shading button to hide the shading, if desired.

Protecting and Using the Form

Your form is almost ready to distribute. One more step will make sure that your template stays intact and that users have access only to the field controls. After you're sure that everything is exactly the way you want it, click the Protect Form button on the Forms toolbar. When you do this, you will no longer have access to most toolbar and menu options. However, you can still save your template, and that's exactly what you want to do next.

When users open a protected form, they will only be able to click on the field controls. Pressing Tab and Shift+Tab will move forward and backward through the fields. They will have limited access to toolbars and other options. They can enter their information, send it to the printer, and name and save the document.

After protecting your form, it's always smart to test the form by filling it out to check that the tab order is correct. *Tab order* is the order in which the fields are activated when you press Tab. Depending on how you created the table and positioned the items in it, it may not tab logically through the fields. To correct this, you may have to insert blank cells or reposition items on the form. You may also find that you made a field's length too short or that you didn't include all the options in a drop-down list. Use the form as if you were one of your potential users; if possible, ask a colleague to test the form for you. It's amazing how easy it is to overlook something when you already know what data is expected in a field.

If you need to edit the form, be sure to open the template and not just a copy of the form. To open the template, choose File ➤ Open, change the Files of Type control to Document Templates (*.dot), locate the form in the appropriate template folder (the default folder is C:\Program Files\Microsoft Office\Templates), and click Open. You can then turn on the Forms toolbar and click the Protect Form button. You will again have free rein to do whatever you want to the form (within reason, of course!).

PROTECTING AND TESTING THE FORM

1. Click the Protect Form button on the Forms toolbar to restrict user access to just the field controls on the form.

2. Test the tab order by pressing Tab through the form and making sure it proceeds in a logical order.

3. Correct any tab-order problems by rearranging fields or inserting blank cells in the table.

4. Enter data in each field and see what happens if a user enters incorrect data (too much or too little, for example).

5. To edit the form, choose File ➤ Open, change Files of Type to Document Template (*.dot), select the template from the template folders, and click Open.

6. Turn on the Forms toolbar (choose View ➤ Toolbars ➤ Forms) and click the Protect Form button to turn protection off.

7. Make editing changes as desired, click Protect Form again, and save the template.

SKILL
4

USING AN ONLINE FORM

1. Choose File ➤ New and choose the form from the New dialog box.

2. Press Tab and Shift+Tab to navigate through the fields.

3. Save or print the new document as desired.

Hands On

1. Design a form similar to the one shown in Figure 4.11. It can be the same form or one of your own design.

   a) Create a new blank template to hold your form.

    b)   Enter and format the form title and other information.

    c)   Create a table to hold the body of your form. Use each type of field controls where appropriate. Set the options for each control, including length for text fields.

    d)   Set the Text format of one of the text fields for Title Case.

    e)   Protect, save, and close the form when you have finished designing it.

2. Open the form as if you were a user (choose File ➢ New) and enter data in each field. Note any problems with the form. Close the form without saving changes.

3. Reopen the template and turn off form protection. Make any needed editing changes identified when you tested the form. Turn on protection, save, and retest the form.

4.4: Adding References to Your Documents

Adding footnotes, endnotes, tables of contents, and indexes makes your documents easy to follow and helps your readers find what they are looking for. When you plan ahead, Word 2000 takes the headache out of these additional touches, providing one more way for your work to stand out.

Adding Footnotes and Endnotes

When you want to provide readers with more information about your topic, Word 2000 gives you options for inserting both *footnotes*, which appear at the bottom of the page, and *endnotes*, which appear at the end of the document. Word automatically numbers the notes for you *and* calculates how much space footnotes will need at the bottom of the page. Where was this feature when we were typing term papers?

    To insert a footnote or an endnote, position the insertion point where you'd like the *reference mark* (footnote or endnote number) to appear and choose Insert ➢ Footnote. The Footnote and Endnote dialog box opens. Select the type of note you want to insert.

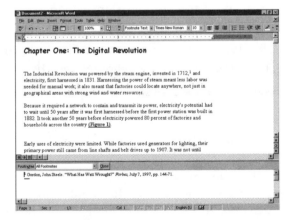

You can choose traditional automatic numbering (1, 2 ,3) or insert a custom mark or symbol. After you make your numbering selection, Word inserts the reference mark and, depending on the current view, either opens a note pane (Normal view) or takes you to the actual location where the note will appear in your document (Print Layout view):

It's much easier to work with notes in Normal view because you can enter your note in the pane and click Close when you are finished. In Print Layout view, you must find your way back to where you inserted the reference mark. In either view, when you want to review your note, all you have to do is point to the reference mark. The mouse pointer will change to a note, and a second later, the note will appear.

> The Trillium Extended Stay Treatment (TEST) is an innovative, cost-effective program designed to provide the additional support that patients need when transitioning from residential treatment to outpatient services. Today, all patients are discharged from residential treatment to return home as they begin participation in day-treatment or intensive Patients will be assisted in securing the Extended Stay Treatment will continue to live at Trillium prompt appointment times and Trillium's treatment. The primary difference between these patients and doctors will communicate directly with the residential program will be the amount of medical care that t primary care physicians about the responsible for seeing their primary care physicians in the ar patients' condition. significant medical concerns arise during the course of their stay.

Just move the mouse pointer away, and the note disappears.

CREATING FOOTNOTES AND ENDNOTES

1. Switch to Normal view. Place the insertion point where you want the reference mark to appear.

2. Choose Insert ➤ Footnote.

3. Indicate whether you want automatic numbering or a custom mark. You can type in a custom mark or choose one from the Symbol font sets.

4. Enter your note in the Footnotes or Endnotes box that opens at the bottom of the screen. Click Close when you are finished entering your note.

5. To view the note, point to the reference mark in your document. The note will appear as a yellow ScreenTip.

Revising Footnotes and Endnotes

Now that you have footnotes and endnotes scattered through your text, you may need to edit one of the notes. Just double-click any reference mark in Normal view to open the Footnotes or Endnotes window at the bottom of the screen. All notes of the same type appear in the same window—just scroll to the one you want to edit, make your changes, and click Close.

Deleting Notes

When you want to delete a note entirely, click before or after the reference mark and press the Backspace or Delete key twice—the first time will select the reference mark and the second time will delete both the mark and the note.

1. To revise a note, double-click any reference mark to open the note pane (in Normal view). Make changes and click Close.
2. To delete a note, select and delete the reference mark in the body of the document.

Using Bookmarks

Especially when you are working with long documents, it's useful to be able to mark a location in the text that you want to return to later. This could be a place where you need to insert some additional information before finishing the final draft. Or if your document will be read online, the location could refer to a piece of text you want readers to be able to jump to quickly. Whatever the reason, by inserting bookmarks you can easily move to specific text or objects in a document without having to scroll.

To insert a bookmark, select the text, graphic, table, or other object you want to mark. Choose Insert ➢ Bookmark. The Bookmark dialog box opens so you can name the bookmark. Names must be one word but you can use upper and lower case:

Click Add to add the bookmark and close the dialog box. (You can also delete bookmarks here by selecting the bookmark and clicking Delete.) To find bookmarks easily in the dialog box, sort them alphabetically or by their relative location in the document.

To see the bookmarks in your text, you can either go back to the Bookmark dialog box or choose Tools ➤ Options and click Show Bookmarks on the View page. The bookmarks will be displayed in brackets:

[EXECUTIVE SUMMARY]

The brackets are nonprinting characters, so if you're working a lot with bookmarks, it's handy just to leave them turned on.

When you want to go to a bookmark, choose Go To from the Browse Object menu at the bottom of the vertical scroll bar. Select Bookmarks from the Go To What list, and then click the drop-down arrow next to the Enter Bookmark Name text box to see a list of the bookmarks in your document:

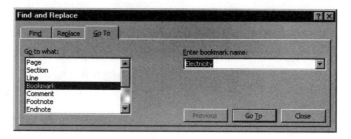

Select the bookmark you want to go to, click Go To and *voilà*, you are there. The Go To dialog box stays open until you close it, so to move to another bookmark, choose it from the list, and click Go To again.

When you close the Go To dialog box, you can use the browse buttons to move through all your bookmarks.

INSERTING, VIEWING, AND DELETING BOOKMARKS

1. Select the item you want to bookmark.

2. Choose Insert ➤ Bookmark and either accept the entire selected name or enter another name (names must be one word). Click Add.

3. View all the bookmarks in a document by choosing Tools ➤ Options ➤ View and clicking Show Bookmarks.

continued ▶

4. To jump to a bookmark, open the Browse Object menu, choose Go To, select Bookmark, and choose the bookmark from the Enter Bookmark Name drop-down list. Click Go To.

5. To delete a bookmark, select the bookmark and click Delete.

Indexing for Easy Reference

You can make lengthy documents more user-friendly by creating an index of key words and phrases. Although marking index text is a manual process, Word 2000 automates the creation of the index and will update it on request. When you're ready to mark your first entry, select the text you want to include in the index and press Alt+Shift+X to open the Mark Index Entry dialog box:

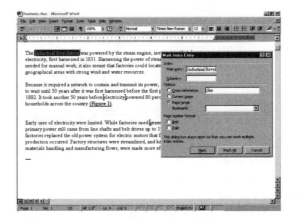

You can accept the selected text as the index entry or edit it any way you prefer. You can also add two subentries. Type the first subentry in the Subentry box, type a colon, and enter the second subentry. Click Mark to mark this specific selection, or select Mark All to mark every occurrence of the text string for indexing. The Mark Index Entry dialog box will stay open while you return to your document and select the next text you want to appear in the index. When you click back in the dialog box, the selected text will appear in the Mark Index Entry text box.

If you want this entry to refer to another entry, click Cross-Reference and after the word *See* type the name of the other entry, or type the word *also* and the name of the other entry. Because the cross-reference will only occur once in the index, you can Mark but not Mark All cross-references. To include a range of pages in the Index (such as `Formatting Text, 13-17`), you must first select the range and give it a bookmark name. You can then choose Page Range in the Mark Index Entry dialog box and select the name of the bookmark.

When you're ready, move to the last page of your document. Insert a hard page break, then enter a heading for the index. Use a heading style if you want the index heading included in your table of contents later. Press Enter a couple of times to leave some space after the heading, and choose Insert ➢ Index and Tables. The Index and Tables dialog box will open and you can choose how you'd like your index formatted, previewing your choices in the Print Preview pane:

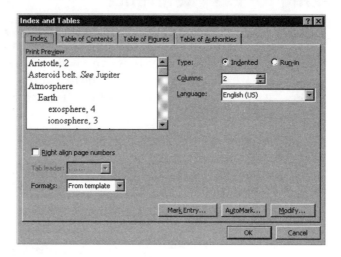

When you've made all your formatting choices, click OK. Your index will be generated automatically at the insertion point.

It's a good idea to go through each entry in the index and make sure it says what you want it to say and that the references are accurate. If you find any errors, you can fix them in the index or in the Index Entry (XE) fields inserted in the document, but any changes made to the index itself will be lost if you regenerate the index. After you make your changes to the XE fields, go to Insert ➢ Index and Tables again to regenerate the index. Word will select the existing index and ask you if you want to replace it.

CREATING AN INDEX

1. Select the first text you want to include in the index.
2. Press Alt+Shift+X to open the Mark Index Text dialog box.
3. Type or edit the text in the Main Entry box.
4. Enter subentries in the Subentry box, placing a colon between second- and third-level entries.
5. Choose Mark to mark a specific selection, or select Mark All to mark all occurrences of the text in the document.
6. To make additional entries, select the text and click in the Mark Index Entry dialog box.
7. To include a cross-reference, choose Cross-Reference from the dialog box and type in the cross-reference text (**See [name of entry]**); choose Mark.
8. To include a range of pages, create a bookmark from the beginning to the end of the range, choose Range of Pages from the Mark Index Entry dialog box, and select the name of the bookmark you created.
9. To generate the index, move to a blank page, insert any heading text you want, choose Insert ➤ Index and Tables, and choose the desired formatting options. Click OK to create the index.
10. To regenerate the index, choose Insert ➤ Index and Tables and click OK again or click in the index and press the F9 key.

SKILL
4

Generating a Table of Contents

After creating an index, a table of contents (TOC) is a breeze: that is, of course, if you used heading styles when you created your document. If you didn't, the breeze just turned into gale-force winds—you need to go back through your document and apply styles to any text you want included in your table of contents.

To create the table of contents, move to the beginning of your document and insert a page break. Move to the blank page and choose Insert ➤ Index and Tables. Click the Table of Contents tab and choose from a number of built-in formats for your TOC.

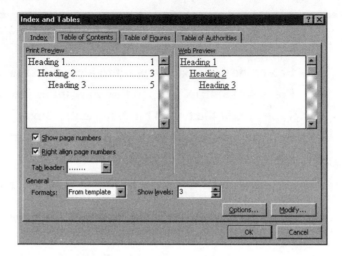

Choose a format and click OK. Add a heading, and your TOC should look something like the one in Figure 4.15.

Table of Contents

FIGURE 4.15: Table of Contents

Modifying a TOC

You can edit directly in the TOC itself. When you click the TOC, it looks like the whole thing is selected, but you can still select text within it and make changes. If you decide that you want fewer heading levels to appear in your TOC, choose Insert ➢ Index and Tables ➢ Table of Contents and decrease the number of heading levels. You can also change the tab leader by selecting a different one from the Tab Leader list. When you click OK, the TOC will regenerate with the requested number of levels. In some documents you may even want two TOCs—one with all heading levels and one with only the first-level headings.

CREATING A TABLE OF CONTENTS

1. Apply heading styles to all the headings you want included in the TOC.
2. Create and move to a blank page at the beginning of the document.
3. Choose Insert ➢ Index and Tables. Click the Table of Contents tab.
4. Choose the format you want for your TOC, the number of heading levels, and the tab leader.
5. Click OK to generate the TOC.
6. Click in the TOC and edit or reformat it directly or make changes to the headings in your document; regenerate the TOC by repeating steps 3–5.

SKILL 4

Hands On

1. Open an existing document or create a new document that has at least three headings and related paragraphs (be sure to apply styles to the headings):

   a) Switch to Normal view and add at least two footnotes and two endnotes to the document.

   b) Switch to Print Layout view and view the footnotes and endnotes at the bottom of the page.

      c) Point to one of the footnotes and read the note in the ScreenTip above the footnote marker.

      d) Delete the first footnote and the first endnote.

2. Using the same document you used in the first exercise:

      a) Create a bookmark to the first paragraph.

      b) Use Go To to move to the bookmark you created.

3. Using the same document:

      a) Go through the document and mark index entries for key terms, names, and other important words.

      b) Move to the end of the document, insert a page break, and generate the index.

4. Again in the same document:

      a) Move to the top of the document and insert a blank page for a table of contents.

      b) Generate the table of contents.

      c) Make changes to one or more of your headings and regenerate the TOC.

4.5: Working Together on Documents

If you work in a networked office where people collaborate on written projects, Word 2000 offers a number of useful workgroup features. You can track document changes, save multiple versions within a document, and even edit a document simultaneously with your colleagues.

Creating Master Documents

As a policy manual, personnel handbook, or similar document gets longer, it uses more resources to open, save, or print. It takes forever to scroll down a couple of pages and editing becomes a nightmare. With a little foresight, you can avoid this dilemma by starting with an outline and then dividing the document into various subdocuments. You—and others in your workgroup—can then work with sub-documents as autonomous entities. However, at any point, you can work with the entire master document, so you can have continuous page numbering, add headers and footers, create a table of contents, attach an index, and insert cross-references—all the stuff that contributes to another kind of nightmare if you try to do it with unrelated documents.

What if you're already 10 chapters into an unruly document? Word 2000 can combine separate documents into one *master document* and divide one long document into several *subdocuments*. So there's no excuse for working with a document that's out of control—the remedy is right at your fingertips.

Creating a New Master Document

To create a new master document from scratch, open a new document, and then click the Outline View button. Word displays the Master Document toolbar to the right of the Outlining toolbar. Create an outline just as you normally would (see Skill 3.5), using the same heading level for each section that you want subdivided into its own document.

When you have finished creating the outline, select the headings and text you want to split into subdocuments. Click the Create Subdocument button, and Word will create individual documents using the first part of the heading text for the document name. The master document will show the subdocuments in a distinct box with a small file document icon in the upper left corner:

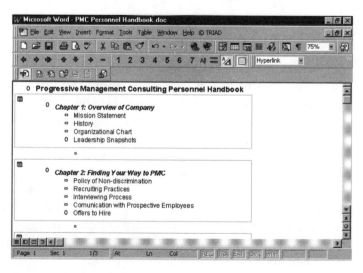

You can double-click any of the document icons to open a subdocument. Any changes you make in the subdocument are reflected in the master document when you save the subdocument.

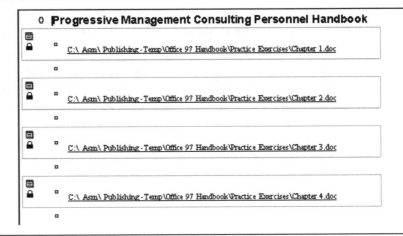

The primary purpose of creating a master document is to be able to work with discrete sections of the document. It makes sense, then, to collapse the master document so that just the document names are visible. Clicking the Collapse button on the Master Document toolbar will collapse the document, as shown in Figure 4.16. If you want to see all the text in the entire document, click the same button again (it's now the Expand button).

FIGURE 4.16: A collapsed master document

When the master document is collapsed, point to any of the subdocuments and double-click to open it. When you want to return to the master document, just close and save the changes you made to the subdocument. You'll notice that the link to the subdocument changes color to show that you have already edited that document.

Subdocuments can only be opened for editing by one person at a time—if another person tries to open the same subdocument, they can only open a read-only copy. You can also lock people out from making changes to the master document or any subdocument by expanding the master document, selecting the document or documents you want to lock, and clicking the Lock Document button on the Master Document toolbar. This prevents anyone from making changes after a document is completed.

When the master document is expanded, you can work with it as if it were one document by just switching to Normal or Print Layout view. You can apply page numbering, headers and footers, a table of contents, an index, and references and adjust styles just as you would in a normal document. Just make sure you're in the master document before making any of these changes, or you can easily have a real mess on your hands.

Converting Existing Documents and Making Changes

For a document to be converted to a master document, you must apply heading styles so you can work with it in Outline view. After you have applied heading styles, you can switch to Master Document view and follow the same steps you would to create a new master document. If you have several documents that you want to combine into one master document, you need to first create a new master document with a couple of (temporary, if need be) subdocuments.

After you create the master document, move the insertion point to where you want to insert an existing document, and click the Insert Subdocument button on the Master Document toolbar. You'll be taken to the Insert Subdocument dialog box where you can select the document you want to insert.

You can merge two subdocuments into one, split one subdocument into two, delete a subdocument, or convert a subdocument into master document text. Table 4.1 shows you how to accomplish these tasks:

TABLE 4.1: Converting Subdocuments

Task	Action	Click
Merge two subdocuments	Select the two subdocuments	
Split one subdocument	Position insertion point at split point	
Delete a subdocument	Select the subdocument	Press the Delete key
Convert a subdocument to master document text	Select the subdocument	

SKILL
4

CREATING MASTER DOCUMENTS FROM EXISTING DOCUMENTS

1. Open the existing document and apply heading styles to the major sections of the document.

2. Click the Outline View button, and click the Create Subdocument button.

3. To insert another document, position the insertion point where you want the document inserted and click the Insert Subdocument button.

4. Save the master document.

Saving Multiple Versions of a Document

Whether you're working with a master document or an isolated document, you can save multiple versions of a document within the document itself and switch back and forth between versions.

To save a version, choose File ➤ Save As, and in the Save As dialog box, click the Tools button. Click Save Versions to open the Save Version dialog box, where you can enter comments describing this version for later reference:

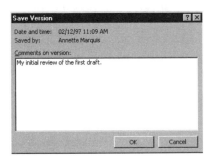

To view or switch between saved versions, choose File ➤ Versions. This dialog box allows you to open a different version, to delete a version that is no longer relevant, and to view comments about a version:

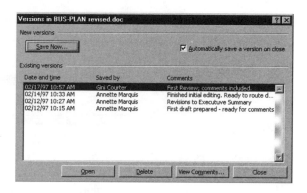

You can enable the Automatically Save a Version on Close check box to assure that a version is preserved every time the document is edited. This option is particularly helpful when the document will be edited by several people consecutively. Although the most recently saved version will open by default, you can always go back to a pervious version.

Tracking Changes to a Document

Although saving each version of a document is helpful, it's still difficult to identify where all the changes were made. Word 2000 will track each change to a document and allow you to accept or reject individual revisions or all revisions in one fell swoop. The easiest way to begin tracking changes is to right-click on the TRK on the status bar:

You can track changes in three ways:

- In the background with no visible queues
- On the screen
- In the printed document

To indicate which option you want, choose Highlight Changes from the pop-up menu. Choose Track Changes While Editing to turn on tracking. Then indicate whether you want the changes visible on the screen or in the printed document.

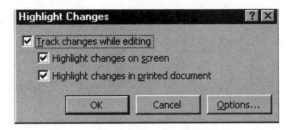

Clear both check boxes if you don't want the changes to be visible in either place. Click OK to close the dialog box and initiate tracking. You'll notice that TRK on the status bar is now enabled. If you choose to have changes visible on the screen, your documents will include a trail of every change. Text you insert will be a different color and will be underlined. Text you delete will be struck through. A vertical line in the margin will indicate lines where text has been changed. Figure 4.17 shows a document that has been edited with Highlight Changes on the Screen turned on.

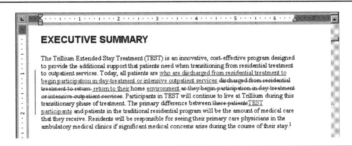

FIGURE 4.17: Tracking changes in a document

As other people open the document, changes they make will appear in different colors (as many 16 authors can work on one document before colors repeat). If you would prefer that all inserted text appear in one color and all deleted text in another, you can set the colors yourself by choosing Options from the pop-up menu or the Highlight Changes dialog box. The Track Changes dialog box lets you set color options for Inserted Text, Deleted Text, Changed Formatting, and Changed Lines.

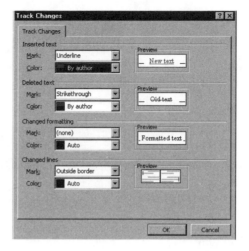

By Author means that every author will be given a different color. Any other choice assigns a specific color to a function rather than to an author. You can also change the type of mark that is used. For example, you can choose to have inserted text appear in italics rather than underlined. To see who is responsible for an editing change, just point to the marked text to see a ScreenTip that indicates the type of change, who made it, and the time and date it was made.

TRACKING CHANGES TO A DOCUMENT

1. Right-click TRK on the status bar (or choose Tools ➤ Track Changes) and choose Highlight Changes.

2. Click the Track Changes While Editing check box and choose whether to highlight changes on-screen and/or highlight changes in the printed document.

3. Click Options if you want to set a specific color for each type of revision—inserting, deleting, formatting, and borders.

4. When Tracking Changes is turned on, the status bar indicator is black. Double-click it to turn tracking off; double-click it again to turn tracking back on.

Accepting or Rejecting Changes

After a document has been edited, you can accept or reject changes. Right-click the status bar TRK indicator and choose Accept or Reject Changes. The Accept or Reject Changes dialog box allows you to scroll through each individual change and accept or reject them as a group or individually:

If you want to accept or reject all the changes without reviewing them, click the Accept All or Reject All button. Word will ask if you are certain—click Yes to confirm your choice.

If, on the other hand, you want to review each individual revision, click Find to move through the document. Revisions will be selected one at a time, and you can choose to accept or reject each one. Word starts reviewing where the insertion point is currently located, so if you reach the end of the document without having gone through all the changes, Word will ask if you want to go to the beginning to catch the rest of them. It will also tell you when you have reviewed all the revisions. Click OK and then click Close to close the Accept or Reject dialog box. If you don't want any more marked revisions, make sure you turn off tracking.

ACCEPTING OR REJECTING CHANGES

1. Right-click the status bar Tracking indicator (or choose Tools ≻ Track Changes) and choose Accept or Reject Changes.

2. Click Accept All or Reject All if you don't want to review individual changes.

3. Click Find to review changes one by one. Word will select the change—click the Accept or Reject button and click Find again to move on to the next change.

4. Click Undo to reverse an accept or reject decision that you made.

5. Click Close to exit the Accept and Reject dialog box. Remember to turn off tracking if you do not want further changes tracked.

Inserting Comments

When you're creating or editing a document with others, it's often valuable to be able to make comments that aren't part of the printed document but can be viewed on-screen. Word's Comments feature fits the bill. You can insert comments, view comments from one or all reviewers, and print the comments.

To insert a comment, move the insertion point to where you want to position the comment and choose Insert ➤ Comment. The word immediately preceding the insertion point is highlighted, and your initials and a comment number appear in the text. A comment box then opens at the bottom of the screen:

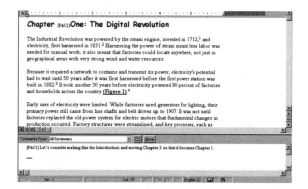

Enter your comment and click Close. To view the comment, just hover over the highlighted word for a second—the insertion point will change to an I-beam with a note attached, and a second later the comment will appear above the text:

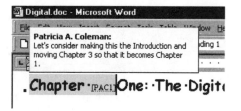

If you're going to be working a lot with comments, turn on the Reviewing toolbar, which includes buttons to insert, edit, and delete a comment and to move to previous and next comments.

1. Click where you want the comment to be inserted and choose Insert ➤ Comment.
2. Type your comment in the Comment box and click Close when you are finished.
3. Point to the comment to view it.
4. Turn on the Reviewing toolbar (choose View ➤ Toolbars ➤ Reviewing) to move between, edit, or delete comments.
5. To print the comments, choose File ➤ Print and choose Comments from the Print What drop-down list.

Highlighting Text

Word's highlighter is one of the easiest tools to use when you want to make sure that whoever's reviewing a document notices a particular section of text. Imagine using a highlighter pen, and you know almost everything you need to know to use this formatting feature.

 You can choose from 15 highlight colors. Just click the Highlight button drop-down arrow to select a color.

1. Click the Highlight button and drag over the text to be highlighted.
2. Triple-click to highlight an entire paragraph.
3. Click the Highlight button again to turn Highlighting off.

Adding Comments Using Document Summary Information

Every Windows document has a Properties sheet that tracks information about the document—when it was created, who created it, when it was last modified, and so on. You can also enter detailed information about the document that other users can view from the Open dialog box—without actually opening the document. To add to the document properties, choose File ➣ Properties and click the Summary tab:

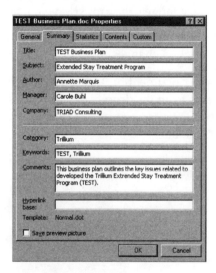

SKILL
4

ADDING COMMENTS USING DOCUMENT SUMMARY INFORMATION

1. Click File ➣ Properties and click the Summary tab.
2. Enter information and comments in fields as desired.
3. Click OK to close and save the Properties sheet.
4. To view the properties of an unopened document, choose File ➣ Open, and select the document.

Protecting Documents

Word 2000 provides several ways to protect your documents from unscrupulous eyes. You can:

- Restrict the access of anyone who doesn't have the password to open the document

- Require users to open read-only copies

- Recommend that users open the document as read-only so that, if they make changes, they must save it using a different name

- Prevent changes to a document you route for review, except for comments or tracked changes

To apply document protection, open the Save As dialog box. Click the Tools button and from the drop-down list choose General Options to open the Save dialog box. You can also access this page by choosing Tools ➤ Options and clicking the Save tab.

When you enable the Password to Open control, users will be prompted to input the password. Without the password, they will not be able to open the document.

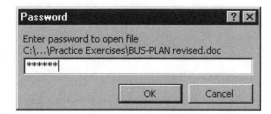

If they know the password, the document will open, and they can modify it and save the changes. If they do not know the password, the document will not open and they are told why.

If you want users to be able to view but not change the original document, enter a Password to Modify. Users who don't know the password can only open the document as read-only and must save any changes under a different name. Click the Read-Only Recommended check box if you want to remind yourself or others that this document should not be modified and that it would be preferable to open it as read-only:

SKILL
4

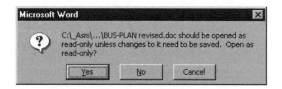

Whichever password option you choose, the password will not be visible on the screen as you type—Word will ask you to reenter the password for verification. Word then gives you a stern warning that password-protected documents cannot be opened if you forget the password. Take this warning seriously. If you forget the password for a document, it's gone for good. To change or delete a password, open the document and reenter or delete the password from the Save dialog box.

PROTECTING DOCUMENT WITH PASSWORDS

1. In the Save As dialog box, click the Tools button and choose General Options to open the Save dialog box, or choose Tools ➢ Options and click the Save tab.

continued ▶

2. Enter a Password to Open if you want users to be unable to open the document without a password. Click OK and reenter the password to confirm it. Click OK again and save the document.

3. Enter a Password to Modify if you want to allow all users to open the document as read-only but require a password to modify the original document. Click OK and reenter the password to confirm it. Click OK again and save the document.

4. Click the Read-Only Recommended check box if you want to suggest to users that they open the document as read-only to prevent accidental changes to an original document. Click OK and save the document.

5. To change or delete a password, open the document with the password, go to the Save dialog box, and enter a new password or delete the existing one.

Routing Documents

Being connected to your colleagues—by a local or wide-area network or through electronic mail—makes sharing and exchanging documents a snap. Word 2000 even includes a routing slip that you can attach to an outbound document. To attach a routing slip, choose File ➢ Send To ➢ Routing Recipient:

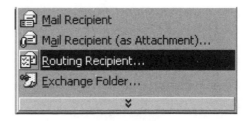

Click the Address button on the Routing Slip:

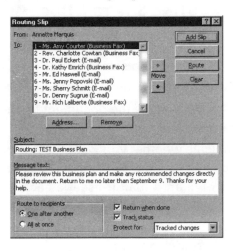

You can then access your address books or Outlook contact lists to identify the people you want to see the document. (If you do not have any names in an address book, see Skill 9 about setting up Outlook contact lists). Move selected names to the To column and click OK to return to the Routing Slip. Enter information in the Subject field and include any message you'd like to send. Recipients can receive the document in sequence, or it can be routed to everyone at the same time. Word assumes that you'll probably want the document returned when everyone's seen it and that you'd like to track its status along the way, so you'll receive an automatic e-mail message when someone sends the document on to the next person.

After you've prepared the routing slip, click Route on the slip to send the document to the first person on the list, or close the Routing Slip and choose File ➤ Send To ➤ Next Routing Recipient/Other Routing Recipient. Next Routing Recipient opens the Send dialog box, which lets you choose to send the document to the next person on the list or to send the document without using the routing slip:

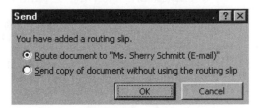

ATTACHING A ROUTING SLIP TO A DOCUMENT

1. Choose File ➤ Send To ➤ Routing Recipient.

2. Click Address to select names from an address book or contact list.

3. Enter a subject and a message.

4. Choose to route the document to one recipient after another or to all recipients at once.

5. Indicate whether you want the document returned when the last person is finished with it and whether you want the status tracked (you'll receive an e-mail message each time it moves to a new person).

6. Protect the document for Tracked Changes, Comments, or Forms, or turn off protection by choosing None.

7. Click Route to send the document to the first person on the list. Click Add Slip to save the slip with the document.

8. To send the document, choose File ➤ Send To and choose either Next Routing Recipient or Other Routing Recipient.

Hands On

1. Create a master document using a newly created outline for a project you are working on. Be sure to apply the Heading style to each major topic before creating the subdocuments.

   a) Save the master document and collapse it.

   b) Edit one of the subdocuments, close, and save it. Expand the master document and view the edited document.

   c) Insert a new document into the master document. In the master document, edit and save changes to the inserted document.

   d) Select and delete a subdocument from the master document.

   e) Save and close the master document and any open subdocuments.

2. Open an existing document:

   a) Turn on Track Changes. Make the changes visible on the screen.

b) Make changes to the document, inserting and deleting text. Save a version of the document. Make additional changes to the document and save another version.

c) Insert a comment and highlight some important text.

d) Choose File ➤ Properties and input Document Summary information describing the document.

e) Protect the document for Tracked Changes and save another version of the document. Turn on Automatically Save Version on Close.

f) If you're on a network and have names in an address book, prepare a Routing Slip for the document. If possible, send the document to a colleague and ask him or her to make changes and send the document back to you.

g) Open the Versions dialog box and view the Existing Versions. Close the Versions dialog box. Using Accept or Reject Changes, review each change made to the document and accept or reject each as you deem appropriate. Turn off Track Changes and save the final version.

Are You Experienced?

Now you can...

- ☑ **Create, sort, and use data sources**

- ☑ **Merge data sources with main documents to create merged documents, labels, and envelopes**

- ☑ **Build online forms**

- ☑ **Create indexes and tables of contents**

- ☑ **Save document versions, track revisions, and protect documents**

Creating Excel Worksheets

- ➔ **Entering data in Excel**
- ➔ **Working with numbers**
- ➔ **Changing worksheet layout and other formatting**
- ➔ **Printing and previewing**
- ➔ **Using functions and references**
- ➔ **Working with ranges**
- ➔ **Using charts to express information graphically**

If you're new to Microsoft Office 2000, you might want to work through Skill 1, "Working in Office 2000" and then return here to begin work in Excel. Throughout this skill, we use Excel practice worksheets to illustrate concepts. If you would like to use the practice worksheets, you can create them based on the illustrations in the text or download them from the Sybex Web site: `http://www.sybex.com`. You may also choose to practice these skills using your own worksheets, immediately applying the skills to your work.

5.1: Entering and Editing Cell Entries

Welcome to Excel 2000, the number cruncher! If you've used earlier versions of Excel, you'll find a bundle of new features that are welcome additions to Excel. If you're moving to Excel from another spreadsheet program, you're in for a real treat. Simply put, Excel 2000 is the best spreadsheet program ever designed: a powerful program with plenty of features to help you harness that power in your workplace.

The Excel Application Window

The Excel application window (see Figure 5.1) includes the standard title bar and command bars. Below the command bars is a strip that contains the *name box* and the *formula bar*.

The Excel status bar displays information about current selections, commands, or operations. The right end of the status bar displays NUM if the keyboard's Num Lock is on.

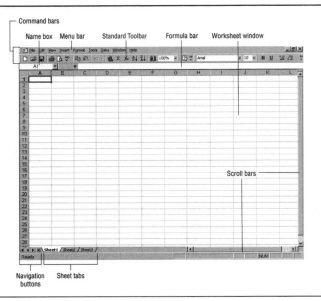

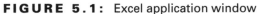

FIGURE 5.1: Excel application window

Workbooks and Worksheets

When you launch Excel, the Excel application window opens with a new Excel *workbook*. A workbook is a multi-page Excel document. Each page in the work-book is called a *worksheet*, and the active worksheet is displayed in the document window. At the left end of the horizontal scroll bar are *sheet tabs* and *navigation buttons*. Use the sheet tabs to move to another worksheet and the navigation buttons to scroll the sheet tabs.

Each worksheet is divided into columns, rows, and cells, separated by *gridlines*, as shown in the Payroll worksheet in Figure 5.2. *Columns* are vertical divisions. The first column is column A, and the letter A appears in the *column heading*. The horizontal *rows* are numbered. Each worksheet has 256 columns (A through IV) and 65,536 rows—plenty of room to enter all your numbers!

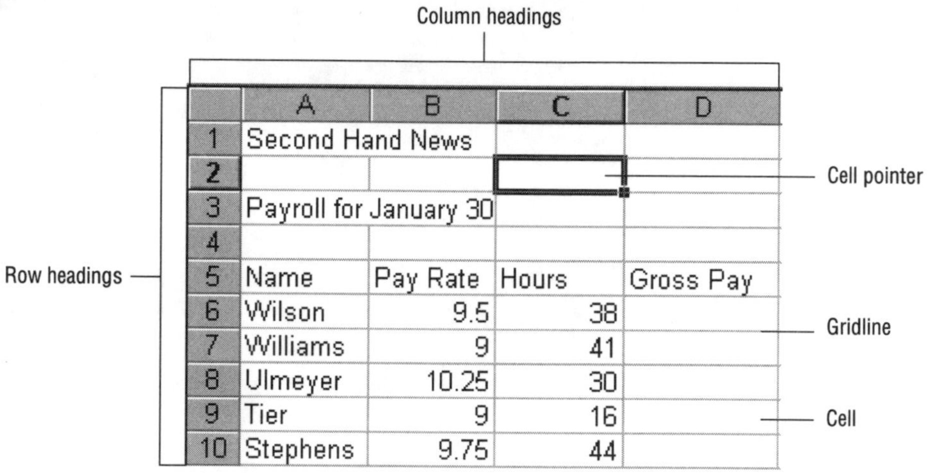

FIGURE 5.2: Payroll worksheet

A *cell* is the intersection of a row and a column. Each cell has a unique address composed of the cell's column and row. For example, the cell in the upper left corner of the worksheet, with the text *Second Hand News* (see Figure 5.2), is cell A1. Even though some of the text appears to run over into cell B1 in the next column, it is really entered in cell A1. The *active cell*, C2 in Figure 5.2, has a box around it called the *cell pointer*, and the headings in the active cell's column (C) and row (2) are outdented or "lit up." When you enter data, it is always placed in the active cell.

Moving the Cell Pointer

To move the pointer one cell to the left, right, up, or down, use the keyboard arrow keys. Table 5.1 shows other frequently used keyboard commands.

TABLE 5.1: Keystrokes to Move the Cell Pointer

Key(s)	To Move
PgDn	Down one screen
PgUp	Up one screen
Home	To column A in the current row
Ctrl+Home	To cell A1

To activate a cell with the mouse, simply click the cell. If you want to see other areas of the worksheet, use the scroll bars. To scroll up or down one row, click the up or down arrow at the ends of the vertical scroll bar. Use the arrows at either end of the horizontal scroll bar to scroll one column to the left or right. To move up, down, left, or right one window, click the empty space above, below, or to the left or right of the scroll bar's scroll box:

Click here to scroll   Click here to move over one window

Column: A

Drag the scroll box to scroll more than a couple of rows or columns. As you drag, a *ScrollTip* shows the location you are scrolling over. Note that scrolling doesn't change the active cell—scrolling lets you view other parts of the worksheet, but the active cell is wherever you left the cell pointer. To scroll large distances, hold the Shift key while dragging the scroll box, and Excel will scroll farther for each movement of the mouse.

SKILL
5

Entering Text and Numbers

You can enter three types of data in a worksheet: numbers, formulas, and text. *Numbers* are values you may want to use in calculations, including dates. Dates are often used in calculations to determine, for example, how many days to charge for an overdue video or how many months of interest you have earned on a deposit. *Formulas* are calculations. *Text* is any entry that isn't a number or a formula. To enter data in a cell, first activate the cell, and then begin typing the data. As soon as you begin entering characters from the keyboard, three things happen: an insertion point appears in the cell, the text you are entering appears in the cell and the formula bar, and the formula bar buttons are activated.

If you make a mistake while you are entering data, click the Cancel button (the red X) to discard the entry you were making and turn off the formula bar buttons. You can also cancel an entry by pressing the Esc key on the keyboard. Clicking the Enter button (the green checkmark) finishes the entry and turns off the formula bar buttons. Pressing the Enter key on the keyboard is the same as clicking the Enter button, except the Enter key also moves the cell pointer down one cell.

Excel has an *AutoComplete* feature that keeps track of text entered in a column and can complete other entries in the same column. For example, if you have already typed Jones in cell A1 and then enter the letter J in A2, Excel will automatically fill in ones to make Jones. If Jones is the correct text, simply finish the entry by pressing Enter, moving to another cell, or clicking the Enter button. If it is not correct, just continue entering the correct text to overwrite the AutoComplete entry. AutoComplete resets each time you leave a blank cell in a column.

Revising Text and Numbers

You can change an entry in a cell in two ways. If you activate the cell and type the new entry, the old entry will be replaced. This is the easiest way to change a number (for example, 15 to 17) or to replace text with a short word. If the original entry is long and requires only minor adjustment, you might prefer to edit it. Click on the cell and edit the entry in the formula bar, or double-click on the cell to open it for editing and edit directly in the cell. Use the mouse or the keyboard to edit the entry. When you are finished, you must press Enter or click the Enter button to complete the entry—you can't simply move to a new cell.

To delete the contents of a cell completely, activate the cell, and then press the Delete key on the keyboard or right-click and choose Clear Contents from the shortcut menu. (Don't choose Delete—that deletes the cell, not just the entry in the cell.)

Selecting Multiple Cells

In Excel, at least one cell is always selected: the active cell. A group of cells is called a *range*. To select a range, move to the first cell in the range (check to be sure the mouse pointer is the large cross used for selecting), hold down the mouse button, and drag to the last cell you want to select before releasing the mouse button.

To select all the cells in a column or row, click on the column heading or row heading. To select multiple columns or rows, select one heading then drag to select the others. When you point to row or column headers to select them, be sure that your mouse pointer looks like the fat selection cross as you do this, not a thinner black cross. To select the entire worksheet, click the Select All button, the gray rectangle at the upper left corner of the worksheet above the row headings.

If the cells, columns, or rows you want to select are noncontiguous (not next to each other), select one of the ranges you want to select, and then hold down the Ctrl key while selecting the others.

Hands On

1. In a new workbook, create the worksheet shown here. Save the workbook as *Cyclops Proposal* for future use.

	A	B	C
1	Cyclops Database Proposal - Draft		
2	Hardware		
3			
4	Item	Quantity	Price
5	PCs	19	1565
6	Server	1	4175
7	Scanners	2	685
8	Printers	4	499

2. In the Cyclops Proposal workbook, click Sheet 2 and create the second worksheet shown below. Resave Cyclops Proposal before closing it.

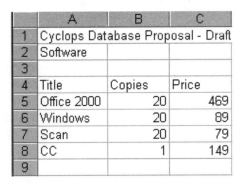

	A	B	C
1	Cyclops Database Proposal - Draft		
2	Software		
3			
4	Title	Copies	Price
5	Office 2000	20	469
6	Windows	20	89
7	Scan	20	79
8	CC	1	149
9			

3. In an existing worksheet:

    a) Use the drag technique to select all the numbers in a worksheet.

    b) Select all the text in the worksheet.

    c) Select columns A and C only.

    d) Select rows 1 and 3 and column C.

5.2: Working with Numbers

You use a *formula* every time you want to perform a calculation in Excel, so you'll appreciate some of the formula features built into Excel 2000. Formulas are what make a spreadsheet a spreadsheet: the driving force behind the magic of Excel.

Excel uses standard computer operator symbols for mathematical and logical operators, as shown in Table 5.2:

TABLE 5.2: Mathematical and Logical Operators

Operation	Operator symbol
Addition	+
Subtraction	–
Multiplication	*
Division	/
Exponentiation (to the power of)	^
Precedence (do this operation first)	enclose in ( )
Equal to	=
Not equal to	<>
Greater than	>
Less than	<

Creating Formulas

You can create formulas in a number of ways, but some are more efficient than others. We'll begin with simple formulas that have one math operation. For example, the Second Hand News Payroll worksheet (see Figure 5.2) needs a formula to multiply Wilson's pay rate times the hours worked in order to calculate gross pay. You can approach this formula in two different ways. The first method is the highly reliable point-and-click method for which Excel is known.

ENTERING A POINT-AND-CLICK FORMULA

1. Activate the cell where you want the result to appear.

2. Type **=**.

3. Click on the first cell you want to include in the formula.

4. Type an operator.

5. Click on the next cell in the formula.

6. Repeat steps 4 and 5 until the entire formula is entered.

7. Finish the entry by pressing Enter or clicking the Enter button on the formula bar. (Don't just move to another cell—Excel will include it in the formula!)

**SKILL
5**

The other method is the traditional spreadsheet approach: typing in the formula using the cell addresses of each cell you want to include in the formula. Typing in a formula is the least desirable way to create a formula; no matter how well you type, it is the most error-prone method. It's much too easy to glance at the wrong column or row, even when you're only working with a few numbers. When you have thousands of numbers in the middle of a worksheet, the chance of error increases. If you need to reference widely disparate cells, consider naming the cells (see Skill 5.7) and then referring to the names.

NOTE NOTE NOTE NOTE NOTE NOTE NOTE NOTE NOTE NOTE NOTE NOTE NOTE NOTE NOTE
Excel 200 allows you to use labels in formulas, such as =pay rate*hours. **To activate this feature, formerly referred to as natural language formulas, choose Tools ➢ Calculations and check the Accept Labels in Formula check box.**

Using the Formula Palette

Whatever formula construction method you use, you can use the *Formula Palette* to view the progress of your formula as it's being constructed. To activate the Formula Palette, click Edit Formula (the = sign button) in the formula bar rather than pressing the = key on the keyboard. For more about the Formula Palette, see Skill 5.6.

WARNING WARNING WARNING WARNING WARNING WARNING WARNING WARNING

Formulas are dynamic, so the results automatically change each time the numbers in the underlying cells are revised. Typed-in numbers don't change unless they are edited. This is the reason for the first of two Very Important Excel Rules: *Never* **do math "in your head" and type the answer in a cell where you or other users would reasonably expect to have a formula calculate the answer.**

Complex Formulas

Complex formulas involve more than one operation. For example, you might have separate columns for hours worked in the first week of the pay period and hours worked in the second. You'll want to add the hours together before multiplying by the pay rate: = (Hours Week 1 + Hours Week 2) * pay rate. When you have more than one operation in a formula, you'll need to know about the Order of Operations.

The *Order of Operations* is a short set of rules about how formulas are calculated:

- Formulas are calculated from left to right: 15/3+2 is 7, never 3.

- Multiplication and division are always done before any addition or subtraction. Excel will make two left-to-right passes through the formula in the preceding paragraph and do the multiplication on the first pass. Then, it will come back through and add the hours worked in the first week to the gross pay for the second week. Calculating the gross pay this way would not make your employees happy.

- Any operation in parentheses is calculated first. If you want the hours for the two weeks added together first, just throw a set of parentheses ( ) around the addition part of the formula. Notice that you never need to include parentheses if you're only doing one operation; they only kick in when you need to tell Excel how to order two or more operations.

Filling Formulas

Now that you understand formulas, you may be tempted to quickly create all the other gross pay formulas. Don't—there's a much faster way. The formula for each employee's gross pay is the same: hours * pay rate. Since you've already created one working formula, all you need to do is *fill* it to the other cells.

The square box in the lower right corner of the cell pointer is called the fill handle. As you move the mouse toward the cell pointer, the mouse pointer changes shape to a black cross to let you know that you can use the mouse for a fill operation.

The mouse pointer assumes several shapes as you move it around the worksheet. When the mouse pointer is a large cross, you can use it to activate or select cells.

If you move the mouse toward the border of the active cell, the mouse pointer will change to an arrow. When the pointer is an arrow, you can use the pointer to move the cell (you'll learn more about moving cells in Skill 5.3). You'll want to look at the mouse pointer frequently while working in Excel. A mouse movement of $\frac{1}{32}$ of an inch is the difference between selecting, moving, and filling.

Filling is a kind of copying. Begin by activating the cell that has the formula you want to copy. Move the mouse pointer toward the fill handle until the mouse pointer changes to the fill pointer shape. Press the mouse button and drag the fill handle down to select the cells you want to copy the formula to. Release the mouse button, and the formula will be filled to the other cells.

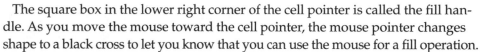

FILLING A FORMULA

1. Select the cell that contains the formula you want to copy to other cells.

2. Drag the fill handle to select the cells where you want the formula copied.

3. Release the fill handle to fill the formula.

 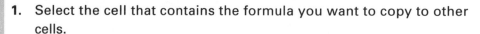

A common mistake that users make when they're new to fill operations is to include the wrong cells in the initial selection. At this point in your fill career, if all the selected cells don't include formulas, you've selected incorrectly.

Totaling Columns and Rows

Excel has a one-step method for creating row and column totals using the Auto-Sum button on the Standard toolbar. Begin by selecting the cells that contain the numbers you want to total; you can include the empty cell that should contain the total in the selection. Then click the AutoSum button. Excel will add a formula to the empty cell (whether or not you selected it) and calculate the total. If you would like a blank row before the totals, simply select two extra cells. Excel always places the total in the last empty cell selected. If you want to create totals for multiple rows or columns and a grand total, select all the numbers before clicking AutoSum, as shown in the Tickets worksheet in Figure 5.3. In this example, Excel will create formulas in row 9 and column E for each selected row and column. In cell B9, the formula will be =sum(B5:B8), telling Excel to sum (total) the values in the range of cells B5 through B8.

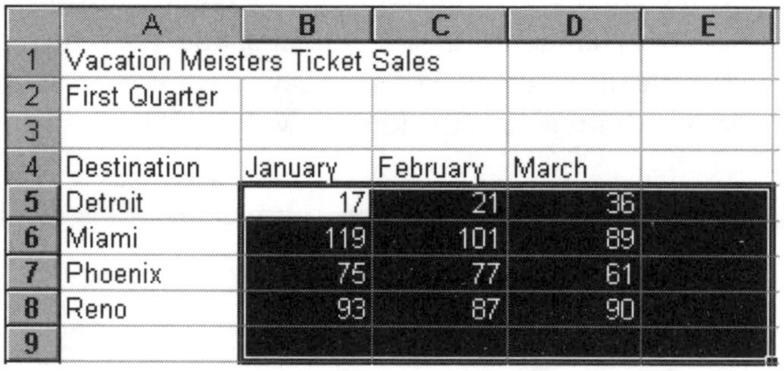

	A	B	C	D	E
1	Vacation Meisters Ticket Sales				
2	First Quarter				
3					
4	Destination	January	February	March	
5	Detroit	17	21	36	
6	Miami	119	101	89	
7	Phoenix	75	77	61	
8	Reno	93	87	90	
9					

FIGURE 5.3: Using AutoSum to total rows and columns

USING AUTOSUM TO TOTAL ROWS AND COLUMNS

1. Select the cells that contain the numbers you want to total and a blank row and/or column to hold the totals.
2. Click the AutoSum button on the Standard toolbar.

Revising Formulas

You might want to revise a formula for two reasons: you entered an incorrect formula, or you've added new data and need to change the formula to reflect the new entries. You can move to the cell that contains the formula and create a new formula, overwriting the original formula, or you can edit the existing formula.

When you double-click a cell with a formula to open it for editing, Excel paints each cell address or range address in the formula a different color and places a border of the same color around the cell or range. The border is called a *Range Finder*. In this example, B10 in the formula and the Range Finder around cell B10 are blue; green is used for C10:

| Stephens | 9.75 | 44 | =B10*C10 |

This makes it easy to see whether a formula refers to the correct cells. If you want to change the formula reference to C10 so that it refers to another cell, you can use the keyboard or the Range Finder. To use the keyboard, select C10 in the formula and then either click on the cell you want to replace it with or type the replacement cell's address. If the formula you're revising uses row labels instead of cell addresses, select the column or row label and type the correct label to replace the original entry. To use the Range Finder, grab the border of the Range Finder and move it to the correct cell. (You're moving the Range Finder, so the mouse pointer should be an arrow.) If you need to include additional or fewer cells in a range, drag the selection handle at the lower right corner of the Range Finder to extend or decrease the selection; the pointer will change to a fill pointer. When you are finished editing the formula, press Enter or click the Enter button.

SKILL 5

WARNING WARNING WARNING WARNING WARNING WARNING WARNING WARNING

If the cell reference you want to change is a range, the reference will include the first cell in the range, a colon, and the last cell in the range, like this: B10:B15. To revise this reference in a formula, select the entire reference, and then move into the worksheet and drag to select the cells for the new formula, or move and then extend the Range Finder.

Unions and Intersections   Unions and intersections are two special types of ranges. A *union* is all the cells in two separate ranges. If you want, for example, to add a group of numbers in C2 though C8 and those in C20 through C28, the ranges would be (C2:C8,C20:C28). By using a comma to separate the two ranges, you're indicating that you want all cells from both ranges.

An *intersection* is just what it sounds like: a place where two ranges come together or overlap. For an intersection, use a blank space instead of a comma. The intersection (C2:C10 A10:J10) refers to just one cell: C10, where the two ranges overlap.

Formatting Numbers

Excel lets you present numbers in a variety of formats. *Formatting* is used to identify numbers as currency or percentages and to make numbers easier to read by aligning decimal points in a column. You can format selected cells using the Formatting toolbar, the Format Cells dialog box, or the shortcut menu. When you format a number, you change its appearance, not its numeric value. The default format for numbers, General, doesn't display zeros that don't affect the actual value of the number. For example, if you enter 10.50, 10.5 has the same numeric value, so Excel doesn't display the extra, or *trailing*, zero.

Using the Formatting Toolbar

To format cells with the toolbar, first select the cells, and then click a button to apply one of the formats shown in Table 5.3.

 NOTE NOTE NOTE NOTE NOTE NOTE NOTE NOTE NOTE NOTE NOTE NOTE NOTE NOTE

The Formatting toolbar is the toolbar displayed on the right side of the Personal toolbar. To see all the buttons on the Formatting toolbar, choose View ➢ Toolbars ➢ Customize. Click the Options tab and clear the Standard and Formatting Toolbars Share One Row check box.

TABLE 5.3: Numeric Formatting from the Formatting Toolbar

Button	Style	Example
$	Currency Style	Displays and lines up dollar signs, comma separators, and decimal points: 75.3 as $75.30
%	Percent Style	Displays number as a percentage: 0.45 as 45%
,	Comma Style	Same as Currency, but without dollar signs: 12345.6 as 12,345.60
+.0 .00	Increase Decimal	Displays one more place after the decimal: .45 as .450
.00 +.0	Decrease Decimal	Displays one less place after the decimal: 0.450 as 0.45

If decreasing the number of digits eliminates a nonzero digit, the displayed number will be rounded. For example, if the number 9.45 is displayed with only one decimal place, it will be rounded to 9.5. If you display 9.75 with no digits following the decimal, Excel will display 10.

Formatting affects only the display of a cell, not the cell's contents. To view the contents of a cell, click on the cell and look at the formula bar. The number entered in the cell appears in the formula bar exactly as entered regardless of the format that has been applied to the cell.

APPLYING NUMERIC FORMATS FROM THE FORMATTING TOOLBAR

1. Select the cells to be formatted.
2. Click a button on the Formatting toolbar to apply a format to the selected cells.
3. Click on any cell to turn off the selection.

SKILL
5

Excel has more number formats that you can select from the Format Cells dialog box. Select the cells you want to format. Then open the dialog box: either choose Format ➤ Cells from the menu bar, or right-click to open the shortcut menu and choose Format Cells. The Format Cells dialog box has separate pages for Number, Alignment, Font, Border, Patterns, and Protection. The Number page of the Format Cells dialog box is shown in Figure 5.4. If the Number page is not active, click the Number tab.

The Number page includes a list of format categories (see Table 5.4) and controls for the number of decimal places, thousands separator, and treatment of negative numbers. First choose a category, and then fill in the other options.

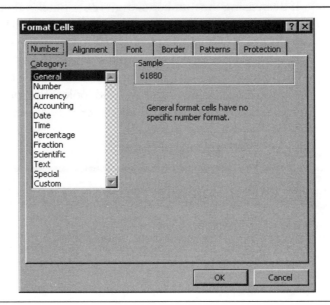

FIGURE 5.4: The Format Cells dialog box

TABLE 5.4: Numeric Formatting in the Format Cells Dialog Box

Category	Description
General	The default format.
Number	Like General, but you can set decimal places, use a thousands separator, and include negative numbers.
Currency	Numbers are preceded with a dollar sign immediately before the first digit. Zero values are displayed.
Accounting	Dollar signs and decimal points line up. Zero values are shown as dashes.
Percentage	The same as the Percent toolbar button.
Scientific	Numbers are displayed in scientific notation: for example, 1.01E+03.

TIP TIP TIP TIP TIP TIP TIP TIP TIP TIP TIP TIP TIP TIP TIP TIP TIP TIP TIP TIP TIP TIP TIP TIP

If you point to the button on the Formatting toolbar with the dollar symbol, the ScreenTip indicates it is the Currency Style button. However, when you apply this button's format, Excel applies the Accounting format, with dashes for zeros and the dollar signs lined up. Go figure!

The Format Cells dialog box includes six more specialized formatting categories. Date formats are used for dates and times. If you select the Date category, you can also select a format for the date from a scrollable list box. The Fraction category allows you to choose from formats based on either the number of digits to display in the divisor (1, 2, or 3) or the fractional unit (halves, quarters, tenths, and so on). Special and Text both convert a number to text.

Special includes formats for kinds of numbers that aren't really mathematical values: Zip Code, Zip Code + 4, Phone Number, and Social Security Number. You wouldn't want to add or multiply any of these numbers—they are informational labels just like a last name.

Text changes a number to text, so it is no longer a number and can't be used in calculations. This is fine if the number is really a label. For example, you might need to include employee numbers in a worksheet: 8712, 0913, 7639. But how do you get Excel to leave the 0 in employee number 0913? All the regular numeric formats strip off leading zeros. To keep the leading zero in 0913, format the cell for text *before* entering the number. You won't be able to include the employee numbers in a calculation, but you wouldn't want to anyway, so it's no loss.

SKILL
5

WARNING WARNING WARNING WARNING WARNING WARNING WARNING WARNING

Unlike the other formatting categories, Special and Text *change the underlying value of the number*. If you format a number with Special or Text, you will no longer be able to use the number in mathematical operations—unless you first reformat the cells in some other format. If you have only a few numbers that need to be treated as text, you can enter them manually. Simply type an apostrophe (') before the number, and Excel will treat the number as text.

Custom allows you to select from or make an addition to a list of formats for numbers, dates, and times (see Skill 6.1).

Using the Format Cells Dialog Box

1. Select the cells to be formatted.
2. Choose Format ➤ Cells, or right-click and choose Format Cells.
3. Click the Number tab.
4. From the Category list, choose the appropriate formatting category.
5. Set other available options, such as the color of text and the background of cells.
6. Click the OK button to apply the format and close the dialog box.

Hands On

1. Apply suitable formatting to a worksheet that includes currency entries: for example, the Hardware and Software worksheets of the Cyclops Proposal workbook.

2. Use a worksheet that contains dates and numbers (like the Tickets worksheet in Figure 5.3) to practice using the date and numeric formats.

5.3: Changing Worksheet Layout

As you have seen, the way you initially enter data in a worksheet doesn't necessarily produce the most attractive or useful presentation. You'll almost always want to make adjustments to the layout.

Adjusting Column Width and Row Height

By default, Excel columns are slightly more than eight characters wide. If the data in a worksheet is wider or much narrower than the column, you'll want to adjust the *column width* so it is wide enough to contain the data, but not so wide that data seems lost. You can adjust column width manually or use AutoFit to fit the column width to the existing data.

To adjust the width of a column manually, begin by pointing to the border at the right side of the column header. The mouse pointer will change to an adjustment tool, shaped like a double-headed arrow. Drag the edge of the column header to the desired width, and then release the button. If you double-click on the column header border instead of dragging the border, Excel will AutoFit the column, making the column slightly larger than the widest entry in the column.

You can select several columns and size them all at the same time. By dragging the header border of any selected column, all columns will be sized to the same width. Double-clicking the header border of any of the selected columns will size each column individually, to fit the data in the column. You can also select the column(s) you want to adjust and select AutoFit from the menu (choose Format ➤ Column ➤ AutoFit Selection).

WARNING WARNING WARNING WARNING WARNING WARNING WARNING WARNING

The second Very Important Excel Rule: *Never* **leave blank columns between columns in a worksheet. Blank columns create problems with charts, sorting, and many other advanced features. Instead, adjust column widths to provide adequate space for and between entries.**

You can adjust row height the same way you adjust column width. If you move the pointer to the lower edge of a row heading, the pointer will change to an adjustment tool. Double-click to adjust the row height to fit the font size; drag to manually increase or decrease size.

ADJUSTING COLUMN WIDTHS

1. Select the column(s) you want to adjust.
2. Position the mouse pointer at the right edge of one of the selected columns' headings. The pointer will change shape to a double-headed arrow.
3. Double-click to have Excel adjust the widths of the selected columns to fit the contents of the columns.
4. Click anywhere in the worksheet to turn off the selection.
5. To adjust column widths manually, drag the right border of a column's heading to make the column wider or narrower.

SKILL
5

Inserting and Deleting Rows and Columns

To insert a column between the current columns A and B, begin by selecting column B. Right-click and select Insert from the shortcut menu or choose Insert ➤ Columns from the menu bar to insert a column. To insert multiple columns simultaneously, select more than one column before inserting. For example, you can insert three columns by first selecting B, C, and D. You can insert rows in the same fashion.

TIP TIP TIP TIP TIP TIP TIP TIP TIP TIP TIP TIP TIP TIP TIP TIP TIP TIP TIP TIP TIP TIP TIP TIP TIP

To quickly insert a single row or column, select the row or column heading by right-clicking. As soon as the row or column is selected, Excel immediately opens the shortcut menu.

Deleting rows and columns is much like inserting. Begin by selecting one or more rows or columns. To clear the contents but leave the emptied row in place, press the Delete key on your keyboard. To delete the contents *and* remove the row or column, choose Edit ➢ Delete from the menu bar. When you delete a row or column, all information is deleted, including cells that may not be in the part of the worksheet you can see.

TIP TIP TIP TIP TIP TIP TIP TIP TIP TIP TIP TIP TIP TIP TIP TIP TIP TIP TIP TIP TIP TIP TIP TIP TIP

You can use some nifty keystroke combinations to see if there is more data in a row or column. Select an occupied cell, hold Ctrl and press →. The cell pointer moves to the last occupied cell to the right of the original cell. If you press Ctrl+ → again, the cell pointer stops to the left of the first occupied cell. Ctrl+·↑, ↓, and → work the same way. Ctrl+End moves you to the outer limit of the used portion of the worksheet: a cell in the last used row and column.

INSERTING AND DELETING ROWS AND COLUMNS

1. Select the row or column where you want the new inserted column to appear.

2. Right-click and choose Insert (or choose Insert ➢ Rows from the menu bar) to insert a row. To insert a column from the menu bar, choose Insert ➢ Columns.

3. To delete a column or row, first select it. Then, right-click and choose Delete, or choose Edit ➢ Delete from the menu bar.

Inserting and Deleting Cells

Sometimes, you'll need to add or delete cells in part of a worksheet without inserting or deleting entire rows or columns. For example, Figure 5.5 shows a section of a worksheet for a network switchover project. Tasks are listed in columns A–D, and project components (like software) in column E. If you needed to add some tasks for March 10, you can't insert rows, because it would leave blanks in the components list in column E. Instead, you can insert cells in columns A-D.

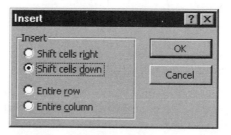

	A	B	C	D	E
1	Cyclops Software Division				
2	Windows NT Network Conversion Project				
4	Date	Task	Days	Resource	Project Components
5	10-Mar	Install NT Server 1	1.0	Ken	Windows NT Server
6	10-Mar	Install NT Server 2	1.0	Jody	Windows NT Client - 25
7	11-Mar	Switch sales printers	0.5	Ken	Innoculan Server
8	11-Mar	Switch service printers	0.5	Ken	Carbon Copy
9	12-Mar	Backup CS Sales files	0.3	Jody	
10	12-Mar	Backup CS Service files	0.5	Jody	

SKILL
5

FIGURE 5.5: Network switchover worksheet

Select the range where new cells should be inserted, and then right-click and choose Insert. When you insert or delete rows and columns, Excel automatically moves the surrounding rows and columns to fill the gap. If you insert or delete cells, Excel needs more instruction to know how to move the surrounding cells, so the Insert or Delete dialog box opens:

If you choose Shift Cells Down, the cells in the selection and all cells below them in the same columns are shifted. If you choose Shift Cells Right, cells in the same row(s) are moved to the right. Notice that you can also use this dialog box to insert rows or columns.

Moving and Copying Cell Contents

Basic move and copy techniques in Office 2000 are discussed in Skill 1.5; however, you'll notice a few differences when copying and moving cells and ranges of cells in Excel:

- If you paste cells on top of existing data, the existing data will be overwritten, so make sure that there are enough blank cells to accommodate the selection you want to paste. For example, if you want to move the contents of column E to the right of column A without overwriting column B, begin by inserting a blank column between A and B.

- *Cut and paste* and *copy and paste* operate differently in Excel than in other Office 2000 applications. You can't copy now, do a few other things, and then paste later. You must paste the data immediately; if you don't, the cut (or copy) operation is canceled.

- When you cut a cell in Excel, it is copied to the Clipboard but is not removed from the worksheet until you paste it in its new location by pressing Enter or clicking the Paste button.

- When you get ready to paste, just click on the first cell, row, or column where you want pasted cells, rows, or columns to appear. If you select more than one cell to paste into, the selected range must be exactly the same size as the range you want to paste, or an error will occur.

- When you cut a selection, you can only paste it once, so you can't use cut to make multiple copies. You can *copy* and paste repeatedly. When you press Enter at the end of a paste operation, Excel empties the Clipboard, so use the Paste button to paste the first, second, and so on copies that you want. Press Enter to place the final pasted copy.

If you want to move or copy data from one worksheet to another, cut or copy the selection, and then click the sheet tab for the sheet that you want to paste into. Click in the appropriate cell, and then press Enter to paste. If you want to move or copy data from one workbook to another, both workbooks must be open. Select and cut or copy the data, and then choose Window from the menu bar and select the destination workbook from the list of open workbooks. Click in the destination cell and press Enter.

Moving and Copying Cells with Cut/Copy and Paste

1. If there is data below or to the right of the paste area, begin by inserting enough blank cells, rows, or columns for the data you want to move or copy.

2. Select the data you want to move or copy. To move, click the Cut button, choose Edit ➤ Cut, or right-click and select Cut from the shortcut menu. To copy, click the Copy button, choose Edit ➤ Copy, or right-click and select Copy from the shortcut menu.

3. Select the first cell, row, or column where you want to place the moved or copied data.

4. Press Enter to move or copy the data to its new location.

TIP TIP TIP TIP TIP TIP TIP TIP TIP TIP TIP TIP TIP TIP TIP TIP TIP TIP TIP TIP TIP TIP TIP TIP

A new feature in Office 2000, the Office Clipboard, allows you to save up to 12 items on the Clipboard and then paste them one at a time or all of them at once. To turn on the Clipboard toolbar, choose View ➤ Toolbars ➤ Clipboard.

Using Drag-and-Drop

When you're moving or copying cells between worksheets or workbooks, it's easiest to cut or copy and paste. Another method, called *drag-and-drop*, works well when you can see the cells to be copied and their destination on one screen. After you select the cells, move the mouse so that it points to any part of the cell pointer except the fill handle (the mouse pointer will change to an arrow). Hold down the right mouse button and drag the cells to their new location. When you release the mouse button, a shortcut menu opens that lets you select whether you want to move or copy the cells.

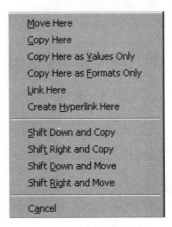

You can also move cells by dragging with the left mouse button. To copy with the left mouse button, hold the Ctrl key down, drag and drop the selected cells, then release the Ctrl key.

MOVING AND COPYING CELLS WITH DRAG-AND-DROP

1. Select the cells, rows, or columns to be moved or copied.
2. Point to any part of the cell pointer. The mouse pointer will change to an arrow shape.
3. To move the selection, drag it and drop it in its new location. To copy a selection, hold the Ctrl key while dropping the selection.

Naming a Worksheet

Because a workbook contains multiple worksheets, it is not always easy to remember which sheet contains what data. Excel allows you to give each worksheet a descriptive name so that you can locate it instantly within the workbook.

Naming a Worksheet

1. Double-click the sheet tab to select it.
2. Type a new name for the worksheet and press Enter.

Selecting Worksheets

You can move, copy, delete, and enter data in selected worksheets. To select one worksheet, click the sheet tab. To select more than one worksheet, hold the Ctrl key while selecting each worksheet. To select all worksheets in a workbook, right-click on any tab and choose Select All Sheets from the shortcut menu.

Using Grouped Worksheets

Skill 5

When more than one worksheet is selected, the worksheets are *grouped*. Data entered into one sheet is entered into all sheets in the group, making it easy to enter the same title on five sheets in the same workbook. However, this also means that you need to remember to immediately ungroup worksheets when you are finished entering, moving, or copying common data. Otherwise, entries you make on one worksheet will be made on all worksheets, overwriting the existing entries on the other sheets in the group.

Ungrouping Worksheets

To ungroup worksheets, right-click on any grouped worksheet tab and choose Ungroup Sheets from the shortcut menu. Or click on any worksheet in the workbook that is not included in the group.

Grouping and Ungrouping Worksheets

1. To select one worksheet, click the sheet tab.
2. To select more than one worksheet, hold the Ctrl key while selecting each worksheet.

continued ◗

3. To select all worksheets in a workbook, right-click on any tab and choose Select All Sheets from the shortcut menu.

4. To ungroup worksheets, right-click on any grouped worksheet tab and choose Ungroup Sheets from the shortcut menu.

Copying and Moving Worksheets

You can copy or move one or more selected worksheets within and between workbooks. To move worksheets within the same workbook, drag the sheet's sheet tab to the new location (marked by a small triangle just above the tab) and drop it:

To copy a worksheet in the same workbook, hold the Ctrl key while dragging. The copy will have the same name as the original sheet, followed by the copy number:

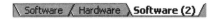

You can copy or move a worksheet to a new workbook or to an existing workbook.

COPYING AND MOVING WORKSHEETS

1. To move a worksheet within the same workbook, drag the sheet's sheet tab to the new location (marked by the triangle) and drop it. Hold down the Ctrl key while dragging to copy the worksheet.

2. To move or copy between workbooks, select the worksheet you want to copy, then either choose Edit ➢ Move or Copy Sheet from the menu bar. Select the name of the workbook you want to copy the sheet to. Click Create a Copy to copy it. Click OK.

Inserting and Deleting Worksheets

To insert a new worksheet, choose Insert ➢ Worksheet from the menu bar. To delete one or more selected sheets, choose Edit ➢ Delete Sheet from the menu bar, or right-click on the sheet(s) and choose Delete from the shortcut menu. When you delete a worksheet, a dialog box will open, asking you to confirm the deletion.

TIP TIP TIP TIP TIP TIP TIP TIP TIP TIP TIP TIP TIP TIP TIP TIP TIP TIP TIP TIP TIP TIP TIP TIP

Excel includes three worksheets in every new workbook. If you frequently find yourself adding sheets to workbooks, you might want to increase the default number of sheets in a new book. Select Tools ➢ Options from the menu bar, and change the Sheets in New Workbook setting on the General page of the Options dialog box.

Hands On

1. Practice naming worksheets in your workbooks. For example, name Sheet 1 in Second Hand News Payroll.

2. Use cut and paste to alphabetize a list within a worksheet. For example, alphabetize the Second Hand News Payroll worksheet by employee last name.

3. In an existing workbook such as the Cyclops Proposal workbook:

   a) Adjust column widths where needed.

   b) Insert blank rows between column labels and data.

   c) Practice moving cells, columns, and rows using cut and paste, copy and paste, and drag-and-drop techniques.

   d) Name all used worksheets.

   e) Move worksheets so they are ordered by sheet name.

4. In a new workbook, group all three sheets. Enter and format a title and some data; then ungroup the sheets and enter data on one sheet only.

5. Open a new workbook:

   a) Name each of the sheets in the workbook by clicking each sheet tab and entering a name; then press Enter.

   b) Hold Ctrl and select the first two sheets by clicking their sheet tabs.

c) Move to cell A1 in the first sheet and enter your name.

d) Click on the second sheet and notice that your name has also been entered in A1.

e) Right-click on either grouped sheet and choose Ungroup Sheets to turn off grouping.

5.4: Other Formatting Options

You have additional ways in which you can enhance the appearance of a worksheet. You can call attention to certain cells by the way text is aligned in them, you can even rotate text, and you can add borders, fill color, and font colors.

Aligning Text

 By default, Excel left-aligns text and right-aligns numbers. You can use the buttons on the Formatting toolbar to override the defaults and align text and numbers at the left, center, or right within cells:

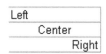

Excel has a fourth alignment called Merge and Center, which *merges* selected cells into one cell and centers the contents of the top left selected cell across the new merged cell. Worksheet titles are often merged and centered.

 To merge and center a title, select the cell containing the title and the cells in the same row for all the used columns in the worksheet; then click the Merge and Center button. Excel only centers the text in the top left cell of the selection, so if your worksheet's title is in more than one row, merge and center each title row separately.

There are more alignment options that aren't accessible from the toolbar but are set in the Alignment page of the Format Cells dialog box. Some of the more unique alignments, including text rotation, are illustrated in Figure 5.6. The Alignment page of the Format Cells dialog box is shown in Figure 5.7.

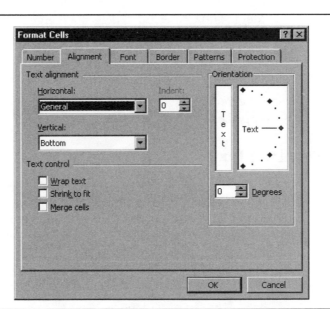

	A	B	C	D	E
1	V E R T I C A L	Text Rotated 45°		The text in this cell is justified horizontally and vertically.	
2	L M E R	Text centered vertically and horizontally	The text in this cell is wrapped.		
3	G	Left, 0 indent	Merged and centered		
4	E	Left, 1 indent			
5	D	Left, 2 indent	Shrunk to fit in this cell		

FIGURE 5.6: Text alignments

FIGURE 5.7: Alignment page of the Format Cells dialog box

Horizontal Alignment and Indenting

There are seven types of Horizontal alignment:

General is the default alignment: text to the left and numbers to the right.

Left (Indent) aligns the contents of the cell at the cell's left edge, just like the Formatting toolbar button. However, if you choose Left in the dialog box, you can also specify a number of characters to indent in the Indent box.

Center and **Right** are identical to the Formatting toolbar buttons.

Fill "fills" the cell with the current contents by repeating the contents for the width of the cell. If, for example, "-" is the contents of the cell and you choose Fill for the alignment, "————" will appear in the cell.

Justify wraps the text within the cell and adjusts the spacing within each line so that all lines are as wide as the cell, providing a smooth right edge, like text in a newspaper column.

Center across Selection is applied to a range of cells. The contents of the leftmost cell are centered across all the cells selected. This is similar to Merge and Center, but it does not merge the cells.

Vertical Alignment

The default vertical alignment is Bottom. Top and Center are used to float the contents nearer the top or middle of the cell. Justify adds space between the lines in a wrapped cell.

Rotating Text

In the Orientation section, use the tools to orient text vertically or to rotate text. To orient text vertically, click the box with the vertical word Text in it. To rotate text to another orientation, either use the Degrees spin box or drag the Text indicator in the Orientation tool. Rotating text lets you create a splashy column or row label. Vertically orient and merge text (see below) to label a group of row labels.

Merge, Shrink to Fit, and Wrap Text

If you want a vertical title to cross several rows (such as the label *Vertical Merged* in column A of Figure 5.7), select the title and several additional cells below the title. Click the Merge Cells check box to merge the cells. Shrink to Fit reduces the size of the type within selected cells so the contents fit. Wrap Text wraps the contents of a cell if it would exceed the cells' boundaries. Both Shrink to Fit and Wrap Text use the current column widths. If you narrow or widen a column after you shrink or wrap a label, you'll need to reshrink or rewrap.

ALIGNING TEXT

1. Select the range of cells to be formatted.
2. Choose Format ➤ Cells from the menu bar or right-click and choose Format from the shortcut menu.
3. Click the Alignment page tab.
4. Choose horizontal, vertical, orientation, merge, and wrap options, and then click OK.

Borders and Color

Effective use of fonts, discussed in Skill 1.6, can help make worksheets easier to understand. Borders and color provide further ways to highlight information in a worksheet. A *border* is a line drawn around a cell or group of cells. *Fill color* is used to highlight the background of part of a worksheet; *font color* is applied to text. Even if you don't have access to a color printer, you might still want to use color in worksheets that you or others use frequently. Color distinguishes between similar looking worksheets; for example, the Sales Department's budget could have a blue title, and Production's title could be burgundy.

The Borders, Fill Color, and Font Color buttons are found on the Formatting toolbar. All three buttons are combination buttons that include a menu opened by clicking the drop-down arrow attached to the button.

Borders can completely surround a group of cells, surround each cell individually, provide an underline, or double-underline the selected range. Selecting a border from the menu assigns it to the button and applies it to the selected cells. After you assign a border to the button, the next time you click the Border button, the same border style will be applied to your currently active cell or range of cells. The Fill Color and Font Color buttons also have attached menus and are used the same way.

If you have a lot of borders, colors, or font colors to apply, you can open any or all of the menus as separate windows that float on your worksheet. Open the menu, and then point to the dark gray bar at the top of the menu. The bar will turn the same color as your program title bar; if you hover for a moment, a ScreenTip "Drag to make this menu float" will appear. Drag the menu into the worksheet and release the mouse button. Close the menu with its Close button.

ADDING BORDERS, COLORS, AND FONT COLORS

1. To apply a Font Color or Fill Color, select the cells to be formatted. Click the Color button's drop-down and select a color from the menu.

2. To add a border, select the cells to be formatted. Click the Borders button's drop-down and select a border from the menu.

TIP TIP TIP TIP TIP TIP TIP TIP TIP TIP TIP TIP TIP TIP TIP TIP TIP TIP TIP TIP TIP TIP TIP TIP
If you need to apply several formatting changes to a group of cells, you may find it easier to use the Format Cells dialog box. Click the page tabs to move from page to page and set the desired formats for the selected cells. When you are finished, click OK to apply all the chosen formats to the selection.

Hands On

1. Create an "alignment sampler" similar to Figure 5.6.

2. Use alignments, fonts, borders, and colors to format the Cyclops Proposal Software and Hardware worksheets.

3. In an existing worksheet, use borders to separate numeric data from totals.

5.5: Printing in Excel

Print Preview, Page Setup, Page Break Preview, and Print are interrelated. Print Preview lets you see how each page of the workbook will appear when it is printed. Page Setup is used to change the margins, print quality, print area, and print features. Page Break Preview displays the current page breaks and allows you to adjust them. Print prints the specified number of copies of selected worksheets or workbooks.

Print Preview

When you click the Print Preview button, the preview window displays the current worksheet as it will appear when it is printed, as shown in Figure 5.8.

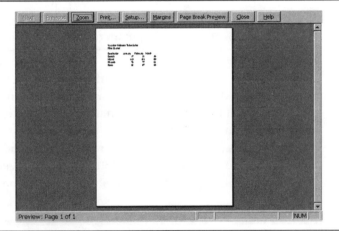

SKILL 5

FIGURE 5.8: Excel Print Preview window

If the worksheet is wider or longer than one page, the Previous and Next buttons let you move between pages. (If the worksheet fits on one page, these two buttons are disabled.) The preview window's Zoom button toggles between full-page view and a magnified view of the worksheet. The full-page view lets you see the general layout of the page. Use the magnified view to look at specific details.

Adjusting Margins in Print Preview

The Print Preview Margins button displays the current margin settings. Point to any of the margin lines, and the pointer will change to an adjustment tool, as shown in Figure 5.9. Press the mouse button, and the status bar will indicate the name and current setting for the margin. Drag a margin to adjust it.

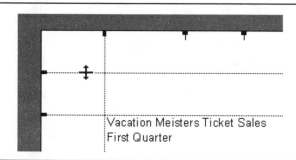

Vacation Meisters Ticket Sales
First Quarter

FIGURE 5.9: Adjusting margins in Print Preview

Excel's default margins are $^3/_4$" on each side, and 1" on the top and bottom, with a $^1/_2$" header and footer margin. Headers and footers print in the $^1/_2$" of space between the header/footer margin and the regular margin. The top and bottom margins define the limits of the printed worksheet, and the header and footer margins define the areas where the header and footer will print. If you use headers and footers, the top and bottom margins need to be inside the header and footer margins, or part of the worksheet will print on top of the header and footer.

ADJUSTING MARGINS IN PRINT PREVIEW

1. Click Print Preview to open the preview window.
2. Click the Margins button to display page margins.
3. Drag the margin you wish to change to its new location.

Changing Page Setup

To change page setup, choose File ➤ Page Setup from the menu bar to open the Page Setup dialog box. (If you're already in Print Preview, click the Setup button; from Page Break Preview, right-click and choose Page Setup from the shortcut menu.) The Page Setup dialog box splits page layout into four tabbed pages that contain Page, Header/Footer, Margins, and Sheet settings.

Page Settings

Use the Page options of the Page Setup dialog box, shown in Figure 5.10, to set orientation, scaling, paper size, and print quality.

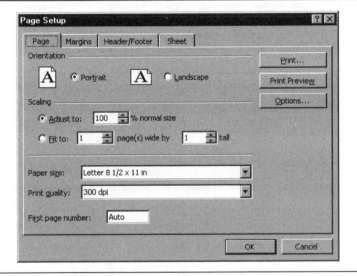

FIGURE 5.10: Page settings in the Page Setup dialog box

Orientation is the direction of print in relation to the paper it is printed on. Portrait, the default setting, places the short edge of the paper at the top and bottom. If your worksheet is wider than it is long, consider using landscape orientation.

Scaling is used to reduce or enlarge the print. If you simply need to make the print larger, use the Adjust To control and choose a size greater than 100%. The Fit To control instructs Excel to reduce a worksheet that exceeds a specific number of pages so it will fit.

SKILL
5

Use the Paper Size control if you are using a different paper size from the default (for example, legal paper). Print Quality is measured in dpi: dots per inch. Higher dpi means higher print quality, but there is a trade-off: it takes longer to print at higher dpi. The First Page Number control is used to set an initial page number other than 1.

TIP TIP TIP TIP TIP TIP TIP TIP TIP TIP TIP TIP TIP TIP TIP TIP TIP TIP TIP TIP TIP TIP TIP

The Options button appears on every page of the Page Setup dialog box. The button opens the Windows property sheet (or the manufacturer's property sheet if there is one) for the printer that's currently selected.

CHANGING PAGE SETTINGS

1. Open the Page Setup dialog box by choosing File ➤ Page Setup or by clicking the Setup button in the Print Preview window. Click the Page tab.

2. Change settings for Orientation, Scaling, Paper Size, Print Quality, or First Page Number.

3. Click OK to apply the settings.

Headers and Footers

A header appears at the top of each page of a document. Footers are printed at the bottom of the page. The default setting is no header or footer. If you want a header or footer, choose or create it in the Header/Footer page in the Page Setup dialog box, shown in Figure 5.11.

The currently selected header and footer are displayed in the two preview panes. To choose a different predesigned header, click the Header drop-down list. Choose a footer the same way, using the Footer drop-down list. When you select a different header (or footer), the preview pane will reflect the change.

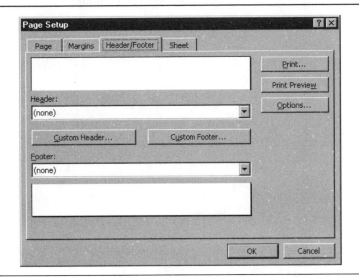

FIGURE 5.11: Header/Footer page of the Page Setup dialog box

To create a new header, click the Custom Header button to open the Header dialog box, shown in Figure 5.12. The header is separated into three sections: left, center, and right. Click in any section to place information in that portion of the header. You can enter text (like your name) or insert a placeholder from Table 5.5.

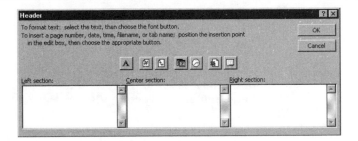

FIGURE 5.12: The Header dialog box

TABLE 5.5: Header and Footer Placeholders

Button	Button Name	Placeholder
	Page Number	Current page number
	Total Pages	Total number of pages printed
	Date	Date worksheet was printed
	Time	Time worksheet was printed
	File Name	Name of workbook
	Tab	Name of worksheet

When the file is printed, Excel will replace each placeholder with the actual page number, date, time, workbook, or worksheet name.

To format header text, including placeholders, select the text and click the Font button to open the Font dialog box. When you are finished creating the header, click OK to return to the Header/Footer page of the Page Setup dialog box and add the new header to the drop-down list.

NOTE NOTE NOTE NOTE NOTE NOTE NOTE NOTE NOTE NOTE NOTE NOTE NOTE NOTE

You can open the Header and Footer dialog box directly, rather than going through Page Setup, by selecting View ➢ Header and Footer, just as you do in Word.

SELECTING AND CREATING HEADERS AND FOOTERS

1. Choose File ⪴ Page Setup from the menu bar.
2. In the Page Setup dialog box, select the Header/Footer page.
3. Click the Header drop-down list and select a header, or click Custom Header to create a header. Click the Footer drop-down and select a footer, or click Custom Footer to create a footer.
4. Press Enter to return to the Page Setup dialog box.

Setting Margins in the Page Setup Dialog Box

The preview in the Margins page of the Page Setup dialog box (see Figure 5.13) displays the margins as dotted lines. You can change the margins here using the spin box controls for each margin.

SKILL
5

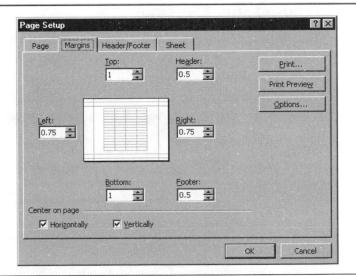

FIGURE 5.13: Margins page of the Page Setup dialog box

Use the Center on Page controls to center the printed worksheet horizontally between the side margins or vertically between the top and bottom margins. As you change settings on the Margins page, the preview will change to reflect the new margin settings.

CHANGING MARGINS IN PAGE SETUP

1. In the Page Setup dialog box, select the Margins page.
2. Using the spin box controls, set the top, bottom, left, and right margins.
3. If you are using a header or footer, use the Header and Footer spin boxes to set the distance for the header and footer margins.
4. Use the Center on Page check boxes to center the printed worksheet.

Changing Sheet Settings

The Sheet page (see Figure 5.14) contains settings that relate to the sheet features that will appear in the printed copy, including the print area, repeating rows and columns, and gridlines.

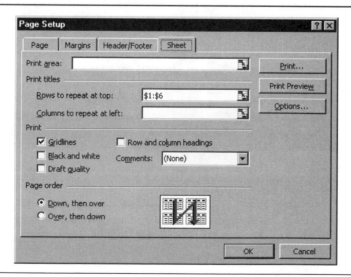

FIGURE 5.14: Sheet settings

The Print Area, Rows to Repeat, and Columns to Repeat controls are only enabled when you open the Page Setup dialog box from the menu (choose File ➢ Page Setup or View ➢ Header and Footer). If you go to Page Setup from Print Preview or the Print dialog box, you won't be able to change these three settings.

Print Area   By default, Excel prints from the home cell (A1) to the last occupied cell in a worksheet. To specify a different range, type the range in the Print Area control, or select the print area with the mouse. If the Print Area includes noncontiguous cells, each contiguous range will print on a separate page.

TIP TIP TIP TIP TIP TIP TIP TIP TIP TIP TIP TIP TIP TIP TIP TIP TIP TIP TIP TIP TIP TIP
The easiest way to set the Print Area is from the menu bar. Select the cells to be printed, and then choose File ➢ Print Area ➢ Set Print Area from the menu bar. When you want to print the entire worksheet again, choose File ➢ Print Area ➢ Clear Print Area.

SKILL
5

Print Titles   Prints column and row labels on each page of the printout. Specify these rows or columns in the Rows to Repeat at Top and Columns to Repeat at Left text boxes. (Excel requires a *range* with a colon for these entries, even if it's only one row or column.)

Print or Hide Gridlines   Determines whether gridlines will be printed but does not affect their display in the worksheet. Turning off the print gridlines gives your worksheet a cleaner appearance and can make it easier to read.

TIP TIP TIP TIP TIP TIP TIP TIP TIP TIP TIP TIP TIP TIP TIP TIP TIP TIP TIP TIP TIP TIP
To turn off screen gridlines, choose Tools ➢ Options and clear the check mark in the Gridlines option on the View page of the Options dialog box.

Draft Quality   Chooses draft mode to print the worksheet without gridlines or graphics.

Black and White   If you used colors in the worksheet but won't be printing on a color printer, click this control to speed up the print process.

Row and Column Headings   The row numbers and column letters will be included in the printout. This is a useful feature when you are editing or trying to locate an error in a worksheet.

Page Order   Establishes the order in which multi-page worksheets are printed.

If you find it difficult to select cells with the Page Setup dialog box in the way, click the Collapse Dialog button to minimize the dialog box while you select cells. Click the Expand Dialog button to return to the Print Setup dialog box.

CHANGING SHEET SETTINGS

1. Choose File ➢ Page Setup, or from Print Preview, click the Setup button to open the Page Setup dialog box. Click the Sheet page tab.

2. Specify ranges for a Print Area and rows and columns to be repeated as titles on each printed page by entering them from the keyboard or by using the mouse.

3. Enter option settings in the Print and Page Order sections.

4. Click OK.

TIP TIP TIP TIP TIP TIP TIP TIP TIP TIP TIP TIP TIP TIP TIP TIP TIP TIP TIP TIP TIP TIP TIP TIP TIP TIP

You can set Page Setup options for multiple worksheets by grouping (selecting) the worksheets before opening the Page Setup dialog box. Remember to ungroup the worksheets after you've changed the Page Setup.

Page Break Preview

Page Break Preview, shown in Figure 5.15, is a view of the worksheet window that shows you what will be printed and the order in which the pages will be printed. To turn on Page Break Preview, click the Page Break Preview button in Print Preview, or choose View ➢ Page Break Preview from the menu bar. In Page Break Preview, areas that will be printed are white; cells that won't be printed are gray. Each printed page is numbered. You can quickly change the range to be printed by dragging the edge of the page break with your mouse to include or exclude cells.

	A	B	C	D	E	F
1	Vacation Meisters Ticket Sales					
2	First Quarter					
3						
4	Destination	January	February	March		
5	Detroit	17	21	36		
6	Miami	119	101	89		
7	Phoenix	75	77	61		
8	Reno	93	87	90		
9						
10						

FIGURE 5.15: Page Break Preview

SKILL 5

If a worksheet prints on multiple pages, you can adjust the breaks by dragging the page break. To add a manual page break, select the first column or row you want to appear in the page after the break. Right-click and choose Insert Page Break from the shortcut menu:

> Insert Page Break
>
> Reset All Page Breaks
>
> Set Print Area
>
> Reset Print Area
>
> Page Setup...

To remove a manual page break, right-click in the row below the horizontal page break or in the column to the right of the vertical page break, and choose Remove Page Break from the shortcut menu. To remove all manual page breaks, right-click any cell and choose Reset All Page Breaks from the shortcut menu. In Page Break Preview, you can also remove a page break by dragging it outside the print area.

To return to Normal view, choose View ➤ Normal from the menu bar. Note that you can also go directly from the worksheet to Page Break Preview from the View menu.

PREVIEWING AND ADJUSTING PAGE BREAKS

1. From the Print Preview window, click the Page Break Preview button.

–OR–

1. From the worksheet window, choose View ➢ Page Break Preview.
2. Using the mouse, drag the page break to extend or limit the range of cells to be printed.
3. Choose View ➢ Normal to close Page Break Preview.

Changing Print Settings

If you click the Print button on the Standard toolbar, Excel prints one copy of the selected worksheet(s) using the default print settings, including any settings you have changed in the Print Setup dialog box. To choose a printer, to specify what to print, and to set the number of copies, use the Print dialog box, shown in Figure 5.16. Choose File ➢ Print to open the Print dialog box.

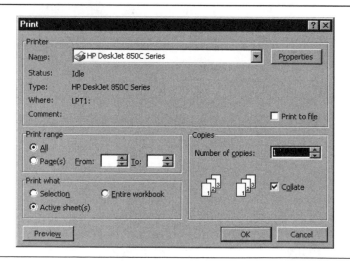

FIGURE 5.16: The Print dialog box

Click the Name drop-down list to select a different printer from the default. Click the Properties button to view or change the printer's settings.

Use the Print Range controls to print some, but not all, of the pages of a multi-page print job, and use the spin boxes to specify a starting and ending page to print. You cannot specify noncontiguous pages in Excel, so if you want to print pages 1–4 and 6–8, you either have to print twice or choose the cells on those pages and specify them as your print area.

In the Print What control, specify which part of the worksheet or workbook you want to print. The Selection option provides another way to override the default print area: select the cells you want to print, and then print the selection. Choose Workbook to print all used worksheets in the active workbook.

TIP TIP TIP TIP TIP TIP TIP TIP TIP TIP TIP TIP TIP TIP TIP TIP TIP TIP TIP TIP TIP TIP TIP TIP TIP

To print some, but not all worksheets in a workbook, select the sheets before opening the Print dialog box, and then choose Active Sheets.

SKILL
5

Use the Number of Copies spin box to print more than one copy of the selection, worksheet, or workbook. If you are printing multiple copies of more than one page, use the Collate control to print the pages in order. Two copies of a three page worksheet will print 1–2–3, then 1–2–3. With Collate turned off, the same print request will print 1–1, 2–2, and 3–3.

CHANGING PRINT SETTINGS

1. Choose File ➤ Print to open the Print dialog box.
2. Select a printer from the Printer Name drop-down control.
3. Select what you wish to print: a selection, active worksheets, or the current workbook.
4. Set the number of copies using the Copies spin box, and turn Collate on or off for multi-page print jobs.
5. Specify a page range or leave the default as All.
6. Click OK to print and return to the worksheet.

Checking Worksheet Spelling

Misspelled words automatically cast doubt on the accuracy of the rest of a worksheet. Excel includes two tools to help you correct spelling errors. AutoCorrect automatically fixes common typos, and Spelling checks all the text in a worksheet to ensure that it is error-free. (Of course, you still need to examine all the numbers in a worksheet to verify that you've entered data and formulas correctly.)

If you are not in the home cell when you begin the spelling check, Excel will check from the cell pointer to the end of the worksheet, and then ask if it should return to the top of the worksheet and finish checking. When Spelling is complete, Excel will notify you that it has finished checking the entire sheet. Spelling is a shared feature of all the Office 2000 products, so words you add to the dictionary or to AutoCorrect are added to the common custom dictionary you use with Word, PowerPoint, and Access. For more information on AutoCorrect and Spelling, see Skill 1.4.

Hands On

Open the Cyclops Proposal workbook or another workbook of your choice.

1. In the first worksheet:

    a) Preview the worksheet.

    b) Center the worksheet horizontally and vertically on the page.

    c) Check spelling.

    d) Create a header that includes your name, and a footer with the current date and time left-justified and the sheet name right-justified.

    e) Preview and print the worksheet.

2. In the second worksheet:

    a) Use Page Break Preview to extend the print area to include two blank columns and one blank row.

    b) Change the paper orientation to landscape.

    c) Change the top margin to 1.5 inches so the worksheet can be placed in a notebook.

    d) Check spelling.

    e) Add a horizontal page break so the worksheet prints on at least two pages.

f) Print the worksheet title and column labels on each page.

g) Preview and print the worksheet.

5.6: Using Functions and References

In Excel, a function is a predefined formula, and you can save a lot of time by using functions. You can also save time by using references to other cells, rather than including all the calculations that produce the results in those cells.

Using Functions

In Skill 5.2 you used the SUM function (by clicking the AutoSum button) to total numbers. Excel includes hundreds of other functions that you can use to calculate results used in statistics, finance, engineering, math, and other fields. *Functions* are structured programs that calculate a specific result: a total, an average, the amount of a monthly loan payment, or the geometric mean of a group of numbers. Each function has a specific order, or *syntax*, that must be used for the function to work properly. Functions are formulas, so all functions begin with the = sign. After the = is the *function name*, followed by one or more *arguments* separated by commas and enclosed in parentheses.

=SUM(D6:D11)

Excel's functions are grouped into 10 categories, as indicated in Table 5.6.

TABLE 5.6: Excel Functions

Category	Examples
Financial	Calculates interest rates, loan payments, depreciation amounts
Date & Time	Returns the current hour, day of week or year, time, or date
Math & Trig	Calculates absolute values, cosines, logarithms
Statistical	Performs common functions used for totals, averages, and high and low numbers in a range; advanced functions for t-tests, Chi tests, deviation
Lookup & Reference	Searches for and returns values from a range; creates hyperlinks to network or Internet documents
Database	Calculates values in an Excel database table

Skill 5

TABLE 5.6: Excel Functions *(continued)*

Category	Examples
Text	Converts text to uppercase or lowercase, trims characters from the right or left end of a text string, concatenates text strings
Logical	Evaluates an expression and returns a value of TRUE or FALSE, used to trigger other actions or formatting
Information	Returns information from Excel or Windows about the current status of a cell, object, or the environment
Engineering	Included with Office 2000, but must be installed separately from the Analysis Toolpack

You don't have to learn all the functions—but you should know the common functions and have enough knowledge about other functions so that you can find them as you need them. SUM is the only individual function included on the Standard toolbar. You can access all the functions (including SUM) using the Formula Palette.

Entering Functions

Before entering a function, make sure the cell where you want the results to be displayed is activated. Click the Edit Formula (the = sign) in the formula bar to open the Formula Palette. The Name box (to the left of the formula bar) will change to a Function box, displaying the name of the last function that was used (SUM), as shown in Figure 5.17.

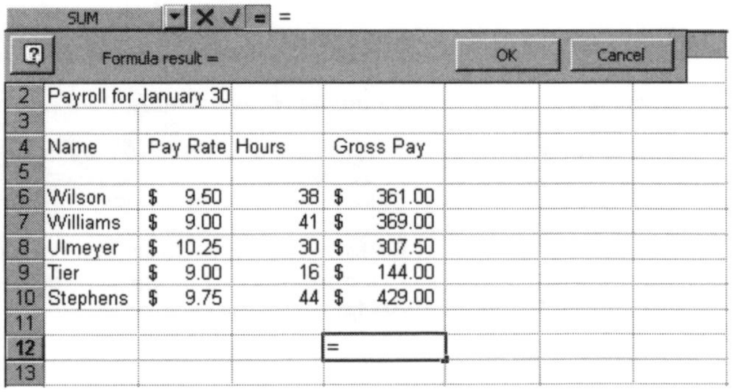

FIGURE 5.17: Formula Palette and Function box

Click the Function box drop-down list to choose from recently used functions.

If the function you want is on the list, select it, and Excel will move the function to the formula bar and the Formula Palette. The Formula Palette includes a description of the function and one or more text boxes for the function's arguments, as shown in Figure 5.18. For common functions that use a single range of cells as an argument, Excel "guesses" which numbers you might want to sum or average and places the range in the argument text box. Required arguments are bold, like Number 1 in Figure 5.18. These text boxes must be filled in to successfully use the function.

SKILL
5

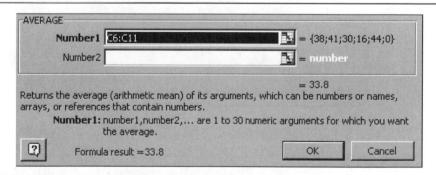

FIGURE 5.18: Function Palette (AVERAGE function)

In Figure 5.18, you can't tell whether the range in the Number 1 text box is correct because the Formula Palette covers the cells. Click the Collapse Dialog button to shrink the Formula Palette.

Confirm that the correct cells are selected, or use the mouse to select the correct cells, before expanding the palette with the Expand Dialog button. After you have selected all the required arguments, click OK to finish the entry and close the

Formula Palette. As with any formula, the results of the function are displayed in the active cell; the function itself is displayed in the formula bar when the cell is active.

If the function you want is not listed in the Function box, choose More Functions at the bottom of the list to open the Paste Function dialog box, shown in Figure 5.19.

If you're using a function that you rarely use, you can open this dialog box directly by clicking the Paste Function button on the Standard toolbar.

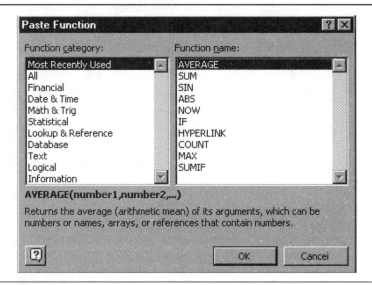

FIGURE 5.19: The Paste Function dialog box

Select a function category from the left pane of the dialog box, and then scroll the right pane and select a function. If you need more information, clicking the Office Assistant button opens the Assistant, which will offer help on the selected function. Click the OK button to choose the selected function and return to the Formula Palette.

USING FUNCTIONS

1. Activate the cell where you want the result of the function to appear.
2. Click the Edit Formula button on the formula bar.

continued

3. Choose a function from the Function Box drop-down list.

–OR–

3. If the function does not appear on the list, choose More Functions to open the Paste Function dialog box. Choose a Category in the left pane and a function from the right pane. Click OK to return to the Formula Palette.

4. In the Formula Palette, select the Number 1 text box. Click the Collapse Dialog button to move the dialog box, and then select the cells you want to include in the argument. Click the Expand Dialog button to return to the Formula Palette.

5. Click the OK button to complete the entry.

Relative and Absolute Cell References

SKILL
5

When you copy a formula from one cell to another, Excel automatically adjusts each cell reference in the formula. Most of the time, this is exactly what you want Excel to do. However, there are exceptions. For example, Vacation Meisters would like to know the percentage of tickets sold for each destination city. You'd calculate a city's percentage by dividing the city's total into the grand total for all cities.

In Figure 5.20, a formula was entered to divide the total Detroit tickets (74) into the grand total (866). The formula for Detroit is fine—but it's obviously wrong when filled to the other cities.

	A	B	C	D	E	F	G
1		Vacation Meisters Ticket Sales					
2		First Quarter					
3							
4	Destination	January	February	March	Total	Average	Percent of Total
5							
6	Detroit	17	21	36	74	25	9%
7	Miami	119	101	89	309	103	143%
8	Phoenix	75	77	61	213	71	288%
9	Reno	93	87	90	270	90	87%
10							
11	Total for Month	304	286	276	866		
12	Average for Month	76	72	69	217		
13	Minimum for Month	17	21	36	74		
14	Maximum for Month	119	101	90	309		

FIGURE 5.20: Calculating percentages

So what happened? The formula in G6 was =E6/E11. When it was AutoFilled from G6 to G7, Excel changed each cell reference, just as it did with the totals you filled earlier. You can see which cells were referenced in each formula by double-clicking on a formula. The formula in G7 was changed to =E7/E12, and the change from E11 to E12 created the problem. Rather than dividing Miami's total into the total for all destinations, it divided it into the average in cell E12. The formulas for Phoenix and Reno have a similar problem.

When you fill this formula, you want E6 to change to E7 *relative* to the formula's new location, but you don't want E11 to change at all. The reference to E11 should be *absolute*—not changeable.

You can instruct Excel to not change the reference to E11 by making it an absolute cell reference. Absolute cell references are preceded with dollar signs: E11. The dollar signs "lock in" the cell reference so Excel doesn't change it if you fill or copy the formula to another cell. The dollar sign in front of the E instructs Excel not to change the column; the dollar sign in front of the 11 locks in the row. So as you fill the formula to the other cities, E6 will change to E7, E8, and E9, but E11 will always be E11.

You create the absolute cell reference in the original formula. If you never intend to fill or copy the formula, you don't need to use absolutes, and absolutes won't fix a formula that doesn't work correctly to begin with. Remember, the original formula in G6 worked just fine. If you are typing the formula, just precede the column and row addresses with a $. You can also create the absolute cell reference using the F4 key, as you will see in steps below.

CREATING AN ABSOLUTE CELL REFERENCE

1. Place the cell pointer where you want the results of the formula to appear.

2. Begin entering the formula. After you indicate the address of the cell that contains the absolute value, press the F4 key once to add $ to the row and column of the cell reference.

3. When the formula is complete, press Enter or click the green check mark.

4. Fill the formula to the appropriate cells.

You can also create a *mixed reference*, making part of a cell address absolute and part relative, by locking in either the column or the row. Use mixed references when you want to copy a formula down *and* across and to have a reference change relatively in one direction but not in the other. For example, E$5 will remain E$5 when copied down because the row reference is absolute, but can change to F$5, G$5, and so on when copied across because the column reference is relative.

TIP TIP TIP TIP TIP TIP TIP TIP TIP TIP TIP TIP TIP TIP TIP TIP TIP TIP TIP TIP TIP TIP TIP TIP

The Absolute key (F4) is a four-way toggle. The first time you press it, it locks both the column and row: E11. Press again, and only the row is locked: E$11. The third time you press, the column is locked: $E11. Press a fourth time, and both row and column are relative: E11.

Hands On

1. Open the Cyclops Proposal Software or other similar worksheet and make the changes indicated below:

	A	B	C	D	E
1	Cyclops Database Proposal - Draft				
2	Software				
3					
4	Title	Copies	Price	Total	Percent
5	Office Pro 97	20	$469	$9,380	73%
6	Windows 95	20	$89	$1,780	14%
7	McAfee Scan	20	$79	$1,580	12%
8	Carbon Copy	1	$149	$149	1%
9					
10	Total Software Cost			$12,889	

2. In the Cyclops Proposal Hardware or other similar worksheet, make the changes indicated below:

	A	B	C	D	E
1	Cyclops Database Proposal - Draft				
2	Hardware				
3					
4	Item	Quantity	Price	Total	Percent
5	PCs	19	$ 1,565	$ 29,735	80%
6	Server	1	$ 4,175	$ 4,175	11%
7	Scanners	2	$ 685	$ 1,370	4%
8	Printers	4	$ 499	$ 1,996	5%
9					
10	Totals	26		$ 37,276	

5.7: Naming Ranges

You can apply a *name* to refer to a cell or a range of cells, rather than using cell addresses as references. Names provide multiple benefits:

- Names are more descriptive and easier to remember than cell addresses.

- When a cell moves, the name moves with it.

- You can use a name in place of a cell or range address in a formula or function argument, just like a row or column label.

- When you copy a formula that uses a name, the effect is the same as using an absolute cell reference.

Naming Ranges

Names can be a maximum of 255 characters and can include letters, numbers, underscores, and periods. The name must begin with either a letter or the underscore character. You cannot use spaces, commas, exclamation points, or other special characters. Names cannot be valid cell addresses: F1998 cannot be used as a name. Names are not case-sensitive: *INTEREST RATE* and *interest rate* are the same name. The traditional practice is to exclude spaces and to mix uppercase and lowercase letters, beginning each word within the name with an uppercase letter: InterestRate. A name can't be repeated within a workbook, so you can't use the same name on two different sheets in the same workbook.

You can name a range in three ways. The easiest is to select the range (which can include noncontiguous cells) and then click in the Name box to the left of the formula bar. Click the box, not the drop-down arrow. Type the name for the range, and then press Enter.

NAMING A RANGE USING THE NAME BOX

1. Select the range to be named.
2. Click in the Name box.
3. Type a valid name for the range and press Enter.

You can name ranges and change or delete existing range names using the Define Name dialog box, shown in Figure 5.21. The dialog box displays a list of the names you are already using in any sheet in the workbook.

SKILL
5

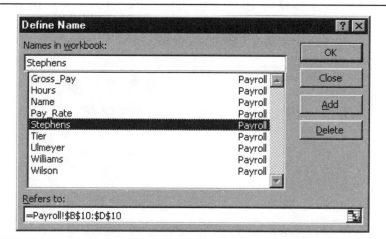

FIGURE 5.21: Define Names dialog box

DEFINING, CHANGING, AND DELETING RANGE NAMES

1. To define a name, select the range of cells you want to name.

2. Choose Insert ➤ Name ➤ Define from the menu bar.

3. In the Names in Workbook text box, type a valid range name; then click Add.

4. To change a name, select the name from the Names in Workbook list. Select the name in the Names in Workbook text box; overtype the old name with the new name, and then click Add.

5. To delete a name, select the name from the Names in Workbook list, and then click the Delete button.

6. When you are finished, click OK.

Excel automatically allows you to use the row and column labels to refer to cells. However, you might want to refer to a range by using a different column or row of text. Use the Create Names dialog box (see Figure 5.22) to *assign* a name to one cell from text in another cell even if the text is not a row or column label.

FIGURE 5.22: The Create Names dialog box

Excel edits labels as needed to make them valid names. If the label for a column or row contains spaces, Excel will replace the space with an underscore, thus `Interest_Rate`. If the cell contents begin with a number, like `8-Mar` or `4 bags`, Excel will add an underscore to the beginning of the name: `_8-Mar` or `_4_bags`. However, Excel will not create a name from a cell that contains *only* a number (like 1998, 78, or 1254.50). Excel will let you go through the motions, but it won't create the names.

CREATING NAMES FROM A ROW OR COLUMN OF TEXT

1. Select the range to be named. Include the cells you want to use as names as either the top or bottom row, or the first or last column selected.

2. Choose Insert ≻ Name ≻ Create from the menu bar to open the Create Names dialog box.

3. In the Create Names In text box, select the row (Top or Bottom) and/or column (Left or Right) that contains the labels you want to use to name the selected range.

4. Click OK to apply the names and close the dialog box.

Using Names

You can enter a name anywhere a regular cell reference is valid. For example, you can type in the name of a range as an argument for a function: =SUM(Totals). Names also serve a valuable navigation function, particularly in large workbooks and worksheets. To move to and select a named range anywhere in the workbook, click the down arrow in the Name box, and select the name from the list.

Hands On

1. Using the Cyclops Proposal Software worksheet or another worksheet:

   a) Practice naming ranges using both Name ≻ Create and Name ≻ Define.

   b) Move to a named range.

5.8: Creating Easy to Understand Charts

Charts are graphical representations of numeric data. Charts make it easier for users to compare and understand numbers, so charts have become a popular way to present numeric data. Every chart tells a story. Stories can be simple: "See how our sales have increased," or complex: "This is how our overhead costs relate to the price of our product." Whether simple or complex, the story should be readily understandable. If you can't immediately understand what a chart means, it isn't a good chart.

Charts are constructed with *data points*—individual numbers in a worksheet—and *data series*—groups of related data points within a column or row. In the Vacation Meisters Tickets worksheet (see Figure 5.20 earlier in this skill), each of the numbers is a data point. There are many possible sets of data series in this worksheet. One set includes four data series—one for each city's row. Another set includes a data series for each month's column. Each column or row of numbers is a series.

Pie Charts

Use *pie charts* to show the relationships between pieces of an entity. The implication is that the pie includes *all* of something: all the tickets sold in a month or all the tickets sold in the first quarter (see Figure 5.23). The pie chart isn't appropriate for illustrating *some* of anything, so if there's not an obvious "all" in the data you're charting, don't use a pie.

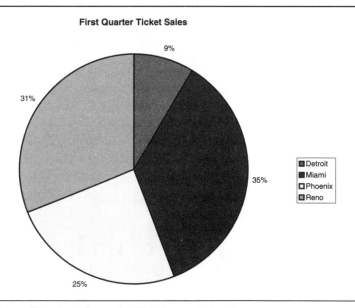

FIGURE 5.23: Pie chart from the Tickets worksheet

A pie chart can only include one data series. If you select more than one data series, Excel uses the first series and ignores all others. No error message appears, so you won't necessarily know that the chart doesn't show the data you intended to include unless you examine the chart carefully.

NOTE NOTE NOTE NOTE NOTE NOTE NOTE NOTE NOTE NOTE NOTE NOTE NOTE NOTE NOTE

Pie charts almost always show relationships at a fixed point in time—the end of the year, a specific month, day, or week. It is not impossible to create a pie chart with more than one time frame; however, this kind of information would be better represented in a series chart.

When you create a pie chart, Excel totals the data points in the series and then divides the value of each data point into the series total to determine how large each data point's pie slice should be. Don't include a total from the worksheet as a data point; this doubles the total Excel calculates, resulting in a pie chart with one large slice (50% of the pie), as shown in Figure 5.24.

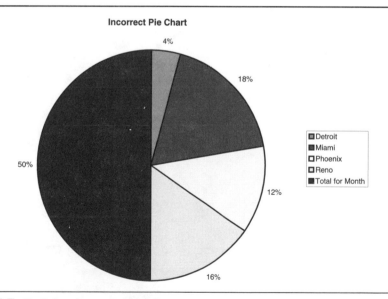

FIGURE 5.24: Incorrect pie chart

Series Charts

In a *series chart*, you can chart more than one data series. This lets you compare the data points in the series, such as January *vs.* February, Reno *vs.* Phoenix. Series charts are open-ended: there is no requirement that the data shown is all the data for a month or year. There are several types of series charts. You can give the same set of data a very different look by simply changing the chart type.

Line and Area Charts

The series chart shown in Figure 5.25 is a *line chart* showing the relationship between ticket sales and each city during the first quarter. Each data series is a city. Line charts are available in a 2-D version (as shown) or a in 3-D version that is sometimes called a ribbon chart. An area chart is a line chart with the area below the line filled. Line charts and area charts are typically used to show one or more variables (sales, income, price) changing over time.

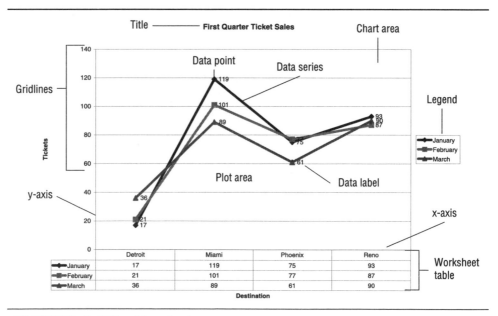

FIGURE 5.25: Line chart

Column and Bar Charts

Figure 5.26 shows the same information presented as a *bar chart*. The bars give added substance to the chart. In the line chart (Figure 5.25), the reader notices the trend up or down in each line and the gaps between the lines. The bar chart makes all ticket sales seem more substantial, but it also makes the difference between destinations even clearer—like why doesn't anyone vacation in Detroit?

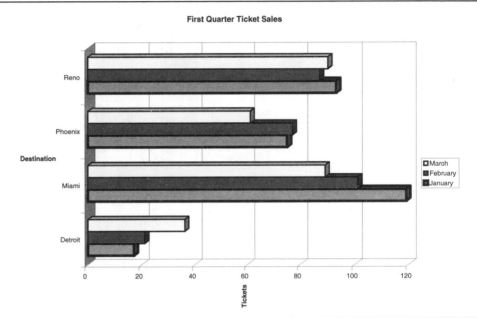

FIGURE 5.26: Bar chart

Line and area charts share a common layout. The horizontal line is called the X-axis, and the vertical line is the Y-axis (the same X- and Y-axes you may have learned about in algebra or geometry class when plotting data points). In a bar chart, however, the axes are turned 90 degrees so the X-axis is on the left side.

Column charts are the same as bar charts, but with the X-axis at the bottom. There are three-dimensional varieties of bar and column charts, which add depth to the regular chart. Cylinders, cones, and pyramids are variations of a column chart. Excel also offers another style of bar and column chart—the stacked chart. A stacked 3-D column chart, using the same data as Figures 5.25 and 5.26, is shown in Figure 5.27. In a stacked chart, parallel data points in each data series are stacked

SKILL
5

on top or to the right of each other. Stacking adds another dimension to the chart, since it allows the user to compare sales between as well as within time periods—like providing a column chart and a pie chart for each time period.

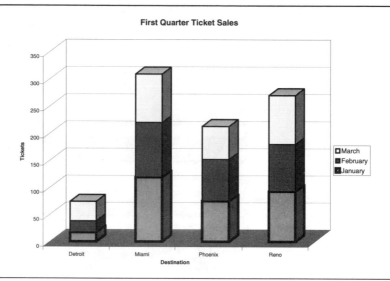

FIGURE 5.27: Stacked 3-D Column Chart

The 3-D charts have three axes. In a 3-D column chart, the X-axis is on the bottom. The vertical axis is the Z-axis; the Y-axis goes from front to back, providing the "third dimensional" depth in the chart. Don't worry about memorizing which axis is which in each chart type; there are ways to know which is which when you're creating or editing the chart.

Creating a Chart

The easiest way to create a chart is by using the Chart Wizard. Begin the charting process by selecting the data to be used in the chart. With the exception of the chart's title, everything that appears in the chart should be selected somewhere in the worksheet. Make sure that the ranges you select are symmetrical: if you select four labels in rows 9–12 of column A, select data points from the other columns in rows 9–12. If you select labels in columns A–D of row 5, the data series you select should also be in columns A–D.

If you include blank rows or extra empty columns in your selection, you'll have empty spaces in your chart. Remember that you can hold the Ctrl key to select noncontiguous ranges of data. If you select some cells you don't want to include, press Esc and start again.

When you have your text and numbers selected, click the Chart Wizard button on the Standard toolbar to open the Chart Wizard. In the first step of the Chart Wizard, choose a chart type in the Chart Type list box (see Figure 5.28). If the type of chart you want isn't listed, check out the chart types on the Custom Types tab. For more information about a chart type, select the chart type, click the Chart *Wizard's Office Assistant button*, and choose Help With This Feature. The Assistant will offer to provide a sample of the selected chart.

After choosing a chart type in the left pane, choose a subtype in the right pane. To see a rough sample of the type and subtype using your data, use the mouse pointer to press the Press and Hold to View Sample button in the Chart Wizard. When you've selected a type and a subtype, click Next to continue.

SKILL
5

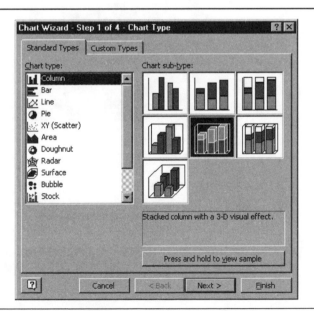

FIGURE 5.28: Chart Wizard, Step 1

In the second step, shown in Figure 5.29, you have an opportunity to make sure the range you selected is correct. If it isn't, click the Collapse Dialog button and re-select the proper range before continuing. Choose Rows or Columns in the Series In option group. The preview will change to reflect the range and series arrangement you specify. Click Next.

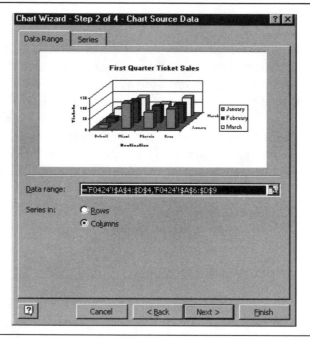

FIGURE 5.29: Chart Wizard, Step 2

In the third step, use the tabs to change options for various aspects of the chart:

Titles   Enter titles for the chart and axes

Axes   Display or hide axes

Gridlines   Display gridlines and display or hide the third dimension of a 3-D chart

Legend   Display and place a legend

Data Labels   Display text or values as data labels

Data Table   Show the selected range from the worksheet as part of the chart

As you change options, the chart preview will reflect your changes. When you've finished setting options, click Next to continue.

TIP TIP TIP TIP TIP TIP TIP TIP TIP TIP TIP TIP TIP TIP TIP TIP TIP TIP TIP TIP TIP TIP TIP

Every chart needs a title. The title provides information that is not already included in the graphical portion of the chart. The chart's picture, legend, and title taken together should answer any questions about the timing, location, or contents of the chart.

In the last step of the Chart Wizard, you can place the chart on the current worksheet or on a new, blank sheet in the same workbook. If the chart is placed on its own sheet, it will print as a full-size, single-page chart whenever it is printed. If you add it to the current worksheet as an object, it will print as part of the worksheet, but it can also be printed separately. Don't spend a lot of time deciding whether to place the chart in this worksheet or its own worksheet. You can easily move it later. Enter a new sheet name, or choose As Object In, and click Finish to create and place the chart.

SKILL
5

CREATING A CHART

1. Select the cells to be included in the chart.

2. Click the Chart Wizard button on the Standard toolbar.

3. In the first step, select a chart type and subtype; then click Next.

4. In the second step, verify that you have selected the correct range, and choose to have the series represented by rows or by columns. Click Next.

5. In the third step, use the tabs to move to the various options for the chart. On the Title tab, enter a chart title. Set other options as you wish, and then click Next.

6. In the fourth step, either enter the name for a chart worksheet or leave the default setting to place the chart as an object in the current worksheet. Click Finish.

TIP TIP TIP TIP TIP TIP TIP TIP TIP TIP TIP TIP TIP TIP TIP TIP TIP TIP TIP TIP TIP TIP TIP
You can always move a chart object to its own worksheet or make a chart an object in another worksheet. Select the chart or chart object, right-click, and choose Location from the shortcut menu to open the Chart Location dialog box.

Moving, Sizing, and Printing Chart Objects

If you place the chart as an object in the current worksheet, you might find that you'd like to move or resize the chart—especially if the chart is too small or if it covers part of the worksheet data. If you need to, moving or resizing a chart in Excel is a snap!

When the chart is placed in the worksheet, it is selected: it has square *handles* on the corners and sides. If the chart isn't selected, clicking once on the chart selects it. To deselect the chart and return to the worksheet, click once on part of the worksheet that isn't covered by the chart.

Once the chart is selected, you can move it by pointing to the chart and holding the mouse button down until the pointer changes to a four-headed arrow. Drag the chart to its new location. To change the chart's size, move the mouse pointer to one of the chart's handles. Press the mouse button and drag the handle to stretch or shrink the chart. Handles on the sides of the chart change the size in one direction (width or height). To increase width and height in proportion, use a corner handle.

TIP TIP TIP TIP TIP TIP TIP TIP TIP TIP TIP TIP TIP TIP TIP TIP TIP TIP TIP TIP TIP TIP TIP
You might want to turn on Page Break Preview when sizing and moving charts to make sure they remain within the boundaries of a page. Page Break Preview isn't an option while a chart is selected, so click anywhere in the worksheet to deselect the chart, and then choose View ➢ Page Break Preview.

MOVING AND SIZING CHARTS

1. If the chart isn't selected, click once on the chart to select it.

continued ▶

2. To move the selected chart, point to the chart. Hold down the mouse button until the pointer changes to a four-headed arrow. Drag the outline of the chart to its new location. Release the mouse button to drop the outline and move the chart.

3. To size the chart, move the mouse pointer to one of the handles. Hold down the mouse button and drag the handle to change the size of the chart.

Even if you placed your chart as an object in the current worksheet, you can still print it separately. If the chart is selected when you print, it will print by itself on a full page. If the worksheet is selected, the worksheet prints, including the chart object.

SKILL
5

PRINTING CHART OBJECTS

1. To print a worksheet, including a chart object, activate any worksheet cell before printing.

2. To print a chart object as a full-page chart, select the chart before printing.

Hands On

1. Create any or all of the charts shown in this skill. Place at least one chart as an object in the current worksheet.

2. Create a pie chart to illustrate the Cyclops Proposal Software worksheet. Place the chart on the same page as the worksheet. Move and size the chart appropriately, and then print the entire worksheet.

3. Create a series chart to illustrate the Second Hand News Payroll information. Include a data table. Place the chart in a separate worksheet. Print the chart.

4. Select the row and column labels and all the regular numbers (not the formulas) in the Tickets worksheet. Open the Chart Wizard, and choose each of the chart types in turn to see how it would chart your data.

5.9: Editing and Formatting Charts

Creating a chart in Excel is really easy, and often you can use one of Excel's preformatted charts right "out of the box." But you can also customize charts so that they reflect exactly the emphasis and information that you want to convey.

Adding a Data Series

Excel's charting tools allow you to modify charts quickly and easily. You can, for example, create a simple series chart and then add another data series using drag-and-drop. (You can't add individual data points, just data series.)

ADDING DATA SERIES TO A CHART

1. In the worksheet, select the data series to be added.
2. Drag the series and drop it in the chart.

Deleting a Data Series

A chart is a collection of graphic objects. To access the objects, first select the chart. Then click on the object you want to select. The selected object (data point, data series, title, and so on) will have handles. When an object is selected, you can delete or format the object.

DELETING A DATA SERIES FROM A CHART

1. In the chart, select the data series or any data point in the series.
2. Press the Delete key on the keyboard.

Modifying and Formatting Charts

The *chart area* (see Figure 5.25) is a rectangular area within the chart window bounded by the chart border. Changing the size of the chart window changes the size of the chart area. All objects in a chart must be within the chart area. The *plot area* is bounded by the axes and contains the columns, lines, wedges, or other objects used to represent the data points. Objects within the plot area have fixed locations and cannot be moved or individually sized. For example, the X-axis labels must be located near the X-axis. You can, however, resize all the objects in the plot area by increasing or decreasing the plot area itself. (There's an exception to this rule; see "Exploding Pies" later in this skill.) Objects outside the plot area and axes can be sized or moved to other locations in the chart area. The title and legend can be placed above, below, or in the plot area. Any object in a chart can be selected and then formatted or deleted, with the exception of individual data points. Data points can be formatted, but only data *series* can be added or deleted. To select a data point, first select the data series, and then click once on the data point.

SKILL
5

Using the Chart Toolbar

Common formatting options are available on the Chart toolbar, as indicated in Table 5.7. To display the Chart toolbar, right-click any toolbar, and click Chart. Select the chart object you want to format from the Chart Objects drop-down list, and then use the toolbar buttons to format the object or the entire chart.

TABLE 5.7: Chart Toolbar Buttons

Button	Button Name	Function
	Format Object	Opens the Format dialog box for the selected object.
	Chart Type	The drop-down opens a menu of chart types; clicking the button applies the type indicated on the button face.
	Legend	Displays or hides the legend.
	Data Table	Displays or hides the data table.
	By Row	Uses the selected worksheet rows as a data series.
	By Column	Uses the selected worksheet columns as data series.
	Angle Text Downward	Angles selected text downward.
	Angle Text Upward	Angles selected text upward.

Double-click on any object to open the formatting dialog box for the object. For example, double-clicking any column in a data series opens the Format Data Series dialog box, shown in Figure 5.30.

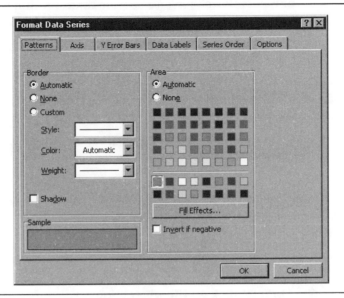

FIGURE 5.30: The Format Data Series dialog box

There are five or six pages in this dialog box. Each contains a group of settings for the selected data series. Depending on the chart type, the dialog box may include a tab for Shape and not include Axis or Y Error Bars tabs.

Patterns   Used to set the color and pattern for the series.

Axis   If the chart has more than one series, this option allows you to add a second vertical axis at the right end of the plot area scaled to this data series.

Y Error Bars   Adds a graphic display of the standard error; used to approximate sampling error when the data in a chart is a statistical sample being applied to a larger population.

Data Labels   Adds a descriptive label or the numeric value for each data point in the series.

Series Order   Allows you to reorder the series in a chart; this is especially helpful with 3-D charts, in which the selected range is charted in reverse order.

Options   Settings for the bar or column overlap, gap, and color variation.

SKILL
5

For more information on a specific control within the Data Series dialog box, click the dialog box Help button, and then click on the control.

Similar options are available when you double-click a selected data point, the plot area, chart area, or other chart object.

TIP TIP TIP TIP TIP TIP TIP TIP TIP TIP TIP TIP TIP TIP TIP TIP TIP TIP TIP TIP TIP TIP

You can select any object or series: right-click, then select Format... from the shortcut menu. Chart Type is always a shortcut menu option, giving you access to all the types and subtypes. If the entire chart is selected, Chart Options appears on the menu.

FORMATTING CHART OBJECTS

1. Select the chart.
2. Double-click on the object you want to format, or select the object, right-click, and choose Format.... to open the appropriate dialog box.
3. Change formatting options, and then click OK to apply the changes and close the dialog box.

Inserting and Formatting Titles

If you decide to insert a title, select the chart, right-click, and open the Chart Options dialog box from the shortcut menu to open the Titles page of the dialog box. You can edit or format existing titles (including placeholders) in a selected chart without having to use the Chart Options from the shortcut menu. To change the text in a title, click once to select the title, and then edit the selected text.

TIP TIP TIP TIP TIP TIP TIP TIP TIP TIP TIP TIP TIP TIP TIP TIP TIP TIP TIP TIP TIP TIP

To wrap a title into multiple lines, place the insertion point where you want the second line to begin, hold the Ctrl key, and press Enter.

Double-click on a title (or select the title, right-click, and choose Format Title from the shortcut menu) to open the Format Chart Title dialog box. Use the controls in the Patterns, Font, and Alignment pages to format the title as you would format other text.

TIP TIP TIP TIP TIP TIP TIP TIP TIP TIP TIP TIP TIP TIP TIP TIP TIP TIP TIP TIP TIP TIP TIP TIP

To change all the fonts used in a chart, double-click in the chart area and change fonts in the Format Chart Area dialog box.

Exploding Pies

If you want to emphasize specific data points in a pie chart, you can *explode* the pie chart by moving one or more pieces of the pie farther from the center (see Figure 5.31). Usually, you'll move one or two individual slices to emphasize specific data points in the chart. In Figure 5.31, the Detroit slice has been exploded. Although you can select an exploded pie in the Chart Wizard, the Wizard explodes all slices of the pie or the first slice, depending on which explosion sample you choose. It's easiest to create an unexploded pie of the type you wish and then edit the chart to explode select slices.

SKILL
5

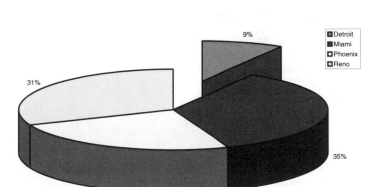

FIRST Quarter Ticket Sales

FIGURE 5.31: Exploded pie chart

If you want to explode all the slices in an existing chart, select the chart, and then select the pie in the plot area. Excel will put handles on the outside edge of each slice of the pie. Drag any slice away from the center to explode all the pie slices. To explode a single slice, first select the chart, and then click on the pie to select the data series. With the series selected, click to select the slice you want to explode. Drag the slice away from the center. When you explode all slices in a pie, each slice gets smaller as you increase the space between the slices. If you explode slices individually, the other slices remain centered in the plot area, and the slices don't get smaller.

Hands On

1. Create or open a 2-D pie chart. Change the pie to a 3-D pie. Explode one slice. Change the color and pattern of all the slices.

2. Create or open a series chart object. Move the chart to its own worksheet. Format each series. Edit the text and then format the chart's title (insert a title if it doesn't have one).

Are You Experienced?

Now you can...

- ☑ **Enter data in Excel**
- ☑ **Format numbers and create formulas**
- ☑ **Format cells and worksheets**
- ☑ **Work with ranges**
- ☑ **Create and edit charts**

Taking Excel to the Max

- ➔ **Using formats and creating custom formats**
- ➔ **Working with financial and statistical functions**
- ➔ **Sorting, filtering, and analyzing data**
- ➔ **Auditing worksheets**
- ➔ **Using and creating templates**
- ➔ **Linking worksheets**

In this skill, you'll learn about features that separate casual users from Excel experts, proficiencies that make other users wonder, "How did they *do* that?" You'll also learn advanced functions that allow you to replace manual processes with one-step formulas. Throughout the skill, we'll use Excel practice worksheets to illustrate concepts.

6.1: Using Custom and Special Formats

You already know how to apply formats from the toolbar and the Format Cells dialog box. In this section, you'll kick your skills up a few notches with four tools for specialized formatting: AutoFormat, styles, conditional formatting, and custom formats.

Using AutoFormats

Excel includes a number of canned worksheet designs, including formal business, list, and 3-D formats. If you're in a hurry, the predesigned formats allow you to quickly apply a standard format to all or part of a worksheet. Before you Auto-Format, select the cells to be formatted. This will usually include all the text and numbers in your worksheet, but you might want to apply an AutoFormat to titles or data only. Choose Format ➢ AutoFormat from the menu bar to open the Auto-Format dialog box. Click the Options button to expand the dialog box to display the formatting elements you can apply, as shown in Figure 6.1. For example, you might choose not to apply column widths if you've already adjusted column widths and don't want them changed. As you select formats and turn the Formats to Apply options on and off, the selected worksheet will change to reflect your choices.

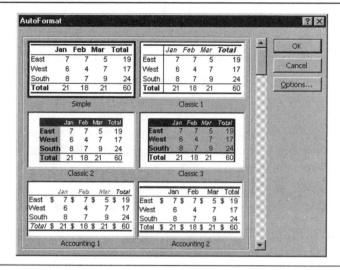

FIGURE 6.1: The AutoFormat dialog box

AUTOFORMATTING A WORKSHEET

1. Select the portion of the worksheet you want to AutoFormat.
2. Choose Format ➤ AutoFormat from the menu bar to open the AutoFormat dialog box.
3. Choose a format.
4. Click the Options button to show Formats to Apply. Deselect any options you don't want to include.
5. Click OK to apply the selected formats.

Working with Styles

AutoFormats are composed of *styles*: specifications about one or more formatting options. Most AutoFormats include several styles: for example, Arial 14-point teal bold for the title; Arial 12-point, accounting format, for the numbers; Arial 12-point bold with a top border for totals.

Creating Styles

Although you can't create your own AutoFormats, you can create individual styles and apply them to ranges in a worksheet. You can create a style in two ways: from existing formatted entries, or by specifying formatting options as you create the style. If the formatting you want to save as a style already exists in the worksheet, select a range that includes the formatting; if not, select a cell that's close to what you want so you'll have less formatting to modify.

CREATING A STYLE

1. Select cells that are the same as, or similar to, the style you want to create.

2. Choose Format ➣ Style from the menu bar to open the Style dialog box as shown in Figure 6.2.

3. Enter a new name for the style.

4. Use the check boxes to disable formatting features that should not be included in the style.

5. Click the Modify button and change any format options you wish in the Format Cells dialog box. Click OK to close the dialog box.

6. Click the Add button to add the new style. Click Close to close the dialog box, or click OK to apply the style to the current selection and close the Style dialog box.

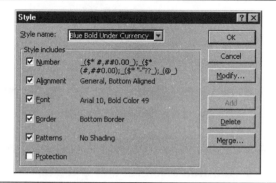

FIGURE 6.2: The Style dialog box

Using Styles

Applying a style that already exists in a workbook is easy. Select the range you want to format, and then choose Format ➤ Style to open the Style dialog box. Choose the style you want from the Style Name drop-down list, and then click OK.

If the style you want to apply is in a different workbook, you can merge the style into the current workbook and then apply it.

APPLYING A STYLE

1. Select the cells you want to apply the style to.
2. Choose Format ÿ Style to open the Style dialog box.
3. Select the style from the Style Name drop-down list, and then click OK.

–OR–

1. If the style you want to apply is in a different workbook, open the workbook.
2. Return to the workbook you want to apply the style in, and then choose Format ➤ Style ➤ Merge.

continued❯

3. Select the workbook the style is in, and then click OK to merge the styles from the selected workbook into the current workbook.

4. Select the style from the Style Name drop-down list, and then click OK.

Deleting and Editing Styles

Styles hang around forever unless you delete them. To delete a style, open the Style dialog box, select the style from the Style Name drop-down list, and click the Delete button. To change an existing style, choose the style from the Style Name drop-down list. Change any formatting options you wish, and then click the Add button to add the changes to the style.

Using Conditional Formatting

With *conditional formatting*, you can apply formats to selected cells based on a *condition*. A condition is an expression that, when evaluated, is either true or false. Examples of conditions are: Hourly Rate greater than $10.00, State equal to CA, and Cost between 2000 and 3000.

For any given cell, each of the conditions will either be true or false: the value in the cell either is or is not greater than $10.00, equal to CA, or between 2000 and 3000. You can apply font attributes, borders, or patterns to cells based on whether the condition is true or false. In Figure 6.3, for example, all values greater than 200 are bold and have a border.

Interest Rate					
10%					
	Amount Borrowed				
Loan Life (Years)	$5,000.00	$10,000.00	$15,000.00	$20,000.00	$25,000.00
						M
1	$420.14	$840.28	$1,260.42	$1,680.56	$2,100.69	O
2	$210.94	$421.88	$632.82	$843.76	$1,054.71	N
3	$141.21	$282.42	$423.63	$564.84	$706.05	T
4	$106.35	$212.69	$319.04	$425.38	$531.73	H
5	$85.43	$170.86	$256.28	$341.71	$427.14	L
6	$71.48	$142.97	$214.45	$285.94	$357.42	Y
7	$61.52	$123.05	$184.57	$246.10	$307.62	
8	$54.06	$108.11	$162.17	$216.22	$270.28	P
9	$48.25	$96.49	$144.74	$192.99	$241.23	M
10	$43.60	$87.20	$130.80	$174.40	$218.00	T

FIGURE 6.3: Loan Payment worksheet with conditional formatting

To apply conditional formatting to a selection, choose Format ➤ Conditional Formatting from the menu bar to open the Conditional Formatting dialog box, shown in Figure 6.4.

FIGURE 6.4: The Conditional Formatting dialog box

From the first drop-down list, choose Cell Value Is to base the formatting on the value in the cell or Formula Is to base the formatting on a formula that returns a value of true or false. Don't let this confuse you; it doesn't matter whether the cell contains a typed-in value or a formula. If you want the format to be applied based on the number or text that appears in a cell, use Cell Value Is. You'll only use Formula Is with specialized functions such as the Date and Logical functions.

In the second drop-down list, choose one of the conditional operators: Between, Not Between, Equal To, Not Equal To, Greater Than, Less Than, Greater Than or Equal To, or Less Than or Equal To. In the condition text box, either type in a constant (such as 200), select a cell in the worksheet, or enter a formula. (There's more about the second and third options under "Using Cell References in Conditions" below.)

Now click the Format button to open an abbreviated version of the Format Cells dialog box. Some of the formats are disabled (such as font type and size), so you know you can't use them for conditional formatting. You can, however, pile on borders, shading, and different colors to make cells jump off the page. Choose the format options you want to apply when the condition is true, and then click OK to return to the Conditional Formatting dialog box. Click OK to close the dialog box, and the formats will be applied to the appropriate cells.

What if you want more than one alternate format? For example, you might want to show sales increases over last month in blue and decreases in red. In this case, you need two conditions. Create the first condition in the Conditional Formatting dialog box, and then click the Add button (see Figure 6.4) to add another condition.

SKILL
6

Using Cell References in Conditions

You can compare the value in a cell to the value in another cell in the worksheet. For example, you might select a cell that shows an average and apply a conditional format to all the numbers that are above average. In this case, each cell you conditionally format will refer to the cell that contains the average, so you'll use an absolute cell reference. Simply click on the cell with the average to place the absolute reference in the condition text box.

Using relative references in conditional formats isn't much trickier. In the section of the Tickets worksheet shown below, February sales that were greater than January sales are bold and shaded:

	A	B	C
1	**Vacation Meisters Ticket Sales**		
2	First Quarter		
3			
4	Destination	January	February
5			
6	Detroit	17	**21**
7	Miami	119	101
8	Phoenix	75	**77**
9	Reno	93	87

To decide what kind of reference to create, think about how you would create a formula for each cell in column C to compare it to the value in column B. Each cell needs its own formula relative to column B, so to create this condition, make sure that you use relative cell references. In this example, select the cells, open the Conditional Formatting dialog box, and choose Cell Value Is and Greater Than. Click in the conditions text box, then click cell B6. B6 is added as an absolute cell reference: B6. Use the F4 key to change the reference to a relative reference.

Extending Conditional Formatting   You don't have to apply conditional formatting to all the cells in a range at once. You can create conditional formats for one cell and tweak them until they're exactly what you want. Then select the entire range you want to format, including the formatted cell. Choose Format ➤ Conditional Formatting, and the dialog box will open, displaying the format you created. Just click OK, and the format will be adjusted and applied to the other selected cells.

Using Formulas As Conditions

Now add one more flourish: you can compare a cell to a formula. For example, you only want to bold and shade a cell in column C if the value is at least 3 greater than the value in column B. If sales didn't go up by at least three tickets, it's not a substantial enough increase to warrant special formatting. So instead of using the condition `greater than B6`, create the condition `greater than B6+3`. Use formulas like this to format the sales that went up more than 20 percent or individual items that represent more than 5 percent of the total budget.

CONDITIONALLY FORMATTING CELLS

1. Select the cells you want to format.
2. Choose Format ➤ Conditional Formatting from the menu bar to open the Conditional Formatting dialog box.
3. Choose Cell Value Is (most of the time) or Formula Is.
4. Select a conditional operator.
5. In the condition text box enter a value, cell reference, or formula.
6. Click the Format button. Set up a format for this condition, and click OK.
7. If you have additional conditions or formats, click the Add button and repeat steps 3–6 for each condition.
8. Click OK to close the dialog box and apply conditional formatting.

SKILL
6

Using Formatting Codes

Excel includes a huge number of formats, but you might need a particular format that isn't part of the package. You can create *custom formats* to handle specialized formatting needs. A common use of custom formats is creating formats that include a text string: 10 mpg, $1.75/sq ft, or $3.00/dozen. You create custom formats in the Format Cells dialog box. But before you open the dialog box, let's look at the codes you'll use to create custom formats.

Codes for Numbers

Each of the codes shown in Table 6.1 is a placeholder for a digit or a character. You string together a number of placeholders to create a format. If a number has more digits to the right of the decimal than there are placeholders, the number will be rounded so it fits in the number of placeholders. For example, if the format has two placeholders to the right of the decimal, 5.988 will be rounded to 5.99.

NOTE NOTE NOTE NOTE NOTE NOTE NOTE NOTE NOTE NOTE NOTE NOTE NOTE NOTE

Excel differentiates between significant digits and insignificant digits. A significant digit is part of a number's "real value." In the value 3.70, the 3 and 7 are significant; the zero is an insignificant digit, because removing it doesn't change the real value of the number. Only zeros can be insignificant. Insignificant zeros after the decimal are called trailing zeros. Different placeholders display or hide insignificant zeros.

TABLE 6.1: Number Format Codes

Code	Use	Example
#	Displays significant digits	###.## formats 3.50 as 3.5 and 3.977 as 3.98
0	Displays all digits; place-holders to the right of the decimal are filled with trailing zeros if required	##0.00 formats 3.5 as 3.50 and 57.1 as 57.10
?	Displays significant digits and aligns decimal or slash placeholders	???.?? displays 3.50 as 3.5, 57.10 as 57.1, and 3.977 as 3.98, and aligns decimals
/	Displays a number as a fraction	# ??/?? displays 7.5 as 7 1/2
,	Thousands separator, also used to format numbers as if they were divided by a thousand or a million	##,### displays 99999 as 99,999 ##, displays 9,000 as 9 ##,, displays 9,000,000 as 9
( )	Parentheses, used to format negative numbers	(##,###) formats –99999 as (99,999)
-	Hyphen, used to place a hyphen in a number	000-000 formats 123456 as 123-456
" "	Indicates a text string	### "/per hour" formats 100 as 100/per hour

You can add color to a format. Type the name of the color in brackets at the beginning of the format: [BLUE], [GREEN], [RED].

There are a couple of approaches to conditional formatting within a custom format. If you include two formats, separated by a semicolon, Excel uses the first format for positive numbers and the second for negative numbers. The format ##,###; [RED]##,### will format negative numbers in red. If you have three sections of format, the third format is used for zero. The format [BLUE]##; [RED]##; [WHITE]## will display blue positive numbers, red negative numbers, and white zeros. On a white background, this makes zeros disappear. A fourth section can be used for text that appears in the cell (see "Codes for Text" below).

You can enter a condition in brackets, followed by the two formats to be used based on whether the condition is true or false. A common use for a conditional custom format is formatting zip codes when some have nine digits and others have five. The condition [>99999] will be true for nine-digit zip codes, so the format [>99999]00000-0000;00000 will format both nine-digit and five-digit zip codes correctly, including leading zeros.

Codes for Dates and Times

Use the format codes shown in Table 6.2 to create date and time formats. The m code is used for both months and minutes. Excel treats the m as a month code unless it appears directly after a code for hours or before a code for seconds.

TABLE 6.2: Date and Time Format Codes

SKILL
6

Code	Use	Examples
m	Months as ##	Formats January as 1 and December as 12
mm	Months as 00	Formats January as 01 and December as 12
mmm	Months as three-letter abbreviation	Formats January as Jan
mmmm	Month named spelled out	Formats Jan as January
mmmmm	Month's first letter	Formats January as J and December as D
d	Days as ##	Formats 1 as 1 and 31 as 31
dd	Days as 00	Formats 1 as 01 and 31 as 31
ddd	Days as weekday abbreviation	Formats 1/1/99 as Fri
dddd	Days as weekday	Formats 1/1/99 as Friday
yy	Years as 00	Formats 1999 as 99
yyyy	Years as 0000	Formats 1/1/99 as 1999
h, m, s	Hours, minutes, and seconds as ##	Formats 3 as 3

TABLE 6.2: Date and Time Format Codes *(continued)*

Code	Use	Examples
hh, mm, ss	Hours, minutes, and seconds as 00	Formats 3 as 03
AM/PM	12-hour clock, uppercase	h AM/PM formats 3 as 3 AM
am/pm	12-hour clock, lowercase	hh am/pm formats 3 as 03 am
a/p	12-hour clock, short form	hh:mm a/p formats 3 as 3:00 a

If you don't include one of the versions of am/pm, Excel bases time on the 24-hour clock.

NOTE NOTE NOTE NOTE NOTE NOTE NOTE NOTE NOTE NOTE NOTE NOTE NOTE NOTE NOTE
According to Microsoft, Excel 2000 is fully Y2K compliant. Additional date formats for displaying four-digit years have been added. Choose Format ➤ Cells, click the Number tab, and then scroll through the Type list to see them. For more information, go to `http://www.microsoft.com/technet/topics/year2k/default.htm.`

Codes for Text

If you want to include text along with a number in a cell, put quotes around the text string or precede the text with a backslash (\). If you want to include a format for text entered in a cell, make it the final section in your format. The @ symbol stands for any text typed in the cell, so [BLUE]@ will format text in the cell in blue. If you don't include a text format, text entered in the cell is formatted according to the defaults or the formatting applied with the toolbar and Format Cells dialog box.

Spacing Codes

You'll use spacing codes for two reasons: alignment and filling. In some formats, negative numbers are surrounded by parentheses. If you use parentheses in a custom format, you need to add a space to the end of the positive format that will line up with the right parenthesis in a negative value. (This keeps the decimal points lined up.) To create a one-character space in a format, include an underscore: ##,##0.00_.

You can fill any empty space in a cell by entering an asterisk (*) and then a fill character in the number format. For example, the accounting format begins with an underscore and a dollar sign, followed by an asterisk and a space before the digit placeholders: _$* #,##0.00. This ensures that the dollar sign is one space from the left edge of the cell, and that all the room between the dollar sign and digits is filled with spaces.

Creating a Custom Format

When you decide on a format you want to create, you can enter the custom format in the Format Cells dialog box.

CREATING A CUSTOM FORMAT

1. Select the cells to be formatted. Choose Format ➢ Cells from the menu bar or right-click and choose Format Cells from the shortcut menu.
2. On the Number page of the Format Cells dialog box, choose Custom from the category list.
3. Enter a format in the Type text box.
4. Click OK to apply the custom format.

SKILL
6

To delete a custom format, select it from the Type list, and then click the Delete button in the Format Cells dialog box.

Hands On

1. Use AutoFormat to format an existing worksheet.

2. Create conditional formats in an existing worksheet. Create at least one format that includes two or more conditions.

3. In an existing worksheet, create:

   a) A custom format that includes a text string.

   b) A custom format that includes different colors for positive and negative numbers.

   c) A custom format that prints the word "Zero" if the value in a cell is 0.

6.2: Using Financial and Statistical Functions

Excel has more than 50 built-in financial functions, and you don't have to be an accountant to find ways to use them. You can use the financial functions to determine how much your monthly car payments will be, how long you'll be paying on your student loan, or how much you can afford to finance on a new home. If you have a small business, the financial functions give you five ways to calculate depreciation and several tools to manage the profit you invest in various stocks and bonds. In addition, Excel includes a fistful of statistical functions. Most are better appreciated by statisticians, but in the second part of this section, we'll tell you about those that you'll find useful.

Excel's Financial Functions

The financial functions use a variety of arguments, but these are the most common:

FV (future value)   What a loan or investment will be worth at a future time when all payments have been made

NPER (number of periods)   The number of months, years, days, or other periods for an investment or loan

PMT (payment)   The amount you periodically receive from an investment or are paid on a loan

PV (present value)   The initial value of an investment or loan

RATE   The interest rate on a loan; the discount or interest rate on an investment

The amount of a periodic payment, present value, interest rate, and the total number of payments have a fixed relationship to each other. If you know any three of these, you can use one of the Excel financial functions to calculate the fourth:

NPER   Calculates the number of periods

PMT   Calculates the payment amount

PV   Returns the present value for the amount loaned or invested

RATE   Returns the interest rate

With these four functions, you can determine how much interest you paid on a loan or how much income you would receive from an annuity. The worksheet in Figure 6.5 uses the PMT function to calculate a monthly payment for various present values at an interest rate entered by the user.

LOAN PAYMENT CALCULATOR					
Enter an interest rate here:	12%				
Loan Life (in years)	$5,000.00	$10,000.00	$15,000.00	$20,000.00	$25,000.00
1	$444.24	$888.49	$1,332.73	$1,776.98	$2,221.22
2	$235.37	$470.73	$706.10	$941.47	$1,176.84
3	$166.07	$332.14	$498.21	$664.29	$830.36
4	$131.67	$263.34	$395.01	$526.68	$658.35
5	$111.22	$222.44	$333.67	$444.89	$556.11
6	$97.75	$195.50	$293.25	$391.00	$488.75
7	$88.26	$176.53	$264.79	$353.05	$441.32
8	$81.26	$162.53	$243.79	$325.06	$406.32
9	$75.92	$151.84	$227.76	$303.68	$379.61
10	$71.74	$143.47	$215.21	$286.94	$358.68

FIGURE 6.5: Loan Payment Calculator worksheet

When you work with financial functions, you need to make sure that all the arguments in a function are based on the same period: a day, month, or year. For example, in Figure 6.5 the payments are monthly payments, but the number of periods and the user-entered interest rate are based on years. In the PMT function arguments, then, NPER has to be multiplied by 12 and RATE divided by 12 so that all the arguments are based on a period of one month, as shown in Figure 6.6. (Pasting the PMT function in a cell opens this dialog box.)

SKILL
6

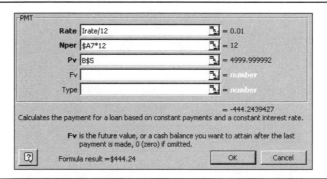

FIGURE 6.6: PMT arguments for the Loan Payment Calculator worksheet

Businesses must select a depreciation method as assets are placed in service, and the method can't be changed later. The worksheet in Figure 6.7 uses several of the depreciation functions to model methods a business could use to depreciate assets.

	A	B	C	D	E	F
1	**Asset Depreciation Model**					
2						
3		Name of Asset	PC Workstation			
4		Years of Useful Life	5		Cost	$2,340.00
5		Month Purchased	5		Salvage Value	-
6						
7		Annual Depreciation				
8	Year	Declining Balance	Double Declining Balance	Straight Line	Sum of the Years Digits	
9	1	$1,365.00	$936.00	$468.00	$780.00	
10	2	$975.00	$561.60	$468.00	$624.00	
11	3	$0.00	$336.96	$468.00	$468.00	
12	4	$0.00	$202.18	$468.00	$312.00	
13	5	$0.00	$121.31	$468.00	$156.00	

FIGURE 6.7: Asset Depreciation worksheet

The depreciation functions use other arguments: the years of useful life of the asset (similar to NPER), how much the asset will be worth when it's past its useful life (salvage), and the number of months the asset was in service the first year. The arguments for the Declining Balance function are shown in Figure 6.8.

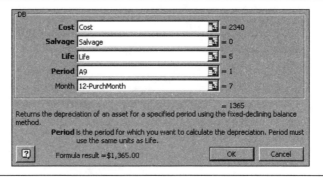

FIGURE 6.8: Arguments for Declining Balance function

Working with Statistical Tables

Statistics functions are great tools if you're taking a statistics course, but you're more likely to use the everyday statistics functions such as AVERAGE, MIN, MAX, and:

COUNT   Returns the number of numbers in a selected range

MEDIAN   Another kind of average, used to calculate the value in the middle of a range

MODE   Returns the value that occurs most frequently

If you don't have a statistics background, don't worry. All three of these functions are useful and easy to understand.

Using COUNT, MEDIAN, and MODE

The COUNT function tells you how many numbers are in a selected range. COUNT is used to calculate the number of survey responses in Figure 6.9.

AVERAGE returns a value called the arithmetic mean—the total of all the values in a range divided by the number of values in the range. But there are two other types of averages: MEDIAN and MODE. MEDIAN tells you which value is the middle value in a range, and MODE tells you which value occurs most frequently, as shown in Figure 6.9.

**SKILL
6**

Question: How much would you be willing to pay for this product?	
Survey Number	**Response**
109871	30
109874	30
109880	40
109881	150
109889	40
109899	30
110001	40
110051	30
110060	33
Number of Responses	9
Mean Average	47
Median	33
Mode	30

FIGURE 6.9: Functions that return averages

Enter arguments for the financial and statistical functions as you would any other function. The Hands On exercises below are designed to provide practice with these functions.

Hands On

1. In this exercise, you'll create and then modify the Loan Payment Calculator worksheet shown in Figure 6.5.

   a) Enter the titles and labels shown in Figure 6.5. Apply formatting as indicated in the figure.

   b) Name cell C3 irate.

   c) In cell B7, click the = button to open the Formula Palette. Click the Function drop-down list and choose More Functions. Select the PMT financial function and enter the required arguments, as shown in Figure 6.6. Notice that RATE uses an absolute reference, while NPER and PV are mixed references. NPER should change when filled down rows, but remain unchanged when filled across columns; the opposite is true for PV.

   d) Enter a monthly interest rate in C3 to test the function. The monthly payment amounts will all be negative (because you're sending, not receiving, these payments). Edit the formula to begin =-PMT so that the payment value is positive. Fill the formula in B7 to the other monthly payment cells.

   e) Test the worksheet by entering different interest rates and amounts. Notice the changes in the monthly payments.

   f) For more practice with the PMT function, rebuild the worksheet so that the periods in column A are months rather than years.

2. For more practice, create the Depreciation Model worksheet shown in Figure 6.7. In the double declining balance function, leave the optional factor argument blank.

3. Create the worksheet shown in Figure 6.9.

4. Open any worksheet that includes an average. Calculate the mode, median, and count for the same range as the average.

6.3: Tracking Data with Excel

You've worked with Excel's spreadsheet and charting features. In the next two sections, you'll use Excel's database capabilities to create and manage lists. A *database* is a list with a specific structure, defined by its *fields*: the categories of information it contains. A telephone directory, for example, is a printout of a computer database whose fields include last name, first name, middle initial, address, and telephone number. An individual listing in the phone book is a *record* in the database, containing a single set of the fields: one phone user's last name, first name, middle initial, address, and telephone number. Each field must have a unique *field name*: LastName, last name, LASTNAME, and LastNameforListing are all possible field names for a field containing last names. In Excel, fields are columns, and each record is an individual row.

The Traverse Tree Sales worksheet (shown in Figure 6.10) is an Excel database. Each field is a separate column. Field names (Month, County, Type, Quantity, and Bundles) are used as column labels. Each individual row is a record.

TRAVERSE TREE SALES				
County Cooperative Tree Orders				
Deliver for Distribution 15th of Month				
Month	County	Type	Quantity	Bundles
Apr-98	Genesee	White Pine	37000	74
Apr-98	Oakland	Blue Spruce	22500	45
Apr-98	Oakland	White Pine	15500	31
Apr-98	Oakland	Concolor Fir	13500	27
Apr-98	Genesee	Blue Spruce	12500	25
Apr-98	Oakland	Scotch Pine	11000	22
Apr-98	Genesee	Frazier Fir	6500	13
May-98	Lake	Blue Spruce	42500	85
May-98	Lake	White Pine	32000	64
May-98	Lake	Frazier Fir	14500	29
May-98	Kalkaska	Blue Spruce	13500	27
May-98	Lake	Concolor Fir	12000	24
May-98	Kalkaska	Concolor Fir	10000	20
May-98	Kalkaska	Frazier Fir	7500	15
Sep-98	Lake	Blue Spruce	31000	62
Sep-98	Lake	White Pine	26500	53

FIGURE 6.10: The Traverse Tree database

Microsoft Access is designed specifically to create databases and allows you to create and manage incredibly large numbers of records, limited only by the amount of space on your hard drive. Excel databases are limited to the number of rows in a worksheet: 65,536. Despite these and other limitations, Excel's list management features are powerful tools for creating small databases and manipulating smaller sets of records from larger databases.

Creating a database is as simple as creating any other worksheet, but there are two additional rules for worksheets that you intend to use as databases:

Blank rows   Signal the end of a database. Don't leave a blank row between column headings and data records. Do leave a blank row after all records and before totals, averages, or other summary rows.

Field names   At the top of columns. Field names must be in a single cell and unique within a worksheet. Be consistent: label every column.

Any worksheet you've already created can be used as a database, but you might have to delete or add rows or edit column labels to meet these requirements.

Sorting a Database

Database software must allow you to do two distinct things with data: organize, or *sort*, the data in a specific order (for example, alphabetized by state), and separate, or *filter*, the data to find specific information (for example, all your customers who live in Oregon).

To sort the data in a database, first select any cell in the database (do not select the column or only that column will be sorted); then choose Data ➢ Sort from the menu bar to have Excel select the records in the database and open the Sort dialog box, shown in Figure 6.11.

FIGURE 6.11: The Sort dialog box

Excel will select all cells above, below, to the right, and to the left of the cell you selected until it encounters a blank column and row. Excel will examine the top row of the database and assign it as a record by including it in the selection, or deselect it, assuming it is a row of column headings. The last section of the Sort dialog box lets you correct an incorrect selection by specifying whether you have a header row.

TIP TIP TIP TIP TIP TIP TIP TIP TIP TIP TIP TIP TIP TIP TIP TIP TIP TIP TIP TIP TIP TIP TIP TIP

If you didn't select a cell within the database before choosing Data ➢ Sort, Excel will open a dialog box and warn you that there was no list to select. Click the OK button in the dialog box, select a cell in the database, and choose Data ➢ Sort again.

You can sort a maximum of three levels using the Data Sort dialog box. Records can be sorted in *ascending order* (A–Z or 1–100) or *descending order* (Z–A or 100–1). In the Sort By text box, enter or use the drop-down to select the field name you want to sort by. Choose a sort order. If some of the records have the same value in the Sort By field, use the first of the two Then By text boxes to select the field you want to sort by when there is a tie in the primary sort field. For databases with many similar records (like the family reunion mailing list), you might want to add a tertiary sort. When you have made all the sort selections, click the OK button to sort the database according to the specifications you entered.

Skill
6

TIP TIP TIP TIP TIP TIP TIP TIP TIP TIP TIP TIP TIP TIP TIP TIP TIP TIP TIP TIP TIP TIP TIP

You can sort a database that includes no column headings—just records. However, the drop-down lists in all the database dialog boxes will list Field 1, Field 2, and so on rather than the field names.

Sorting Using the Menu Bar

1. Select any cell within the database.
2. From the menu bar, choose Data ➢ Sort.
3. Select the field you want to sort by from the Sort By drop-down list.
4. Use the Then By drop-down lists to select secondary and tertiary sort fields.
5. Click the OK button to sort the database.

You can also sort a database using the sort buttons on the Standard toolbar. Select a single cell within the *column* you want to sort by. Click the Ascending Sort or Descending Sort button to sort the database. This is an easy way to sort, but it has one major drawback: Excel doesn't allow you to verify that the correct cells have been selected as the database. It's best to sort each database once using the Sort dialog box and ensure that that the correct rows and columns have been selected before using the toolbar.

SORTING USING THE TOOLBAR

1. Select any cell within the database in the column you want to sort by.
2. Click the Ascending or Descending Sort button.
3. For secondary, tertiary, and other sorts, use the Ascending and Descending Sort buttons to work through the sorts in reverse order.

Filtering a Database

Many times you'll want to work with a database *subset*: a group of records in the database. A *filter* is used to select records that meet a specific criterion and temporarily hide all the other records. You enter criteria to set the filter.

Select any cell in the database and choose Data ➤ Filter ➤ AutoFilter to set up an AutoFilter. Excel reads every record in the database and creates a filter criteria list for each field. Click the drop-down arrow that appears next to each field name (see Figure 6.12) to access the field's criteria list.

Month	County	Type	Quantity	Bundles
Apr-98	Genesee	White Pine	37000	74
Apr-98	Oakland	Blue Spruce	22500	45
Apr-98	Oakland	White Pine	15500	31
Apr-98	Oakland	Concolor Fir	13500	27
Apr-98	Genesee	Blue Spruce	12500	25
Apr-98	Oakland	Scotch Pine	11000	22

FIGURE 6.12: Database with an AutoFilter

All   The default criteria setting in each field, meaning that the contents of the field are not being used to limit the records displayed.

Top 10   Used in numeric fields to display the top or bottom ten, five, or any other number or percentage of values.

Custom   Prompts you to create a custom filter (see "Creating a Custom Filter" below) for choices that don't appear on the list.

When you apply a filter, all the records not included in the subset are hidden, as shown in Figure 6.13, where the records are being filtered on Lake County. The number of records found and the total number of records in the database are displayed in the status bar. Each record retains its original row number; the row numbers of filtered records appear in blue. The field criteria drop-down arrow for the filtered field turns blue, to show that it is being actively used to filter the database.

Month	County	Type	Quantity	Bundles
May-98	Lake	Blue Spruce	42500	85
May-98	Lake	White Pine	32000	64
May-98	Lake	Frazier Fir	14500	29
May-98	Lake	Concolor Fir	12000	24
Sep-98	Lake	Blue Spruce	31000	62
Sep-98	Lake	White Pine	26500	53

FIGURE 6.13: Filtering a database

Filter on more than one field to select, for example, all the Scotch Pine sales in Oakland County. Set the criteria using each field's drop-down list. Only records that meet all the criteria you selected will be included in the filtered subset. To redisplay the entire database, change the filter criteria for all filtered fields back to All, or simply choose Data ➤ Filter ➤ Show All. You'll know at a glance that all filters are set to All because the drop-down arrows and the row headings will all be black again.

TIP TIP TIP TIP TIP TIP TIP TIP TIP TIP TIP TIP TIP TIP TIP TIP TIP TIP TIP TIP TIP TIP TIP TIP

Sometimes, the field criteria drop-down list has so many entries that it runs off the top or bottom of the screen. You can scroll down to see a list that runs off the bottom. If the list runs off the top, insert several blank rows above the column labels to force the filtered list down the screen.

APPLYING AND USING THE AUTOFILTER

1. Select any cell in the database.
2. Choose Data ➤ Filter ➤ AutoFilter to turn on the filter.
3. Click on the drop-down arrow for the field you want to use to filter, and choose a filter from the criteria drop-down list.
4. To see all the records in the database, reset all filter criteria to All.

Creating a Custom Filter

When you filter using the drop-down criteria, you are always looking for records that exactly equal specific criteria or fall in a Top 10 criterion. Custom filters give you access to other ways to set criteria:

- All records with fields that are NOT equal to a criterion
- Records that are greater than or less than a criterion
- Records that meet one condition OR another.

To create a custom filter, choose Custom from the drop-down criteria list to open the Custom AutoFilter dialog box, shown in Figure 6.14.

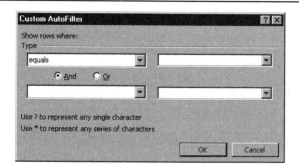

FIGURE 6.14: The Custom AutoFilter dialog box

The first drop-down under Show Rows Where opens a list of operators. The list includes regular logical operators such as Equals and Is Greater Than or Equal To, but as you scroll the list, you'll notice other operators that allow you to look for entries that do or do not begin with, end with, or contain a string.

The right drop-down list displays the record entries in the field from the field criteria list. To find all records that are NOT in Lake County, choose <> (not equal to) as the operator, and select Lake from the drop-down. You can also enter text in the criteria control. In the bottom of the dialog box, notice that you can use the * and ? wildcards to broaden the search string. To find all orders for Oakland and Ottawa counties, you could:

- Use the wildcard character and search for Equals O*

- Use the Begins with Type and search for Begins with O

The AND and OR options are used when you want to filter by more than one criterion in a column. AND is used to establish the upper and lower ends of a range and is almost always used with numeric entries: Quantity is greater than 100 AND Quantity is less than 201 leaves only the quantities between 100 and 201. OR is used to filter by two different criteria: Lake County OR Oakland County. If you use AND when you mean OR, you'll often get a *null set*: no records. (There are no records in Lake County AND Oakland County—it's one or the other.) If you use OR when you mean AND, you'll get all the records. (Every record is either less than 201 OR greater than 100.)

SKILL
6

CREATING A CUSTOM FILTER

1. If the AutoFilter is not turned on, turn it on (choose Data ➤ Filter ➤ AutoFilter). Choose Custom from the filter criteria drop-down list to open the Custom AutoFilter dialog box.

2. Set the operator (Type) for the first criterion.

3. Enter or select the first criterion from the drop-down list.

4. Set an operator, and enter or select the second criterion.

5. Set AND for a range; set OR to filter for more than one possible value.

6. Click OK to apply the custom filter.

The filter criteria drop-down lists don't appear when you print a database, so there usually isn't a reason to turn the AutoFilter off until you are done working with a database. To turn the AutoFilter off, choose Data ➤ Filter ➤ AutoFilter again.

Working with Filtered Records

You can work with the filtered set of records in a number of ways. If you print the database while it is filtered, only the filtered records will print; so you can quickly generate reports based on any portion of the information in the Excel database. Filtering is also useful when you need to create charts using part of the data in the database. Filter the records you want to chart, and then select and chart the information as you would normally. When you create a chart based on a filter, you need to print the chart before changing the filter criteria. Changing the criteria changes the chart. If you need to create a permanent chart, see the following section on creating a subset database.

Creating a Subset

At times you will want to work with or distribute a subset of the database. For example, you might have a database with 5,000 records—but only 700 of them pertain to your current project. It would be easier to work with a smaller database that included only the 700 records you need. You can copy the filtered subset to the Clipboard and paste it in a new location in any open workbook to create a new database containing only records from the filtered subset.

CREATING A NEW DATABASE FROM A FILTERED SUBSET

1. Filter the active database to create a filtered subset.
2. Select the filtered database, including the column labels and any other titles you wish to copy.
3. Click the Copy button or choose Edit ➤ Copy.
4. Select the first cell where you want the new database to appear.
5. Press Enter to paste the database.

Extracting a Subset

If you prefer, you can create a subset by *extracting* the subset's records from the database using Excel's Advanced Filter. The Advanced Filter requires you to establish a *criteria range* that includes the column labels from your database and one or more criteria that you enter directly below the labels.

The criteria range is the heart of advanced filtering. If the criteria range is incorrect, the extracted data will be wrong—so take your time with this. The column labels must be precisely the same as they are in the database, so begin by copying the column labels to another location in your workbook (a separate worksheet that you name Criteria is good).

Then, type the criteria you want to establish. For example, if you want to extract records where the Quantity is over 10000, enter >10000 in the cell just below the Quantity column label. If you have more than one criterion in a single column (for example, County = Genesee or County = Oakland), use one cell for each criterion:

Month	County	Type	Quantity	Bundles
	Genesee			
	Oakland			

There are two ways to filter for two criteria in separate columns, based on whether you want to use AND or OR. Enter criteria on the same row for an AND condition:

Month	County	Type	Quantity	Bundles
	Genesee		>20000	

Place criteria on separate rows for an OR condition:

Month	County	Type	Quantity	Bundles
	Genesee			
			>20000	

In this example, criteria are established to find quantities over 20,000 in Oakland County or over 10,000 in Lake County:

Month	County	Type	Quantity	Bundles
	Oakland		>20000	
	Lake		>10000	

SKILL
6

You can't create this last criterion with an AutoFilter in one pass. You would need to find each county separately. A need to mix AND and OR conditions is one of the two reasons to use an Advanced Filter.

You'll need to refer to the criteria range in the Advanced Filter dialog box, so you might want to name it.

When the criteria range is set, click anywhere in the database and open the Advanced Filter dialog box (choose Data ➤ Filter ➤ Advanced Filter) to see the second reason to use an Advanced Filter: you can instruct Excel to return only unique records, as shown in Figure 6.15.

FIGURE 6.15: The Advanced Filter dialog box

Excel will automatically select your database for the List Range text box. Select the Criteria Range text box and identify your criteria range, including the column labels. Choose whether you want to filter the records in their current location (as AutoFilter does) or extract the records by copying them to another location. If you choose another location, the Copy To text box will be enabled so that you can select the first cell of the range where the filtered records should be copied. (As with any copy operation, just select one cell—if you select a range, it must match exactly the range required by the extracted data. Be sure that there is room in the destination area for the incoming data.) You can enter a cell in any open work-book in the Copy To text box, so you can put the filtered subset of your database in a different workbook or a different worksheet than the original database. If you want to eliminate duplicate records from the filtered list, turn on the Unique Records Only check box. Finally, click OK and Excel will filter in place or extract data as you have indicated.

TIP TIP TIP TIP TIP TIP TIP TIP TIP TIP TIP TIP TIP TIP TIP TIP TIP TIP TIP TIP TIP TIP TIP TIP TIP

You've got a database with 10,000 records, many of them duplicate records. Don't eliminate the duplicates manually. Set up a criteria range without criteria and use the Unique Records Only option to extract a list without duplicates.

When you use the Advanced Filter to filter in place, the filtered subset will have blue row numbers, just as it does with AutoFilter. To turn the filter off, choose Data ➢ Filter ➢ Show All.

USING THE ADVANCED FILTER

1. Copy the database column labels to another location.
2. Enter criteria in the cells directly under the column labels.
3. Select any cell in the database, and choose Data ➢ Filter ➢ Advanced Filter to open the Advanced Filter dialog box.
4. Check to ensure Excel has accurately identified the database range. If not, adjust it in the List Range text box.
5. Enter the criteria range in the Criteria Range list box.
6. Choose the Filter in Place or Copy To option.
7. If you are extracting (copying) the filtered list to another location, enter the upper left cell of that location in the Copy To text box.
8. Enable or disable the Unique Records Only check box.
9. Click OK to create the filter.

SKILL
6

Creating Subtotals

You can create subtotals based on any field in the database. A *subtotal* is not necessarily a sum; it can be an average, count, minimum, maximum, or other statistical calculation based on a group of records. Before subtotaling, you need to sort the database on the field you want to subtotal. For example, if you want to subtotal each month's orders, first sort by month. Then, select a cell anywhere in the database and choose Data ➣ Subtotals to open the Subtotal dialog box, shown in Figure 6.16.

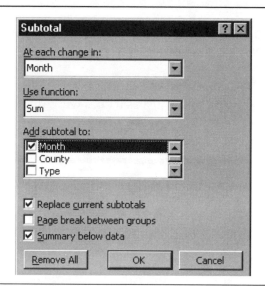

FIGURE 6.16: The Subtotal dialog box

In the At Each Change In control, select the field the database is sorted on. The trigger for Excel to insert a subtotal is a change in this column. If you choose an unsorted field, you'll get a multitude of subtotals (interesting, but useless). Select a type of subtotal from the Use Function drop-down list. In the Add Subtotal To control, select each field you want to subtotal. You can subtotal more than one field at a time, but you have to use the same function: average three fields, sum three fields, and so on.

Use Replace Current Subtotals if you have subtotaled earlier and want to replace the former set with new subtotals. If you want both sets of subtotals to appear (for example, sums and averages), deselect this option. If you are going to print the worksheet with subtotals and want each subtotaled set of records to print on a separate page, click the Page Break between Groups check box. Selecting Summary Below Data places a summary (grand total, grand average) row at the bottom of the database. When you have entered the information for subtotals, click the OK button to add subtotals, as shown in Figure 6.17. To remove subtotals from a worksheet, open the Subtotal dialog box again (see Figure 6.16) and click the Remove All button.

Month	County	Type	Quantity	Bundles
Apr-98	Genesee	White Pine	37000	74
Apr-98	Oakland	Blue Spruce	22500	45
Apr-98	Oakland	White Pine	15500	31
Apr-98	Oakland	Concolor Fir	13500	27
Apr-98	Genesee	Blue Spruce	12500	25
Apr-98	Oakland	Scotch Pine	11000	22
Apr-98	Genesee	Frazier Fir	6500	13
Apr-98 Total			118500	
May-98	Lake	Blue Spruce	42500	85
May-98	Lake	White Pine	32000	64
May-98	Lake	Frazier Fir	14500	29
May-98	Kalkaska	Blue Spruce	13500	27
May-98	Lake	Concolor Fir	12000	24
May-98	Kalkaska	Concolor Fir	10000	20
May-98	Kalkaska	Frazier Fir	7500	15
May-98 Total			132000	
Sep-98	Lake	Blue Spruce	31000	62
Sep-98	Lake	White Pine	26500	53
Sep-98 Total			57500	
Grand Total			308000	

FIGURE 6.17: Traverse Tree Sales subtotals

SKILL
6

CREATING SUBTOTALS

1. In your database, sort the records on the field you want to trigger the subtotal.
2. Select any cell in the database.
3. Choose Data ≻ Subtotals from the menu bar.
4. Select the sorted field from the At Each Change In drop-down list.
5. Select a type of subtotal.
6. Select the numeric fields to be subtotaled when the value of the At Each Change In field changes.
7. If necessary, change the settings for Replace Current Subtotals, Page Break between Groups, and Summary Below Data.

continued ▶

8. Click OK to generate subtotals.

9. To remove subtotals, choose Data ➤ Subtotals, and then click Remove All.

Hands On

1. Open any worksheet that can be used as a database, or create the Traverse Tree Sales worksheet in Figure 6.10. The values in Bundles are formulas (Qty/500). Sort the database:

   a) Using the Sort dialog box

   b) Using the toolbar buttons

   c) By one field

   d) By two fields (primary and secondary sort)

2. Open any worksheet that can be used as a database. Filter the database:

   a) By a value in a field

   b) Using a Top 10 filter in a numeric field

   c) Using a custom filter with the Begins With or Contains type

   d) Using a custom filter and AND or OR

3. Open any worksheet that can be used as a database. Create at least two types of subtotals. Remove the subtotals.

6.4: Analyzing Data with Excel

Often when you enter data in Excel, you want to use it to provide information on which you can make a decision. In other words, the data itself is a means to an end. Using data forms and PivotTables are both excellent tools for analyzing data.

Using a Data Form

Data forms provide an easy way to enter or search for data yourself, and a bullet-proof way to let a less accomplished user enter data. Select any cell in a database, and choose Data ➤ Form to open a data form. The first record in the database will be displayed in the data form. The data form for Traverse Tree Sales (see Figure 6.10) is shown in Figure 6.18.

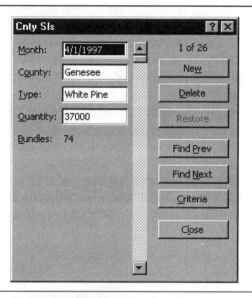

FIGURE 6.18: Traverse Tree Sales data form

Because data forms have a portrait orientation, they're particularly helpful when the columns in your database exceed the width of the screen. Using the form allows you to see all the database fields at once without scrolling horizontally. In the form, use the vertical scroll bar or the up and down arrow keys to browse the records. Use the Tab key to move between fields in the form; pressing Enter moves to the next record. You can change the contents of a field by editing the text box next to the field name. The contents of *calculated fields* (like the Bundles field) are displayed without a text box, because you can't edit them. However, if you change a value that a calculated field is based on, Excel will recalculate the field. To discard changes made to a record, click the Restore button before moving to another record.

Adding and Deleting Records

Clicking the New button or scrolling to the last record of the database opens the New Record form. Enter each field in the appropriate text box control. When you have entered information for the last field, press Enter or click the New button again if you want to keep entering new records. Press the up arrow or click the scroll bar to close the New dialog box.

To delete the record currently displayed in the data form, click the Delete button. A dialog box will appear, warning that the record will be permanently deleted. Pay attention to the warning—clicking Undo will not bring the record back. Click the OK button to delete the record's row from the database.

Searching for Records

You can use the data form to search for individual records that meet specific criteria. This is like filtering, but you view the records one at a time. Click the Criteria button to open the Criteria form. Enter the field contents you are searching for in the appropriate text box. Click the Find Next button to find the first record that matches the criteria. Each time you click Find Next, you move to the next record that is a match. The Find Prev button lets you move up to the previous matching record. The Criteria form is a good tool to locate specific records that you need to delete.

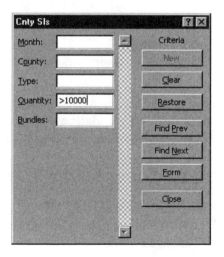

When you have criteria set, you can use the Find Next and Find Prev buttons to move between records based on criteria, and you can use the scroll bar or up and down arrows to move between all the records in the database. If you want to erase the search criteria, click the Criteria button again. Click the Clear button to delete the criteria, and then click the Form button to return to the form.

You can enter criteria in more than one text box. Excel joins the two criteria with AND, so will only find records that meet both criteria. You can't search for records that meet either criteria (OR). For advanced searching, use a filter.

SEARCHING FOR RECORDS

1. Open the data form if it is not already open.
2. Click the Criteria button.
3. Enter the search criteria for one or more fields in the text box controls.
4. Click Find Next to find the first record that meets the criteria. Use Find Next and Find Prev to view the records that meet the search criteria.
5. Click the scroll bar to view all records in the database.

SKILL
6

Creating PivotTables

PivotTables are a powerful tool for data analysis. A *PivotTable* summarizes the columns of information in a database in relationship to each other. The Traverse Tree Sales database shown in Figure 6.19 is a small database, but it would still take time and effort to answer the following questions accurately:

- How many trees of each type were delivered each month?
- How many Blue Spruces were delivered each month?
- How many White Pines were delivered in 1998?
- What was the average number of each type of tree sold in Oakland County?

You could sort the list and then add subtotals to answer any one of these questions. Then, to answer any other question, you would have to sort and subtotal again. A single PivotTable will allow you to answer all the above questions and more.

TRAVERSE TREE SALES				
County Cooperative Tree Orders				
Deliver for Distribution 15th of Month				
Month	County	Type	Quantity	Bundles
Apr-98	Genesee	White Pine	37000	74
Apr-98	Oakland	Blue Spruce	22500	45
Apr-98	Oakland	White Pine	15500	31
Apr-98	Oakland	Concolor Fir	13500	27
Apr-98	Genesee	Blue Spruce	12500	25
Apr-98	Oakland	Scotch Pine	11000	22
Apr-98	Genesee	Frazier Fir	6500	13
May-98	Lake	Blue Spruce	42500	85
May-98	Lake	White Pine	32000	64
May-98	Lake	Frazier Fir	14500	29
May-98	Kalkaska	Blue Spruce	13500	27
May-98	Lake	Concolor Fir	12000	24
May-98	Kalkaska	Concolor Fir	10000	20
May-98	Kalkaska	Frazier Fir	7500	15
Sep-98	Lake	Blue Spruce	31000	62
Sep-98	Lake	White Pine	26500	53

FIGURE 6.19: The Traverse Tree Sales database

Using the PivotTable Wizard

Select any cell in a database, and choose Data ➤ PivotTable and PivotChart Report to launch the PivotTable and PivotChart Wizard. In the first step, you tell the Wizard what kind of data you have: data in a single Excel database, data from an external source such as Microsoft Access, data that you want to consolidate from several worksheets or sources, or an existing PivotTable or PivotChart. You also specify whether you want to create a PivotTable or a PivotChart with a Pivot-Table. Clicking Next moves you to the second step.

In the second step, verify the range of the database. A flashing line should appear around a suggested range of cells. Use the scroll bars to verify that the entire database—including the field names—is selected. If there is no range selected, or if the range is incorrect, select the correct range before clicking the Next button.

In the third step, you tell the Wizard whether you want to place the PivotTable in a new worksheet or an existing worksheet. The default destination is a new worksheet. If you want to place the PivotTable in an existing worksheet, click the Existing Worksheet control. Then enter a cell address for the upper left corner of the PivotTable in the text box.

Click the Layout button to open the dialog box shown in Figure 6.20. A Pivot-Table contains four areas: the Page number, the Column labels, the Row labels, and the Data. Each area has a corresponding layout area in the Layout dialog box.

At the right side of the dialog box is a group of *field buttons,* one for each field name in the database. You design the PivotTable layout by dragging the field buttons into one of the four sections of the layout area. The Row, Column, and Data areas must have fields assigned to them; Page is an optional area.

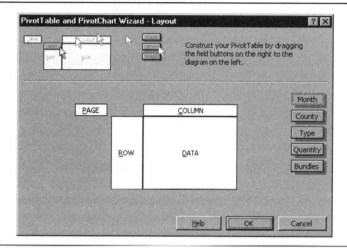

FIGURE 6.20: The Layout dialog box of the PivotTable and PivotChart Wizard

Place fields you want to compare in the Row and Column areas. For example, you might want to compare sales regions by month or types of trees sold by county. The Row and Column areas are somewhat interchangeable; however, your PivotTable is easier to use if it isn't too wide. When the table is created, Excel will examine the fields you choose. Each unique entry becomes a row or column heading in the PivotTable. If you have five unique entries in column A, but 10 in column C, using column A for Column and C for Row will create a PivotTable report that fits on a screen. If you put column C in the Column, you will have ten columns of data, which is too wide to view without scrolling.

If you need to create separate reports for values in one or more columns, drag those field buttons to the Page area. The Page area works like a filter in the completed PivotTable.

Information in the data area is mathematically summarized, so numeric fields are generally placed in the Data layout area. (You could place a non-numeric field and COUNT the number of entries.) For Traverse Tree Sales, we could place either Quantity, Bundles, or both in the data area.

As you drop a field button in the Data area, Excel will indicate the type of summary that will be done with the data. SUM is the default. To change the type of summary, drag the field button to the Data area, and then double-click on the field button to open the PivotTable Field dialog box. Choose the type of summary you want to use from the scroll list.

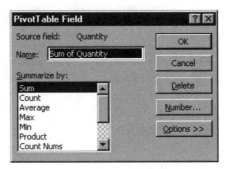

The default numeric format in a PivotTable is General. You can click the Number button in the PivotTable Field dialog box to format the numbers for this field, or you can wait and format the completed PivotTable. Clicking the Option button extends the PivotTable Field dialog box so that you can perform custom calculations (see "Using Custom Calculations in PivotTables" later in this skill). Click OK to close the dialog box and return to the Layout dialog box of the PivotTable and PivotChart Wizard. When you are finished laying out the PivotTable, click OK to return to step 3 of the PivotTable and PivotChart Wizard.

Click the Options button to open the PivotTable Options dialog box, shown in Figure 6.21. You can name the PivotTable just as you name any other range of cells. If you don't name it, Excel will give it a riveting name such as PivotTable1. For more information about any other option, click the dialog box Help button, and then click on the option. When you are finished setting options, click OK to return to the PivotTable and PivotChart Wizard.

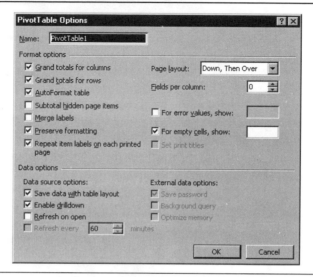

FIGURE 6.21: The PivotTable Options dialog box

Click Finish to close the Wizard and create the PivotTable Report, as shown in Figure 6.22. The PivotTable toolbar will also open.

Sum of Quantity	Month			
County	Apr-98	May-98	Sep-98	Grand Total
Genesee	56000			56000
Kalkaska		31000		31000
Lake		101000	57500	158500
Oakland	62500			62500
Grand Total	118500	132000	57500	308000

FIGURE 6.22: A PivotTable Report

Using the PivotTable Toolbar   If the PivotTable toolbar does not appear, turn it on by choosing View ➢ Toolbars ➢ PivotTable. The PivotTable toolbar lets you change the completed table's layout and options:

SKILL
6

Using Custom Calculations in PivotTables Excel 2000 allows custom calculations in the Data fields of a PivotTable. You create custom calculations in the Layout dialog box of the third step of the PivotTable and PivotChart Wizard. In the diagram, double-click the field button you want to calculate to open the Pivot-Table Field dialog box. Click the Options button to extend the dialog box, and then choose one of the functions from the Show Data As drop-down list:

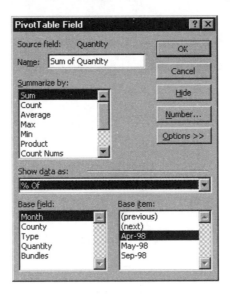

Many of the functions use a *Base field* and a *Base item*. Base fields and Base items are like criteria: the Base field is a column in your database, and the Base item is a value from that field.

If your PivotTable is already completed and you want to change a summarization method, click the PivotTable drop-down list on the PivotTable toolbar, and select Field Settings to open the PivotTable Field dialog box.

CREATING A PIVOTTABLE REPORT

1. Select any cell in the database.

2. Choose Data ➤ PivotTable and PivotChart Report from the menu bar to open the PivotTable and PivotChart Wizard.

3. Select the type of data source you will be using for the table, and specify that you are creating a PivotTable. Click Next.

4. Verify that the entire database is selected. If it is not, select the correct range for the database. Click Next.

5. Specify whether you want to put the PivotTable in a new or an existing worksheet, and click the Layout button to open the Layout dialog box.

6. Drag field buttons to the PivotTable layout areas. You must place a field in the Data, Column, and Row areas, but Page is optional.

7. To choose another summary method for a data field, double-click the field button in the data area to open the PivotTable Field dialog box. Select a summarization method from the Summarize By list. To use a custom calculation, click the Options button to extend the dialog box, and then choose a function and Base field and Base item if required. Click OK to return to the Layout dialog box of the PivotTable and PivotChart Wizard. Click OK.

8. Enter a starting cell location for the table, or leave the location blank to have Excel insert a new worksheet for the table.

9. Click the Options button to open the PivotTable Options dialog box. Enter a name for the table or leave the default name. Select the options you want to use, and then click OK.

10. Click the Finish button to close the Wizard and create the Pivot-Table Report.

SKILL
6

TIP TIP TIP TIP TIP TIP TIP TIP TIP TIP TIP TIP TIP TIP TIP TIP TIP TIP TIP TIP TIP TIP TIP TIP

A chart that contains thousands of bars or columns for the rows in a database is meaningless. Instead, base your chart on a PivotTable. Don't begin by selecting a cell that includes a field button, because as you drag away, the button will move. Begin at the lower right corner and end on the field button.

Creating PivotTables from External Data Sources   If you have data that resides outside Excel in an ODBC (Open Database Connectivity) or OLE (Object Linking and Embedding) DB compliant database such as Microsoft Access or Oracle, you can create a PivotTable without bringing the data into Excel. For information about setting up an ODBC or OLE DB connection, refer to *Mastering Excel 2000*, also from Sybex.

Changing PivotTable Layout

You might need to summarize a database in a number of ways. Rather than creating a new PivotTable, you can change the layout of an existing PivotTable. The field buttons you placed in the Page, Column, and Row areas are in the PivotTable. You can change the table by dragging a field button to another area, and Excel will update the PivotTable. For example, if you want to view the data in Figure 6.22 by county and date, you can drag the County button to the Column area and the Month button to the Row area. The PivotTable will change to reflect the new layout.

To remove a field from the PivotTable, in the Layout dialog box drag the field button out of the PivotTable area. To add a field to the PivotTable, select any cell in the table and choose Data ➤ PivotTable and PivotChart Report or click the PivotTable Wizard button on the toolbar to open step 3 of the Wizard; click the Layout button to open the Layout dialog box. Add, delete, or rearrange the field buttons, and then click OK to return to the Wizard. Click Finish to return to the PivotTable.

CHANGING PIVOTTABLE LAYOUT

1. Rearrange the table by dragging field buttons from one area to another.
2. To delete a field, drag the field button from the diagram and drop it outside the diagram.

continued ▶

3. To add a field, select any cell in the PivotTable Report and choose Data ➤ PivotTable and PivotChart Report to reopen the Wizard. Click the Layout button to open the Layout dialog box. Add fields, and then click OK and Finish.

Keeping the PivotTable Up-to-Date   A PivotTable is dynamically linked to the database used to create the table. If you edit values within the database, simply choose Data ➤ Refresh Data, or click the Refresh Data button on the Pivot-Table toolbar; Excel will update the PivotTable to reflect the database changes. However, if you add rows or columns to the database, you *cannot* simply refresh the data. You must return to the PivotTable and PivotChart Wizard and identify the new range of records that should be included in the table. If you don't, the PivotTable values won't include the added data. To update the range being used by the PivotTable, choose Data ➤ PivotTable and PivotChart Report from the menu bar or click the PivotTable menu in the toolbar and choose Wizard. The PivotTable Wizard will open at step 3. Reselect the database, or hold Shift and extend the current selection. Click the Finish button to close the PivotTable and PivotChart Wizard and return to the updated PivotTable.

SKILL
6

Creating Separate PivotTables

Rather than printing different departments' or counties' PivotTables on different pages, you might want to create a series of PivotTables: one for each department or county. You can do this in one step. First, make sure that the field you want to create each table for (such as County) is in the Page area of the diagram in the Layout dialog box. Select any cell in the PivotTable and right-click to open the context menu and select Show Pages, or click the PivotTable menu on the toolbar and select Show Pages to open the Show Pages dialog box. Choose the field that you want to create individual PivotTables for, and then click OK. Excel will insert new worksheets and create a PivotTable for each unique entry in the selected field. Check it out—Excel also names the sheets.

CREATING SEPARATE PIVOTTABLES BASED ON A VALUE

1. Arrange the PivotTable layout so that the field that you want to use to separate the tables is in the Page area.
2. Select any cell in the table, right-click, and choose Show Pages.
3. Choose the field you want to create separate PivotTables for, and click OK.

Drilling Down in a PivotTable

Even though the cells in the Data area contain summary information, you can *drill down* through a PivotTable to view all the detail that underlies an individual summary figure. Double-click on any non-zero value in the Data area, and Excel opens a new worksheet to display the records that were used to create that cell of the summary. Figure 6.23 shows the results of drilling down in the cell for Genesee County in April 1998.

Month	County	Type	Quantity	Bundles
4/1/98	Genesee	White Pine	37000	74
4/1/98	Genesee	Frazier Fir	6500	13
4/1/98	Genesee	Blue Spruce	12500	25

FIGURE 6.23: Drilling down to details

DRILLING DOWN IN A PIVOTTABLE

Double-click on the Data area cell that contains the summary you want to examine in more detail.

You Are Here: Data Mapping in Excel

Use Excel's data map feature with geographic data: countries, states, or zip codes. With data map, you can create amazing, shaded maps to illustrate any figures that are tied to major geographic areas. The map in Figure 6.24 shows the population by state from the U.S. Census of 1990.

State	Population (000)
Alabama	4089
Alaska	570
Arizona	3750
Arkansas	2372
California	30380
Colorado	3377
Connecticut	3291
Delaware	680
District of Columbia	598
Florida	13277
Georgia	6623
Hawaii	1135
Idaho	1039
Illinois	11542
Indiana	5610

FIGURE 6.24: Population data map

SKILL 6

TIP TIP TIP TIP TIP TIP TIP TIP TIP TIP TIP TIP TIP TIP TIP TIP TIP TIP TIP TIP TIP TIP TIP

Excel 2000 comes with extensive demographic information, including population figures by age range and gender for the world, U.S. states, Australian territories, and Canadian and Mexican provinces. All this information is contained in the `mapstats.xls` **file. You'll find the file in the** `Program Files\Common Files\Microsoft Shared\Datamap\Data` **folder.**

You can create a data map from any worksheet that contains a column of geographic data: country, state, and province names, zip codes, or postal codes. If you use zip codes, first format them as text. Select the column of geographic data and the columns that contain the numeric data you want to map. Click Insert ➤ Object and double-click Microsoft Map to have Excel begin analyzing your data. If there's any ambiguity about your data, you will be prompted to select a map. Excel always asks which U.S. map you want if you use U.S. state information.

Select a map, then click OK. Click on your worksheet. The data map appears in your worksheet, the Microsoft Map Control opens, and the Microsoft Map command bars replace the Excel menu bar and toolbar, as shown in Figure 6.25.

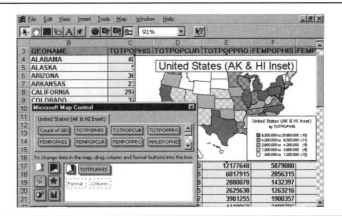

FIGURE 6.25: Data map and Control panel

You can display or hide the Map Control with the Show Map Control button on the toolbar. The Map Control is similar to the PivotTable layout page. If you begin by selecting multiple columns of data, you can see how each looks by dragging the column's button into the box in the control. If you drop one button on top of another, the first button is returned to the list above the box. If you drop a button in an empty spot, both buttons will be represented in the data map. To remove a data category, drag the column button out of the box, and drop it back in the category area.

The buttons in the left side of the control are format buttons. Drag a format button into the space next to a column to format it. When you remove a column, its format is automatically removed and vice versa. Table 6.3 lists the name and description for each format button.

TABLE 6.3: Data Map Formats

Button	Name	Description
	Value Shading	Shows numeric data in different shades
	Category Shading	Shows text data in different shades; used to show membership in a region or category
	Dot Density	Shows numerical data as dots; larger quantities equals more dots
	Graduated Symbol	Shows numerical data as symbols; larger quantities equals larger symbols
	Pie Chart	Places a small pie chart over each area of the map to represent local data
	Column Chart	Places a small column chart over each area of the map to represent local data

You can combine different formats to show multiple categories of information in the same data map. The data map in Figure 6.26 shows the total population with value shading, and the population separated into age groups in the pie charts.

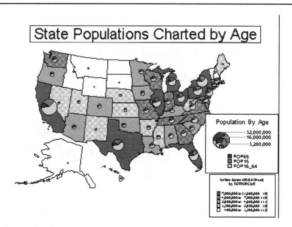

FIGURE 6.26: Combination data map

The data map, like a chart, is an object embedded in your worksheet. Use the handles to move and size it as you would any other object. Click anywhere in the worksheet to close the object and return to the worksheet.

CREATING A DATA MAP

1. Select the columns of data you want to map, including the column that contains zip codes, state or country names, or other geographic reference data.
2. Click the Data Map button on the Standard toolbar.
3. Drag an area in the worksheet for the data map.
4. Select a map if you are prompted to do so.
5. In the Microsoft Map Control, drag column and format buttons into the box to add information to the map. Drop one column on another to replace it; drop a column in an empty space to add a column. Delete columns by dragging them back to the column button area.
6. Move and size the data map object as desired.

Beefing Up the Data Map

Right-click the data map, and choose Features from the shortcut menu to see a list of other features that are attached to the map.

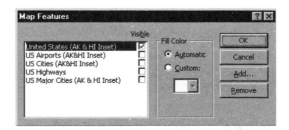

To add a feature that does not appear on the list, right-click the data map and choose Add Features. This makes it available to select or deselect in the Features dialog box.

Once you're happy with the map's overall appearance, use the tools on the Data Map toolbar to reposition the map, make labels, and insert pushpins.

Printing Data Maps

Data maps print as objects in a worksheet; you can't print them separately. Of course, you can always move or copy a data map into a blank worksheet if you don't want it to print on its original worksheet.

Hands On

1. Open any worksheet that contains a database with text or dates in more than one column. (The Traverse Tree Sales worksheet shown in Figure 6.10 works very well if you don't have a worksheet already.) Practice using PivotTables by:

   a) Creating a PivotTable that uses the SUM function in the Data area

   b) Changing the SUM function to AVERAGE or COUNT

   c) Altering the PivotTable layout in the worksheet by moving columns and rows

   d) Adding and deleting a column or row

   e) Creating a custom calculation in the Data area (try one of the "% of" functions)

   f) Drilling down through a value

   g) Making separate PivotTables based on a value in a column.

2. Add one or two new records to the database, then reset the range for the PivotTable.

3. Edit a record in the database and note the changes in the PivotTables based on the database.

4. Using your own worksheet or one you copy from `mapstats.xls`, create and modify a data map. Use the Zoom, Center Map, and Grabber tools. Change some of the data underlying the map, then refresh the map.

SKILL
6

6.5: Auditing Worksheets

You know how to use Excel to create flashy worksheets and reports, complete with bar and pie charts. Excel makes numbers look believable—even when results are so incorrect that no one should believe them. Part of creating a worksheet is checking the completed worksheet for errors, before you or other people rely on the results for decision-making.

Checking for Errors

You can make two kinds of errors when creating a worksheet. One is a data entry error: typing the wrong number, misspelling a word or name, or forgetting to type both parentheses in a pair. You can use Excel's Spelling tools to check for misspellings, and Excel will let you know when you miss a parenthesis, but there is no software tool that can check to be sure you enter all your numbers correctly. You can ensure that a number is in an acceptable range, but you also need to use your personal observation tools.

Resolving Logical Errors

The other kind of error is a logical error: adding rather than subtracting, or multiplying the wrong numbers. Some logical errors violate Excel's rules about how formulas are constructed and result in an error message in the cell or an interruption from the Office Assistant. Those errors are the easy ones to catch and correct. But errors that don't violate Excel's internal logic are the really nasty ones, because nothing jumps out and says, "This is wrong!" If you are familiar with the data, you can check the logic yourself to make sure the results make sense. If you are not conversant with the data yourself, find someone who is and review the worksheet with them before relying on it for critical operations or reporting.

Working with Error Codes

Excel has eight standard error codes that pop up in cells to let you know that a formula requires your attention. The first is the ###### error, which may be telling you that the data is too wide for the column. This is easy to fix (hardly an error, but you get the idea). The codes, listed in Table 6.4, give you information about what caused the error.

TABLE 6.4: Error Codes

Error Code/ Error Name	Cause
#####	1. Data is too wide for the cell, or 2. You subtracted one date from another, and the result is a negative number. Double-check your formula.
#DIV/0 Division by Zero	The number or cell reference you divided by is either zero or blank. If you see this in cells you just filled, you needed an absolute cell reference in the original formula.
#N/A Not Available	1. You omitted a required argument in a function, or 2. The cell that contains the argument is blank or doesn't have the kind of entry the function requires.
#NAME	1. You misspelled the name of a range or function, or 2. You referred to a name that doesn't exist, or 3. You used text in a formula or format without putting it in quotes, or 4. You left out the colon in a range (B3D7 instead of B3:D7).
#NULL	You referred to an intersection that doesn't exist by using a space between two ranges in an argument.
#NUM	1. You used text or a blank cell in an argument that requires a number, or 2. You entered a formula that creates a number too large or too small for Excel to handle.
#REF Invalid Reference	You deleted some cells that this formula requires, so the formula can't find the cell that it refers to. You may have deleted some cells by pasting other cells over them.
#VALUE	You entered text when a formula requires a number or a value such as True or False.

SKILL
6

Resolving Circular Cell References

Circular cell references result in immediate messages from Excel. A circular cell reference occurs when a formula refers to the cell that it is in. For example, when the formula =SUM(J15:J20) is in cell J20, Excel tries to add J20 to itself over and over again. This is called iteration. Excel will iterate 100 times; then it will give up and show an error message letting you know you have a circular cell reference.

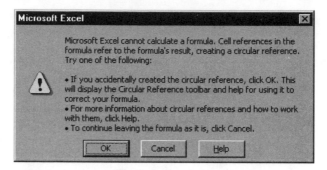

Click OK, and Help opens with information about circular references. (Help only opens the first time you create a circular reference in a session.) Excel places a blue dot next to the formula that created the circular reference and displays `Circular:` and the reference for the offending cell in the status bar. If Help opened, clicking the cell with the circular reference opens the Circular Reference toolbar (or you can turn it on from the View menu).

The drop-down list in the toolbar displays the current circular reference; clicking the drop-down list shows all the circular references in all open workbooks. The first two buttons on the toolbar are used to trace dependents and precedents. *Dependents* are cells with formulas that rely on the cell in the drop-down list; *precedents* are the cells that are referred to in this cell's formula. Click the Trace Precedents button, and Excel will show you the precedent cells, as shown in Figure 6.27.

Month	County	Type	Quantity	Bundles
Apr-98	Genesee	White Pine	37000	74
Apr-98	Oakland	Blue Spruce	22500	45
Apr-98	Oakland	White Pine	15500	31
Apr-98	Oakland	Concolor Fir	13500	27
Apr-98	Genesee	Blue Spruce	12500	25
Apr-98	Oakland	Scotch Pine	11000	22
Apr-98	Genesee	Frazier Fir	6500	13
May-98	Lake	Blue Spruce	42500	85
May-98	Lake	White Pine	32000	64
May-98	Lake	Frazier Fir	14500	29
May-98	Kalkaska	Blue Spruce	13500	27
May-98	Lake	Concolor Fir	12000	24
May-98	Kalkaska	Concolor Fir	10000	20
May-98	Kalkaska	Frazier Fir	7500	15
Sep-98	Lake	Blue Spruce	31000	62
Sep-98	Lake	White Pine	26500	53
				0

FIGURE 6.27: Tracing precedents

The arrow shows that all the cells in the column, including cell E22, are included in the formula in E22. Click the Remove All Arrows button, and Excel will turn the arrows off. Then move to the circular reference cell and fix the formula so that it does not include a reference to itself.

TIP TIP TIP TIP TIP TIP TIP TIP TIP TIP TIP TIP TIP TIP TIP TIP TIP TIP TIP TIP TIP TIP TIP TIP

If there's a circular cell reference anywhere in an open workbook, CIRCULAR appears on the status bar. Use the drop-down list in the Circular Reference toolbar to find the reference.

In the example we've used so far, the circular reference was easy to find, because the formula referred directly to the cell it was stored in. Indirect circular references are harder to find. For example, Excel reports a circular reference in J24. When you trace the precedents, the formula in E12 refers to cells E4:E11. So where is the problem? A formula in cells J15:J22 refers to J24 or refers to another cell whose formula refers to J24. This is an indirect circular reference. Just continue clicking the Trace Precedents button, and you'll eventually find a formula that refers to the cell where the circular reference was reported.

SKILL
6

RESOLVING A CIRCULAR REFERENCE

1. If the circular reference error dialog box is open, click OK to clear the dialog box and open the Circular Reference toolbar, or open the toolbar (choose View ➤ Toolbars) from the menu bar.

2. Choose the circular reference cell from the drop-down list on the toolbar.

3. Click the Trace Precedents button to see the cells that the formula refers to. Continue clicking Trace Precedents until an arrow points back to the cell with the reference.

4. Fix the formula in the original cell (or, if necessary, in a precedent cell) to remove the circular reference.

5. Click Remove All Arrows, and close the Circular Reference toolbar.

Minimizing Data Entry Errors

You're entering payroll. You're in a hurry. Instead of entering Jill Jones' 10 hours, you enter 100. When payday rolls around, Jill is a very happy person. You, on the other hand, are not. A helpful tool called *data validation* allows you to build business rules into each cell so that grossly incorrect entries result in error messages. Business rules are the policies and procedures, formal and informal, that govern how a business operates. Examples of business rules include: no refunds after 30 days; no one ever works more than 80 hours; and all employees must be at least 16 years of age.

To create a validation rule, select the cell or range of cells that have the same business rule. Then choose Data ➤ Validation to open the Data Validation dialog box, shown in Figure 6.28. The dialog box has three pages: Settings, Input Message, and Error Alert. The business rule you want to enforce goes on the first page. On the second page, you can enter a prompt that lets users know how to enter data in the cell. And on the third page, you can enter a message that a user will see when invalid data is entered.

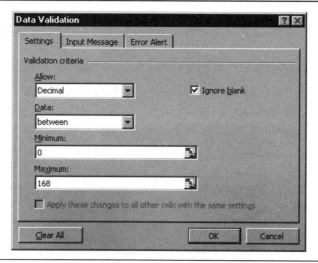

FIGURE 6.28: The Data Validation dialog box

Let's use the error in entering payroll hours mentioned above as an example. In the Settings page, select the type of value that's an acceptable entry for this cell from the Allow drop-down list. There are two possible choices: Whole Number and Decimal. When you select either, additional text box controls will open so you can enter values. In the Data drop-down, choose the operator that you need. In Figure 6.28, we've used the Between operator because there is an upper and a lower limit that employees can work. Enter values for the Minimum and Maximum values. No one can work less than 0 hours. If no maximum is established in the workplace, you could use 168. It's not possible to work more than 168 hours in a week—that's all there are. Notice that you can use the value in another cell as the minimum or maximum. If the Ignore Blank check box is checked, the user can leave the cell blank. Turn off the check mark if entries are required in all the selected cells.

The Input Message page lets you display a message (like a ScreenTip) to tell the user how to enter data in the cell. The message is displayed each time a user selects one of the cells in the range. This is great help if you have a number of users working infrequently with this worksheet. However, if the same people use the worksheet over and over, input messages become cloying. If you want to enter an Input Message, do so. If you add a title, it will appear in bold above the message. You can't just enter a title. The message only appears if there is some text in the Input Message text box.

TIP TIP TIP TIP TIP TIP TIP TIP TIP TIP TIP TIP TIP TIP TIP TIP TIP TIP TIP TIP TIP TIP TIP

Input Messages are great additions to worksheets you build for other people to use, even if you don't want to validate the data they enter in a cell. On the Settings page, leave the default Any Value setting, and then enter your message on the Input Message page.

Use the Error Alert page to build an error dialog box like the dialog boxes used throughout Excel. Choose one of three styles—Stop, Warning, or Information—based on the severity of the error. The Information style is a casual notice. A Warning is a bit more severe, and Stop uses the same icon that users see when a problem-ridden program is about to shut down; it really catches people's attention. Include an error message and a title if you wish.

You don't have to include an error message. You might prefer to enter data and then have Excel show you all the data that isn't valid. Whether you show error messages is a matter of practicality. If someone else is entering data in the worksheet, you should probably let them know when the data is incorrect so they can immediately find the correct data and enter it. Sometimes, the person entering data isn't in a position to correct it; in that case, you might want to dispense with the error message and handle the validation afterward (see the next section, "Using the Auditing Toolbar").

SKILL 6

VALIDATING DATA AND PROVIDING INPUT MESSAGES

1. Select the cells you want to validate.

2. Choose Data ➤ Validation to open the Data Validation dialog box.

3. If you want to set validation rules, on the Settings page set validation criteria for entries allowed, data, and minimum and/or maximum.

4. If you want to include an Input Message, enter a message and optional title on the Input Message page. Make sure the Show Input Message When Cell Is Selected check box is checked.

5. If you want to display a user message when invalid data is entered, choose a Style and enter an Error Message and optional title on the Error Alert page. Make sure the Show Error Alert after Invalid Data Is Entered check box is checked.

6. Click OK.

7. Test the input message, validation, and error message by entering invalid data in one of the cells you selected.

To remove Data Validation or Input Messages, select the cells, open the dialog box, and click the Clear All button to clear all three pages of the dialog box.

Using the Auditing Toolbar

The Auditing toolbar includes the tracing tools from the Circular Reference toolbar, a tool to check the precedents for error codes, and a button to circle any entries that violate the validation rules you established. The Auditing toolbar is one-stop shopping for error checking in your worksheet. Turn on the toolbar from the Tools menu (not the View menu) by choosing Tools ➤ Auditing ➤ Show Auditing Toolbar.

Hands On

1. In any worksheet you're not too attached to, add a formula that includes a circular cell reference. Use the Circular Reference toolbar to view the precedents and resolve the error. Create a NAME error by entering a formula that uses a named range that doesn't exist (like =hours*rate when there is no range named rate). Open the Auditing toolbar and trace the error.

2. In any worksheet, add Data Validation, including input messages and error alerts. Test the validation, messages, and alerts by entering invalid data. When the error alert appears, continue and enter the invalid data. Then use the Circle Invalid Entries button on the Auditing toolbar to identify the invalid data.

3. In any worksheet, use the Data Validation dialog box to add several input messages without validating the entries in the cell. Add a comment to another cell. Delete the comment and clear the input messages.

6.6: Using and Constructing Templates

Templates are workbook models that you use to create other workbooks. Templates let you quickly construct workbooks that are identical in format, giving your work a consistent look. Excel includes some templates; you can create others for your personal use or for novice users in your workplace. An Excel template can include text, numbers, formatting, formulas, and all the other features you already use. When you open a template, a copy is opened, and the original template is not altered.

**SKILL
6**

Working with Existing Templates

Excel includes predesigned templates that you can use or modify. To open a template, choose File ➤ New from the menu bar to open the New dialog box. (You can't simply click the New button on the Standard toolbar. The New button opens the default template: an empty workbook.) Click the Spreadsheet Solutions tab to view the built-in Excel templates. Some templates are included in the Typical Excel installation; others have to be custom installed, but they can always be added later. Click once on any template icon to preview the template. To open an existing template, select the template in the Spreadsheet Solutions window, and then click OK.

Entering Data

The Invoice template, shown in Figure 6.29, is a typical template. There are two worksheets in the template: Invoice and Customize Your Invoice. Each template includes a special toolbar. As you use each template, its toolbar is added to the list in the Toolbars dialog box. The Invoice toolbar initially appears as a palette in the worksheet window. You can move the toolbar if you wish. To view the entire worksheet template, click the Size to Screen button on the Invoice toolbar. Clicking the button again returns the worksheet to its original size.

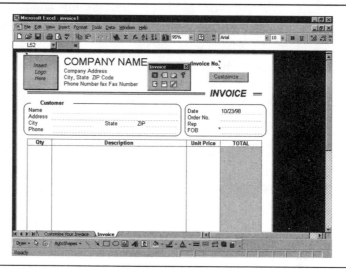

FIGURE 6.29: Invoice Template

Cells with a red triangle include comments called CellTips to explain the information you should enter in the cell. To view a comment, move the mouse pointer over the cell. You can click the Hide Comments/Display Comments button on the Invoice toolbar to suppress or enable comment display. Click the New Comment button to add your own comment to the template.

The canned templates include sample data that you can examine as a guide to enter your data. To view the sample data, click the Display Example/Remove Example button on the template's toolbar. To enter data in the template, turn off the example. Activate the cell, and then enter the information. Cells with a light-blue back color contain formulas, so don't enter information in shaded cells.

Customizing the Template

The Invoice sheet includes placeholders for generic title information: the company name, a place for a logo or picture. To add your personal information, click the Customize button in the Invoice worksheet to move to the Customize Your Invoice worksheet. At the top of the worksheet is a Lock/Save Sheet button. *Locking* a template prevents users from accidentally changing the customized information in this workbook, but it does not alter the template. You can always choose to customize again and unlock the template if you want to change it.

Or you can save a copy of the template that includes the custom information you entered. It's more convenient to permanently alter the template by saving. To lock or save template changes, click the Lock/Save Sheet button. A dialog box opens so that you can select locking or locking and saving:

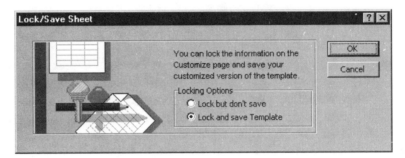

SKILL
6

CUSTOMIZING A TEMPLATE

1. Activate the Customize worksheet.
2. Enter your custom information as indicated in the worksheet.
3. Click the Lock/Save Sheet button.
4. Choose Lock But Don't Save or Lock and Save Template; then click OK.

Creating a Template

You can create a template for workbooks that you use frequently. For example, you might use Excel to complete a weekly payroll and put all the payroll worksheets for one month into a separate workbook. Rather than constructing a new workbook each month, you can create a monthly payroll template. At the beginning of each month you can create a new workbook from the template. Your template will differ from a regular workbook in four specific ways.

- The completed workbook will be saved as a template rather than as a workbook.

- It will contain only the text, formulas, and formatting that remain the same each month.

- The template will include visual formatting clues and comments to assist users.

- It will be saved in the Office 2000 Templates folder.

You can create a template from scratch or base it on an existing workbook. If you're using an existing workbook, first make sure that all the formulas work and that numbers and text are formatted as you want them. Then remove the text and numbers that will be entered each time the template is used. Don't remove formulas—although the results of the formulas change, the formulas themselves remain the same. If you're creating a template from scratch, you still need to enter (and then remove) values to test the template's formulas before saving it.

Now, use borders and shading to let users know where they should—and shouldn't—enter text or other information. The Invoice template is a good model. Add comments (choose Insert Comment from the shortcut menu) to provide CellTips where users might have questions about data entry. Remove any extra worksheets from the template to improve its overall appearance. When you're finished formatting the worksheet, choose File ➤ Save As, and save the workbook as a Template type. (Excel templates have the .xlt extension.)

TIP TIP TIP TIP TIP TIP TIP TIP TIP TIP TIP TIP TIP TIP TIP TIP TIP TIP TIP TIP TIP TIP TIP TIP
You can create a folder within the templates folder to hold your personal templates. Other than the General tab, tabs in the New dialog box represent folders in the Templates folder.

SAVING A TEMPLATE

1. Click the Save button or choose File⊱ Save As.
2. In the Save As Type control, choose Template from the drop-down list. The Save In control will change to the default Templates folder.
3. Enter a name for the template in the File Name text box control.
4. Click the Save button.

When you choose File ⊱ New, the template will be included on the General page or the specific folder you saved it in. The template itself will not be altered when you or other users create new workbooks. To modify a template, open the template from the Templates folder with File ⊱ Open rather than File ⊱ New. When you are finished editing, save and close the template.

Hands On

1. Use another of the templates (such as Expenses) included with Excel 2000. Customize the template with your company's information. Save the customized template.

2. Create a template that calculates and totals gross pay, taxes, and net pay for 10 employees based on information entered by the user. Users should enter the following information for each employee: Social Security number, last name, first name, hourly rate, tax rate (as a percentage), and hours worked.

3. Modify the template in Exercise 2 to allow for payroll deduction of employee contributions to National Public Radio. The deduction amount will be entered with the employee information and deducted from the pay after taxes are calculated. Total the contribution column.

SKILL
6

6.7: Linking and Referencing

A link is a reference to a cell or range in another workbook. Links are commonly used to avoid double-entering workbook information.

Linking Workbooks

Suppose that in your company, departments are responsible for their own budgets. As the time to finalize the coming year's budget approaches, each manager is working furiously on his or her budget. The vice president for finance has a master budget that is a roll-up of the department budgets. It's not practical to put all the department worksheets and the master budget in one large workbook, because many people would need to use the workbook at the same time (see Skill 6.8 for another way to work with the workbook). By linking the workbooks, the changes made by the department managers can be immediately reflected in the vice president's master budget workbook.

Each link establishes a relationship between two workbooks. The vice president's workbook is called the dependent workbook, because the value that the v.p. sees depends on a value in another workbook. The external workbook that contains that value is called the *source workbook*.

You can create a link in two ways: by using an open workbook or by referring to a workbook on disk. The first method is much easier. It's the same as creating any other reference in a formula, but you need to switch to the source workbook before selecting the cell to reference in the formula.

Before creating the formula that includes a link, open the source workbook. Begin entering the formula in the dependent workbook with an =. At the point in the formula where you want to include a cell reference from the source workbook, choose Window on the menu bar and select the source workbook. In the source workbook, click on the cell that you want to reference, and it will be included, as shown in Figure 6.30.

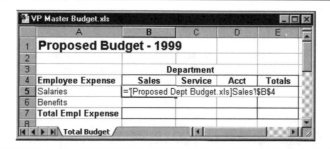

FIGURE 6.30: Creating a link

Notice that the cell reference includes the workbook and worksheet names as well as the cell address:

$\times$ $\checkmark$ = ='[Proposed Dept Budget.xls]Sales'!B4

You may prefer to arrange the source and dependent workbooks so that you can see the results cell and the cell to be referenced at the same time. With both workbooks open, choose Window ➢ Arrange to open the Arrange Windows dialog box:

Choose how you want the open workbooks arranged, and then use each workbook window's sizing tool to further size and arrange the windows.

SKILL
6

 TIP TIP TIP TIP TIP TIP TIP TIP TIP TIP TIP TIP TIP TIP TIP TIP TIP TIP TIP TIP TIP TIP TIP TIP

You can also arrange copies of a single workbook so that you can work in two different areas of the workbook in separate windows. First, choose Window ➢ New Window, and then open the Arrange Windows dialog box and arrange the windows.

CREATING A LINK TO AN OPEN WORKBOOK

1. Open both the dependent workbook and the source workbook.
2. In the dependent workbook, begin entering your formula.
3. To include a reference to the source workbook, open the Window menu and select the source workbook.

continued ▶

4.   In the source workbook, locate and select the cell you want to include in the formula.

5.   Finish creating the formula as you normally would.

If the workbook is not open, you must provide all the information that Excel needs to find the source workbook, including the full path. For example, if you want to refer to cell D4 in the Sales sheet of the Proposed Dept Budget workbook, stored in the Sales Management folder on the C: drive, the reference would be: `'C:\Sales Management\[Proposed Dept Budget.xls]Sales'!D4`. There are a lot of places to make a mistake when typing an entry like this. Try to create links with open source workbooks whenever possible.

Linking with Paste Link

If you simply want to refer to a cell in another workbook (as opposed to using it in a formula), create a link with Copy and Paste Link. Open both workbooks, and then select and copy the cell(s) from the source workbook. Activate the destination workbook, and choose Edit ➤ Paste Special from the menu bar to open the Paste Special dialog box. A normal paste pastes the formula(s) from the Clipboard. Here, you can paste values, formula, formats, and other cell attributes or perform a math operation during the paste:

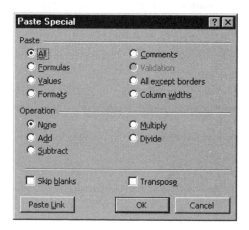

Click the Paste Link button, select a destination for the pasted selection, and then press Enter to paste the link to the source workbook.

Updating Links

When you open the dependent workbook and the source workbook is not open, Excel will ask if you want to update the links. If both workbooks are open, changes in the source workbook are automatically updated in the dependent workbook. If, however, the source workbook can be opened by other users, they could be making changes to the workbook while you are working with the dependent workbook. In this case, the links will not be updated automatically; you have to instruct Excel to update the links.

With the dependent workbook open, choose Edit ➤ Links to open the Edit Links dialog box:

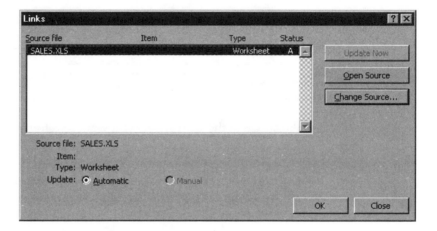

From the Source File list, choose the source workbook that you want to update. Click the Update Now button to update the dependent workbook with information from the latest saved version of the source workbook.

UPDATING LINKS

1. In the dependent workbook, choose Edit ➤ Links.
2. Click Update Now.

SKILL
6

Formulas That Span Worksheets

In Excel, you can reference ranges that occur in the same cell or group of cells on two or more worksheets. For example, Figure 6.31 shows the January worksheet for reporting types of media sold at various locations. The February and March worksheets have exactly the same layout. The FirstQuarter worksheet summarizes the figures from the three monthly worksheets. You can total all worksheets at one time with a 3-D cell reference.

	A	B	C	D	E
1	Media Sales by Location and Type				
2	Sales in Units - 1998				
3					
4	Location	Disk	CD	Video	Total
5	Temple Street	110	141	67	318
6	Mt. Vernon	45	90	104	239
7	Cambridge	211	300	41	552
8	Milton	351	313	0	664
9		717	844	212	1773

FIGURE 6.31: Media Types worksheet

First, make sure that the worksheets you want to reference are next to each other. Then simply create the formula as you normally would, using AutoSum. To insert a 3-D argument, hold Shift and select the worksheets that include the cells you want to insert in the argument. (The sheet with the formula will also appear to be included; just ignore it.) Then, select the cell(s) that you want to include and finish creating the formula:

Formulas with 3-D references can be filled like other formulas.

CREATING A 3-D REFERENCE IN A FORMULA

1. In the results cell, begin constructing the formula.
2. To include the 3-D reference, click the sheet tab of the first sheet of the 3-D range.

continued ▶

3. Hold Shift, and select the last sheet you want to refer to.
4. Select the cell or range of cells to include in the formula.
5. Finish the formula, and press Enter.

You might want to use 3-D names if you're creating a lot of three-dimensional cell references. For example, if cell B10 in three worksheets is the value for April's Salaries, you could name all three cells SalaryApr.

DEFINING 3-D RANGE NAMES

1. Choose Insert ➤ Name ➤ Define from the menu bar.
2. In the Names in Workbook text box, type the range name.
3. Delete any reference in the Refers To text box, and type an =.
4. Click the sheet tab for the first worksheet you want to reference.
5. Hold Shift and select the sheet tab for the last worksheet to be referenced.
6. Select the cell or range to be named.
7. Click Add to add the name, and then click OK to close the dialog box.

SKILL
6

Hands On

1. Create the worksheet shown below for the Sales department. Re-create or copy the Sales worksheet to two separate workbooks. Edit the worksheet for the Accounting and Service departments. Save all three workbooks.

	A	B	C	D
1	**Proposed Budget - 1999**			
2				
3	**Employee Expense**	**1998 Budget**	**1998 Actual**	**1999 Proposed**
4	Salaries	147,000	148,540	151,000
5	Benefits	39,690	38,790	40,770
6	**Total Employee Expense**	186,690	187,330	191,770

a) In a new workbook, create the Budget Summary worksheet shown in Figure 6.30. Use links to refer to the figures in column D of the three departmental workbooks.

b) Close all four workbooks. Open the Accounting department workbook and change the proposed salaries and benefits for 1999. Close and save the Accounting department workbook.

c) Open the Budget Summary workbook. Do not update the links. Note the figures for Accounting. Update the links.

d) Open and arrange all four workbooks.

2. In a new workbook, create at least three periodic worksheets (see Figure 6.31) and one total worksheet. Use 3-D cell references to total the periodic worksheets on the total worksheet.

6.8: Working with Others in Excel

Excel 2000 was designed to allow multiple users to view and modify a single workbook simultaneously. If you want others to be able to use a workbook while you have it open, you need to share the workbook and ensure that it is stored on a network or shared drive that other users can access.

Sharing Workbooks

To share a workbook, you use the Share Workbook dialog box (choose Tools ➤ Share Workbook):

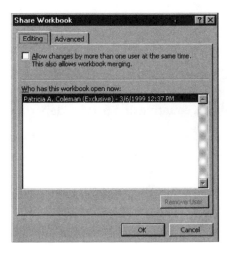

Before you make any changes in this dialog box, note that the current user has exclusive rights to this workbook. On the Editing page, click in the Allow Changes check box to make the file accessible to other users. Then activate the Advanced page to set options for tracking changes and resolving conflicts.

Tracking Changes

Tracking changes is only available in shared workbooks. If you choose to track changes in a *change history*, select the number of days each change should be kept. If you don't want to track changes, tell Excel not to keep a history. Whether you track changes or not, you need to determine when changes are updated. The default only updates changes when the file is saved. This means that each time you (or another user) save, Excel will save your changes and update your workbook with changes made by other users. Or you can choose to have your workbook updated automatically every set number of minutes; by choosing the Save My Changes option, your changes will be saved when the update occurs. (If you update changes automatically, other users still won't see your changes until you save; however, they can also choose to see saved changes automatically rather than waiting until they save.)

When two or more users make different changes in the same cell, it causes a conflict. Set the Conflicting Changes option to indicate how conflicts should be resolved. Excel can prompt you to resolve conflicts, or it can automatically accept the saved changes. The Personal view contains your print and filter settings for the workbook. These settings do not affect other users' view of the workbook. Use the check boxes to include or exclude these settings when the workbook is saved.

SHARING A WORKBOOK

1. With the workbook open, choose Tools ➢ Share Workbook from the menu bar.
2. On the Editing page, enable Allow Changes by More Than One User.
3. On the Advanced page, set Track Changes, Update Changes, Conflicting Changes, and Personal View options.
4. Click OK to close the dialog box.

When you close the dialog box, Excel will save the workbook as a shared workbook; if you haven't previously saved it, the Save As dialog box will open. If you return to the Shared Workbooks dialog box, you'll notice that you no longer have the workbook open Exclusively, as other Excel 2000 users can now open it.

TIP TIP TIP TIP TIP TIP TIP TIP TIP TIP TIP TIP TIP TIP TIP TIP TIP TIP TIP TIP TIP TIP TIP TIP
Excel tracks workbook users by name. If the name listed in the Editing page is incorrect, you can change it on the General page of the Options dialog box (choose Tools ➢ Options).

You can restrict who can open and use the data in a workbook by setting a password to open or save the workbook. Choose File ➢ Save As, and then choose Tools ➢ General Options button in the Save As dialog box to open the Save Options dialog box.

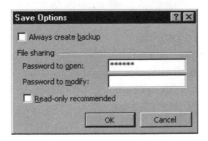

Enter passwords that users (including you) must enter to open or modify the workbooks. Click OK to return to the Save As procedure. Make sure you keep track of the password; if you lose it, you lose the open or modify rights to the file.

Working in a Shared Workbook

When Tracking Changes is enabled, each change made is noted in a comment, and changed cells are flagged. For example, if you delete the value in a cell, a triangle appears in the upper left corner of the cell. When you move the mouse pointer over the cell, a comment tells you who changed the cell, when they changed it, and what the former value in the cell was. Excel assigns a different triangle color to each user who modifies the workbook, so you can visually inspect the workbook to find all the changes made by one user. When you save the workbook, you accept the changes, so the triangle and comment disappear.

> **Patricia A. Coleman, 10/23/1998 11:52 AM:**
> Changed cell E21 from '=D21/500' to '54'.

Some Excel 2000 features aren't available in shared workbooks. However, you can use the features before you share a workbook, or you can temporarily unshare the workbook, make changes, and then turn sharing on again. For instance, while a workbook is shared, you can't:

- Delete worksheets

- Add or apply conditional formatting and data validation

- Insert or delete ranges of cells (you can still insert and delete individual cells, rows, and columns), charts, hyperlinks, or other objects (including those created with Draw)

- Group or outline data

- Write, change, view, record, or assign macros

See Excel's Online Help for the complete list of limitations of shared workbooks.

SKILL 6

Resolving Conflicts

If changes you are saving conflict with changes saved by another user, you'll be prompted to resolve the conflict (unless you changed the Conflicting Changes setting in the Advanced page of the Share Workbook dialog box). In the Resolve Conflicts dialog box, you can review each change individually and accept your change or others' changes, or accept/reject changes in bulk.

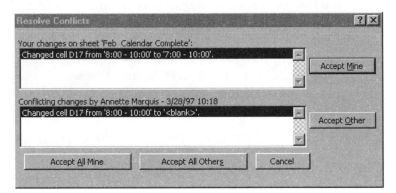

Viewing the Change History

You can examine all the changes saved in a workbook since you turned on the change history. Choose Tools ➤ Track Changes ➤ Highlight Changes to open the Highlight Changes dialog box. In the dialog box, select the time period for the changes you want to review, and specify the users whose changes you want to see. If you only want to see changes for a particular range or sheet, select the range you want to view. You can view the changes on screen or on a separate worksheet in the workbook.

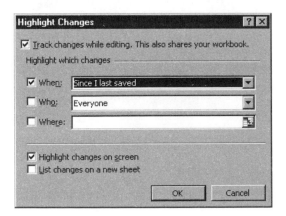

VIEWING THE CHANGE HISTORY

1. Choose Tools ➤ Track Changes ➤ Highlight Changes.
2. In the Highlight Changes dialog box, set the When, Who, and Where options.
3. Enable or disable viewing on screen or in a separate worksheet.
4. Click OK.

When you view the history on a separate worksheet, you can filter the changes to find changes made by different users or on specific dates, as shown in Figure 6.32. When you remove a workbook from shared use, the change history is turned off and reset. If you want to keep the changes, select the information on the History worksheet and copy it to another worksheet before unsharing the workbook.

Action Number	Date	Time	Who	Change	Sheet	Range	New Value	Old Value	Action Type	Losing Action
1	1/17/99	6:14 PM	Annette Marquis	Cell Change	Cards	J3	2	<blank>		
2	1/17/99	6:14 PM	Annette Marquis	Cell Change	Cards	J3	<blank>	2		
3	1/17/99	6:34 PM	Gini Courter	Cell Change	Cards	J3	1	<blank>		
4	1/17/99	6:50 PM	Annette Marquis	Cell Change	Cards	J3	2	<blank>	Won	3
5	1/17/99	6:52 PM	Annette Marquis	Cell Change	Cards	J3	<blank>	2		

The history ends with the changes saved on 1/17/1999 at 6:52 PM.

FIGURE 6.32: Viewing the change history

SKILL 6

Merging Workbook Changes

If you anticipate many conflicting changes in a shared workbook, or if you want users to be able to make changes independently and then review all changes at once, you should make and distribute copies of the shared workbook. To create the copies, use Save As and give each copy of the workbook a different name. Then you can merge the copies when users are done with their changes. You can only merge workbooks that have the same change history, so it's important that none of the users turns off sharing while using the workbook. Also, the history must be complete when you merge the workbooks. If, for example, you set the number of days for the history at 30 days and users keep the workbooks for 32 days, you won't be able to merge the workbooks. Before you make copies of the shared workbook, make sure you set the history to allow enough time for changes and merging. If you're uncertain, set 600 days or an equally ridiculous length of time.

MERGING SHARED WORKBOOKS

1. Open your copy of the shared workbook that you want to merge changes into.
2. Choose Tools ➤ Merge Workbooks. If you haven't saved your copy of the workbook, you'll be prompted to do so.
3. In the Select Files to Merge into Current Document dialog box, choose the copy of the shared workbook that has the changes you wish to merge. (Use Ctrl or Shift to select multiple workbooks from one location.) Click OK.

Are You Experienced?

Now you can...

- ☑ **Take advantage of Excel's advanced formatting features**
- ☑ **Use financial and statistical functions**
- ☑ **Sort, filter, and analyze data**
- ☑ **Create PivotTables and data maps**
- ☑ **Check worksheets for errors with auditing tools**
- ☑ **Use templates, and create your own templates**
- ☑ **Link workbooks and create 3-D cell references**
- ☑ **Track changes to shared workbooks**

SKILL 7

Creating PowerPoint Presentations

- ➔ Creating a presentation
- ➔ Modifying visual elements
- ➔ Adding objects
- ➔ Applying transitions, animations, and linking
- ➔ Preparing handouts
- ➔ Presenting a slide show

7.1: Creating a Basic Presentation

When you make your next presentation—whether it's to demonstrate a product, outline a project, or sell an idea—PowerPoint offers a way to take the focus off you and put it where it belongs—on what you have to say! In this skill, you'll learn how to create a polished presentation with minimal effort.

What Is PowerPoint?

Use PowerPoint to create electronic slide shows that can liven up even the most apathetic crowd. If you don't want to give your presentation electronically, you can create vivid overhead transparencies and valuable audience handouts that will rival the most polished presenters. With PowerPoint, you can create presentations that run automatically. Automated presentations are often used as kiosks at trade shows, and such presentations are also seeing increased use on the Internet.

Creating Your First Presentation

Every PowerPoint presentation consists of a series of *slides*: text or objects displayed on a graphic background, as shown in Figure 7.1. You create your presentation by adding text and objects to slides.

You'll go through a series of steps for every presentation you create in PowerPoint:

1. Create the presentation, entering and editing text, and rearranging slides.

2. Apply a presentation design. Modify the design if necessary.

3. Format individual slides if you wish.

4. Add objects to the presentation.

5. Apply and modify transitions, animation effects, and links for electronic presentations.

FIGURE 7.1: The PowerPoint slide

6.   Create audience materials and speaker notes.

7.   Rehearse and add slide timings.

8.   Present the presentation.

When you launch PowerPoint, the PowerPoint dialog box opens:

You can create a new presentation or open an existing presentation. To help you become familiar with PowerPoint, you'll create your first presentation using the AutoContent Wizard. The other creation methods are discussed in Skill 7.2.

Using the AutoContent Wizard

The AutoContent Wizard works like any of the other Wizards in Office 2000. You are taken through a series of steps with additional questions that help design your presentation. In each step, click Next to advance, or click Back to return to a previous step. If you have just launched PowerPoint, choose AutoContent Wizard from the PowerPoint dialog box, and click OK to start the Wizard. If PowerPoint is already running from an earlier presentation, or if you closed the PowerPoint dialog box, choose File ➤ New to open the New Presentation dialog box, and choose the AutoContent Wizard, as shown in Figure 7.2.

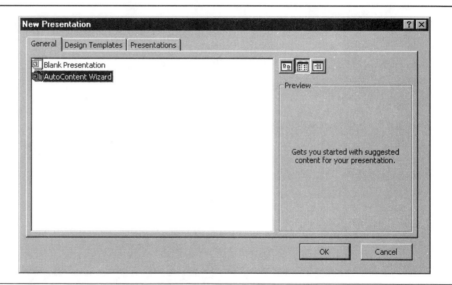

FIGURE 7.2: The New Presentation dialog box

The first step explains the Wizard. In the second step, choose a presentation type. Clicking one of the category buttons (see Figure 7.3) displays a list of types in the list box.

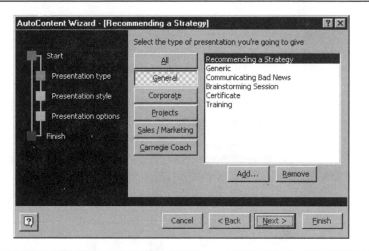

FIGURE 7.3: Choosing a presentation type

In the third step, specify the type of output you want. The first four output options determine which set of design templates you'll choose from. For example, the On-Screen Presentations use colored backgrounds; the Color Overhead templates have no backgrounds, but colored graphic images.

In the fourth step, supply a title for your presentation, and specify whether it will have a footer. After you enter the presentation options, you're done with the Wizard. Click Next, and then click Finish to open the presentation.

SKILL
7

USING THE AUTOCONTENT WIZARD

1. Choose AutoContent Wizard from the New Presentation dialog box or the PowerPoint dialog box.
2. Click Next to move beyond the first screen.
3. Choose a presentation type from the list provided. Click Next.
4. Specify the type of output. Click Next.
6. Enter a title for your presentation, and specify whether you want a footer. Click Next.
7. Click Finish to close the Wizard and open the presentation in Normal view.

Viewing Slides

The PowerPoint window includes a few features that aren't included in other Office 2000 applications. In Figure 7.4, the AutoContent Wizard has just closed and the presentation has been opened in *Normal view*, one of five ways to view a presentation.

Five view buttons appear at the left end of the horizontal scroll bar; the Normal View button is pressed in.

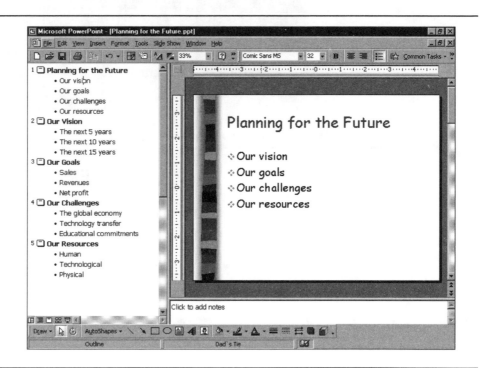

FIGURE 7.4: The Normal view

Each view provides a different way to look at and work with your presentation. In Normal view, presentation text appears in the Outline pane on the left, the slide appears in the Slide pane on the right, and an area for notes is visible at the botton in the Notes pane. You can edit the content of the presentation in either the Outline pane or the Slide pane.

In *Outline view*, which is shown in Figure 7.5, presentation text appears in the main pane on the left, and the slide display in miniature in the pane on the right. In this view, you can also edit in either pane, but working with the miniature slide is a bit difficult, of course. You can also add notes in Outline view. See the section "Adding Notes to the Notes Page" for information about how and why you do this. To display the Outlining toolbar, choose View ➢ Toolbars ➢ Outlining.

To display a slide, click its topic in the outline. Use the scroll bars to scroll through the outline.

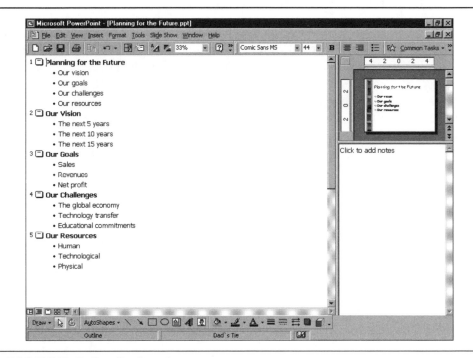

FIGURE 7.5: Outline view

Slide view lets you work with slides one at a time. Click a slide's icon to display that slide. You can edit text or place objects on slides and immediately see the impact of your changes and additions. Some users prefer to do all their editing in Slide view.

Slide Sorter view allows you to see a screen full of slides at one time. You can swap slides around, delete slides, and add special effects. You cannot edit text or place objects on slides in this view.

Slide Show view is the final button in this group. Click this button to see how a slide will look in full-screen mode. Click the icon in the lower left of the screen, and choose from the shortcut menu to go to the next or the previous slide. Press the Esc key on the keyboard if you want to leave the slide show before the last slide.

When you switch from one view to another, the current slide remains current, regardless of view. If you are on slide 5 in Slide view and switch to Outline view, the 5th slide will be selected. Clicking the Slide Show button begins the Slide Show with slide 5.

Developing a Presentation

In the early stages of your presentation's development, you'll probably want to work in Normal view or in Outline view. Each has advantages. In Normal view, you can edit the text in the left pane or the right pane, and you can work with graphical elements in the right pane. In Outline view, you can enter and edit text and rearrange bullet points, paragraphs, and slides.

In Outline view or in the Outline pane of the Normal view, each slide has a number in the left margin and a slide icon. The slide title is located next to the slide icon. Indented below the title is the body text.

Entering and Editing Text

You will want to replace the contents of the slides created by the Wizard before making substantial formatting changes. To change the contents, edit text as you would in Word. If you click in the left margin, the cursor changes to a four-headed arrow because you can drag the selected line to move it. There are five levels below the slide title:

> 1 ▢ **Slide Title**
>   • Level 1
>   – Level 2
>   ▪ Level 3
>   – Level 4
>   » Level 5

When you reach the end of a line and press Enter, the next line is on the same level as the previous line; if you position the insertion point at the end of a slide's title and press Enter, you will insert a new slide. Press the Tab key or click the Demote button to move to a lower level. By default, each level below the title is automatically bulleted. Press Tab or click Demote again, and you'll be at the second level. Press Enter at the end of a bulleted line, and you will get another line at the same level. Text entered at any level other than the title level is a point or a subpoint. To move back a level, either hold Shift and press Tab or click the Promote button.

Checking Spelling   PowerPoint includes two spelling features. To correct spelling as you type, right-click on words with a red wavy underline to see suggested correct spellings. to check the spelling for an entire presentation, click the Spelling button on the Standard toolbar. (For more information on spelling, see Skill 1.4.)

Using Find and Replace   Use PowerPoint's Find feature to locate a text string in your presentation. Choose Edit ➤ Find to open the Find dialog box:

In the Find What text box, enter the text string that you want to find, and then set the Find options.

If you use Find in Normal, Outline, or Slide view, clicking Find Next will move to and select the next text string that matches the Find What string. In Slide Sorter view, there isn't a Find Next button; instead, the button is Find All. Clicking Find All selects all the slides that contain the Find What string.

You can replace each occurrence of one text string with another. Choose Edit ➤ Replace, or if the Find dialog box is already open, click the Replace button in the Find dialog box. Enter the string you want to find in Find What and the string you want to replace it with in Replace With:

SKILL
7

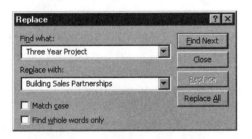

To replace all the occurrences, click Replace All. Or, you can work through the replacements one at a time. To find the next occurrence, click Find Next. Click Replace to make the replacement, and click Find Next to move to the next possible replacement. When you've replaced all occurrences of the text string, a message box appears to let you know that PowerPoint has searched the entire presentation and there aren't any more occurrences of the text string. A similar dialog box opens to let you know if the text string you entered in Find What doesn't appear in the presentation.

Selecting Text, Lines, and Slides

Select text in PowerPoint just as you do in Word or Excel. Double-click a word, or drag across one or more words to select them. To select a point or title, click the bullet or slide icon or triple-click anywhere in the point or title. If you select a first-level point that has second-level points underneath it, the second-level points will also be selected. Selecting the title selects the entire slide.

Inserting, Deleting, and Moving Points and Slides

To move a point (and all the subpoints underneath it), select the point. If you click a slide's icon, the entire slide—title and any body text—is selected. Move into the left margin, and your mouse pointer will change to a four-headed arrow:

Using the four-headed arrow, drag the selection toward its new location, and a horizontal line will appear in the outline. Drag and drop the horizontal line, and the selected point(s) or slide will move to the new location.

Working in Slide View

Some people prefer to work on one slide at a time. Slide view gives you a better feel for how the slide will actually look when complete.

Most slides include two text boxes, one for the title and one for the body text. When you click on the title or body, a frame appears around the text box. You can point to the frame and drag the text box to another location on the slide. To format the text in the box, select the text by clicking or dragging as you would in Outline view or Normal view, and then change formats using the Formatting toolbar or Format menu.

WORKING IN SLIDE VIEW

1. Click the Slide View button to move to Slide view. Click a slide icon to move to the slide you want to format.

2. Click on the text box for the title or body to select it. Use the handles to resize the text box. Drag the box to move it to a new location, or click the Delete key to delete the box.

3. Select and format text using the Formatting toolbar or the Format menu.

Using the Slide Sorter

In Slide Sorter view, shown in Figure 7.6, you work with entire slides. You can't rearrange the text *on* a slide, but you can move or copy entire slides.

Click once on a slide to select it, or select multiple slides by holding Ctrl while clicking. A selected slide has a dark border around it, like Slide 1 in Figure 7.6. To move a selected slide, drag the slide toward its new location. A gray vertical line will appear. Drag and drop to move the line, and the selected slide, to the new location. To copy a slide, hold the Ctrl key on the keyboard while dragging; release Ctrl after dropping the slide in place. To delete slides in Slide Sorter view, select the slides, and then press the Delete key on the keyboard.

SKILL
7

TIP TIP TIP TIP TIP TIP TIP TIP TIP TIP TIP TIP TIP TIP TIP TIP TIP TIP TIP TIP TIP TIP TIP TIP TIP

In Slide Sorter view, you can't always read the text on a slide. To see just the title, hold Alt and click on the slide. When you release the mouse button, the slide miniature returns to normal.

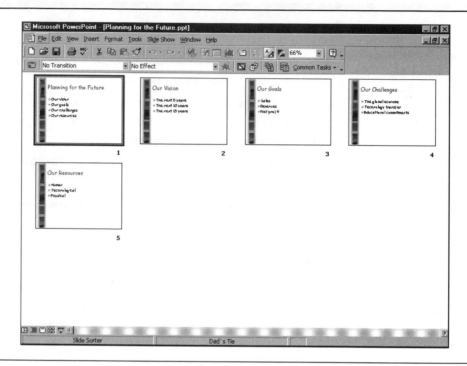

FIGURE 7.6: Slide Sorter view

MOVING, COPYING, AND DELETING SLIDES IN SLIDE SORTER VIEW

1. Click once on a slide to select it.
2. Hold Ctrl and click to select additional slides.
3. Press Delete to delete the slides.

–OR–

3. Drag selected slides to a new location to move them. Hold Ctrl while releasing the mouse button to copy the slides.

Adding Notes to the Notes Page

You can use Notes Pages for speaker notes during a presentation, but you can also use them to keep track of other information about particular slides as you're creating a presentation: data that needs to be verified or alternative information or wording you've considered adding to the slide. You can add notes in three ways:

- In Normal view, simply type them in the pane on the bottom right (see Figure 7.4, earlier in this chapter).

- Choose View ➤ Notes Page to open Notes Page view, as shown in Figure 7.7.

- In Slide Show view, right-click to open the shortcut menu, and select Speaker Notes to open the Speaker Notes dialog box, as shown in Figure 7.8. Enter your note, and click Close to return to the Slide Show. To check the spelling or format of notes, open Notes Page view.

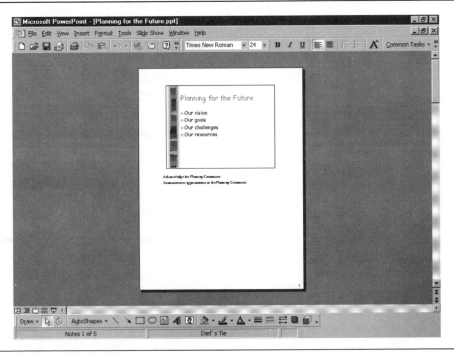

FIGURE 7.7: Notes Page view

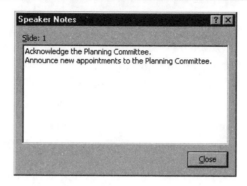

FIGURE 7.8: The Speaker Notes dialog box

Notes Page view opens with a view of a single page (see Figure 7.7). The slide is at the top of the page; the bottom half of the page is a single text box where you can type your notes.

 Change the Zoom percentage so that you can actually see what you're typing, and then click in the text box and enter your notes. When you're finished entering notes for a slide and want to add notes to another slide, select the slide from another view, and choose View ➤ Notes Page again.

ADDING NOTES IN NOTES PAGE VIEW

1. Click the Notes Page View button to open Notes Page view.
2. Click the text box and type the text for the note on the current slide.

Hands On

1. Use the AutoContent Wizard to create a presentation of your choice.

   a) Add a note to one of the slides in Notes Page view.

   b) Move, copy, and delete slides in Slide Sorter view.

   c) Edit the existing text in Outline view or Normal view to add your content. Add a new slide with a title and subpoints.

d) Add text to a slide in Slide view.

e) View the presentation in Slide Show view.

7.2: Building Presentations

The benefit of the AutoContent Wizard is that it helps you to develop your content. If you've already decided what should be in your presentation, you don't need to use the Wizard. You can create a presentation in other ways:

- Using a design template, which gives you a "look" without burdening you with text to alter or delete

- Borrowing the design from an existing presentation, which is useful if the presentations in your department should share a common design

- "Working from scratch"—entering your text first, and then applying a design

- Importing and modifying an existing Word outline

You can always apply another design template or presentation design to an existing presentation.

Using Design Templates or Blank Presentations

You can use the design elements from any presentation or template in a new presentation. To create a presentation using a design template, either choose Design Template in the dialog box that opens when you launch PowerPoint, or choose File ➤ New from the menu bar to open the New Presentation dialog box. Click the Design Templates tab, and select a template. You'll see the sample title slide in the Preview area, as shown in Figure 7.9. Double-click a design template or click OK to choose the selected template.

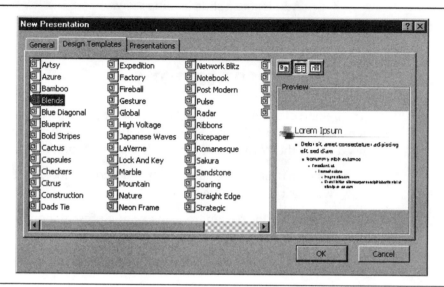

FIGURE 7.9:   The Design Templates tab in the New Presentation dialog box

The Presentations tab contains the presentation types, which are the same as those you see in the AutoContent Wizard. Click an icon to see a preview, as shown in Figure 7.10.

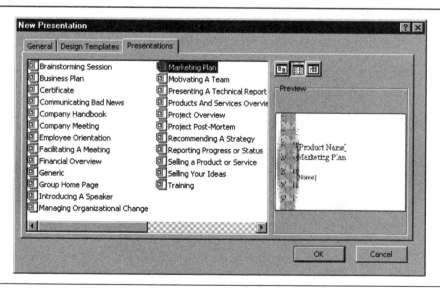

FIGURE 7.10:   The Presentations tab in the New Presentation dialog box

The difference between a design template and a presentation type is that the template contains only the design; the presentation type also contains placeholder content.

To create a presentation without a design, choose Blank Presentation when you launch PowerPoint, or choose Blank Presentation from the General tab in the New Presentation dialog box.

Selecting Slide Layouts

If you begin a presentation with a design template or choose to create a blank presentation, the New Slide dialog box opens, as shown in Figure 7.11.

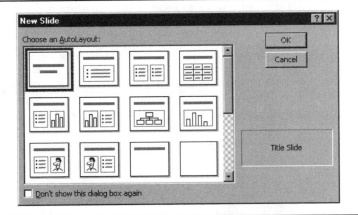

FIGURE 7.11: The New Slide dialog box

In the New Slide Dialog box, you select an AutoLayout for each new slide. When you click the thumbnail for the layout, a description appears. No choice that you make in this dialog box is carved in stone; you can always change a slide's layout. Notice that there is a scroll bar in this dialog box; there are other layouts you might want to look at. Select the Title Slide layout for the first slide in the presentation, and click OK. The slide opens in Normal view.

Enter a title for your presentation and, optionally, a subtitle. You can use the text boxes on the slide, or you can work in the left pane. To use a text box, simply click inside it, and enter the text you want. Your text will also appear, as you type it, in the pane on the left.

When you finish the first slide, choose New Slide from the Common Tasks toolbar. This opens the New Slide dialog box again so that you can select a layout for the second slide. To change the layout of a slide, select the slide and choose Slide Layout from the Common Tasks menu to reopen the Slide Layout dialog box.

Using Existing Presentations

If you want to use the design from an existing presentation, begin by choosing any design template or a blank presentation. Then click Apply Design Template in the Common Tasks dialog box. When the Apply Design Template dialog box opens (see Figure 7.12), set the Look In control to the folder that contains the presentation. Change the Files of Type drop-down list at the bottom of the dialog box to All PowerPoint Files. Select the presentation that has the design you want to use, and click Apply. Use the same method to apply any of the design templates in the Presentations folder to an existing presentation.

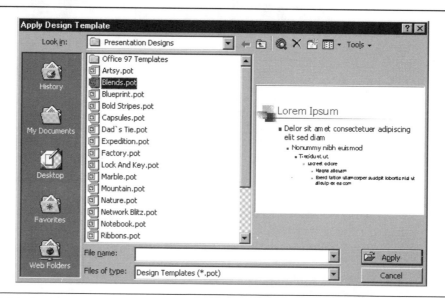

FIGURE 7.12: The Apply Design Template dialog box

Applying a Design to a Presentation

1. Choose Apply Design Template from the Common Tasks toolbar to open the Apply Design Template dialog box.

2. If the presentation you want to use is not a template, change the Look In control to the folder where the presentation is stored. Change the Files of Type drop-down control to All PowerPoint Files.

3. Select the presentation or design template you want to apply.

4. Click Apply.

Using Slides from an Existing Presentation

Applying a design template uses a presentation's background, fonts, and formatting without any of the content. You can take entire slides from an existing presentation and add them to another presentation using the Slide Finder. Choose Insert ➤ Slides from Files to open the Slide Finder. Click the Browse button and select the file that contains the slides you want to add to your presentation; then click the Display button to add thumbnails of the slides to the Slide Finder, as shown in Figure 7.13.

SKILL
▼ 7

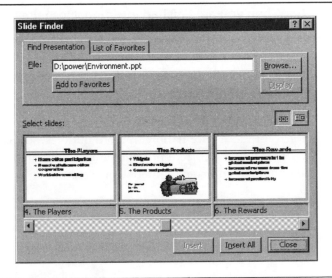

FIGURE 7.13: The Slide Finder

The slides appear with each slide's number and title below the slide. Use the horizontal scroll bar to move through the slides in order. To work more quickly, click the Show Titles button in the dialog box to display a list of slide titles with a single preview pane.

Click the Show Slides button to return to the thumbnails view. Select and then insert the slide or slides you want (hold Shift or Ctrl to select multiple slides). When you insert a slide, the text and any objects (such as a picture or chart) on the slide are imported. The slide's design is *not* imported into the current presentation.

INSERTING SLIDES FROM OTHER PRESENTATIONS

1. Position the insertion point (in Outline view or Normal view) or slide selector (in Slide Sorter view) where you want to insert slides.

2. Chose Insert ➤ Slides from Files to open the Slide Finder.

3. Select the presentation that includes the slides you want to insert.

4. Click the Display button to view the slides.

5. Select the slide(s) you want to insert, and then click Insert to insert the slides in the current presentation. If you want to insert all the slides, click the Insert All button.

6. The Slide Finder remains open, so you can move to a different location in the active presentation and insert other slides.

7. When you are finished inserting, close the Slide Finder.

Using Word Outlines

You can import a Word outline (see Figure 7.14) to create a PowerPoint presentation. (For more information on Word outlines, see Skill 3.5.) The outline will be inserted into the current presentation, so you can use the outline as the total presentation, or add some content to a presentation you're already working on.

◊ **Building Sales Partnerships**
  ▫ *a presentation by the Sales and Marketing Staff*
◊ **Vision**
  ◊ *connect directly to clients:*
      ▫ Fax services
      ▫ EDI
◊ **Goal**
  ▫ *to create at least three new partnerships this fiscal year*
  ▫ *generate four new partnerships each of the next three years*
▫ **Resources Required**
▫ **Utilization of Existing Staff**

FIGURE 7.14: A Word outline

ADDING A WORD OUTLINE TO A PRESENTATION

1. Choose Insert ➤ Slides from Outline from the menu bar.
2. Select the Word document you want to insert.
3. Click Insert.

Hands On

1. Create a new presentation based on a design template.

   a) Apply a new design from an existing presentation.

   b) Apply a new design from the PowerPoint design templates.

   c) Insert a slide using the New Slide dialog box. Add text to the slide.

   d) Insert one or more slides from an existing presentation using the Slide Finder.

   e) If you do not have a Word outline, open Word and create a short outline. Insert the outline into the presentation.

7.3: Modifying Visual Elements

You can customize the visual elements of a presentation in several ways:

- By changing the color scheme
- By editing the Slide Master
- By adding footers
- By replacing or adding a background

Changing the Color Scheme

It's easiest to choose one of PowerPoint's design templates to establish the primary background for your presentation and then change the background or colors to meet your specific needs. Consider the purpose of your presentation when changing colors. For overheads, the lighter the better. Dark backgrounds work well for on-screen presentations, but if you need to show a presentation with room lights on, choose a light background and dark text. Choosing Format ➤ Slide Color Scheme opens the Color Scheme dialog box, shown in Figure 7.15. (You can't change the color scheme in a blank presentation; you must have already applied a design.)

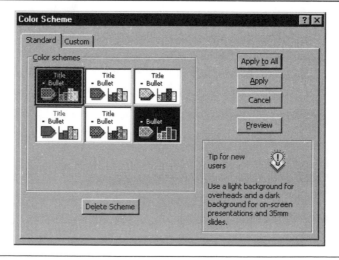

FIGURE 7.15: The Color Scheme dialog box

The dialog box has tabs for Standard and Custom color schemes. The Standard color schemes include the current color scheme, at least one alternate scheme, and one black-and-white choice. You can choose to apply a scheme to the current slide or to all the slides in the presentation. To see how a slide will look, click the Preview button. (You'll have to move the dialog box out of the way to see the impact on the slide.) When you're satisfied, click Apply to change the selected slide or slides or Apply to All to change every slide in the presentation.

If you don't like any of the Standard schemes, you can create your own. Select the scheme that's closest to what you want and click the Custom tab on the Color Scheme dialog box, shown in Figure 7.16. Select the color you want to change and click the Change Color button to open the Colors dialog box. Choose a color from the array of colors presented, or if you want to mix your own, click the Custom tab, and use the slider bar. If you wish, you can save the color scheme for future use with the current design by adding it to the schemes shown on the Standard tab (see Figure 7.15).

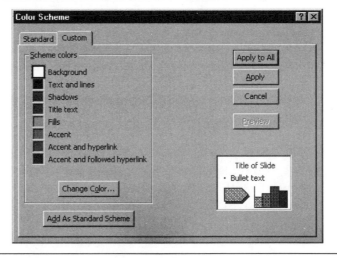

SKILL
7

FIGURE 7.16: Custom color schemes

APPLYING A COLOR SCHEME

1. Choose Format ➤ Slide Color Scheme to open the Color Scheme dialog box.

2. Click the color scheme you want to apply.

3. To create your own scheme, click the Custom tab to change specific colors in the color scheme. Click the color you want to change and click the Change Color button. Repeat this step for each color you want to change.

4. Choose Preview to see the changes before applying them. Click Apply or Apply to All to apply the scheme to the current slide or all slides in the presentation.

Modifying the Slide Master

Every design includes a *Slide Master* (see Figure 7.17) that identifies the position of the text and graphic objects, the style of the fonts, the footer elements, and the background for all slides. There are one or two Slide Masters for each presentation; some designs include separate slide and title Slide Masters. Any change that you make to the Master will be reflected in each slide that is based on the Master. For example, if you want a graphic object (a logo perhaps) to appear on every slide, you could attach it to the Master rather than inserting it on each slide. To change the title font for all slides, change it on the Master. To open the Master, either choose View ➤ Master ➤ Slide Master or hold the Shift key and click the Title Master View button. (The name of the Slide View button changes to Title Master View when you hold down the Shift key.)

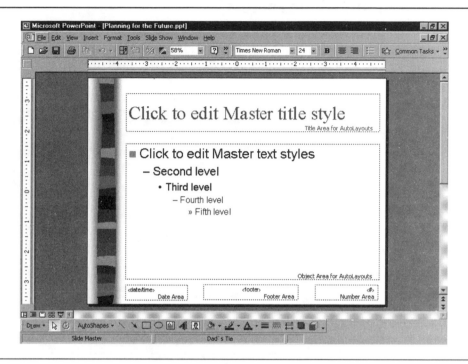

FIGURE 7.17: The Slide Master

EDITING A SLIDE MASTER

1. Choose View ➤ Master ➤ Slide Master or hold Shift and click the Title Master View button to open the Slide Master.

2. On the Master, click any text box to edit its contents. Use the buttons on the Formatting toolbar to format text. Select and move or delete placeholders, including graphic objects and text boxes.

Adding Slide Footers

The Slide Master includes a footer area. You can have a date, slide number, or other footer appear on every slide by changing it in the Master. Choose View ➤ Headers and Footers from the menu bar to open the dialog box shown in Figure 7.18.

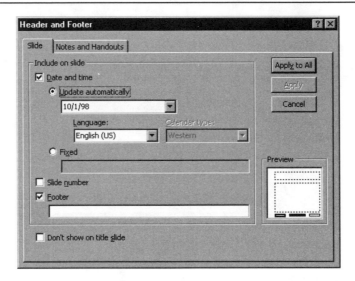

FIGURE 7.18: The Header and Footer dialog box

For Date and Time, choose Update Automatically or Fixed to add a changing or fixed date to each slide. Click the Slide Number text box to show the slide number. If you want footer text, click the Footer check box and type the footer in the text box.

SETTING SLIDE FOOTERS

1. Choose View ➢ Header and Footer to open the Header and Footer dialog box.
2. Turn on items you want displayed on all slides.
3. Turn on Don't Show on Title Slide if you don't want the footer to appear on the first slide in the presentation.
4. Choose Apply to apply to the active or selected slide, or choose Apply to All to apply to every slide in the presentation. (If you open the dialog box from the Slide Master, you can only choose Apply to All.)

Customizing the Background

When you choose to apply a design template, the template includes the color scheme and background color. But the background may have a shaded effect, a pattern, or a texture. A picture or a graphic object may also be part of the background. All these characteristics form the background of the slide. Any text or objects that you place on the slide are positioned on top of the background.

To change the background, choose Format ➢ Background to open the Background dialog box, shown in Figure 7.19. For individual slides, you can choose to Omit Background Graphics from Master. (This means that Master background graphics won't be applied on the selected slide.) By omitting background objects, your slide can retain the same basic appearance as the other slides, but won't detract from other graphics, such as charts, that you might add to the slide. If you omit background graphics, you also omit the footer.

SKILL
7

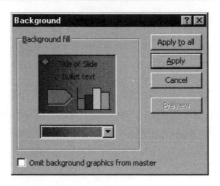

FIGURE 7.19: The Background dialog box

To make changes in the background fill, click the drop-down arrow in the Background Fill area of the dialog box to open a drop-down menu of fill choices.

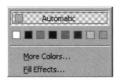

Choosing Automatic fills the background with the default fill color. Selecting a color from the eight color-scheme colors or choosing More Colors (which opens the Color Picker) changes the background fill color. Choosing Fill Effects opens the Fill Effects dialog box, shown in Figure 7.20.

In this dialog box, you can select from four types of fills: Gradient, Texture, Pattern, or Picture. On the Picture page, you use the Browse button to select a picture to apply to a background. PowerPoint supports many different graphic formats, from Windows MetaFiles to JPEGs. Whether you choose a picture or texture, pattern or gradient, it's a good idea to preview the fill before applying it.

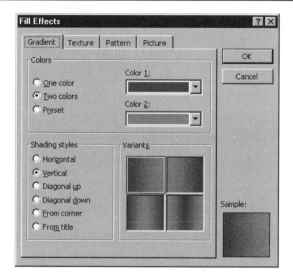

FIGURE 7.20: The Fill Effects dialog box

CUSTOMIZING BACKGROUND FILLS

1. Choose Format ➤ Background to open the Custom Background dialog box.

2. Click the Omit Background Graphics from Master check box to remove the background graphics from a particular slide or all the slides.

3. Click the drop-down arrow next to the blank text box to select the fill options that you want to change. Choose from shadowed, patterned, or textured fill, or choose a picture from the Clipart folder. To return to the original fill, choose Automatic from the drop-down list.

SKILL
7

Hands On

1. In an existing presentation:

    a) Change the color scheme.

    b) Create and apply a custom color scheme.

    c) Open the Slide Master. Change the font for the slide title.

    d) Add a footer that contains the current date and your name.

    e) Change the Background Fill for the Slide Master.

    f) Change the Fill for a single slide.

    g) Turn off objects from the Master on a single slide.

7.4: Formatting and Checking Text

The design templates that come with PowerPoint were created by professional graphic artists and, therefore, reflect the principles that are commonly applied to the choice of typeface, size, and attributes. You can, however, format text to suit yourself, using the techniques you use in any Windows application. And, as you would with anything you plan to distribute or present, you'll want to proof spelling, grammar, and style.

Formatting Text

When you format text on individual slides, the formatting takes precedence over formatting from the Slide Master. Even if you apply a new design, formatting applied to individual slides won't change, so you should make sure you are pleased with the design before formatting individual slides. You can apply standard text enhancements that you know from other Windows applications to your PowerPoint slides. Select the text to be formatted, and then change font typeface, size, and attributes using the Formatting toolbar or the Format menu.

Formatting always appears in Slide view. In Outline view and Normal view, you can decide whether to display formatting. The Show Formatting button on the Formatting toolbar toggles between displaying and hiding text formatting.

Two buttons that do not appear in other Office applications are the Increase Font Size and Decrease Font Size buttons. Each click changes the font size in standard increments. The increment increases as font size increases. For example, fonts between 12 and 48 points are changed in 2-point increments; 10 points and smaller change in 1-point increments.

Add a shadow to text by clicking the Text Shadow button; change the color of the text by clicking the Font Color button on the Drawing toolbar. When you select the desired text, and then click the down arrow to see the dialog box associated with this button, the colors from the current color scheme are displayed. Selected text can be left-, center-, or right-aligned or justified. Left, Center, and Right alignment are options on the Formatting toolbar. To justify selected text, choose Format ➤ Alignment ➤ Justify from the menu bar.

Replacing Fonts

You use the Replace Font dialog box to substitute one font for another, throughout the presentation. You might choose to replace fonts to change the look of a presentation, but there is a more pressing reason to use the dialog box. If you open a presentation on a computer that doesn't have the presentation's fonts installed, another font is automatically substituted—unless the fonts were embedded in the presentation. And the substitute font doesn't have to be good-looking; occasionally, it isn't even readable. Rather than changing various levels of the Master, you can have PowerPoint change each occurrence of the font.

SKILL
7

REPLACING FONTS IN A PRESENTATION

1. Select a text box that includes the font you want to replace.
2. Choose Format ➤ Replace Fonts to open the Replace Font dialog box.
3. Select a replacement font.
4. Click OK.

Adjusting Line Spacing

In PowerPoint 2000, you can add or subtract space between lines and before or after paragraphs in a text box, much as you add leading in desktop publishing. Rather than entering extra blank lines between points or subpoints, adjust the line spacing.

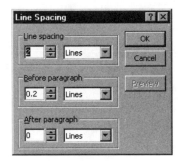

Adjusting Tabs and Indents

The indent distance when you press the Tab key is preset at one-half inch. You can see the default tab stops in Slide view on the ruler.

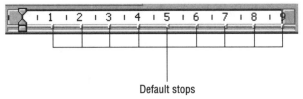

Default stops

CHANGING DEFAULT TABS

1. In Slide view, display the ruler (choose View ➢ Ruler).
2. Select the text that you want to change tabs for.
3. On the ruler, drag the first default tab stop to its new position. All other tab stops will adjust so that the distance between each tab stop is the same.

The distances between the left edge of a text box and each level of bulleted text are also preset. When a text box with levels of text is selected, the upper and lower indent markers show on the ruler. Each level of text has its own set of indent markers:

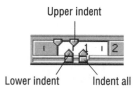

Upper indent

Lower indent   Indent all

CHANGING INDENTATION

1. In Slide view, select the text you want to set indents for.
2. If the ruler isn't displayed, turn it on (choose View ➤ Ruler).
3. Drag the upper indent marker to change the indent for the first line of a paragraph.
4. Drag the lower indent marker to set the indent for other lines in a paragraph.
5. To change the indent for an entire paragraph, drag the square box beneath the lower indent marker to move both the upper and lower markers at the same time.

SKILL
7

Checking Presentation Styles

PowerPoint automatically chceks your presentation for consistency, style, and punctuation. When it encounters a style violation, a light bulb appears on the slide or next to the Office Assistant. Click the light bulb to review the reason for the flag. Once you decide how you want to handle the style violation, you have to make the changes manually.

To specify options for style, choose Tools ➤ Options, and in the Options dialog box, select the Spelling and Style tab. Click the Style Options button to open the Style Options dialog box.

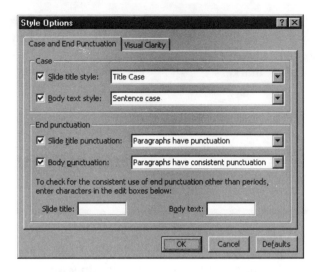

Hands On

1. In an existing presentation:

   a) Change the font and font color to emphasize one word on a slide.

   b) Add a shadow to the title for all slides in the Slide Master.

   c) Replace the body text font with another font.

2. In an existing presentation:

   a) Change the alignment for titles.

   b) Increase the spacing between the paragraphs in a bulleted list.

   c) Change the indentation in the list.

   d) Change the font and font size for several slides, and then review the Help information about the style violation.

7.5: Adding Objects

In PowerPoint, each item on a slide is an object, including text, clip art, a table, a chart, a sound, and a video clip. Objects can enhance and enliven your presentation. Remember, however, that slide real estate is limited; you don't want an overwhelming number of elements competing for audience attention.

Inserting Objects

If you want to insert an object, you'll find it easiest to begin with a slide layout that includes the object. Once you've selected the correct slide layout, just double-click on the object and you'll be taken to the appropriate application to either insert or create the indicated object.

Inserting Clip Art

If you want to use clip art with your presentation, choose Insert ➤ Picture ➤ Clip Art, click the Clip Art button, or select a slide layout with a clip art placeholder (see Figure 7.21) and double-click the placeholder.

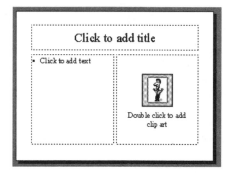

FIGURE 7.21: Slide layout with a clip art placeholder

The Insert ClipArt dialog box will open, as shown in Figure 7.22. The clip art is arranged in categories. Click a category, and then locate the thumbnail for the clip art you want to insert. Select the picture, then click Insert Clip from the pop-up menu. Figure 7.23 shows this menu and your other choices.

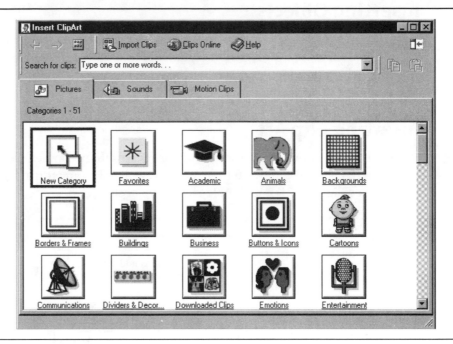

FIGURE 7.22: Inserting clip art

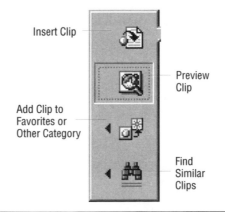

FIGURE 7.23: Pop-up menu

In the slide, click once on the object to select it. When an object is selected, you can drag it to another location on the slide or use the object's handles to resize the object.

ADDING CLIP ART TO A SLIDE

1. Choose Insert ➤ Picture ➤ Clip Art or double-click a clip art place-holder to open the Insert Clip Art dialog box.
2. Select the picture you want to insert and click Insert.

Recoloring a Clip Art Object

When you select a clip art object, the Picture toolbar automatically opens. General use of the Picture toolbar is discussed in Skill 11.2, but one toolbar button is available only in PowerPoint: the Recolor Picture button. Clicking the button opens the Recolor Picture dialog box, shown in Figure 7.24.

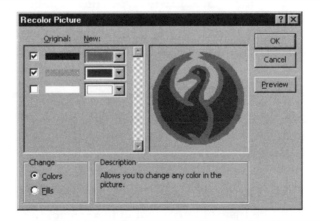

FIGURE 7.24: The Recolor Picture dialog box

In the lower left corner of the dialog box is a Change area. Choose Colors, which changes the colors of lines and fills, or Fills, which doesn't affect lines. To change a color, turn on the check box in front of the color you want to change, then select a new color from the corresponding New drop-down list. The sample will change as you recolor different colors and fills in the clip art.

RECOLORING CLIP ART

1. In the slide, select the clip art object.
2. Click the Recolor Picture button on the Picture toolbar.
3. Choose to change Colors or Fills.
4. Check and choose a new color for each color you want to change.
5. Click Preview to preview the changes in the slide; click OK to apply the changes.

Sound and Motion Clips

PowerPoint includes sounds and motion clips you can play during your slide shows. Some sounds, like the typewriter or laser sound, are included on the Animation Effects toolbar. Other sounds, music, and motion clips are in the Insert ClipArt dialog box. (To find out more about clip art and other objects created with WordArt and Draw, see Skill 11.)

INSERTING A SOUND OR VIDEO FILE

1. Open the slide you want to add an object to.
2. Choose Insert ➤ Movies and Sounds ➤ Sound from Gallery or Movies from Gallery.
3. In the Insert ClipArt dialog box, select the sound or motion clip you want to add. Click Play Clip to preview the selected sound or motion clip.
4. Click Insert Clip to insert the object and place a sound icon or motion clip object on the slide.
5. To play the sound or motion clip, double-click on the icon or object.

TIP TIP TIP TIP TIP TIP TIP TIP TIP TIP TIP TIP TIP TIP TIP TIP TIP TIP TIP TIP TIP TIP TIP
To insert a sound or motion clip that isn't in the Insert ClipArt dialog box, choose Insert ➤ Movies and Sounds, and then select Movie from File or Sound from File. Locate, select, and open the file.

Inserting Charts

In Office 2000, you can create charts in two programs: Excel and Microsoft Graph. If you already have a chart in Excel, you can easily copy it and then embed or link it in a PowerPoint slide or another document using Paste Special. However, if you don't have access to Excel, you can use Microsoft Graph to create charts quickly and easily.

Creating Charts

In PowerPoint, you can open Microsoft Graph in three ways:

- Choose Insert ➤ Chart.

- Click the Insert Chart button on the Standard toolbar.

- Double-click a chart placeholder in an AutoLayout.

NOTE NOTE NOTE NOTE NOTE NOTE NOTE NOTE NOTE NOTE NOTE NOTE NOTE NOTE NOTE NOTE
Microsoft Graph may not be installed by default when you install Office. To install it, choose Start ➤ Settings ➤ Control Panel ➤ Install/Remove Programs. You'll need your Office CD.

**SKILL
7**

In Figure 7.25, you can see that Graph contains two windows:

- A datasheet that includes sample data

- A chart

Replace the labels (text) in the top row and left column with your labels and the values in the remaining cells with your numbers, and you have a basic bar chart. You can close the datasheet at any point to place the chart in your document.

You can resize and reposition the chart object as you would any other object. The chart must be selected to resize it; a selected chart object has hollow handles. Double-clicking the chart opens the chart object so you can edit the individual objects inside the chart object; when you can edit the chart, the object handles are solid, and you cannot move the chart object. To select the entire object again, click in the document to close the object, and then click once on the chart object to select it for moving or sizing.

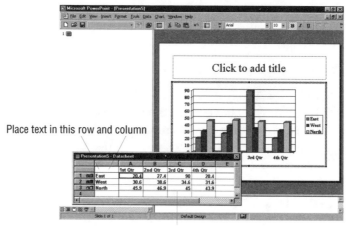

Place text in this row and column

Place numbers here

FIGURE 7.25: Inserting a Microsoft Graph chart object

INSERTING A MICROSOFT CHART

1. In PowerPoint, click the Insert Chart button on the Standard toolbar, choose Insert ➢ Chart, or double-click the chart placeholder on an AutoLayout. In Word, choose Insert ➢ Picture ➢ Chart.

2. Edit the datasheet to include your labels in the first row and column and your values (numbers) in cells in numbered rows and lettered columns.

3. To change the chart type, click the drop-down arrow on the Chart Type button on the Standard toolbar. Choose a chart type from the list.

4. Close the datasheet to embed the chart in your document. Select, then resize or move the chart as necessary.

Using Existing Data

If you already have data, don't re-enter it—you can import or copy data into Microsoft Graph. To import data from an existing file, choose Edit ➤ Import File on the Graph menu or click the Import File button to open the Import File dialog box. Graph can convert data from Excel, text files, SYLK files, Lotus 1-2-3, and CSV (comma-separated files) that can be exported from most spreadsheet and database programs. Choose an appropriate File Type, and then select the file and click Import to place the data in Graph.

If you import data from a spreadsheet, the Import Data Options dialog box will open so that you can select a worksheet or named range to import. Choose Over-write Existing Cells to replace the data in the Graph datasheet. Turn this option off, and the imported data will be appended at the end of the current data in the datasheet.

IMPORTING DATA FOR A CHART

1. In Microsoft Graph, choose Edit ➤ Import File on the menu bar or click the Import File button on the toolbar.

2. Select a file type, then select the file that contains the data in the Import Data dialog box. Click Open.

3. If the file is a spreadsheet, select the worksheet or named range that contains the data you want to import in the Import Data Options dialog box. Turn the Overwrite Existing Cells option on or off, and click OK.

Copying or Linking Existing Data Use Copy and Paste or Paste Special to use existing data from Word or Excel to create a chart. Select and copy the data in its source application. In Graph, select the first cell where you want the data to appear. Choose the upper left cell to overwrite the existing data, or select the left cell in an empty row to append the data. Paste the data, or choose Edit ➤ Paste Link from the Graph menu to link the chart to the table or worksheet.

Formatting a Chart

To change from a bar chart to a pie chart, click the Chart Type button on the toolbar. You'll see 18 chart types to choose from.

While you're formatting the chart, you can hide the datasheet display by clicking the View Datasheet button. Use the By Rows and By Columns buttons to change the basic layout of the chart. With By Rows, each row is a data series, and the column labels (in the first row) are the labels on the X-axis of the chart. By Columns uses each column as a data series; row labels are on the X-axis.

With the chart selected, right-click and choose Chart Options to open the Chart Options dialog box. Use the dialog box options to add titles, scale axes, display gridlines, show and position a legend, display data labels, and include the datasheet as part of the chart object.

FORMATTING A MICROSOFT GRAPH CHART

1. Double-click the chart object to open it for editing. The chart object handles will be solid.
2. Click the Chart Types button drop-down list and select a chart type.
3. Click the By Rows or By Columns button on the toolbar to change the representation of data in the chart.
4. Right-click and choose Chart Options to open the Chart Options dialog box. Enter a chart title, and set options for legends, gridlines, and other general chart features.

To format an individual chart object (for example, the columns, all the data in a row or column, the chart background, or the legend), select the object with the mouse in the chart, or choose the object from the Chart Objects drop-down list on the toolbar. Then double-click the selected object, right-click and choose Format [Object Name], or click the Format Object button on the toolbar to open the Format Object dialog box. The Format Data Series dialog box is shown in Figure 7.26.

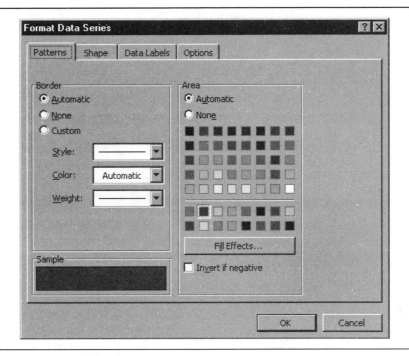

FIGURE 7.26: The Format Data Series dialog box

Formatting Individual Chart Objects

1. Select the object in the chart or in the Chart Objects drop-down list on the toolbar.

2. Right-click and choose Format [Object Name], or click the Format Object button on the toolbar, to open the appropriate Format dialog box.

3. Set options on each dialog box page, then click OK.

Inserting Tables from Word

If you've already created a table in Word that you want to use in a presentation, you can copy it in Word and paste it onto a slide. A table any bigger than three columns by four rows will be too large to show up clearly on a slide, so keep it simple. If you want to create a Word table in the current presentation, choose Insert ➤ Picture ➤ Microsoft Word Table or choose a Table AutoLayout from the New Slide dialog box and double-click the Table icon on the slide. You will be asked how many columns and rows you want:

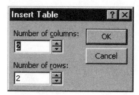

After you select the appropriate number of rows and columns and click OK, PowerPoint displays the Tables.

Enter text for the table as you would in Word. (For a review of Word's table features, see Skill 3.3.)

After you enter the text for the table, click outside the table. You can resize the table using the handles or reposition the table by dragging it to a new location. If you need to edit the table, double-click the table object.

INSERTING A WORD TABLE

1. Select a Slide AutoLayout that includes a table and double-click the table placeholder, or choose Insert ➤ Picture ➤ Word Table.

2. Indicate the number of columns and rows that you want and click OK.

continued ▶

3. Enter the text for the table using Word's table features to format or enhance the table.
4. Click outside the table to close the table object.

Hands On

1. In a new or existing presentation:
   a) Insert clip art on a single slide.
   b) Insert clip art on the Slide Master. Resize the clip art to the size of a small logo and place it in a corner of the slide.
   c) Recolor the clip art on the single slide.
   d) Insert a table from Word.

2. In a new or existing presentation:
   a) Insert a sound file.
   b) Test the playback in Slide Show view.

3. Insert a Microsoft Graph chart object.
   a) Use Import File to get data from an existing Excel worksheet.
   b) Format individual chart elements using the Format Object dialog box.

SKILL
7

7.6: Applying Transitions, Animation Effects, and Linking

An electronic presentation, or Slide Show, is displayed on a computer screen or projected with an LCD projector. Since slides are "changed" by the computer rather than by hand, you can add computerized special effects to a slide show that aren't possible when you use overheads for a presentation. A *transition* is a special effect added to the slide's initial appearance on screen. The slide can appear from the right, dissolve in gradually, or fade through the background of the previous slide.

Some of the design templates also include animated features: for example, one of the background objects may streak into place.

Individual slides can include *animation*—different steps used to construct the slide, one placeholder at a time. For example, the slide can appear with a title only, and bulleted points can be added. You add transitions in Slide Sorter view using the tools on the Slide Sorter toolbar, shown below. While you can add preset text animation in the Slide Sorter, you can't animate other objects, so you'll generally want to work with animation in Slide view.

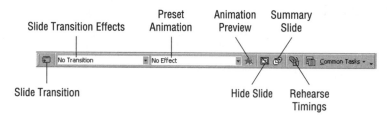

Modifying and Adding Transitions

If a presentation doesn't have transitions, each slide simply appears in place of the previous slide—very vanilla. Most of the PowerPoint design templates include transitions, so there is more pizzazz. To change or add transitions, select the slide(s), then choose a transition from the Slide Transition Effects drop-down list.

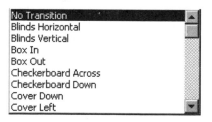

Many of the transitions listed differ only in direction; for example, Cover Up, Cover Down, and Cover Up-Left. When you select a new transition from the list, PowerPoint provides a preview of the transition using the selected slide. (Look fast—it doesn't take long.)

A *transition icon* appears below the lower left corner of a slide with an assigned transition. Clicking this icon shows the transition again in the slide miniature. Take some time to browse the various types of transitions.

ADDING OR CHANGING TRANSITIONS

1.   In Slide Sorter view, select the slide(s) to transition.

2.   Choose a transition from the Slide Transition Effects drop-down list.

Setting Transition Speed and Sound

Each type of transition has a default speed. The default for Wipes, for example, is Fast. You can change the speed for transitions, choose a different transition, or add sound effects to accompany a transition in the Slide Transition dialog box.

 Make sure the slides you want to affect are selected; then click the Slide Transition button on the Slide Sorter toolbar to open the Slide Transition dialog box, shown in Figure 7.27.

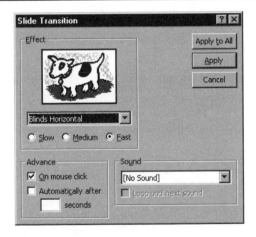

FIGURE 7.27: The Slide Transition dialog box

From the Effect drop-down list, select a transition, and then choose one of the Speed options. In the Advance section, enter timings for automatic slide advances (see Skill 7.8). There is also a drop-down list of Sounds you can add to a transition. If you assign a sound, you can choose to have the sound loop until another

**SKILL
7**

sound is assigned. The last choice on the list, Other Sound, opens a dialog box so that you can select a sound file. PowerPoint uses wave sounds, files with a .wav extension. You'll find some wave files in the Media folder in the Windows folder, but you can purchase CDs of wave files at many computer stores. When you've finished setting options, choose Apply or Apply to All. You can preview effects, including sound, by clicking the transition icon in the Slide Sorter.

CHANGING TRANSITION SPEED AND SOUND

1. In Slide Sorter view, select the slide(s) you want to change.
2. Click the Slide Transition button on the Slide Sorter toolbar to open the Slide Transition dialog box.
3. Choose settings for Effect and Speed (and Sound if you wish).
4. Click Apply or Apply to All.

Adding Animation

Transition effects are used *between* slides; animation effects occur *within* a slide. Each title, bulleted point, or other object on a slide can be added to the slide separately. This allows you to discuss individual points or add illustrations in a particular order during the presentation. In Slide Sorter view, you can apply a group of preset animation settings. Select the slide or slides, and then choose a type of animation from the Preset Animation drop-down menu:

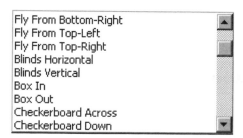

The selected animation will be applied to all text (other than the title) in the slide. Preview the animation by clicking the animation icon in Slide Sorter. If you animate body text, moving to Slide Show view will open the slide with the title and any background objects and graphics. Click anywhere, and the first bulleted point will animate. Click again for each point.

Another group of animation effects are available from the context menu. Right-click on a selected slide in the Slide Sorter, and choose one of the Preset Animations, which include sound:

> ☑ Off
> ──────────
> Drive-In
> Flying
> Camera
> Flash Once
> Laser Text
> Typewriter
> Reverse Order
> Drop-In
> Fly From Top
> Animate Chart
> Wipe Right
> Dissolve
> Split Vertical Out
> Appear

ADDING PRESET ANIMATION TO SLIDES

1. In Slide Sorter view, select the slide you want to animate.
2. Choose a preset animation from the Preset Animation drop-down menu on the Slide Sorter toolbar.

–OR–

2. Right-click on a selected slide and choose a Preset Animation from the shortcut menu.

SKILL
7

Adding Custom Animation

The Custom Animation tools take sound and motion to new heights in electronic presentations. Use the custom animation tools to add sound and motion to individual graphic elements on a slide.

To open the Animation Effects toolbar, switch to Slide view and click the Animation Effects button on the Formatting toolbar.

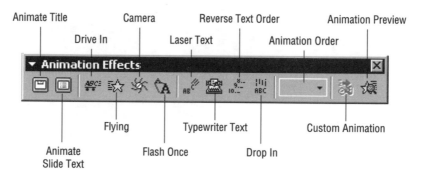

TIP TIP TIP TIP TIP TIP TIP TIP TIP TIP TIP TIP TIP TIP TIP TIP TIP TIP TIP TIP TIP TIP TIP TIP TIP TIP

To move quickly to Slide view, double-click on the slide you want to animate.

To have the slide title drop in from the top, click the Animate Title button. Your slide opens in Animation Preview, and you see the effect of the animation option you selected.

The other Animation Effects buttons are used for specific graphic elements, including text boxes and objects. Select the object you want to animate, then click one of the eight Animation Effects buttons on the Animation Effects toolbar. After you click an effect button, the object will be added to the slide's animation list. When the object is selected, its animation order number appears in the Animation Order drop-down list.

Click the Custom Animation button to open the Custom Animation dialog box, shown in Figure 7.28. Click the Preview button to preview the current animations in order. Select the Order & Timing tab, select an animation in the Animation Order list, and use the Move Up and Move Down arrows to rearrange the order. On the Effects tab, shown in Figure 7.29, assign an animation and, if you wish, a sound. The After Animation drop-down allows you to change the color of animated text as the next animation occurs. You can use this in multi-point slides with rather dramatic effect; for example, you can have each point animate as white text, then change to gray when the next point enters, drawing the viewer's attention immediately to the new point. In the Introduce Text drop-down, you can choose to animate a text box by specific levels or all at once.

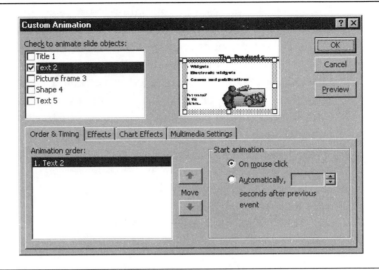

FIGURE 7.28: The Order & Timing tab of the Custom Animation dialog box

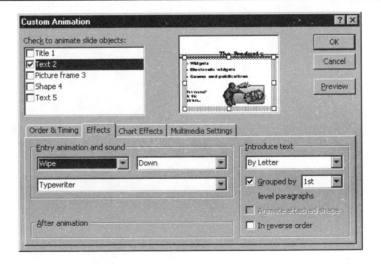

FIGURE 7.29: The Effects page of the Custom Animation dialog box

SKILL
7

The Check to Animate Slide Objects list shows all the objects on a slide. Those that are checked are animated. The Start Animation options, however, refer to the selected object either in the list or in the Animation Order list on the Order & Timing tab. If you want the animation to proceed without mouse clicks, choose the Automatically option and set a number of seconds that should pass between the end of the previous animation and the beginning of the selected animation.

Chart Effects are disabled unless the selected object is a chart. You can introduce an entire chart at one time, or you can have chart elements appear by category, by data series, or individually in the Introduce Chart Elements drop-down list. Chart Effects let you provide dramatic illustrations of numeric data in your presentation.

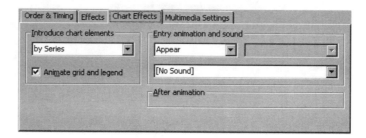

The Multimedia Settings are enabled when a sound or video object is selected. If you choose to assign the media an Animation Order, you don't have to click on the object to play it.

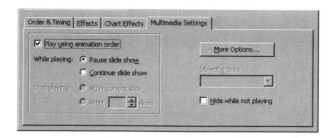

ADDING CUSTOM ANIMATION EFFECTS

1. View the slide you want to animate in Slide view.

2. Click the Animation Effects button on the Formatting toolbar to open the Animation Effects toolbar.

3. Select preset effects from the toolbar.

4. Click the Custom Animation button to open the Custom Animation dialog box.

5. In the Order & Timing tab, use the Move Up and Move Down buttons to change the Animation Order.

6. Select any item in the Animation Order list, and then use the Effects tab to set custom options.

7. Set animation options for charts on the Chart Effects page.

8. Change media playback settings on the Multimedia Settings tab.

9. Click the Preview button to preview changes.

10. Click OK to apply the custom animation changes.

Hiding Slides

Many presentations contain "emergency slides" that are only displayed if certain questions or topics arise during the presentation. Creating, then hiding, a slide gives you some leeway: if the question isn't asked, you don't have to show the slide. If, on the other hand, a member of the audience asks how you plan to raise the $10 million you are talking about spending, you can whip out the hidden slide.

In Slide Sorter view, select the slide you want to hide, and then click the Hide Slide button on the toolbar.

A null symbol appears over the slide's number. To unhide the slide, click the Hide Slide button again.

During the presentation, you can right-click on any slide, and choose Go ➤ By Title. Then from the shortcut menu, click the slide number that is in parentheses (parentheses around a slide number indicate that it is hidden). However, the shortcut menu is very intrusive and lets everyone know you had a hidden slide (so they may begin to wonder what *else* you're not sharing). Hyperlinks provide a slicker way to show hidden slides.

Adding Links to Other Slides

Hyperlinks, like those used to navigate a Web site, can also be used in PowerPoint presentations. Clicking a hyperlink moves the user from the current slide to another slide, another presentation, or a site on the Internet. To create a hyperlink, select the text that will be used as a hyperlink. Normally, this text will tell the user where they're going to end up: `Click Here to Exit the Presentation` or `Click to View More Options`. You don't want to have `Click Here for Hidden Slide`, so select some existing text that forms a logical jumping-off point. With the text selected, right-click and choose Action Settings from the shortcut menu or choose Slide Show ➤ Action Settings from the menu bar to open the dialog box shown in Figure 7.30.

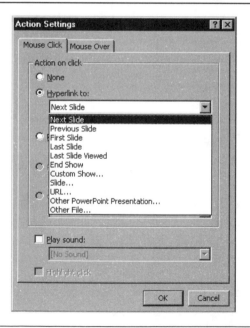

FIGURE 7.30: The Action Settings dialog box

You can activate a hyperlink in two ways: by clicking on it or by moving the mouse over it. Both pages of this dialog box are identical—choose a page based on which mouse action you want to trigger the hyperlink. Click the Hyperlink option, and select the slide you want to link to. Choosing Next Slide shows the next slide, even if it's hidden. To choose a specific slide, choose Slide from the list to open the Hyperlink to Slide dialog box.

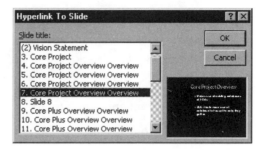

Choose a slide from the list, and then click OK. Click OK in the Action Settings dialog box to create the hyperlink.

CREATING A HYPERLINK TO ANOTHER SLIDE

1. In Slide view, select the text that will be used as a hyperlink.
2. Choose Slide Show ➤ Action Settings or right-click and choose Action Settings from the shortcut menu.
3. Choose the Hyperlink option. From the Hyperlink drop-down list, select the slide you want to link to. For a specific slide, choose Slide... to open the Hyperlink to Slide dialog box. Select a slide, and then click OK.
4. Choose OK to create the hyperlink.
5. Test the hyperlink in Slide Show view.

SKILL 7

When text is turned into a hypertext link, its formatting is changed. The text will be underlined, and a contrasting font color will be applied. You won't be able to change the color or remove the underlining, but you can apply the same color and underline to surrounding text to make the hyperlink blend in. (Of course, you only want to do this if you're running the presentation. Other users won't know it's a hyperlink if it doesn't stand out.)

Hands On

1. In an existing presentation, select one or more slides and:

   a) Apply a new transition.

   b) Change the speed of the transition.

   c) Apply preset animations from the Animation Effects toolbar and the shortcut menu.

2. On a slide in an existing presentation:

   a) Apply custom animation to text.

   b) Apply custom animation to an object.

   c) Change and preview the animation order.

   d) Have one animation follow another without a mouse click.

3. In an existing presentation:

   a) Hide one or more slides.

   b) In Slide Show view, display a hidden slide with the shortcut menu.

   c) Add a hyperlink to the hidden slide.

   d) In Slide Show view, display the hidden slide by using the hyperlink.

   e) Create a hyperlink to move to the last slide viewed, the previous slide, and to exit the presentation.

   f) Test the hyperlinks.

7.7: Preparing Handouts

It's often helpful to give your audience paper copies of your slides so that they have something to refer to later. (They might also choose to add their own notes to these handouts.)

Preparing Handouts and Notes

Handouts are pictures of the slides in a presentation, arranged with either two, three, or six slides to a page to give participants a copy of each slide.

The Handout Master

You use the Handout Master to view the handout layouts. Choose View ➢ Master ➢ Handout Master or press Shift and click the Outline View button to open the Master, shown in Figure 7.31.

The dotted lines show where slides will appear in the layout selected in the Handout Master toolbar. The Handout Master contains areas for the footer, header, and page number. You can click in any of the areas to edit the contents. It's easiest to edit the Master if you change the Zoom ratio to 75% or 100% so you can see the text. Or you can open the Header and Footer dialog box (choose View ➢ Header and Footer) and change settings for any of the areas in the Header and Footer dialog box. The header, footer, number, and date information you enter in the dialog box will replace the appropriate placeholders in the Handout Master when you print handouts.

SKILL
7

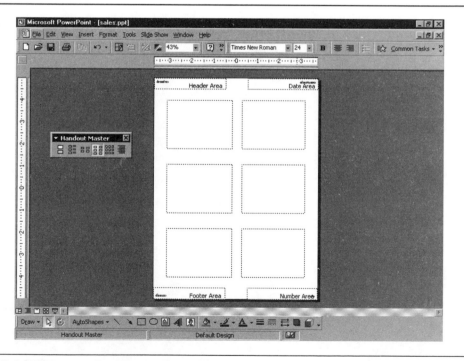

FIGURE 7.31: The Handout Master

Printing in PowerPoint

Clicking the Print button on the Standard toolbar prints the entire presentation in the default setting—usually Slide view. If the slides have a background, this can take up to an hour on an impact printer. In PowerPoint, it's always best to choose File ➤ Print to open the Print dialog box shown in Figure 7.32 so you can select whether to print slides, handouts, notes, or an outline.

The default print setting is to print all slides. If you just want to print some slides, enter the numbers of the slides in the Slides text box. Choose what you want to print (slides, handouts, an outline, notes pages) in the Print What drop-down. If you are printing a color presentation on a noncolor printer, click the Grayscale or Black and White control to speed up the printing process. Click the Frame Slides check box to print a simple box around each slide: a good idea if the slides themselves don't include a border. Then click the OK button to print.

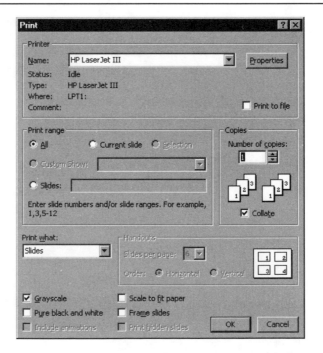

FIGURE 7.32: The Print dialog box

PRINTING IN POWERPOINT

1. Choose File ➤ Print to open the Print dialog box.
2. In the Print Range area, choose the slides to be printed.
3. In the Print What drop-down list, select whether to print slides, handouts, notes pages, or an outline.
4. Set other print options.
5. Click Print.

Creating Handouts in Word

You can use the power of Office 2000 integration to create handouts and reports for a PowerPoint presentation in Word. Write-Up transfers the text and/or slides from the current presentation to a Word document, which you can then edit, format, and print. Choose File ➤ Send To ➤ Microsoft Word to open the Write-Up dialog box:

Select how you want the presentation to appear: in one of the four different handout-style layouts or as an outline. Choose whether you want to paste a copy from your presentation or link the Word document to the presentation. If you choose Paste Link, changes to the presentation will be updated in the Word document; however, you'll lose some of the editing flexibility in Word. (See Skill 11 for more on linking.)

When you have selected Page Layout and Paste options, click OK. PowerPoint will launch Word and export your outline or slides. Edit and print the document as you would a Word document. If you sent slides (instead of an outline), don't worry if it takes a few minutes. Each slide is exported as a graphic object, which takes some time.

TIP TIP TIP TIP TIP TIP TIP TIP TIP TIP TIP TIP TIP TIP TIP TIP TIP TIP TIP TIP TIP TIP TIP TIP TIP

If you're only transferring an outline, click the Grayscale Preview button on the Standard toolbar before opening the Write-Up dialog box for easier formatting in Word.

CREATING POWERPOINT HANDOUTS IN WORD

1. If you intend to "write up" the outline, click the Grayscale Preview button on the Standard toolbar.
2. Choose File ➢ Send To ➢ Microsoft Word to open the Write-Up dialog box.
3. Choose a page layout from the Write-Up dialog box.
4. Select Paste Link or Paste.
5. Click OK to launch Word and create the Write-Up document.

Preparing 35mm Slides and Overhead Transparencies

If you have a desktop slide printer, you can print your slides as 35mm slides for use in a traditional slide projector. Even if you don't, you can still convert the

PowerPoint slides to 35mm. Genigraphics and other service bureaus can take your presentation (or selected slides from it) and convert it to 35mm. To send files to Genigraphics, you use the Genigraphics Wizard. Choose File ➤ Send To ➤ Genigraphics, and the Wizard will walk you through packaging the slides. To print black-and-white or color transparencies, simply insert transparency film in your printer, and then print the slides (without animations) using the Print dialog box.

Hands On

1. In an existing presentation:

   a) Add a header and footer for handouts.

   b) Preview the layouts in the Handout Master.

   c) Print handouts with headers and footers.

2. In an existing presentation with notes:

   a) Export the presentation's outline to Word.

   b) Format the outline in Word to create audience handouts.

   c) Export the slides with notes.

   d) Print the outline and handouts in Word.

7.8: Taking the Show on the Road

You now have the content, design, formatting, and special effects in place for your presentation. But you're not quite ready for prime time. In this section, we'll look at the remaining tasks that you need to take care of before the curtain goes up.

Setting Slide Timings

Once you have added transitions and animation, you are ready to run through your slides in preparation for the actual presentation. Rehearsal is vital—you'd rather discover problems in private than have them projected to a large audience.

Automated vs. Manual Advance

You can advance an electronic presentation in two ways. If the presentation is designed to run "on its own"—for example, in a booth at a trade show—you'll want to advance slides automatically. If your finished presentation will be used to illustrate a verbal presentation, or posted on an intranet, you will usually prefer to advance slides manually. If you use manual advance, your presentation is essentially completed. You'll need to rehearse the presentation a few times, making sure that you know how many times to click on each slide to display all the animations.

Setting Automatic Timings

If you want to use automatic advance, a bit more work is required. You can set slide timings in two ways: through rehearsal, or manually in the Slide Transition dialog box. (You can only enter animation timings by rehearsal.) It's easier to create timings through rehearsal and then alter individual advances manually. Before setting timings, run through the entire slide show two or three times. Make sure that your audience will have time to read the title, read each point, and see how a graphic illustrates the points. It helps to read the contents of each slide out loud, slowly, while rehearsing and setting the timings.

 When you are ready to record timings, click the Rehearse Timings button on the Slide Sorter toolbar. The first slide will appear, and the Rehearsal dialog box will open.

In the dialog box are two timers. The timer on the right shows the total time for the presentation. The left timer shows the elapsed time for the current slide. The Rehearsal dialog box also contains three buttons: Next, Pause, and Repeat. Click the Next button to move to the next slide or animation. If you are interrupted in the middle of rehearsal, click the Pause button; then click Pause again to resume. If you make a mistake while rehearsing a slide, click Repeat to set new timings for the current slide. If you don't catch a mistake before a slide has been advanced, you can either finish and then edit the slide time manually, or close the dialog box and begin again.

When you complete the entire rehearsal for a presentation, you'll be prompted to save the timings. Choosing Yes assigns the timings to the slide transitions and animations. In Slide Sorter view, the timing will appear below the slide. To edit an individual transition time, select the slide, then click the Slide Transition button on the Slide Sorter toolbar. The rehearsed time, which you can edit, will be displayed in the dialog box.

REHEARSING SLIDE TIMINGS

1. In Slide Sorter view, click the Rehearse Timings button.
2. Click the Next button in the Rehearse Timings dialog box to advance each transition or animation. Click the Pause button to Pause rehearsal. Click the Repeat button to try new timings for the current slide.
3. At the end of the rehearsal, choose Yes to record the timings or No to discard them.

Incorporating Feedback

Before showing the presentation, it's a good idea to get some feedback from others. PowerPoint lets reviewers add comments to slides that you display or hide, allowing you to keep the comments with the presentation. Comments do not appear in Slide Show view.

To add a comment, in Slide view, choose Insert ➢ Comment from the menu bar. The Review toolbar will appear. Begin typing, and the comment, including your name, appears on the slide. Use the comment's handles to move or resize the comment. Press Delete to delete the selected comment.

To insert a new comment, click the Insert Comment button on the Reviewing toolbar.

The Show/Hide Comments button displays or hides all comments in the presentation.

INSERTING A COMMENT

1. In Slide view, choose Insert ➢ Comment from the menu bar.
2. Begin typing the comment.
3. Use the handles to move or resize the comment.
4. Click the Insert Comment button on the Reviewing toolbar to insert another comment.

Another way to get feedback about your presentation is to use the Online Collaboration feature. To use this feature, you must be connected to a local area network or an intranet, and all participants must have NetMeeting installed and running on their computers. Using NetMeeting, you can share PowerPoint with others who can then edit your presentation.

COLLABORATING ONLINE

1. Choose Tools ➤ Online Collaboration ➤ Schedule Meeting to open Microsoft Outlook's Appointment form. Complete the form and send it to those you want to invite to the meeting. (See Skill 9 for information on how to do this.)

2. When the time for the online meeting arrives, choose Tools ➤ Online Collaboration ➤ Meet Now to open the Place a Call dialog box.

3. Enter a name or select it from a list. If necessary, click the Advanced button and type the computer name or network address of the person with whom you want to meet.

4. Click the Call button to place the call.

Setting Up the Slide Show

You've designed a good presentation, and the reviewers are raving. Before you present the slide show, choose Slide Show ➤ Set Up Show or hold Shift and click the Slide Show button to open the Set Up Show dialog box, shown in Figure 7.33. In the Show Type area, select a presentation method. In the Advance Slides area, choose Manually or Using Timing, If Present. To show the presentation continuously, choose Using Timings and click the Loop Continuously Until 'Esc' check box. In the Slides area, you can choose to show the entire presentation or part of the slides.

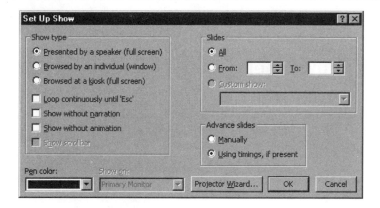

FIGURE 7.33: The Set Up Show dialog box

During the presentation, you can use the mouse pointer to draw on the slides to emphasize a point (see "Drawing on Slides" later in this Skill). You have a choice of colors for the pen. Choose a color that will contrast with both the background and text colors used in the slides.

SETTING UP A SLIDE SHOW

1. Hold Shift and click the Slide Show button to open the Set Up Show dialog box.
2. Select a presentation method.
3. Select an Advance method and Pen Color.
4. If you want the slide show to run continuously, turn on the Loop Continuously check box.
5. Click OK to save the settings.

The slide show settings are saved with the presentation. Clicking the Slide Show View button runs the slide show with the settings in the Set Up Show dialog box.

When you click on the final slide in a Slide Show, you return to the PowerPoint window. To end on a blank slide, choose Tools ➤ Options to open the Options dialog box. Click the View tab, and then click on End with Black Slide.

It's Showtime!

To start the slide show, click the Slide Show view button. When the show begins, a shortcut menu button appears in the lower left or lower right corner of the slide. Clicking the button opens a shortcut menu.

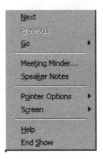

You can choose Previous or Next (or use Page Up and Page Down on the keyboard) to move to the previous or next slide. To move to a specific slide, choose Go ➤ Slide Navigator to open the Slide Navigator dialog box. Select a slide to move to, and click Go To.

Generating Meeting Notes

During the presentation, you can enter minutes or action items in the Meeting Minder. Right-click a slide, and choose Meeting Minder from the shortcut menu to open the Meeting Minder dialog box:

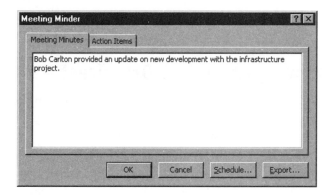

In the Action Items page, enter the "to do" list generated during the meeting, including due dates and the person responsible for the item. If the date or responsible person changes, or if the item is eliminated in later discussion, select the item from the list and edit or delete it.

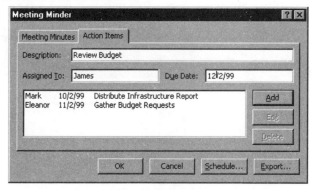

When the presentation is finished, click the Export button to export the minutes to Word, and the action items to Word and/or Outlook.

Drawing on Slides

During the Slide Show, you can use the Pen tool to draw on a slide, underlining or circling an object or text to make a point. Hold Ctrl and press P, or choose Pen from the shortcut menu, and the mouse pointer becomes a pen. Drag to draw on the current slide. Right-click, choose Pointer Options, and choose Arrow, or hold Ctrl and press A on the keyboard to turn the pen off. The drawing isn't saved, so no damage is done to the slide.

Presenting an Online Broadcast

With Online Broadcast, you can show a presentation over a network or the Internet. Members of the audience view the presentation on their computers. One caveat: you must be connected to the Internet through an ISP or connected to a TCP/IP network to use Online Broadcast. If you are not, the option will be disabled on the Tools menu. In addition, each viewer must have a Web browser.

Setting Up and Scheduling a Broadcast

To get started, choose Slide Show ➢ Online Broadcast ➢ Set Up and Schedule to open the Broadcast Schedule dialog box. Click the Set Up and Schedule a New Broadcast option, and then click OK to open the Schedule a New Broadcast dialog box:

Click the Description tab, enter a title for your presentation in the Title text box, and enter a description and contact information. This information will appear in your *Lobby Page*. The Lobby Page is the screen your viewers will see when they join the broadcast. In addition to displaying the information you enter on the Description page, the Lobby Page notifies viewers about how much time is left before the broadcast begins. If the broadcast is delayed, the host of the presentation can display a message about the delay and indicate when the slide show will start. To see how your Lobby Page will be displayed in the browser, click the Preview Lobby Page button.

Select the Broadcast Settings tab. (Your Webmaster or system administrator may have already set these options, or you may need to contact this person about how you set these options.)

Click the Server Options button to open the Server Options dialog box. Enter the pathname of a folder on your network server. When you start your presentation, PowerPoint puts the broadcast-formatted presentation at that location. Click OK.

When all your options are set, click the Schedule Broadcast button to open your e-mail program. Select recipients and compose your message. The URL of the broadcast will automatically be embedded in your message.

Starting and Viewing a Presentation

To start your presentation, open it and choose Slide Show ➤ Online Broadcast ➤ Begin Broadcast.

To view a presentation, open the mail message that notified you of the broadcast, and click the URL. The broadcast will begin automatically. If it is delayed, you can minimize the Lobby Page and continue working at your computer.

PRESENTING AN ONLINE BROADCAST

1. Choose Slide ➤ Online Broadcast ➤ Set Up and Schedule to open the Broadcast Schedule dialog box.

2. Click the Set Up and Schedule a New Broadcast option, and then click OK to open the Schedule a New Broadcast dialog box.

3. Click the Description tab, enter a title for your presentation in the Title text box, and enter a description and contact information.

continued ▶

4. Click the Broadcast Setting tab, and then click the Server Options button to open the Server Options dialog box.

5. Enter the pathname of a folder on your network server, and click OK.

6. Click the Schedule Broadcast button to open your e-mail program.

7. Select recipients, compose your message, and send it.

8. Open your presentation, and then choose Slide Show ➢ Online Broadcast ➢ Begin Broadcast.

Viewing on Two Screens

If you are running Windows 98 or Windows NT and have two monitors that are connected, you can set up a slide show to run in full-screen view on the secondary monitor and view your presentation in Normal view on your primary monitor. To set this up, choose Slide Show ➢ Set Up Show, and in the Set Up Show dialog box, click the Show On drop-down list.

Saving a Presentation for Use on Another Computer

Office 2000 includes a PowerPoint Viewer that you can copy so you can display a presentation on a computer that doesn't include PowerPoint. To bundle your presentation and the viewer in one easy, compressed package, choose File ➢ Pack and Go to launch the Pack and Go Wizard. As you proceed through the Wizard, you'll be asked to select a presentation, a destination drive, linking and embedding options, and whether the file should include the PowerPoint Viewer. If your presentation includes linked objects or fonts that may not appear on the computer used to display the presentation, choose to include linked files and embed fonts.

SAVING A PRESENTATION FOR USE ON ANOTHER COMPUTER

1. Choose File ➢ Pack and Go from the menu bar. Click Next to advance to the second step.
2. Select the active presentation or another presentation you want to pack, and then click Next.
3. Choose a destination drive and/or folder. Click Next.
4. Turn the object-linking and file-embedding options on or off. Click Next.
5. If the destination computer does not have PowerPoint 2000 installed, include the PowerPoint Viewer. Click Next.
6. Click Finish to create the Pack and Go file and copy it to the selected destination drive. If the file will not fit on one disk, you will be prompted to insert additional disks.

UNPACKING A PRESENTATION

1. Insert the disk created by Pack and Go.
2. In Windows Explorer, select the drive where the disk is located, and double-click the pngsetup.exe file.
3. Enter the destination you want to copy the unpacked presentation and viewer to.
4. To start the Slide Show, double-click the PowerPoint Viewer (ppview32.exe), and then click the presentation.

SKILL
7

Hands On

1. Using an existing presentation:
   a) Rehearse and record slide timings.
   b) Set up the slide show.

      c)   Show the presentation with the timings.

      d)   Have a colleague review the timed presentation and add comments.

      e)   Save the presentation for use on another computer.

2.   With an existing, rehearsed presentation, hold an online broadcast conference. (If you're not connected to a network, find a friend with PowerPoint and an Internet connection.) During the presentation:

      a)   Use the Meeting Minder to record minutes and at least one action item.

      b)   Draw on a slide to underline a point.

      c)   Use the Slide Navigator to return to a previous slide.

3.   After the presentation, export the minutes and action items to Word.

Are You Experienced?

Now you can...

☑ **Create a presentation**

☑ **Add objects**

☑ **Apply transitions and animations to spice up the presentation**

☑ **Prepare handouts in PowerPoint or Word**

☑ **Present a slide show in a kiosk, a live presentation, or an online broadcast**

Tracking Data with Access

- → **Planning and creating tables**
- → **Creating, customizing, and using forms**
- → **Modifying field properties**
- → **Sorting, filtering, and querying**
- → **Relating tables**
- → **Designing reports and report snapshots**

In this skill, you'll find information on creating and using Access databases. This skill assumes that you're a knowledgeable computer Windows user; if you are new to Office 2000, you may want to review Skill 1, "Working in Office 2000," then return here to work in Access 2000.

8.1: Planning and Creating Tables

A *database* is a collection of information about groups of items or individuals. Database structure is provided by *fields*—categories of information. For example, a telephone directory is a printout from a database. Fields in a telephone directory include last name, first name, middle initial, address, and telephone number. Each entry in the database for one individual (a last name, first name, middle initial, address, and telephone number) is called a *record*.

Simple database programs only allow you to work with one list of information at a time: one set of fields and records. More capable programs like Access let you group multiple lists together and relate lists to each other, creating a type of database called a *relational database*. In a relational database, each list is stored in a separate *table*; for example, a college database might have a table listing classes offered, another table of information about students, and a third table that lists instructor information.

Designing a Database

Before you begin constructing the database, you need to spend some time designing the database. A bad design virtually ensures that you'll spend time needlessly reworking the database. Database developers often spend as much time designing a database as they do constructing it. To design a database, you should follow these steps:

1. Determine the need or purpose of the database.

2. Decide what kinds of things (tables) the database should include.

3. Specify the fields that comprise the tables and determine which fields in each table contain unique values.

4. Decide how the tables are related to each other, then review and finalize the design.

5. Construct and relate the tables and populate the database with sample data.

6. Create forms, reports, queries, and Data Access Pages to use with the data.

Determining Need or Purpose

Every database begins with a problem or need that can be solved by creating a systematic data-tracking system. You might, for example, need to keep track of certain data about customers. Think about why you need the database: what will it allow you to do better than you do now? Send mailings to existing customers? Track orders? Study current customers to help identify potential new customers? You could create a database for any of these needs, and each would be different.

Deciding What Should Be Included

A customer database could include customers, orders, salespeople who took customer orders, the results of customer surveys, or any combination of these. Determine each type of entity to include; each separate entity will become a table in the database, and all the information about an entity will appear in only one table. It would be redundant to keep the first name, last name, and address of the customer in each of their orders. Customer data belongs in a Customers table, and order data belongs in an Orders table. When the customer moves, you only have to change the address once in the Customers table, not in every future order.

Determining Table Fields

Once you've established the tables you'll be creating, determine what information about each entity should be included. Every field must be part of a specific table. And every field should be atomic: that means that you store data in its smallest logical components. Store street address, city, state, and zip code separately, rather than in one big field, so that you can find all the customers in one state or zip code later on.

Identifying Unique Fields   In a relational database, tables are connected to each other through unique fields: fields with values that occur only once in a table. Social security numbers, for example, uniquely identify one living person. A field or combination of fields that uniquely identifies a specific record in a table is called a *primary key*. Other common primary key fields are the item number in a catalog, an employee ID, and a UPC for retail products.

Deciding How Tables Are Related and Design Review

A relationship ties one table to another by including the primary key from one table in the related table. In the customers example, including a customer's CustomerID number in the Orders table clearly identifies which customer placed the order, so you can find the customer's name and address. For more information on relationships, see Skill 8.5.

After you've planned the tables and relationships, and before you begin constructing tables and typing names and social security numbers, you need to re-examine the structure of the database: tables, fields, and relationships. When you're convinced that the design is well conceived, you'll begin creating tables and setting relationships.

Populating the Database and Creating Forms and Reports

To determine whether the structure accomplishes your objectives and is easy to work with, begin by entering a few records that are a representative sample of the data. Typically, you'll return to the structure and fine-tune it based on your analysis of how the database handled this test data.

Finally, you'll create forms for data entry, reports for output, queries to gather information from more than one table, and maybe even Data Access Pages for working with your database over the Internet. If the database will be used by others, you'll want to have someone who was not involved in the design test the forms and reports to make sure that other people find them easy to use.

Creating a Database

When the Access application window opens, you immediately see the Access dialog box. Access includes a Database Wizard that allows you to customize one of the predesigned databases that come with Access. If a database you want to create is already in the list, you can use the Wizard. You're creating a database from scratch, so choose Blank Database and click OK.

After you click OK, you're immediately prompted to enter a filename and location for the database in the File New Database dialog box. Databases must be saved before you begin creating tables. Access databases get very large very quickly, so we suggest that you save your database on a hard drive or a large removable disk, not a floppy disk. Once you've saved the database, the Database window, shown in Figure 8.1, will open. The Database window has a button on the left-hand navigation bar for each type of object that can be included in an Access database.

Access databases include seven types of objects: tables, forms, reports, queries, macros, Visual Basic modules, and Data Access Pages. Although Access will allow you to name objects any way you wish, we suggest that you follow the Leszynski/Reddick naming convention so that databases you create can be easily understood by other people who work with Access. In the L/R convention, an object name begins with a tag that identifies the kind of object it is: `tbl`, `frm`, `rpt`, `qry`, `mcr`, `bas`, or `dpg`. There are no spaces or punctuation in object names, and the first letter of each word in the name is capitalized. For example, a table of customer orders might be named `tblOrders`; a query showing order information might be called qryCustOrders.

SKILL 8

FIGURE 8.1:   The Database window

Access Projects

When you first started Microsoft Access 2000, you may have noticed the option to create a new database using *pages* and *projects*. Pages refer to Data Access Pages, and you will learn much more about them in Skill 12. Access projects are a way to combine the user-friendly interface of Microsoft Access 2000 with the pure power of a high-end database server, such as Microsoft SQL Server.

SQL Server operates according to the principles of client/server computing. In an Access project, the client, Microsoft Access, requests information from the server, SQL Server. SQL Server is a very powerful enterprise database that responds to the requests from Access by sending back data. Access projects provide a grea way to jumpstart development of new client/server applications in three critical situations:

- Your data is very important. You have zero-tolerance for data loss or temporary unavailability.

- Your data will be used by many people simultaneously. Access tolerates up to 255 users, but performance can become unbearable at much lower numbers if those users are particularly active ones.

- Your database will be very large. Access 2000 cannot manage a file size greater than 2GB.

Creating a Table

Click the Table button on the left hand navigation bar to cause the Table page to open in the Database window. Now, click the New button on the Database window to open the New Table dialog box:

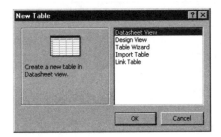

The dialog box lists five ways to create a table:

- In Datasheet view, by entering field names at the top of each column

- In Design view, where you list field names and properties for each field

- With the help of the Table Wizard, which includes suggested field lists for over 100 tables

- By importing a table created from another database or spreadsheet

- By linking (connecting to) a table that exists in another database

Design view is the most flexible place to design new tables, because it lets you specify all the information about each field in the table. When you choose Design view and click OK, a table design window opens. Figure 8.2 shows the table design window with some fields in it.

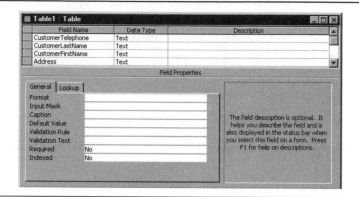

FIGURE 8.2: The Table design window

It is a database convention that field names do not include spaces (even though Access allows it) and that the initial letter of each word is capitalized. Field names should be descriptive, such as CustomerFirstName. The data type indicates the kind of data that can be entered in the field. You can choose from nine data types:

Text   Used for words or non-value numbers (such as phone numbers and social security numbers). It is the default setting because it is used most frequently.

Memo   An open field that is used for comments.

Number   Numbers, or integers, that are negative or positive values (not numbers that have no numeric value, such as social security numbers).

Date/Time   Various formats for dates, times, and combinations of the two.

Currency   Numbers in dollars, or dollars and cents.

AutoNumber   A numeric field automatically entered by Access, used in a primary key field when none of the fields in a table is unique.

Yes/No   A logical field that can have only one of two values: Yes or No.

OLE Object   An object, such as a photograph, that was created in another application.

Hyperlink   Used to store hyperlinks: URL and UNC addresses.

Click the Data Type drop-down list to select a type. Enter the data type, then enter a description for the field if the name is at all ambiguous. The Lookup Wizard, the last option in the Data Type drop-down list, isn't really a data type but is used to let the database user select a value from a list. Once you have selected a data type, press Enter to drop to the next blank row and enter the information for the next field. Continue until all fields are entered.

Selecting a Primary Key

In a customer database, telephone number is often used as a primary key, since it's unusual for two customers to have the same telephone number. If a single field can't serve as a primary key, look at a combination of two fields. For example, in a class registration table, neither the class number nor the student ID could be a primary key, since either could occur several times in the registration table. However, a student would only sign up once for a class, so using both the student ID and class number fields could be a good primary key. If no combination of fields is suitable, then you may need to add an AutoNumber field for a primary key. AutoNumber fields are, by definition, always unique. In the Orders table of a customer database, you could add an OrderID field of type AutoNumber to serve as the primary key for the Orders table.

To set the key, click the row selector (to the left of the Field Name column) to select the field or fields that will serve as the primary key. Right-click and choose Primary Key from the shortcut menu, or click the Primary Key button on the toolbar.

You can't enter data in Design view. Click the Datasheet View button to switch to the table's Datasheet view. You'll be prompted to save the table. Choose Yes; if you choose No, you remain in Design view. Enter a name for the table in the Table Name dialog box, beginning with tbl. If you forgot to assign a primary key, a warning appears. If you click Yes, Access will add an AutoNumber key field to the table. If you want to add or designate your own key field, click Cancel, assign a primary key, and save again.

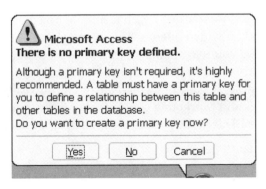

NOTE NOTE NOTE NOTE NOTE NOTE NOTE NOTE NOTE NOTE NOTE NOTE NOTE NOTE

When you change to a different view, the toolbars change to correspond to the view you are in, so don't be surprised if a toolbar looks different when you switch from Design to Datasheet view.

CREATING A TABLE IN DESIGN VIEW

1. With the Tables button depressed on the left-hand navigation bar, click the New button at the top of the Database window.

2. In the New Table dialog box, choose Design View and click OK.

3. In Design view, enter the field name and data type for each field.

4. Select a field or fields to designate as a primary key, and click the Primary Key button on the toolbar or choose Primary Key from the shortcut menu.

5. Save the table. Enter a unique table name when prompted.

6. To begin entering records, click the Datasheet View button on the toolbar, or close the table to return to the Database window.

Using Groups

As a database gets larger and you start adding queries, forms, and reports, it's easy to lose track of which forms are based on which tables and which reports are based on which queries. This is one of the reasons that Microsoft Access 2000 allows you to combine tables and other objects together into *groups*. A group is exactly what its name implies—a logical gathering of similar objects. So, in our example, Accounting could create a group called "Accounting" to hold all of its tables and Marketing could create a group called "Marketing" to hold all of its tables. This greatly reduces the chance of a user confusing similarly named tables.

CREATING A NEW GROUP

1. If the Groups section in the left navigation bar is closed, click the Groups button.
2. Right-click anywhere within the Groups section.
3. From the pop-up menu, choose New Group.
4. Enter the name that you would like to use for your new group.
5. Add shortcuts to tables, queries, forms, etc. to the group by dragging the object from the right pane to the Groups section on the left.

Entering Data in a Table

Datasheet view (see Figure 8.3) looks much like a spreadsheet, and skills that you've learned with Excel or other spreadsheets will serve you well here.

ENTERING RECORDS IN TABLE DATASHEET VIEW

1. Open the table you want to use. If you are not in Datasheet view, click the Datasheet View button.
2. Begin typing the information for the first field. Press Tab to move to the next field. Continue entering field information and pressing Tab until you reach the end of the record. Press Tab again to start another record.

3. To resize columns, move the mouse pointer between the column headings. When the pointer changes to a resizing tool, drag or double-click.

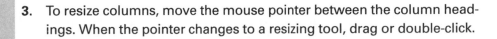

SKILL
8

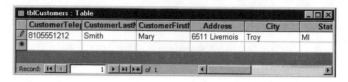

FIGURE 8.3: The Customers Table Datasheet view

When you close the table, you will be asked if you want to save the layout changes made when you adjusted the columns.

Move around in the datasheet using the arrow keys on the keyboard and pan the width of the table with the horizontal scroll bar at the bottom of the screen. The vertical scroll bar at the right screen edge moves up and down through the datasheet. (Scroll bars only appear when there is data that cannot be viewed within the current window.) The navigation buttons at the bottom of the screen are used to move to the first, previous, next, last, or a new record.

Modifying Data in a Table

To edit data, move the mouse over the field you want to edit. The mouse pointer changes to an I-beam, and when you click in the field, an insertion point appears. You can double-click the I-beam to select a single word, then type over a word. To select and overtype the entire field, move the mouse to the left edge of the field. The pointer will change to a selection tool. Click to select the field.

Deleting Records

To delete a record, click the Record Selector to the left of the record's first field to select the entire record, then press the Delete key on the keyboard or click the Delete Record button on the toolbar. (You can drag on the Record Selectors or hold Shift and click to select consecutive records.) Or, right-click the Record Selector and choose Delete Record from the shortcut menu. Deleting records can't be undone, so a dialog box appears, prompting you to confirm the deletion.

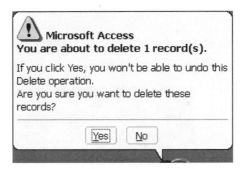

When you are finished entering or modifying table data, close the table. If you have changed table layout, you'll be prompted to save the changes. You will not be prompted to save the data you entered; each record was saved as you entered it.

Saving in a Previous Version

Microsoft Access 2000 allows you to save your work into the format that was used by the previous version of the software, Access 97. Once it is saved in the earlier format, you can no longer use any of the new features of the latest release. If you need to share your database with Access 97 users, this is a valuable enhancement to the product.

Notice that by saving the converted database into a different file, Access is able to keep *your* copy of the information stored in the Access 2000 format that you are currently using. Bear in mind, however, that your disk space usage for that file has now at least doubled and you have two distinct copies of the database, changes made in one are not reflected in the other.

CONVERTING ACCESS 2000 DATABASES TO ACCESS 97 FORMAT

1. Open the Access 2000 database that you would like to convert to Access 97 format.

continued ▸

2. Select Tools ➤ Database Utilities ➤ Convert Database ➤ To Prior Access Database Version.

3. Enter the filename under which you would like to save the converted version of your database, and click Save.

Compacting Your Data

Access 2000 can automatically compact a database every time you close it, reclaiming unused space that can make a database file run slower and take up more disk space.

CONFIGURING ACCESS TO COMPACT ON CLOSE

1. Choose Tools ➤ Options ➤ General from the menu bar.
2. Verify that the check box labeled Compact on Close is checked.
3. Click OK.

MANUALLY COMPACTING YOUR DATABASE

1.   Choose Tools ➢ Database Utilities ➢ Compact and Repair Database.

Hands On

1.   Identify a need for a database in your work or personal life. Using the database design steps listed above, identify tables, fields, field types, and a primary key for each table.

2.   Create the table you feel is most central to the database from Exercise 1. Add two or three records to the table.

3.   Your company needs a database to be used by the Human Resources department to track basic employee data and the results of annual evaluations. Design the database and create tblEmployees.

4.   Pretend that someone in Human Resources is still using Access 97. Save your database into a format that they can use.

5.   Examine the size of your database in the Open dialog box or Windows Explorer. Compact it at least once manually. Check its size again to determine if it has shrunk in size.

Skill 8.2: Creating and Using Forms

SKILL
8

Forms provide a way for users to enter data without having to know how a table is designed. One form can include data from multiple tables, providing one-stop data entry. You can create a customized layout so that a form looks just like its source document: the membership application, customer data form, or other document used to collect the data to be entered in the database. When an entry form closely resembles the source document, data-entry errors are less likely to occur. As with tables, you can create a form in several ways. Access provides three form-creation methods: AutoForms, the Form Wizard, and Form Design view. This section focuses on creating AutoForms and using the Wizard; for information on form design see Skill 8.6.

Creating AutoForms

An *AutoForm* can have one of three different layouts: datasheet, tabular, or columnar. Figure 8.4 shows a Datasheet AutoForm for the Customers table. The AutoForm looks a lot like the table's Datasheet view, right down to the navigation buttons. You can move the columns and rows around, just like in the table.

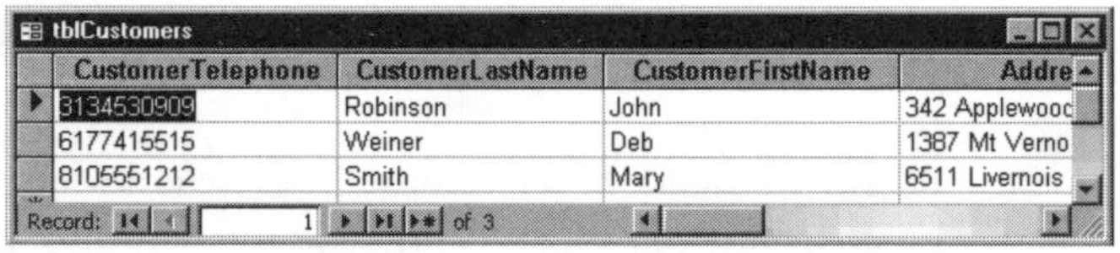

FIGURE 8.4: Datasheet AutoForm

A tabular form for the Customers table is shown in Figure 8.5. Like the Datasheet form, the tabular form presents multiple records, as though you were looking at the table. However, the form itself looks a bit classier.

FIGURE 8.5: Tabular AutoForm

The columnar AutoForm, like the one shown in Figure 8.6, only displays one record at a time. Click the navigation buttons to move between records or to enter a new record. If the primary purpose of a form is data entry or editing one record at a time, a columnar form is best. If you're designing a form to allow users to view multiple records, a datasheet or tabular form is a better choice.

FIGURE 8.6: Columnar AutoForm

CREATING AN AUTOFORM

1   Click the Forms button on the left-hand navigation bar of the Database window, and then click the New button to open the Form dialog box.
2.   Choose an AutoForm from the list.
3.   Select a table from the drop-down list.
4.   Click OK to create the AutoForm.

You can also create a form by choosing the table on the Table page and clicking the New Object button on the toolbar, then selecting Form. (If you choose Auto-Form, you aren't asked which type of AutoForm; you get a columnar form.)

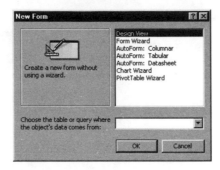

Click the Close control in the form's upper right corner. Access will ask you whether or not you want to save any changes that you have made. Click Yes and you will be prompted for the name that you would like to give to your new form. Enter whatever name you like, but remember the Leszynski/Reddick naming conventions that we showed you at the start of this skill. According to this, a form's name should begin with the letters frm to allow a user to instantly recognize what kind of object it is.

Use AutoForms when you need a form that includes all the information from a single table. If you don't want to display all the fields, or if you need data from multiple tables, you'll use the Form Wizard or Design view.

Entering and Editing in Forms

In a datasheet form, enter and edit information exactly as you would in the table's Datasheet view; select and edit a field by moving to the left edge of the field and clicking. In tabular and columnar forms, drag to select all the text in a field before entering the correct data. To move to the next record on a columnar or datasheet form, tab out of the last *text box control* (any of the depressed areas on a form that display data from a table). In all forms, you can use the navigation buttons to move between existing records and the Delete Record button to delete the selected record.

Printing Forms

Access allows you to print forms just as you see them on the screen. However, you should be aware of a few things before you print. If you click on the Print toolbar button, you will print a form for every record in your database: one hundred records will print one hundred pages. You should only use form printing when you need a copy of a single record in a hurry. (Reports give you many more options for printing multiple records.)

PRINTING THE CURRENT RECORD

1. Select the record you want to print.
2. Choose File ➢ Print from the menu bar to open the Print dialog box.
3. Choose Selected Record(s) under Print Range and click OK.

Sorting Records

Records can be sorted in ascending order (A-Z) or descending order (Z-A). They can be sorted on several levels. For example, you can sort records by last name and then by first name, or by zip code and then by last name within each zip code. Although you can sort records in Form view, it is easiest to see the results if you work directly in a table or in a form's Datasheet view. If you are sorting a table, Access will ask whether you want to save the changes to the table's design when you attempt to close the table. Choosing Yes will save the sort order so that when you open the table again, the records will still be sorted. While a table is sorted, added records are automatically sorted.

SORTING RECORDS

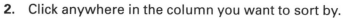

1. Switch to Datasheet view of the table or form.
2. Click anywhere in the column you want to sort by.
3. Click the Ascending or Descending Sort button.
4. To remove the sort order and return records to their original order, choose Records ➢ Remove Filter/Sort.

SKILL
8

Multi-Level Sorting

A *multi-level sort* sorts the records on the first field you specify, then sorts records with the same value using another specified field. In a telephone book, for example, all the Smiths are alphabetized by first name.

SORTING BY MULTIPLE FIELDS

1. Open the desired form or table in Datasheet view.

2. Move the columns you want to sort so they are adjacent. (To move a column, select the column, and then drag it to the desired position.) The column to be sorted first should be on the left, the second level to its immediate right, and so on.

3. Click the Ascending or Descending Sort button on the toolbar.

Sorting in Columnar or Tabular Form view is similar to sorting in Datasheet view, except you cannot apply multi-level sorts. Select the field you want to sort by and click the Sort button on the toolbar. To see the results of the work, move through the records.

Searching for Records

Access provides an easy way to find individual records. Access will even allow you to look for a partial name if you are unsure about how the name is spelled.

To use Access's Find feature, click in the field that contains the data you're searching for, then click the Find button on the toolbar to open the Find dialog box.

Since you already clicked in the field you want to search, you can type in the search string you are looking for and click Find Next. Access will search the field you selected and find the first occurrence of the text you entered. If the search string occurs more than once, you can click the Find Next button again to see the next occurrence. (You might need to move the Find dialog box out of the way to see the search results.) When you have moved to the last record that contains the search string, clicking Find Next again will result in a `Search Item Was Not Found` message.

Access provides a number of options that can help when your search isn't quite so straightforward. Let's say you only remember that the person's name starts with *Has*. You can change the search parameters in a number of ways. You could look for all records starting with *Has* by choosing Start of Field in the Match control. If all you know about the name is that it has a *ch*, you could choose to match Any Part of the Field.

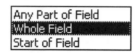

Access provides additional options for searching your data. In order to access these options, you must first click the More button on the Find dialog box. When you do this, the dialog expands to reveal additional options.

You can choose to have Access search either Up or Down through the records. This option saves time when you are confident that the record you are looking for is above or below the record you are on. If you click in the field you want to search before opening the Find dialog box, you'll save having to search through all the fields. To further refine your searches, you can specify that you want to match the case of the string, or match based upon the display format of a field rather than its actual value stored.

Using Wildcards   You can construct search criteria using *wildcards*, symbols that represent one or more characters. Table 8.1 lists wildcard characters you can use in Find:

TABLE 8.1: Wildcard Symbols

Wildcard	Usage	Example
*	Can be used at the beginning or the end of a string to match any number of characters	Par* finds Parker and Parson. *son finds Parson and Williamson.
?	Matches any single alphabetic character	w?ll finds wall, well, and will.
#	Matches any single numeric character	4#5 finds 405, 415, 425, etc.
[ ]	Matches any single character specified in the brackets	w[ai]ll finds wall and will, but not well.

SKILL
8

TABLE 8.1: Wildcard Symbols *(continued)*

Wildcard	Usage	Example
-	Identifies any one of a range of characters in ascending order	[c-h]ill finds dill, fill, gill, and hill, but not kill, mill, etc.
!	Used within brackets to specify any character not in the brackets	w[!a]ll finds well and will, but not wall.

SEARCHING FOR RECORDS

1. In either Form or Datasheet view, click in the field you want to search.
2. Click the Find button to open the Find dialog box.
3. Enter the search string, including appropriate wildcards, in the Find What box and confirm where you're searching in the Look In control. Indicate whether you want to match Whole Field, Any Part of Field, or Start of Field. Set other search options as desired.
4. Click the Find Next button.
5. To find any additional occurrences, click the Find Next button again.
6. Click Close to close the Find dialog box.

Filtering Records

Applying a *filter* to an Access form or table temporarily hides records that don't meet your criteria. You can filter in a table, query, or form. There are three ways to create filters in Access:

Filter By Selection and **Filter Excluding Selection**   Let you create a filter based on a text or value you have selected

Filter By Form   Creates a blank form or datasheet where you can type in the values you want to see

Advanced Filter/Sort   Lets you enter more complex filtering and sorting criteria in a way similar to writing a query

Filter By Selection/Filter Excluding Selection   The easiest way to apply a filter in Access is with Filter By Selection. To find all the records from Indiana, for example, click in the State field or text box control for an Indiana record, then click the Filter By Selection button. Only the records for Indiana will be visible; all others will be hidden. The navigation buttons show only the number of filtered records.

To remove the filter, click the Remove Filter button. If you wish to reapply the filter, click the same button again, which has now become an Apply Filter button. If you want the filter to match only part of a field, select the part of the data you want to see. For example, if you want to see all the companies in area code 317, select the string 317 in the telephone field. You can apply filters to filtered data to narrow the search even further.

If you would like to see all the data except for a certain value—for example, all the companies that aren't in Indiana—locate a record with the value you want to exclude and right-click to open the shortcut menu. Choose Filter Excluding Selection. All the sorting and filtering commands are always just a right-click away.

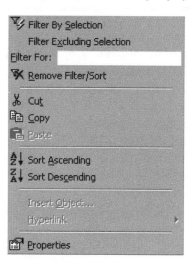

If you have created a filter that you will re-use, apply this filter just before closing the form. Access will ask if you want to save changes to the design of the table. If you answer Yes, the last filter you created is automatically saved. When you open the form again, all the records will be visible, but you can simply click the Apply Filter button to reapply the filter.

FILTERING BY SELECTION OR EXCLUSION

1. Locate a record that contains data matching the data you want to display. Click in or select all or part of the string.
2. Click the Filter By Selection button to see the filtered records.
3. Click the Remove Filter button to remove the filter and make all the records visible again.
4. Click the Apply Filter button to reapply the same filter.
5. To apply a filter to filtered records, select the new filter criteria from the filtered record set, and then click the Filter By Selection button.
6. To see all the records except for the one you've selected and any others that match its criteria, right-click and choose Filter Excluding Selection from the shortcut menu.

Filter By Form   The Filter By Form feature works the same way as the Filter By Selection method, except that you set up your criteria on a blank form or datasheet.

Click the Filter By Form button to open a blank form in Form view or a single row datasheet in Datasheet view. When you click in a field, a drop-down list containing all the values in the field appears. Select the value to use as a filter, then click the Apply Filter button. Using this method, you can apply multiple filters to display records that meet all the criteria you select: an AND filter.

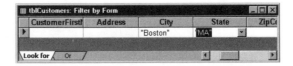

If you would like to see records that meet one or more of the specified criteria but not necessarily all of them (an OR filter), click the Or tab at the bottom of the form before selecting the additional criteria. Selecting part of a field works just as well in Filter By Form as in Filter By Selection.

FILTERING BY FORM

1. In Form or Datasheet view, click the Filter By Form button.
2. Select a filter value you want to see from the drop-down list in one or more fields. To display records that meet one of multiple criteria, click the Or tab.
3. Click the Apply Filter button to view the filtered records.

Hands On

1. Open an existing database. Create tabular, columnar, and datasheet Auto-Forms for one of the tables in the database.

2. Open an existing database. Open a table in Datasheet view and sort the records on one column and on two or more columns. Filter the records by Selection and by Form.

3. Add more records to your Employees table. Sort the records on last name. Filter the records by two or more criteria.

Skill 8.3: Modifying Tables

Sometimes, while working with your database, you will discover that the actual nature of the data that you need to track has changed, or you would like to structure the data fields to add consistency or validation to your data. In cases such as this, you will need to modify the design of an existing table to achieve the results you desire.

SKILL
8

Modifying Field Properties

Every field has properties that control how the field's contents are displayed, stored, controlled, or validated. Some properties are common to all fields, and some properties are only relevant to particular data types. In Table Design view, the field's properties are shown at the bottom of the window. The field properties for the CustomerTelephone field in tblCustomers are shown in Figure 8.7.

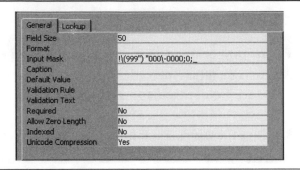

FIGURE 8.7: Telephone field properties

All field types except AutoNumber and OLE Object have the following general properties:

Format Indicates how the field's contents will be displayed.

Caption Provides the label that will be attached to the field on a form or report.

Default Value Specifies values for new entries. Enter the most frequently entered value for the field.

Validation Rule Indicates a range of acceptable entries.

Validation Text Appears in the status bar when the field is active.

Required A Yes/No setting that indicates whether the field must have an entry.

The following general properties apply primarily to text fields:

Field Size Indicates the maximum number of characters allowed in the field. For example, you might set the field size for State to 2.

Input Mask Limits and formats the values that can be entered.

Allow Zero Length A Yes/No setting that determines whether a text string with no length ("") is a valid entry.

Indexed Instructs Access whether or not to create an index for the field. Indexing a field speeds up sorting, searching, and filtering the field's contents. The primary key for a table is always indexed. You should index fields that will be frequently sorted for reports or forms.

Unicode Compression   Unicode is a character encoding scheme capable of encoding every known character. To accomplish this, every character is represented by two bytes instead of one. When this property is set to Yes, Access compresses any character whose first byte is 0 when it is stored and then uncompresses it when it is retrieved, thereby ensuring optimal performance.

Number and Currency fields have one additional general property: Decimal Places, which specifies the number of digits that will be displayed and stored after the decimal.

Setting Input Masks

When a user enters data in the CustomerTelephone field, it would be helpful to have the parentheses and hyphen that are normally found in a telephone number without the user entering them. Formats for data entry are called *input masks*.

To set an input mask, click the Input Mask property box, then click the Build button that appears at the right end of the property box to open the Input Mask Wizard. You will be required to save the table first. In the first step of the Wizard, select the type of input mask you want to add to the field, then click Next.

Input Mask Wizard

Which input mask matches how you want data to look?

To see how a selected mask works, use the Try It box.

To change the Input Mask list, click the Edit List button.

Input Mask:	Data Look:
SIC	98052.999
Social Security Number	531-86-7180
Phone Number	(206) 555-1212
Extension	63215
Password	********
Short Time	18:07

Try It:

[Edit List]   [Cancel]   [< Back]   [Next >]   [Finish]

If you wish, you can alter the input mask by typing or deleting characters in the Input Mask control field. Then select the placeholder that will appear where the user should enter text, and click Next.

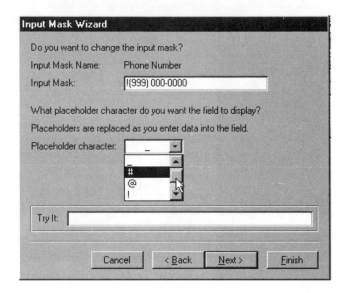

Storing the data with the input mask makes the database file larger but preserves the special format for reports. Choose whether you want the data stored with or without the input mask, and click Finish to close the Input Mask Wizard and add the input mask to the field's Properties sheet.

Setting Key Properties

When a field's Required property is set to Yes, a user must enter data in the field before saving the record. No means that the field is optional. There are three possible values for a field's Indexed property: No, Yes (No Duplicates), and Yes (Duplicates OK). Choosing Yes speeds up searching, sorting, and filtering by creating an index for the field. Yes (No Duplicates) means that the value entered in the field must be unique.

For a single-field primary key, Access will set the Required property to Yes and Indexed to Yes (No Duplicates). With a multiple-field primary key, all fields are required, but duplicates are allowed within a field.

SETTING THE KEY PROPERTIES

1. In Table Design view, select the field in the upper pane.
2. Select No or Yes for Required and No, Yes (Duplicates OK), or Yes (No Duplicates) from the Indexed property in the lower pane.

Validating Entries

Validation is a way to screen data being entered in a table or form. Entering a value in a field's Default property is a passive way to validate data. For more active validation, create a Validation Rule that screens the data, and Validation Text that appears to let the user know what constitutes a valid entry. In Access 2000, you can validate fields and records in tables, and controls in forms.

Field validation is set in a field's Validation Rule property. When you tab or click out of the field, Access checks to make sure the data you entered matches the rule. If not, the Validation Text is displayed.

Record validation is set in the Properties sheet for the table. When you move to a new record, Access checks to make sure the entire record is valid. Record validation is used to compare one field to another to check, for example, that an employee's HireDate occurred before the TerminationDate.

Many field properties set in a table are inheritable. That means that the Validation Rule set in a table passes through to any form control based on the field. To enter a validation rule for a field, select the field in the upper pane in Table Design view, and click in the Validation Rule property box in the lower pane. If the rule is simple (minimum pay rate is $10), enter it using logical operators: >=10. In the Validation Text property box, enter the error message that should appear on the status bar when invalid data is entered.

SKILL
8

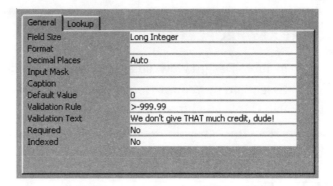

TIP TIP TIP TIP TIP TIP TIP TIP TIP TIP TIP TIP TIP TIP TIP TIP TIP TIP TIP TIP TIP TIP TIP TIP

If you would like a larger space in which to type validation text, right-click in the property box and choose Zoom to open the Zoom box. When you are done entering text, click OK to close the Zoom box.

To validate entire records, open the table's Properties sheet, shown in Figure 8.8. Right-click anywhere in the Design view window and choose Properties from the shortcut menu to open the Table Properties sheet.

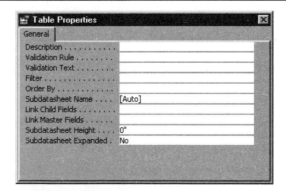

FIGURE 8.8: Table Properties sheet

You can use the Expression Builder, shown in Figure 8.9, to create complex field and record validation rules. To open the Expression Builder, click the Build button at the right end of the Validation Rule text box. With the Builder, you can access common functions and, for record validation, field names from the current table.

For example, suppose that you are a teacher and allow all your students to give themselves a self-evaluation percentile at the end of your course. You could make a rule prohibiting anyone from giving themselves a score in excess of their final *real* score, but how could you enforce that? Figure 8.9 shows one approach you might take to this task using Expression Builder.

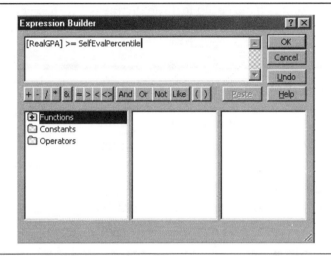

FIGURE 8.9: Expression Builder

If you add validation rules for fields that contain data, you'll be asked whether you want Access to apply the rules to the existing data when you save the table.

VALIDATING DATA ENTRY

1. In Table Design view, select the field you want to validate in the upper pane. Right-click and select Properties to select the table for record validation.

2. In the lower pane, enter a rule in the Validation Rule property box, or click the Build button and create the rule using the Expression Builder.

3. Type the message that you want displayed when invalid data is entered in the Validation Message property box.

Adding Objects to Records

An Access database isn't limited to typed entries. The OLE Object data type allows you to store different types of objects in a database. OLE stands for Object Linking and Embedding, and you can store a variety of objects in an OLE field such as graphics, pictures, sounds, and Word documents. For example, the Customers table could include pictures of customers, the logo for commercial customers, or scanned images of correspondence from customers.

ADDING AN OLE FIELD TO A TABLE

1. Open the table in Design view.
2. Click in an open row, or insert a blank row by right-clicking where you want to insert the field and choosing Insert from the shortcut menu.
3. Enter a name for the field.
4. Choose the OLE Object data type.
5. Save the table design changes.

You can't just type in the OLE object: you have to insert it. During data entry or editing, right-click in the OLE field in the record, and choose Insert Object to open the Insert Object dialog box. You can create an object to place in the field by choosing Create New. If the object already exists on a local or network hard drive, choose Create from File.

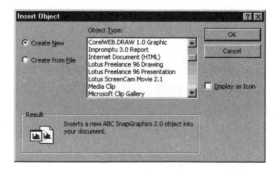

Click the Browse button, and locate the OLE object file. If you want the object in the database to be updated if the disk file changes, choose Link. If, instead, you want a copy of the object in the database, don't choose Link, and the object will be embedded in the database. (See Skill 11 for the advantages and disadvantages of Linking and Embedding.) Click OK to insert the file in the OLE object database field.

The object, the object's type (Word document, MIDI sequence), or an icon representing the object appears in the field. If the type or icon is displayed, double-click on it to open the object in its native format. For example, a Word document will open in Word; a sound or video will open the Windows Sound or Media Player and begin to play.

Working with Name AutoCorrect

In Skill 8.2 you created forms that were intended to help people work easily with the information in your database. Suppose you needed to rename a table upon which one of these forms was based. Would this cause the form to stop working? The answer depends on whether or not you have enabled Name AutoCorrect.

New to Access 2000, AutoCorrect helps repair any damage done to links between database objects during renaming procedures. By default, this feature is turned on for every new database that you create in Access 2000. To verify this, simply select Tools ➤ Options and click the General tab to examine the status of the check boxes in the Name AutoCorrect control.

SKILL
8

You must select the Track Name AutoCorrect Info option *before* renaming your tables for Access to automatically repair your forms. This option simply tells Access to make "mental notes" whenever you rename a database object. The software will not take any immediate steps to repair damaged forms, however. If you want this, you must select the Perform Name AutoCorrect option. If you don't select this option, Access will wait until you *do* select it to make your changes.

If you are worried about the effects of unintentional name AutoCorrections on your data, you can enable Log Name AutoCorrect under Tool ➤ Options ➤ General. This will log all of the changes automatically made by Access to a table named Name AutoCorrect Log. This way, if anything goes really wrong after you rename one of your database objects, you can look at this table for information about what might have gone wrong.

WORKING WITH AUTOCORRECT

1. Choose Tools ➤ Options and click the General tab to access the Name AutoCorrect control.
2. If you would like AutoCorrect turned on, make sure that Track Name AutoCorrect Info and Perform Name AutoCorrect are both selected.
3. If you would like AutoCorrect turned off, deselect Track Name Auto-Correct Info. Any other options in the Name AutoCorrect control should become deselected and unavailable.

Hands On

1. In an existing table:

   a) Add an appropriate input mask to a field.

   b) Review and set FieldLength properties for text fields where data length is known.

   c) Set Required properties where appropriate.

   d) Set the Index property to Yes for the fields that you will sort or filter on most frequently.

2. In an existing table:

   a) Establish a ValidationRule and enter a ValidationMessage for at least one field. Test the rule and message by attempting to enter invalid data.

   b) Set and test a DefaultValue property for at least one field.

3. In a new or existing table:

   a) Modify the table design to include a field with an OLE data type.

   b) Add at least two records to the table that include objects.

   c) In Datasheet view, double-click to open an object.

Skill 8.4: Working with External Data

With Access 2000, you can add copies of tables from other applications to your database or work with tables that exist in a separate database or spreadsheet. Access 2000 can *import* (copy) or *link* (connect to) data from prior versions of Access, other databases like FoxPro and Paradox, spreadsheets like Excel and Lotus 1-2-3, and HTML tables from the Internet or an intranet. The ability to work with data from a variety of sources makes Access a powerful tool in today's workplace, where data can originate in a variety of applications. Before you rekey data that already exists, it's worth your time to see if you can import it directly into Access or transfer it to a program that Access can use.

Importing vs. Linking

Importing data creates a copy of the data in a table in your database. Because a copy is created, the original data isn't affected, and further changes in the original data are not reflected in Access. With linked data, you are working with original data; when the source file changes, the changes are reflected in Access, and changes in Access are reflected in the source file.

Before you can import or link data, you need to decide which you want to do. For example, you're creating a new database and a colleague in another department offers you an Excel spreadsheet that lists all the cities, states, and zip codes for your region. Should you import or link? If you know that the data doesn't need to be updated in another program, you should import it. Cities, states, and zip codes rarely change, so updating isn't an issue with this table. And when you import data, you can change field properties and rearrange or delete fields if you need to, so importing is more flexible from your point of view. If, however, multiple users need access to the original data so that all changes in the data are shared, then you need to link to the data.

TIP TIP TIP TIP TIP TIP TIP TIP TIP TIP TIP TIP TIP TIP TIP TIP TIP TIP TIP TIP TIP TIP

If you share an Access database with other users, you can put the data tables in one database and your forms and reports in another, then link the two databases together to allow multiple users to access the data tables. Access has a Database Splitter Add-In to help you divide a database.

Importing Data

To import external data, choose File ➤ Get External Data ➤ Import to open the Import dialog box. Click the Files of Type drop-down to select the type of file you want to import. Select the file, then click Import.

Importing Data from Spreadsheets and Other Databases

If you choose to import data from Excel or Lotus 1-2-3, the Import Spreadsheet Wizard opens when you click the Import button. You can import worksheets or named ranges from a spreadsheet (see Figure 8.10). If an Excel spreadsheet file contains more than one worksheet or named range, you can choose the one you want. If the file is an Excel 4.0 workbook or a Lotus 1-2-3 notebook, you can't select a page or worksheet, so you have to save each sheet or page in a separate file before opening the Import Spreadsheet Wizard.

In the second step of the Wizard, indicate whether the spreadsheet's first row is data or column labels, then click Next. In the third step, choose whether you want Access to create a new table with this data or place it in an existing table that you've already created. If you choose an existing table, the column labels in the spreadsheet and field names in the table must be identical. The data will be appended to existing table data. In the fourth step, shown in Figure 8.11, indicate whether or not the data in each column is indexed; you can choose to omit some columns of data by skipping them.

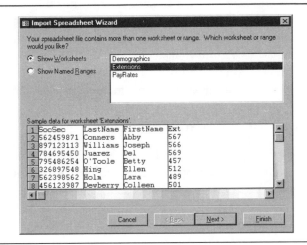

FIGURE 8.10: Import Spreadsheet Wizard

FIGURE 8.11: Choosing columns to import

In the fifth step, either have Access add an AutoNumber primary key, select an existing column as the primary key, or indicate that there is no primary key field. (If the primary key will be more than one field, choose No Primary Key Field and set the primary key in Table Design view after you've imported the data.) In the last step, name the table, and then click Finish. Access will import the data and add the table to your database. After the table is imported, you may want to make some changes in Design view. For example, the social security numbers in Figure 8.11 were imported as numbers; you could change the data type to Text and add an input mask.

When you import from a database other than Access, the Import Database Wizard opens, and the steps are similar to the steps in the Import Spreadsheet Wizard.

Importing from Access

If you import from another Access database, you aren't limited to data. You can import forms, reports, macros, queries, pages, modules, and even relationships. When you choose an Access database in the Import dialog box, the Import Objects dialog box opens, as shown in Figure 8.12. Click the Options button to extend the dialog box to show other available options.

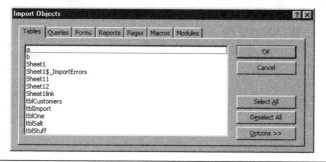

FIGURE 8.12: The Import Objects dialog box

Click the tabs in the dialog box to move from one type of object to another. Click Select All to import all the objects or click to select the specific objects you want to import. Notice that you can choose to import tables including data or the table definitions only. When you've selected all the objects you want to import, click Import to add the objects to the current database.

IMPORTING OBJECTS FROM AN ACCESS DATABASE

1. Choose File ➤ Get External Data ➤ Import.
2. Select the Access database you wish to import from and click Import.

continued ◗

3. Select the object(s) you wish to import. To set import options, click the Options button.

4. Click Import.

Linking to a Spreadsheet or Database

Linking to a table or worksheet is even less complex than importing. You can't change the structure of the linked table or worksheet, so you don't get an opportunity to skip columns.

LINKING TO AN EXTERNAL DATA SOURCE

1. Choose File ➢ Get External Data ➢ Link Tables.

2. Select the type of data source you want to link to in the Files of Type drop-down list.

3. Select the file you want to link to and click Link to open the Link Wizard.

4. Select the worksheet, named range, or table you wish to link to. Click Link.

5. In a spreadsheet, indicate whether the first row contains data or column labels. Click Next.

6. Enter the name you will use to refer to the external table or worksheet, and click Finish.

SKILL
8

You can tell which tables in a database are actually links to other tables. Linked Access tables have a link arrow in front of the Access table icon (see Figure 8.13); other linked file types have other icons with the link arrow. In Figure 8.13, tblExtensions is a linked Excel worksheet, and WebCustomers is a linked HTML table.

FIGURE 8.13: Linked external data

If you decide later that you don't want to be linked to the data, select and delete the link in the Table page of the Database window. The link will be deleted, not the original table.

Hands On

1. In a new or existing database, import data from a spreadsheet or a database other than Access. (If you need a worksheet to import, choose one of the Excel worksheets from the Sybex Web site.) View and, if necessary, change the design of the imported table.

2. In a new or existing database, import at least one table and one form from another Access database.

3. In a new or existing database, link to a table in a worksheet or database. Now delete the link you just created.

Skill 8.5: Creating the Relational Database

Understanding Relationships

A relationship links two tables by specifying a common field that appears in both tables. There are three types of relationships: one-to-one, one-to-many, and many-to-many. If two tables are related in a *one-to-one relationship*, then each record in Table A will have no more than one record in Table B. In the more common *one-to-many relationship*, one record in Table A can be related to many records in Table B: for each class, there are many students.

A *many-to-many relationship* means that a record in Table A can be related to many records in Table B, and a record in Table B can be simultaneously related to many records in Table A. For example, a student enrolled in multiple classes can have many teachers, and a teacher can have many students. Relational databases don't allow you to create many-to-many relationships directly. But these relationships abound in real data. You build linking tables to handle the many-to-many relationships in your database. Linking tables are tables containing the key fields from each table you want to link.

Understanding Foreign Keys

A table's primary key is used to refer to a specific record in the table. If you know a customer's telephone number, you can find out any other information about that customer from `tblCustomers`. Including the CustomerTelephone as a field in an Orders table relates all the information for the customer to the order placed by the customer.

In `tblCustomers`, CustomerTelephone is a primary key. When you include it in an Orders table, it becomes a foreign key. When you relate two tables, you include the primary key from the table on the "one" side of a relationship (the *primary table*) as a foreign key in the "many" table (the *related table*). The foreign key field in the related table must have the same data type as the primary key in the primary table—with one exception. If the primary key uses an AutoNumber data type, then the foreign key field must use the Number type.

There are two ways to create relationships in Access 2000: by placing a lookup field in a table or by creating the relationship directly in the Relationships window.

Setting Lookup Fields

Most databases include two distinct types of tables: those that include primary data and those that hold lists of values used in other tables. These supporting tables are called *lookup tables*. An example is a table that includes the abbreviations for each state.

Once you have a State lookup table, you can use the table to provide data entry choices in the State field of other tables (like tblCustomers). With a lookup field, the user clicks a drop-down arrow and chooses a value from a list rather than typing the state abbreviation. Lookup tables provide two advantages: they provide consistent choices that are easy to use, and you can use them to validate data entry by restricting the user to entries from the table.

If the list of possible entries for a field is short and doesn't change much, you might prefer to create a lookup based on a typed-in list of values rather than a table. For example, if one of the fields in a table is Gender, you might just type in a list of values: Female and Male. It's not likely to change a lot, and it's a short list. If, however, you choose to use a table of possible values, you must create the lookup table before you can use the table to create a lookup field in another table.

Once you've created the lookup table, create the lookup field by opening the table in Design view. Add the Field Name for the new field and choose Lookup Wizard as the data type. If the field you want to look up is already included in the table, change the type to Lookup Wizard. In the first step of the Wizard, choose whether the data in the lookup will come from a typed-in list or an existing table, then click Next.

Typing in a List

If you choose to type in a list, in the next step, you'll choose a number of columns for the list and enter each item that should appear on the list, in the order you want them to appear, as shown in Figure 8.14. (Press Tab at the end of each item.) Then, adjust the width of the column so that it is slightly wider than the longest entry, and click Next. In the last step, enter a label for the lookup column; the label will become the new field name and change to a Text data type when you click Finish.

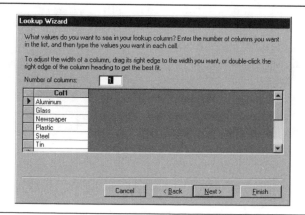

FIGURE 8.14: Entering a lookup list

Using a Lookup Table

If you choose to get the values in your lookup from a table, you'll be prompted to select a table (or query) in the next step of the Wizard. Then you'll choose the columns that you want to include in your lookup. In Figure 8.15, DepartmentID is the primary key of `tblDepts`, so choosing DepartmentID refers to the DepartmentName and DepartmentLocation fields. However, by including DepartmentName as a column in the lookup, users can select a department by name instead of choosing a code or number.

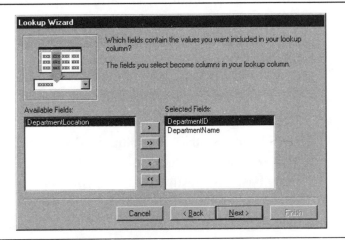

FIGURE 8.15: Choosing fields for a lookup

Then set the width of the column and decide whether the key field should be hidden or displayed. If you don't hide the key column, you need to identify which column you want to use to store data or perform an action. In most cases, you'll want to use the key column. In the last step of the Lookup Wizard, enter a label for the lookup, which becomes the new name for the field. You'll be prompted to save the table so that Access can create the relationship between the table with the lookup field and the table used to provide the field's contents.

SKILL
8

CREATING A LOOKUP FIELD

1. If you want to use a table to populate the list of choices in the lookup field, first create and save the lookup table.
2. Open the table you want to add a lookup field to in Design view.
3. Add a field or change the data type of the existing field to Lookup Wizard.
4. In the first step of the Wizard, choose whether you want to use a table or type in a list of values. Click Next.
5. Select the table to use as a lookup and click Next to choose the fields you want to include. Click Next.

–OR–

5. Select the number of columns to include in the lookup and enter values for each column.
6. Adjust the width of the columns. Click Next.
7. Enter a name for the field and click Finish to create the lookup field. If you base the lookup on a table, you will be prompted to save the current table. Choose Yes.

Working with Relationships

To look at the relationship Access created, open the Relationships window (choose Tools ➤ Relationships). There may be a number of relationships already defined, depending on how many lookups you've created in your database.

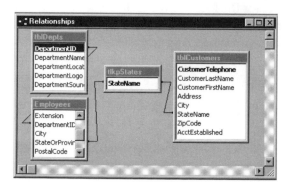

Click the Show All Relationships button to make sure all the relationships are displayed. If you double-click the line that shows the relationship, the Relationships dialog box opens. The primary table and primary key are shown in the left column, and the related table and foreign key are displayed in the second column. The relationship between an employees table and a departments table is shown below.

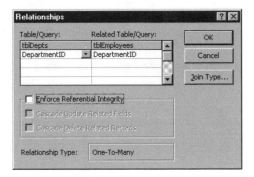

Setting Referential Integrity

Referential integrity ensures that records in a related table have related values in the primary table. Referential integrity prevents users from accidentally deleting or changing records in a primary table when records in a related table depend on them, making sure that there are no orphaned records in the related table: orders without customers, class registrations without students, or pay rates without employees.

When referential integrity is enforced in the relationship between the Departments and Employees tables, three restrictions are applied. First, Access won't allow you to use a DepartmentID in tblEmployees that doesn't already exist in tblDepts. Second, foreign key values (DepartmentIDs) that have been used in the related Departments table protect their matching records in the primary table, so a user can't delete a department in tblDepts that's already been used in tblEmployees. Finally, the actual data in the primary table is protected. A user can't change OPS to Operations in tblDepts because OPS is already referenced in tblEmployees. When you try to enter, delete, or change data that violates the referential integrity rules, Access displays a warning dialog box and ignores the change.

Cascading Updates and Deletes

You can override the second and third restrictions and still maintain referential integrity by enabling Cascade Update Related Fields and Cascade Delete Related Records. When *Cascade Update Related Fields* is enabled, changing the value of a primary key in the primary table automatically updates that value in the foreign key of the related table's matching records. With cascade update enabled, you *can* change OPS to Operations; the change will be automatically reflected in any tblEmployees record that included OPS. When *Cascade Delete Related Records* is enabled, deleting a record in the primary table deletes any related records in the related table. Deleting OPS from tblDepts will delete the record for any employee of the Operations department in tblEmployees.

MODIFYING RELATIONSHIPS AND SETTING REFERENTIAL INTEGRITY

1. Choose Tools ➤ Relationships to open the Relationships window.
2. Move the tables so that you can clearly see the relationship lines.
3. Double-click on the existing relationship lines and set referential integrity, cascade deletes, and cascade updates. Click OK.
4. Close the Relationships window. Save the layout changes.

Creating Relationships

Some of the relationships in a database may not be used for lookups. To create other relationships, make sure that the primary key field in the primary table is included as a foreign key in the related table. Then open the Relationships window.

To create a relationship, make sure that both the primary and related tables are visible. If not, click the Show Tables toolbar button and add the table(s) to the window. Then select the primary key field in the primary table, and drag and drop it on the matching field in the related table. The Relationships dialog box will open so you can set referential integrity.

Drilling Down into Tables

Drilling down into your tables refers to the process of tracing relationships between specific records in different tables to get an extended view of your data. For example, looking up all orders for a given customer in tblCustomers is considered drilling down. Access 2000 allows you to drill down in a couple of different ways.

The traditional way requires manually traversing the relationships between your tables as you look for information. The newer, often better way is through the use of *subdatasheets*. Subdatasheets are basically datasheets-within-datasheets. They take the manual effort out of traversing related tables, and creating them requires little or no additional effort.

Manual Data Inspection

To gain a better appreciation for the wonders of subdatasheets, let's take a brief look at how to manually find related records between tables. We'll use John Smith's record in tblCustomers, shown below, as a starting point. We want to find related records for this entry.

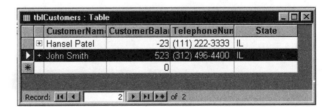

You'll need to know which tables are related to tblCustomers. If you don't, you can find them by looking at the relationships diagram. Here you'll also find the names of the foreign keys in those other tables that are related to your starting table's primary key. In the case of tblOrders, the foreign key is TelephoneNumber.

SKILL
8

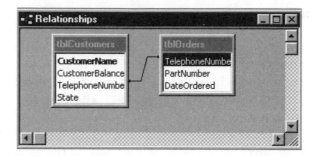

Finally, you must open each of these related tables in Datasheet view and find the rows where the foreign key columns have values that are equal to the value of the primary key column in the starting table. These are the related rows, in the case of our example, the orders placed by customer John Smith.

Using Subdatasheets

The best part about subdatasheets is that most of the work is automatically done for you as you add relationships between tables. Any table that is related through its primary key to one or more other tables contains subdatasheets when viewed in Datasheet view.

At first, the subdatasheets will probably all be collapsed, represented by small plus signs in the left margin of the table.

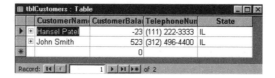

When you click on a plus sign, the immediate result will depend upon exactly how many other tables are related to this one. If there is only one related table, then the row expands to reveal all the rows in the other table that are related to the one you selected. You can now fully view, add, modify, and delete related rows in the other table directly from this datasheet!

On the other hand, if more than one related table is in your database, then clicking a plus sign for the first time opens the Insert Subdatasheet dialog box. Access can only display subdatasheets for one related table at a time, so this dialog box asks you to choose the table or query for which you would like the related rows to be shown.

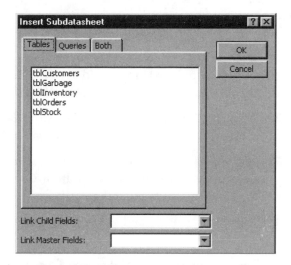

DRILLING DOWN WITH SUBDATASHEETS

1. Specify relationships between tables using at least one primary key in the Relationships diagram.
2. Open a table related via its primary key in Datasheet view.
3. Click on any of the plus signs to access the child rows related to the row in the current table.
4. If more than one table contains rows related to this one, you will first have to choose the table from which you would like to see related rows.

SKILL
8

TIP TIP TIP TIP TIP TIP TIP TIP TIP TIP TIP TIP TIP TIP TIP TIP TIP TIP TIP TIP TIP TIP

The Insert Subdatasheet dialog box lists every table and query available in the entire database, including any that are not even remotely related to the table currently being viewed! Access allows you to select these for subdatasheet use, but the results will range from returning completely blank rows to the utterly bizarre!

Hands On

1. In an existing database, create, populate, and save a lookup table that can be used to supply data for a field in a related table. Create the lookup field in the related table using the Lookup Wizard. Test the lookup field.

2. Examine the relationships in an existing database, and if necessary, enforce referential integrity with or without cascading updates and deletes.

3. In the database you've been creating, add lookup tables you feel would be helpful for data entry and validation. Create any other relationships that are required to maintain data integrity and relate tables.

4. View, add, modify, and delete rows in related tables using subdatasheets.

Skill 8.6: Enhancing Form Design

The simple forms that we have looked at so far are adequate for basic database needs. Fortunately, Access 2000 provides an abundance of features for creating even fancier forms to suit your more advanced applications. In this section, we will show you many ways to improve your form's "look and feel."

Creating Forms for Multiple Tables

The Form Wizard lets you create any of the same forms as AutoForms and also has a few other bells and whistles, like creating forms that display data from more than one related table. The related part is important; if you haven't already created a relationship between two tables, you can't relate them in a form. To easily create a form that includes a subform, press the Forms button on the navigation bar and click New or choose New Form from the New Object drop-down list to open the New Form dialog box. Choose Form Wizard. Because you'll be creating a form that uses more than one table, you do not need to choose a table or to query where the object's data comes from before clicking OK.

In the first step of the Form Wizard, shown in Figure 8.16, use the pick buttons to choose the fields to include on the form. You can access all the tables in the database from the drop-down list in the tables/queries section. When you have selected a table, its fields are displayed in the Available Fields list box, so you can move from table to table to pick fields. When you have selected all the fields you need, click the Next button.

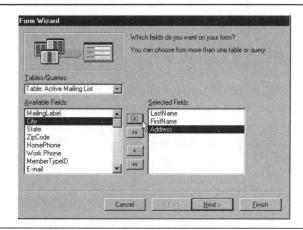

FIGURE 8.16: Selecting fields in the Form Wizard

If you choose fields from unrelated tables, the Form Wizard stops and displays an error message that tells you to cancel the Wizard, set the relationships, and then start the Form Wizard again. If the tables have a one-to-many relationship, you are asked how you want to view your data—whether you want the form's primary focus to be the primary or related table. In the Customers database, switching between By Customers and By Orders changes the sample in the right pane. Figure 8.17 shows the sample form when By Customers is selected.

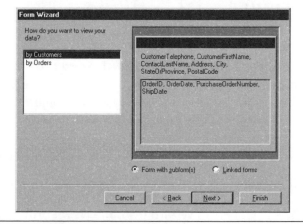

FIGURE 8.17: Form arranged by customers

When the form is arranged by customers, the order data appears in a sunken area of the preview. The customer form includes a datasheet or tabular subform to display order information. A *subform* is a type of "form within a form" that allows you to show related records from different tables when there is more than one record to display. The subform is embedded in the *main form*. The subform in the By Customers form (see Figure 8.17) displays the many order records—a visual representation of the one-to-many relationship between customers and orders. If the main form is already fairly complex, you can choose to display the subform as a linked form, as shown in Figure 8.18. The main form contains a button that opens the linked subform.

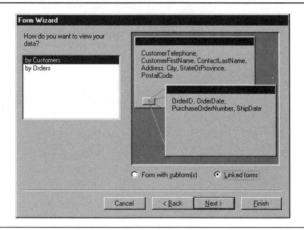

FIGURE 8.18: Linked subform

When the primary focus of the form is the table on the many side of the relationship, there is only one related record to display, so the data from the related table is displayed on the main form. The By Orders layout doesn't include a subform. Each order was placed by one customer, so there is no need for a subform to display multiple customers for a single order.

CREATING FORMS FOR MULTIPLE TABLES

1. Select Form Wizard from the New Form dialog box. Click OK.
2. Select the fields you would like to include on your form.

continued

3. Choose how you'd like to view the form data.

4. Select the type of layout you would like for each form.

5. Choose the style you would like for the form. Click Next.

6. Name the form(s) and click Finish.

Modifying Form Design

The built-in Access forms have limited graphic appeal, but Access 2000 includes many tools to help you make attractive forms. First, open the form in Design view, as shown in Figure 8.19.

FIGURE 8.19: Form in Design view

The Design window includes horizontal and vertical rulers and Form Design and Formatting toolbars. You can activate a Toolbox that will help with adding objects to the form by clicking the Toolbox button on the Form Design toolbar.

The form includes three sections and a number of different controls. The form is separated into three areas:

- A form header at the beginning of the first page of the form, usually used for titles

SKILL
8

- A form footer at the end of the last page of the form, used for user tips or other miscellaneous information

- A detail section, where each record's data is displayed, including the form background; individual areas for data, called text box controls; and a label control for each text box.

In tabular and datasheet forms, labels appear in the form header, and text boxes appear below the labels in the detail section. Any section can include various graphic objects like horizontal lines.

NOTE NOTE NOTE NOTE NOTE NOTE NOTE NOTE NOTE NOTE NOTE NOTE NOTE NOTE NOTE

If the form header and form footer bars aren't visible, choose View ➤ Form Header/Footer from the menu bar to turn them on.

If you want to rearrange a form, it's easiest to begin by enlarging the form's area. Move the mouse pointer to the bottom of the detail section, just above the form footer. The pointer changes to an adjustment tool. Drag the footer bar down to increase the height of the detail area. To increase the header section, move between the header bar and the detail bar, and then drag the detail bar down to open the header area.

Working with Objects

To select an object, click it so that handles appear. If you select a text box, the corresponding label also appears to be selected. Actually, it is only partially selected; it will *move* with the text box, but if you change the *format* of the text box, the label format will not change.

To select multiple objects, move the pointer to either ruler bar. The pointer changes to a bold arrow pointing toward the form. Press the mouse button, and a line drops directly through the form. When you release the button, all the objects the line passed through will be selected. You can also hold the mouse button down and drag the arrow to select a range of objects. If the objects you want to select aren't all in a line, you can select one object, and then hold the Shift key while selecting additional objects. Delete selected objects by pressing the Delete key on the keyboard.

Moving and Sizing Objects   To move an object, first select it, and then move the pointer to an edge of the selected object being sure not to point directly at any of the resizing handles; the pointer changes shape to a small hand. Hold the mouse button and drag the object to its new location. If you move an object beyond the form's current area, the form area will increase.

If you point directly at the handle in the upper-left corner of a text box or label, the hand changes to a finger pointing at the handle. If you drag using the pointing finger, only the object you are pointing at will move. If you point to the text box and drag it, the label will remain in place. If you drag the label, the text box won't move.

Adjust the size of controls as you would any graphic object: by dragging the resizing handles at the corners and sides of the object. Note, however, that changing the size of a text box control does not change the size of its underlying field. To change field size, you must go to the table's Design view and change the field size properties.

TIP TIP TIP TIP TIP TIP TIP TIP TIP TIP TIP TIP TIP TIP TIP TIP TIP TIP TIP TIP TIP TIP

If you have a hard-to-control mouse or want extra precision, select the control and use Shift+arrow keys to resize and Ctrl+arrow keys to move.

Working with Text

Click once on a selected label, and you can edit the text in the label. *Don't* change the field name in a text box control. If you do, data from the table won't appear in that field.

Adding a Title   The detail section is usually reserved for the information from the form's table(s). The header section is used for a form title. Use the Toolbox Label tool to create a title or other text to label the form itself. Click the Label tool and when you move the pointer back into the design area, it changes to a large letter *A* with crosshairs. Move the pointer into the header area, and click where you want to begin entering text. When you are done entering text, click elsewhere in the form to close the label control. You may then select the control and use the Formatting toolbar if you wish to format the title.

Formatting Text   Much of the formatting for controls is the same as text formatting in other Office 2000 applications (see Skill 1 for information on standard formatting.) Select one or more controls, and then choose formatting options from the toolbar, or right-click and select options from the shortcut menu.

Fore color is the color used for text. Some colors, such as dark blue, make a very attractive form that is easy to read. Other colors, such as yellow, are very hard to read and should be used sparingly, if at all.

The *back color* is the color for the fill behind the text. The default for labels is transparent, which means the color from the form background appears as the label's background color. The default background color for text boxes is white.

Conditional Formatting   Sometimes you will want a field to appear differently depending upon certain conditions that vary from one record to the next. For example, if you have a field called CustomerBalance, you might want the number in it to appear red if a customer owed you money, otherwise you'd want it black. Access 2000 can produce this effect through *conditional formatting*.

To use conditional formatting, select the fields that contain the text you want to change and choose Format ➤ Conditional Formatting to open the Conditional Formatting dialog box.

Choose formatting styles in the Default Formatting control area just as you format other fields. Access will apply this formatting whenever one of the conditions specified in the Condition control area is satisfied by the value in the field.

CONDITIONALLY FORMATTING YOUR DATA

1. Switch to Design view of a form and select the field you want to format.
2. Choose Format ➤ Conditional Formatting.

continued ▶

3. To specify how you would want the data to look based on the value in the field, choose Field Value Is from the Conditions List.

4. To specify the way that you would like your data to look when a certain fact is true, set Condition Expression Is and enter an expression representing a test for that fact.

5. To specify the way that you would like your data to look when a user moves the cursor over it, select Field Has Focus.

6. After you set the condition, set the formatting options to reflect how you would like the formatted values to appear.

7. Click Add to apply another condition or Delete to remove an existing condition.

In our example, we want to make the text of the CustomerBalance field turn red whenever a customer owes us money. Since we only need to deal with negative values, we would choose Field Value Is, Less Than, and 0 in our Condition 1 control. We don't need to do anything special to make the text black when the CustomerBalance is 0 or greater, because this is the default.

Changing Borders

Every Access control has a border around it. Borders have three properties: color, line width, and special effect.

Although you can't delete the border, you can effectively disable all three properties by choosing Transparent as the border color. A transparent border has not visible width, color, or effect. This is effective for labels, but text boxes should have no borders so that the form's user knows where to enter data.

You can change border width using the Border Width button on the Formatting toolbar, selecting widths from a hairline thickness to a 6-point width. Typically, a 1- or 2-point border is appropriate; however, the thicker border can be used for graphic design. Borders with special effects also help differentiate control type. There are six special effects that can be accessed from the Special Effects button's drop-down list:

Flat   Appropriate controls that are not designed for data entry

Sunken   Best choice for text boxes for editing or entering data

SKILL
8

Shadowed Good choice for titles

Raised Another useful choice for data entry, titles, or to draw attention to a part of the screen

Etched Good choice for text boxes that cannot be changed

Chiseled Applies a single inverted line underneath the control

When you apply Sunken, Raised, Etched, or Chiseled special effects, you turn off any other choices for border color and line width. Only Flat and Shadowed are affected by the border-color and line-width formatting options.

APPLYING BORDERS AND SPECIAL EFFECTS

1. Select the controls you want to change.
2. Use the Border Color, Border Width, and Special Effects buttons on the Formatting toolbar or the shortcut menu to format the borders for the selected controls.

Changing several controls one by one can be a time-consuming task. Fortunately, you can use the Format Painter to paint all the formatting—color, borders, special effects, and alignment—from one control onto another. If you're going to apply the selected format to more than one other control, double-click to lock the Format Painter on. (For a review of how to use the Format Painter, see Skill 1.6.)

Dividing Pages and Page Sections

A form with a lot of fields or somewhat unrelated fields can be cluttered and hard to use. Access provides two ways to create a form with multiple pages: page breaks and tab controls. Page breaks are cumbersome to use, whereas tab controls provide a simple and nicely designed interface for users.

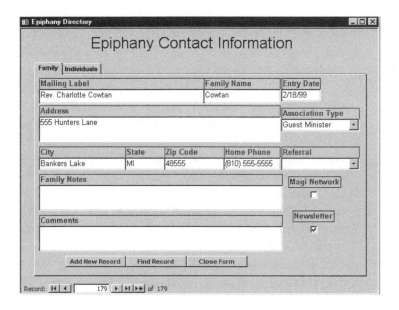

To create a form with tab controls, create a new form in Design view.

CREATING A MULTI-PAGE FORM WITH TABS

1. Select the Tab Control icon from the Toolbox and place it on the form. Resize the control by dragging the handles on its border.

2. To add additional tabs, right-click on the tab control and choose Insert Page.

3. To change the name of the tab, right-click and choose Properties. Enter a name in the Caption box.

4. To add controls to a page, click the page tab and add fields from the Field List or copy controls from another form or add them from the Toolbox.

5. To remove a page, right-click on the page and choose Delete Page.

6. To change the order of the pages, right-click on a page and choose Page Order.

SKILL
8

Relative Sizing and Alignment

The form's background is composed of one-inch horizontal and vertical guide-lines and grid points which make up a grid. If the grid points aren't visible, choose View ➤ Grid (once again, you may need to expand the menu in order for this option to be visible). When you move a control, it automatically lines up with the grid both horizontally and vertically. If you try to place the edge of the control between two grid points, Access moves it to align with one grid point or the other. This is a feature called *Snap to Grid*. Sometimes you might want to place two or more controls so they aren't on a grid point—closer together than the grid allows or not as far apart as two grid points require. To do this, you must first turn off Snap to Grid (choose Format ➤ Snap to Grid). The Snap-to-Grid feature is not one you will need to turn off very often, but working without Snap to Grid is essential for small refinements in your Access forms.

Adjusting Control Alignment, Size, and Spacing

You can manually adjust the size and position of every control on a form. However, Access 2000 automates size and positioning features so you can manipulate multiple controls at one time. Begin by selecting two or more controls, then choose Format ➤ Align or choose Align from the shortcut menu to see the list of options:

Choosing Align ➤ Left will align all selected controls with the control closest to the left edge of the form. Use Align ➤ Top or Align ➤ Bottom to adjust controls on the same horizontal line. Access has trouble differentiating between controls that are overlapped. Separate overlapping controls before attempting to align them to ensure that you only select the controls you want to align.

Sizing Controls

Choosing Format ➤ Size ➤ To Fit or double-clicking any sizing handle will instantly resize labels based on the length of their content. You can select two or more controls and use the other sizing options. Tallest and Shortest refer to vertical height and Widest and Narrowest refer to horizontal width.

Spacing Controls

Spacing allows you to increase or decrease the relative position of selected controls by one grid point either horizontally or vertically. This is valuable if you need to spread out the controls or move them closer together. You can also use Spacing to make sure controls are evenly spaced. Select controls, then choose Format ➤ Vertical Spacing (or Horizontal Spacing) ➤ Make Equal (or Increase or Decrease).

ADJUSTING CONTROL SIZE AND POSITION

1. Select the controls you want to size or position.
2. Choose Format ➤ Size, or right-click and choose Size, to resize the controls.
3. Choose Format ➤ Align, or right-click and choose Align, to align controls in relation to each other.
4. Choose Format ➤ Horizontal Spacing or Format ➤ Vertical Spacing to alter the spacing between the selected controls.

SKILL
8

Rearranging the Tab Order

Tab order—the sequence of controls you move through when pressing Tab—is assigned when the form is created. After you rearrange controls on a form, the tab order may be out of sequence. Users expect to be able to move through the form sequentially, so an inconsistent tab order almost guarantees data-entry errors. Tab order is accessed from the View menu.

ADJUSTING TAB ORDER

1. Choose View ➤ Tab Order, or right-click and choose Tab Order.
2. Click Auto Order to see if Access automatically orders the fields correctly.
3. To change the order of fields manually, select the field(s) you want to move by clicking/dragging the button at the left end of the field. Point to the field(s) and drag them into the proper position.
4. Click OK to save the tab order and close the Tab Order dialog box.

It's important to test how well your forms work each time you make any substantive change. Enter sample data and make sure everything operates as you expect it to.

Formatting Data in Form View

If all you want to change is a color or font, you don't even need to go into Design view. Whenever you use a form to view data in your tables, Access provides you with a Formatting toolbar that gives you access to many design features. Although you can't edit control labels, you can change fonts, colors, and conditional formatting in Form view.

FORMATTING DATA IN FORM VIEW

1. Select whatever data is currently displayed in the field you wish to change.
2. Use the Formatting toolbar to format the selected controls.

–OR–

2. Right-click and select properties from the shortcut menu.
3. Choose Format ➤ Conditional Formatting to make your data's appearance dependant on conditions that you may specify.

Adding Controls to Forms

If you add a field to a table, existing forms won't include the field. To add the field's text box control to the table, open the Field List by clicking the Field List button on the toolbar:

Drag the desired field from the Field List into the form and drop it in place, then format the control.

Changing Properties of Forms and Controls

Every Access object—including tables and forms, controls such as text boxes and labels, and individual fields in a table—has properties. For example, the properties of a text box include its color, font, size, and control source: the table or query that supplies data to the text box. Field properties include size, input masks, and field type. Form properties include the size of the form, how the form can be viewed, and its record source: the table or query the records come from.

It's not essential to know every available property to work successfully in Access. However, whenever an object doesn't behave as you expect it to, it's probably a safe bet to look for a property that might be affecting how the object acts. To view the properties for a control, double-click the control in Design view to open the Properties sheet.

To open the form's Properties sheet, double-click on the Form Select button to the left of the horizontal ruler bar. A form has four categories of properties:

Format refers to properties related to formatting: what the form or control looks like, what buttons and bars are activated, what views are allowed.

Data refers to where the data comes from: the record or control source and whether or not the data can be edited.

SKILL 8

Event includes all the macros and programming code assigned to an object or control.

Other includes any other properties that relate to the object or control including, for example, a field's tab order.

Note that the Properties sheet title bar includes the name of the selected object. If you want to look at properties for one of the form's other controls, don't close the Properties sheet, just click the control.

Changing the Property Settings on Multiple Fields

Often you'll want to change the property settings on multiple controls at the same time. If you select more than one control and open the Properties sheet, only those properties that affect all the selected controls will be displayed. For example, if you selected a label and a text box, there would be no Data or Event properties displayed; the text box has Data and Event properties, but the label does not.

It's helpful to understand a few properties when you are designing forms. If you don't know what a property does, you probably don't know what will happen if you change the setting. Unless you're feeling very adventurous, you should leave strange and unusual property settings intact.

Hiding Form Features

A number of elements are enabled by default on every form, including scroll bars, record selectors, and navigation buttons. All these elements can be turned off, if desired, in the form's Properties sheet. The scroll bars are only needed if parts of the form don't fit on the screen. Record selectors are useful in tables and in some subforms but are not necessary in tabular forms. You have to decide whether it's necessary to have navigation buttons on both a main form and the subform. Turn off features you don't need by opening the form's Properties sheet and changing the undesired item's property setting to No on the Format page. These changes, relatively easy to make, make the form much easier to use.

NOTE NOTE NOTE NOTE NOTE NOTE NOTE NOTE NOTE NOTE NOTE NOTE NOTE NOTE NOTE

A feature unique to datasheet forms is the ability to hide and unhide columns. Simply select the columns that you don't want to display and choose Format ➤ Hide Columns. Be careful not to hide a required field, or the form will in effect become read only. Users will not be able to add records using the form. If you change your mind, just choose Format ➤ Unhide Columns and select the check boxes next to the names of the columns that you would like to display again.

Hands On

1. In an existing database, use the Form Wizard to create two forms that include data from two related tables: a form with a subform, and a form with a single main form.

2. Format the forms created in Exercise 1. Size and align all controls appropriately. Change the borders for text box controls. Edit and format labels as needed. Add and format a form title in the form header area. Turn off form features that aren't required.

3. In an existing database, check the tab order for all forms.

4. Create a datasheet form and hide at least one of the columns, and then make all of them display again.

Skill 8.7: Producing Reports

A *report* is the output of the data in a database. Access gives you the freedom to report your data in a variety of ways. Reports can show all or only some of the data related to a record, and can be based on a table or a query. The flexibility to customize reports based on your personally defined criteria and to organize the data in useful ways—in other words, to make it accessible—is really what gives Access its name. When a report is saved, only the structure of the report is saved—not the data you see in the preview. Data shown in a report is always as current as the records in the database.

Creating a Report

SKILL
8

Most reports are either columnar or tabular reports. A *columnar report*, like the report shown in Print Preview in Figure 8.20, shows each field on a separate line in a single column down the page. The columnar report is the printed version of a columnar form. A *tabular report*, shown in Figure 8.21, is like a tabular form.

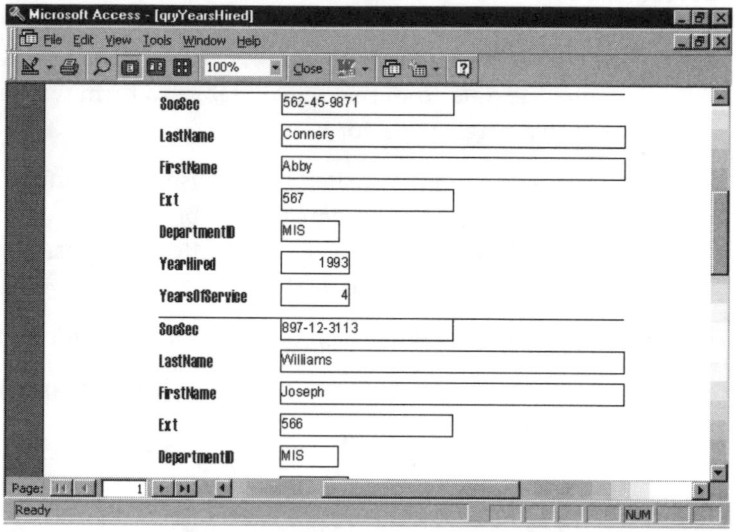

FIGURE 8.20: Columnar report

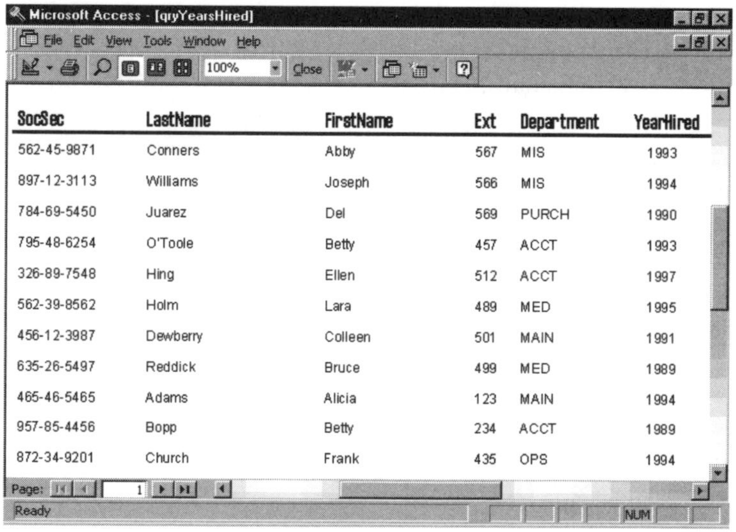

FIGURE 8.21: Tabular report

You can develop reports in five ways:

- In Design view, where you can design a report completely from scratch

- With the Report Wizard, which lets you customize a report

- By choosing one of two AutoReports, which automatically include all of the fields in the table or query you select

- In the Chart Wizard, which walks you through the steps to create a chart

- With the Label Wizard, which creates mailing and other labels

Creating a report in Access is as simple as creating a data form. However, you should have a few additional tricks up your sleeve to format the report so it looks its best and displays precisely the information you want to see. Some reports merely show data in some kind of organized way: an individual data sheet or a listing of names and addresses. But it is through a report that independent bits of data join together to become the compilation of data that managers can use to make decisions, launch studies, and understand their businesses better.

Generating AutoReports

The simplest reports to produce are AutoReports. Just like with forms, there are Columnar and Tabular AutoReports, which provide a good place to start if the data you want is already contained in one table or query. Choose Report from the New Object drop-down list to open the New Report dialog box.

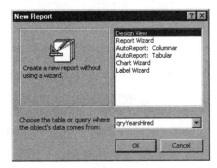

CREATING AUTOREPORTS

1. Choose Report from the New Object drop-down list to open the New Reports dialog box.
2. Choose AutoReport: Columnar or AutoReport: Tabular.
3. Click the drop-down list and choose the table or query on which to base the report.
4. Click OK to produce the report and open it in Print Preview.
5. Print the report, if desired, and close the Print Preview window. You will be prompted to save the report.

Using the Report Wizard

The Report Wizard lets you choose the fields you want in the report— including fields from more than one table—and designate how the data should be grouped, sorted, and formatted. To start the Report Wizard, click Create Report by Using Wizard in the database window (or choose Report from the New Object button on the toolbar, and then choose Report Wizard). You don't have to choose a table at this point—you'll have a chance to do that in the first step of the Wizard. In the Wizard, you'll select, group, and sort the fields in the report; choose a layout and paper orientation; fit the fields to the page; and choose a report style. When you click Finish, Access will create the report and open it in Print Preview.

CREATING A REPORT USING THE REPORT WIZARD

1. Choose Create Report by Using Wizard from the database window, or choose Report from the New Object button on the toolbar and then choose Report Wizard.
2. Choose the table or query on which to base the report. Click the right arrow to move individual fields to the Selected Fields box, or the double arrow to move all the fields. When you have selected all the fields you want from the first table/query, select the next object from the list, if desired.

continued ▶

3. Click Next when you have finished selecting fields.

4. Choose the levels you want to group by, if any. Use the up or down Priority buttons to reverse the order of the grouping levels. Click Next.

5. Choose the fields you would like to sort by, and indicate whether you'd like the records in ascending or descending order. Click Next.

6. Select the layout you'd like for the report, portrait or landscape orientation, and whether you'd like the field width adjusted to fit on one page. Click Next.

7. Select the style you'd like for the report and click Next.

8. Enter a title for the report and choose whether you'd like to open the report in Print Preview or Design view. Click Finish to create the report.

Modifying a Report

Most of what you know about Access form design can be applied to report design. After you open the report in Design view, maximize the report so you have more room to work. Figure 8.22 shows the Years of Service Report in Design view.

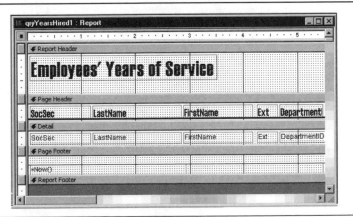

SKILL
8

FIGURE 8.22: Working in Design view

A report has six sections:

Report Header   Appears at the top of the report (page 1) and includes the title and other report information

Page Header   Appears at the top of every printed page of the report

Group Header   Appears at the top of the identified group; there will be a separate group header for each grouping level

Detail   Where the data from the tables/queries will appear

Page Footer   Appears at the bottom of every page

Report Footer   Appears on the last page of the report

You can choose to incorporate any or all of these sections into your report. Use the adjustment tool to increase or decrease the size of the sections.

The Snap-to-Grid, alignment, and size features all work the same as they do in forms (see Skill 8.6). All the colors, lines, borders, special effects, fonts, and other formatting features are also available for your use. You can edit any of the report's labels without worrying about affecting the contents of the report. However, be careful not to edit the text boxes that contain data fields. If you do, the control will no longer be bound to a field, so it won't display data. Most text boxes are in the detail section. However, at least one text box appears in each group header. To be certain that you're editing a label rather than a text box, look at the control's properties.

In Report Design view, there are two preview choices on the View menu: Print Preview and Layout Preview. Print Preview produces the entire report just as it will look when printed.

Layout Preview only shows you sample data. If you have a database with thousands or even hundreds of records, it takes time to produce a preview of all the pages. By using sample data, Layout Preview quickly generates a preview so you that can check design features.

Specifying Date and Page Number Codes

The Page Footer contains a date field that shows today's date and a page number field that shows the current page number out of the total number of pages:

| =Now() | ="Page " & [Page] & " of " & [Pages] |

Each of these controls can be customized if you would like to change their appearance. The date field, which displays today's date, includes the function =Now( ). You can choose different date formats by opening the field's Properties sheet. Click the Format drop-down list on the Format page and then scroll the list to select an option: general date, long date, medium date, or short date. If you want to add a date to a different part of the report or to a report that doesn't already have a date, choose Insert ➤ Date and Time from the menu bar to open the Date and Time dialog box:

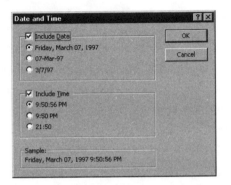

When you set your preferences and choose OK, a text box control with the appropriate code will be inserted at the top of the active report section. Drag the control to its location in the report.

If your report is only one page, you might want to delete the page number field control altogether; select the field and press the Delete key on the keyboard. If you want to change the page number format, it's easier to delete the field and then re-insert a new page number field with the format you want. Choose Insert ➤ Page Numbers to open the Page Numbers dialog box:

SKILL
8

There are two formats: Page N (Page 1) or Page N of M (Page 1 of 2). You can place the page number in the header or the footer and have it aligned on the left, center, or right of the page. For two-sided printing, choose Inside or Outside alignment. You can also suppress the page number on the first page of a multi-page report. When you click OK, a page number field appears in the position on the page that you selected in the Page Numbers dialog box.

MODIFYING A REPORT IN DESIGN VIEW

1. Open the report you want to customize in Report Design view.

2. Select the controls you want to change, then use the Formatting toolbar, the Toolbox, and the Format menu to make the desired design changes.

3. To change the date's format, double-click the date field, open the Properties sheet, and change the date Format to General, Long, Medium, or Short.

4. To insert a new date field, choose Insert ≻ Date from the menu bar, choose the desired settings, and click OK. Reposition the date as desired.

5. To change the page number format, delete the page number field and choose Insert ≻ Page Numbers from the menu. Choose the Page Number settings you want and click OK. Reposition the page number if desired.

Changing Sort Order and Grouping Levels

After you've used the Wizard to create a report, you can change the sort order and grouping levels of the data.

 Click the Sorting and Grouping button on the Report Design toolbar to open the Sorting and Grouping dialog box.

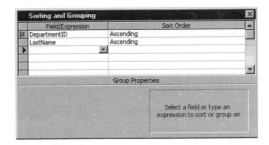

The first item, DepartmentID, is a group level for the report; the Sorting and Grouping icon appears to the left of the Field/Expression column. When you click on the DepartmentID field, you see a Yes under Group Properties, Group Header indicating that there is a group header for the field. The grouped data is then sorted by LastName. If you were to click on the LastName row, you'd see that the Group Header property is set to No, so the report won't include a header for last names.

To rearrange the sorting or grouping order, select a row, then drag-and-drop it into the desired order. To insert a new sort or group level, select the field from the Field/Expression drop-down list. Set Group Header or Footer to Yes if you want to add a header or footer for the group level. To remove a group level, select the row and press the Delete key. You will see the following warning:

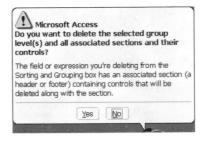

If you click OK, the group level, the group header, and the associated controls will be removed from the report. This does not affect the data displayed in the Detail section of the report.

Adding and Deleting Report Controls

Add and delete report controls just as you add or delete form controls (see Skill 8.6). To add a field to a report, click the Field List button on the Report Design toolbar to open the Field List dialog box, and drag the field into the appropriate section of the report. You might have to format and resize the label and the text box controls once you drop the field into place. To delete a field's text box control from the report, select the text box and press the Delete key on the keyboard.

Using Report Snapshots

A *report snapshot* is a way to capture a report at a given point in time—kind of like taking an electronic photocopy of the report. Report snapshots can be distributed via e-mail, diskette, or the Internet without having to send the rest of your database along with them!

Creating Snapshots

To create a report snapshot, press the Reports button on the database window's left-hand navigation bar and highlight the report that you would like to distribute. Choose File ➤ Export to open the Export Report dialog box.

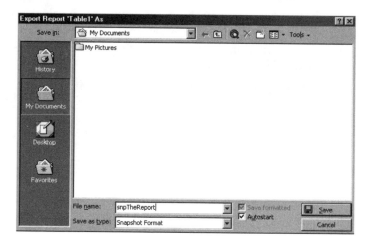

Select Snapshot Format from the Save As Type drop-down list and click the Save button. Access creates your snapshot and saves it under the requested file-name. If you have already installed the Snapshot Viewer application, Access opens your snapshot in it. If not, you are asked whether or not you want to install it.

Distributing Snapshots

You have three ways to distribute a report snapshot after you have created it: by e-mail, by diskette or network drive, or over the Internet or corporate intranet.

- To send the snapshot as an attachment to an e-mail message, choose File ➤ Send from the menu in the Viewer. If you've closed the Viewer, simply select the report you wish to send and click File ➤ Send To ➤ Mail Recipient (As Attachment) from the menu in the database window. Enter the e-mail address of the person to whom you wish to distribute your report snapshot. Your end-users can open your file directly from their e-mail clients by double-clicking its icon in their Attachments list.

- If you are distributing via diskette or a network share, your end-users can open your file directly from Windows Explorer by double-clicking its icon.

- If you are distributing via the Internet or a corporate intranet, your end-users can open your file directly from their browsers by entering its address. If you are using this option, be sure to use a filename with no spaces and give them the full address of the snapshot file.

Viewing Snapshots

To view a report snapshot, you need to have the Microsoft Snapshot Viewer installed on your system. The Snapshot Viewer is available for free download from Microsoft. If you are sending a snapshot to a colleague, it's helpful to include a link to the Microsoft download site so they can access it easily. You can download the Snapshot Viewer from `http://www.microsoft.com/office/000/viewers.htm`.

Hands On

1. In an existing database:
   a) Create a columnar AutoReport.
   b) Create a tabular AutoReport.
   c) Open the tabular AutoReport. Change and format the title.

2. Create a report based on two or more tables using the Report Wizard.

3. Create a report with:
   a) Grouping and group headers.
   b) The page number in the page header, with no number on the first page.
   c) Your name in the footer of each page.

SKILL 8

4. Create a report snapshot and:

   a) View it directly from Windows Explorer.

   b) Mail it to yourself and view it directly from your e-mail client.

   c) If you have access to a Web folder, save the report to a Web folder and view it directly from your browser.

Skill 8.8: Creating Queries

A *query* selects records from one or more tables based on user-specified criteria. You can create five different types of Access queries: select queries, parameter queries, crosstab queries, action queries, and SQL (Structured Query Language) queries.

Queries, like other database objects, can be created a variety of ways. You can enter SQL code manually, use Design view, or use one of the query Wizards. If you're creating a query simply to enter or report data from multiple tables, it is easiest to use the Form or Report Wizard to retrieve the data you want because the Wizard will create the query. If, however, you need to work with a data set independent of a form or report, use the Simple Query Wizard to create a select query.

CREATING A SIMPLE SELECT QUERY

1. From the Query page of the database window, choose New, or click the New Object button and choose New Query. Choose Simple Query Wizard from the list of query options and click OK.

2. From the Tables/Queries drop-down list, choose the table/query that contains the fields you want to include in the query.

3. Select the fields you want to include and click the right arrow or double-click to move the fields into the Selected Fields column.

4. Select any additional tables/queries from the Tables/Queries drop-down list and repeat step 3. Click Next when all fields have been selected.

continued ▶

5. If the fields you selected include a number field, you'll be asked to select a summary or detail query. To see each record, choose Detail. To see totals, averages, or other summaries, choose Summary and set the summation options. Click Next.
6. Provide a name for the query. Click Finish to run the query.

You can sort and filter the query results, which look like the Datasheet view of a table (see Figure 8.23), using the Sort and Filter buttons on the Database toolbar. When you sort, then close a query, you are asked whether you wish to save the changes to the query layout. If you save the changes, you're saving the sorting criteria, and the query will still be sorted the next time it is opened. If you choose not to save the changes, the query returns to its original order.

qryEmplDepts : Select Query

LastName	FirstName	Ext	DepartmentName	DepartmentLocation
OToole	Betty	457	Accounting	Midland
Hing	Ellen	512	Accounting	Midland
Dewberry	Colleen	501	Maintenance	Midland
Holm	Lara	489	Media Arts	West Branch
Reddick	Bruce	499	Media Arts	West Branch
Conners	Abby	567	Information Svcs	Harrison
Williams	Joseph	566	Information Svcs	Harrison
Juarez	Del	569	Purchasing	Harrison

Record: 8 of 8

FIGURE 8.23: Query results set

SKILL 8

Clicking the Design View button opens the query for modification. The query window is separated into two panes. The lower pane uses one column for each field included in the query, indicating the field name, the table the field comes from, whether the query is sorted based on the field, whether the field is shown in the query results, and criteria that have been applied to the field to limit the query results.

The upper pane shows the tables included in the query and the relationship between the tables. If you create a new query from related tables, the relationships will appear as the tables are placed in the upper pane. If you haven't defined the relationships between the tables, you can create relationships in the upper pane the same way you do in the Relationships window. However, these relationships are only created for the query—they aren't automatically placed in the Relationships window. The relationship shown in Figure 8.24 is called a *join*.

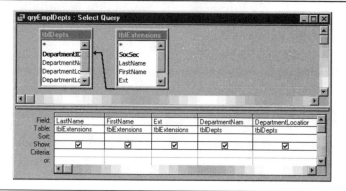

FIGURE 8.24: Query Design view

There are two types of joins: inner joins and outer joins. Outer joins are further divided into right outer joins and left outer joins. Double-clicking the join line opens the Join Properties dialog box.

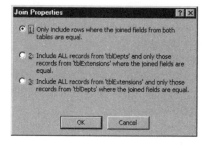

The first join type listed is an inner join, which is the default join in queries. In an *inner join*, the only records displayed in the query are those with identical values in the joined fields. If there are no employees assigned to one of the departments, the department won't be listed; an employee with no department assigned will not be included in the results set.

The second join type is a *left outer join*. With a left outer join, all the records in the primary table in the relationship are displayed, even if they don't have matching entries in the related table.

A *right outer join* includes all the records from the related table (the employee extensions linked from Excel), even if no matching records exist in the primary departments table. The join symbol points from the table that will have all records listed to the table that will only have matching records displayed. All three joins use the same tables and relationships, but each returns a different query results set. To remove a join, select the join and press the Delete key on the keyboard.

Sorting a Query

To sort a query, choose Ascending or Descending in the Sort row of the column you want to sort by. You can sort on multiple fields. Although the fields to sort on don't have to be next to each other, they do need to be in order from left to right. If necessary, rearrange the query so that the primary sort field is to the left of the secondary sort field, and so on.

Printing a Query

When you print a query results set, the results appear in Datasheet view. To improve the appearance of the printed results, create a tabular form or report based on the query.

Creating a Parameter Query

A *parameter query* is a select query that displays a dialog box prompting the user for parameters. Use parameter queries when users frequently need to access a subset of a table or tables. Rather than creating 50 state queries, for example, you can create one parameter query and let the user enter the state abbreviation. You can easily create a parameter query from an existing select query. Open the select query in Design view. Enter a prompt, enclosed in brackets [ ] on the Criteria line of the field you want to use as a parameter:

Skill
8

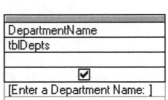

The prompt is the text that appears in the Enter Parameter Value dialog box to tell the user what information should be entered. You can see how the dialog box looks by clicking the Datasheet View button and running the query:

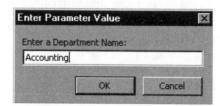

CREATING A PARAMETER QUERY

1. Open an existing select query in Design view.

2. Enter the parameter statement in brackets in the Criteria row of the desired field.

3. Run the query to make sure it works correctly. When the Enter Parameter Value dialog box opens, enter an appropriate value and click OK.

4. If you used an existing select query to create the new query, save the parameters query under a new name.

Creating a Summary Query

A *summary query* is a select query that returns summaries or totals rather than detailed records. If the fields you select in the Simple Query Wizard include numeric fields, you're given the choice to create a detail or summary query. But you can turn any select query into a summary query. First, open the select query that contains the data you want to summarize in Design view.

Σ

Click the Totals button to open the Totals row of the query grid. All fields are automatically set to Group By; the field that you want to base the summary data on should be left with that setting. For other fields, click the Totals drop-down list and choose a summation method. Table 8.2 lists the aggregate functions used in queries.

TABLE 8.2: Aggregate Query Functions

Function	Results	Used with Field Types
Avg	Average of the values in the field	AutoNumber, Currency, Date/Time, Number
Count	Number of records that hold data in this field. Count includes zeros, but not blanks.	All
First	The contents of the field in the first record in the result set	All
Last	The contents of the field in the last record in the result set	All
Min	Lowest value in the field	AutoNumber, Currency, Date/Time, Number, Text
Max	Highest value in the field	AutoNumber, Currency, Date/Time, Number, Text
StDev	Standard deviation of the values in the field	AutoNumber, Currency, Date/Time, Number
Sum	Total of the values in the field	AutoNumber, Currency, Date/Time, Number
Var	Variance of the values in the field	AutoNumber, Currency, Date/Time, Number

In Figure 8.25, the data in the query will be sorted by StateName, grouped by StateName, and the results set will show the number of customer accounts in each state.

SKILL
8

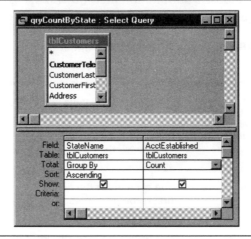

FIGURE 8.25: Summary query using Count

CREATING A SUMMARY QUERY

1. In Design view, open a select query that includes the field you want to base the summary on and the fields you want to summarize.
2. Click the Totals button to open the Totals row of the query grid.
3. Set the Totals row for the field you want to base the summary on to Group By.
4. For every other field, choose an aggregate summarization method from the Totals drop-down list.

Adding Calculations to Queries

The tblExtensions table, shown in Figure 8.26, includes the year each employee was hired in the field called YearHired. The Human Resources department would like to roughly calculate the number of years each employee has worked here.

SocSec	LastName	FirstName	Ext	DeptID	YearHire
587-25-8258	Jilliard	Bill	597	Maintenance	1996
635-26-5497	Reddick	Bruce	499	Media Arts	1989
725-72-5725	Izac	Juara	221	Purchasing	1995
725-72-5853	Hill	Boo	335	Maintenance	1990
784-69-5450	Juarez	Del	569	Purchasing	1990
795-48-6254	O'Toole	Betty	457	Accounting	1993
872-34-9201	Church	Frank	435	Operations	1994

FIGURE 8.26: Records from tblExtensions

To calculate the years of service, create a select query based on the table. In the query's Design view, click in the Field row of an empty column and enter the calculation, or click the Build button on the toolbar to open the Expression Builder.

The built-in Access function Now() returns the current date and time. The function Year() returns the year from a date. By nesting the two functions, you can calculate the current year: Year(Now()). Then, subtract the YearHired from the calculated current year: Year(Now())-[YearHired].

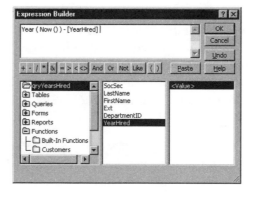

Click OK to close the Builder. Access will name the column Expr1, but you can select the name in query Design view and enter a new name, like YearsOfService. You can base a form or report on a query, so calculated query fields provide the tool you need to calculate many types of values for reporting on screen or on paper.

Adding a Calculation to a Query

1. In the field row of an empty column in the query's Design view, enter the calculation expression.

–OR–

1. Click the Build button to open the Expression Builder. Using the Built-in Functions and list of field names from the active query, create the calculation, and then click OK.
2. If you wish, change the name of the calculated query field from Expr1 to a more descriptive name.

Creating Crosstab Queries

Crosstab queries summarize information about two or more columns in a table or query. (If you want to create a crosstab query that involves more than one table, first use the Simple Query Wizard to create a select query with all the fields you need, then base your crosstab query on the select query rather than a table.) In the example below, we'll create a crosstab query to show the number of new hires by department each year based on the data in `tblExtensions` (see Figure 8.26). The completed query is shown in Figure 8.27.

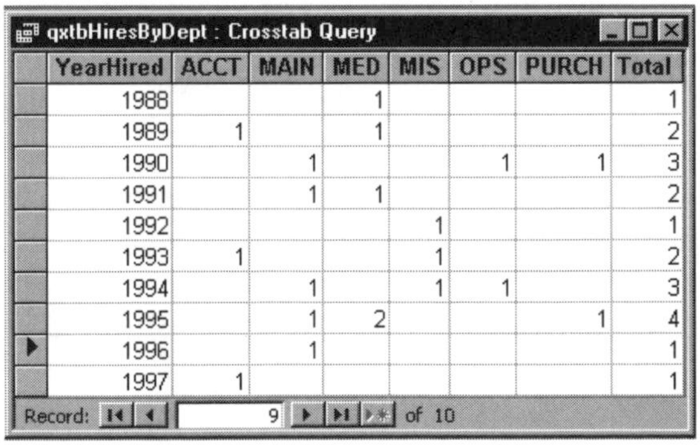

qxtbHiresByDept : Crosstab Query

YearHired	ACCT	MAIN	MED	MIS	OPS	PURCH	Total
1988			1				1
1989	1		1				2
1990		1			1	1	3
1991		1	1				2
1992				1			1
1993	1			1			2
1994		1		1	1		3
1995		1	2			1	4
1996		1					1
1997	1						1

Record: 9 of 10

FIGURE 8.27: Crosstab query results

To create a crosstab query, click the New Object button drop-down list, select New Query, then select the Crosstab Query Wizard. In the first step of the Wizard, identify the table or query that contains the columns you want to summarize, then click Next. The second step of the Wizard asks what field(s) contain the information you wish to present as rows within the query. You can select up to three fields from the table to use as rows. As you select each field, Access adds it to the row headings.

In Figure 8.27, the YearHired field is used for row headings, and the DepartmentID field is for column headings. The only reason to use year as the row heading, rather than column heading, is that there are more years than departments, so placing YearHired on the left side means the completed query is more likely to fit on the width of the computer screen. When you have selected the row headings, click Next. In the next step, select the single field that you wish to use for column headings, then click Next.

This step includes three choices:

- Which field do you want to calculate?

- How do you want to calculate your data?

- Do you want totals for each row?

The field you select (see Figure 8.28) determines the information that will be summarized in the crosstab query's results set, and the type of field you select determines the summary methods you can choose (see Table 8.2). In the last step of the Crosstab Query Wizard, enter a name for the query.

SKILL
8

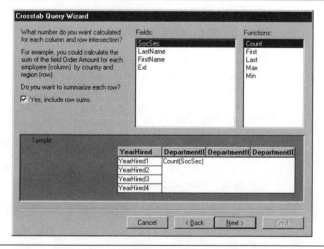

FIGURE 8.28: Selecting a calculated field and function

CREATING A CROSSTAB QUERY

1. In the New Query dialog box, select Crosstab Query Wizard from the list of choices.
2. Select the table or query on which you want to base the query. Click Next.
3. Select the field you want to use as row headings. Click Next.
4. Select the field you want to use as column headings. Click Next.
5. Select the field that contains the numbers you want to calculate, and then choose the function you want to apply. Indicate if you want to summarize each row. Click Next.
6. Enter a name for the crosstab query and click Finish.

Hands On

1. In an existing database:
   a) Create a select query to show information from a single table sorted in a different order than the table.
   b) Add a parameter to the query so a user can look for records based on the value in a particular field.
   c) Create and test a columnar form based on the parameter query.
   d) Create a new query that includes information from more than one table. Change the inner join to each type of outer join and note any differences in the query results sets.

2. In an existing database:
   a) Create a select query that includes a calculated field.
   b) Turn the select query into a summary query to total the calculated field and count at least one other field.

3. In an existing database, create a crosstab query to compare values from two columns in a select query.

NOTE NOTE NOTE NOTE NOTE NOTE NOTE NOTE NOTE NOTE NOTE NOTE NOTE NOTE
Data Access Pages is an exciting new Access feature that allows you to create dynamic Web pages from your Access data. When published to a Web server, Data Access Pages can be viewed and manipulated by other users. For more about creating Data Access Pages, see Skill 12.

Are You Experienced?

Now you can...

- ☑ Create and modify tables in an Access database
- ☑ Save your data into Access 97 format
- ☑ View the data in your tables using simple forms or enhanced design features like conditional formatting
- ☑ Create sophisticated relationships between the tables in your database
- ☑ Drill down into your data using subdatasheets
- ☑ Share your data with other users via reports or report snapshots
- ☑ Retrieve customized sets of data from your tables using queries that you design yourself

SKILL
8

Getting Organized with Outlook

- ➔ **Keeping a list of daily responsibilities**
- ➔ **Tracking contacts**
- ➔ **Sending and receiving e-mail**
- ➔ **Keeping a calendar**
- ➔ **Managing your task list**
- ➔ **Recording notes**
- ➔ **Keeping a journal of events**

With Outlook 2000, you can manage appointments, contacts, meetings, e-mail messages, tasks, projects, files, and notes in one place using a common set of tools. Outlook is a desktop information manager (DIM) rather than the more common personal information manager (PIM), because it is more than "personal." You can manage all your business activities with Outlook 2000.

9.1: Understanding Outlook Basics

Outlook includes six major modules and several minor ones. The major modules are:

Outlook Today   Provides a quick overview of the day's calendar and tasks, along with current e-mail

Inbox   Sends and receives e-mail and faxes

Calendar   Used to schedule appointments, track recurring meetings, plan meetings, and receive reminders of important events

Contacts   Stores names, addresses, and other contact data

Tasks   Keeps a To Do list, assigns tasks to others, and tracks progress on projects

Notes   Computerized sticky notes that can be kept in Outlook or posted on the Windows desktop

You interact with each of the modules using *forms*. Each form window has it own toolbars and menu bar and operates independently. Even closing the main Outlook window doesn't close all the open forms. If a form window is open, you must choose File ➢ Exit or close all module windows to exit Outlook completely. Otherwise, the Outlook application window will close, but form windows will remain open.

NOTE NOTE NOTE NOTE NOTE NOTE NOTE NOTE NOTE NOTE NOTE NOTE NOTE NOTE

Outlooks supports three different mail configurations: Internet Only, Corporate/Workgroup, and No E-mail. Each configuration provides different options. To check or to change your configuration, choose Tools ➢ Mail Delivery ➢ Reconfigure Mail Support. This skill focuses on the Internet Only configuration; if you need more information about options in the Corporate/Workgroup configuration, see *Mastering Outlook 2000*, also from Sybex.

Navigating Outlook

Before you can begin exploring Outlook, you must establish a user profile so Outlook knows who you are, what your e-mail address is, which information service(s) you use, and where you want your data stored. If your profile wasn't established when you installed Office 2000, you will be prompted to establish a profile using the Outlook Setup Wizard.

NOTE NOTE NOTE NOTE NOTE NOTE NOTE NOTE NOTE NOTE NOTE NOTE NOTE NOTE NOTE

If you use a networked computer, your network administrator should be able to help you set up your profile (or may have already done it for you).

When Outlook opens, you may see the Inbox (shown in Figure 9.1) or Outlook Today, a window that provides an overview of current information from the various modules. The vertical Outlook Bar on the left of the window activates other modules: just click an icon on the Outlook Bar to open the module. Use the navigation arrow at the bottom of the Outlook Bar to scroll the list of choices. The Outlook Shortcuts button returns you to the main Outlook Bar where the six main shortcuts are displayed. My Shortcuts and Other Shortcuts buttons open additional lists of shortcuts you can customize and personalize (see Skill 9.7).

Folder Banner

Standard toolbar

Outlook Bar

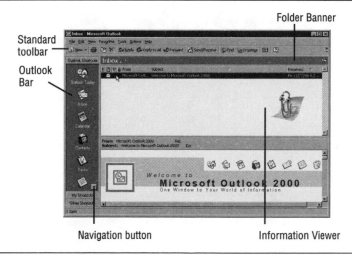

SKILL
9

Navigation button   Information Viewer

FIGURE 9.1: The Outlook Window

OPENING AN OUTLOOK MODULE

1. Click the Outlook Shortcuts button to display Outlook modules.
2. Click the module's icon in the Outlook Bar.

Entering Data

You'll generally enter or edit data in a form. Clicking the New button on the Standard toolbar opens the default form for the module. In the Inbox, for example, it opens a new e-mail form. Open the drop-down list attached to the New button to access all the forms.

Each module also provides easy ways to enter data. For example, when the Tasks module initially opens, it has an area at the top of the Information Viewer where you can click to add a new task.

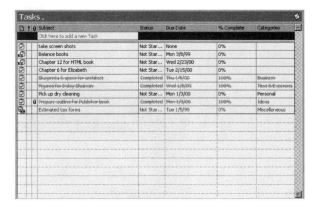

You can click, then type information in this area, or double-click to open a form.

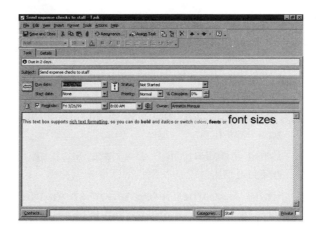

Entering text in an Outlook form is simple. Press Tab to move between fields, and use Backspace or Delete to make corrections. Select text for editing by dragging over it, and then right-click to choose Cut, Copy, or Paste. The Edit menu has an Undo option, but you can only use it to reverse the last thing you did, so use it promptly or you'll have to fix mistakes the hard way.

Outlook supports *rich text formats* in text boxes designed for entering paragraphs of text like the details or comments about a task. If the Formatting toolbar is not visible, choose View ➤ Toolbars ➤ Formatting. (If you have the Share One Row option turned on, the Formatting tollbar may appear on the right side of the Standard toolbar. Toolbar buttons are only enabled in areas that support rich text. You won't find as many formatting choices as you do in Word, but the toolbar buttons include font, font size, color, text enhancement, paragraph alignment, bullets, and indenting.

Using Natural Language for Dates

Entering information in date and time fields is about as free as it can get. You can type 5/2/00 if you wish, but you can also enter `three days before Cinco de Mayo`. Go ahead—try it! Outlook's natural language feature recognizes:

Skill 9

- Abbreviations for months and days (Oct, Mon)

- Dates and times spelled out (May fifth, third of Sep, noon)

- Descriptions of times and dates (yesterday, from today through next Fri, day after tomorrow)

- Holidays that fall on the same date every year (Christmas, Boxing Day, Cinco de Mayo)

ENTERING TEXT IN FORMS

1. Click the Tasks icon to open the task list.

2. Double-click on Click Here to Enter a New Task, or choose File ➤ New ➤ Task from the menu to open a new task form. Enter a Subject. Tab to a date field.

3. Enter a description of a date, such as **tomorrow** or **next Fri,** and press Enter.

4. Enter any other information about the task. Use the drop-down arrows to set options for fields like Priority and Status.

5. When you are finished entering information, choose Save and Close to add the task to the task list and close the form.

Organizing Your Data

Each Outlook record (information about one task, one contact, etc.) is called an *item*. Just as you use forms for data entry, you use views to display existing data. Every module offers ways to organize and to view the items it contains.

Click the Organize button on the main toolbar to view your organization choices in each Outlook module. Your options will appear at the top of the module window, listed on the left side as links; click the organization method you want, then fill in the details.

Changing Your View

The easiest way to alter your view of data is to rearrange the fields. Point to one of the column headers (the field names at the top of the columns) and drag the header horizontally to a new position. Red arrows will appear above and below the row of column headers, showing where the column will be placed.

To adjust the column width, drag the right edge of the column header (as you would in Excel). To delete a field from the display, drag its header into the area above the header row and drop it when a large, black X appears.

Sorting Items in a View   To sort items in a view, click a column header. An upward triangle appears in the column header to show ascending order. Click the header again to reverse the sort order; the triangle will point down.

Grouping Items Together   You can easily group information in an Outlook module using the View menu. To group information by common values, choose View ➤ Current View and select a view that includes By in the name: for example, By Category:

Use the Expand buttons (with plus signs) and Collapse buttons (with minus signs) to display and hide subheadings or subgroups within the grouped view. Your information will be rearranged by column and regrouped by the newly applied view.

TIP TIP TIP TIP TIP TIP TIP TIP TIP TIP TIP TIP TIP TIP TIP TIP TIP TIP TIP TIP TIP TIP TIP TIP

If you were an Outlook 97/98 user, you may be wondering what happened to the Current View drop-down menu and other familiar toolbars buttons. They have been placed on the Advanced toolbar, which you can turn on by choosing View ➤ Toolbars ➤ Advanced.

SKILL
▼ 9

Now that you know how to work in Outlook, we'll move on to the individual modules. You'll be revisiting Tasks again in Skill 9.4.

Hands On

1. Switch between each of the Outlook modules using the Outlook Bar. Explore the menu and toolbar options for each module.

2. Switch to Tasks and:

    a) Add at least three tasks to the list; two or more tasks should have the same subject and category.

    b) Rearrange the order of the Tasks columns. Adjust the column widths if necessary.

    c) Change the view of Tasks three times using different predefined views on the View menu.

    d) Sort tasks by subject, grouped by category.

9.2: Tracking Contacts with Outlook 2000

Of all of the modules that make up Outlook 2000, none is more central than Contacts. Developing a better system for tracking communications is, after all, what most people are looking for in a tool like Outlook.

Adding Contacts

Adding business and personal contacts is one of the first things you'll want to do when you start working in Outlook. It's a way to personalize Outlook and make it immediately useful.

TIP TIP TIP TIP TIP TIP TIP TIP TIP TIP TIP TIP TIP TIP TIP TIP TIP TIP TIP TIP TIP TIP TIP TIP TIP
If you have contacts in another application—Excel, Access, Schedule+, or another database file—you can import the data into Outlook. After you've learned how Contacts works, choose File ➢ Import and use the Import and Export Wizard to import your data.

To enter data, click the Contacts icon in the Outlook Bar to activate the Contacts module, and then click the New Contact button on the Standard toolbar. The Contact form opens with the General page ready to receive your data.

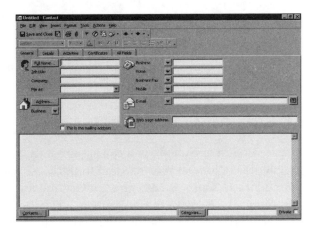

The Full Name and Address fields have buttons that open a secondary form to separate the data into the proper fields. You may enter data here, or use the form to verify that the data was typed in correctly.

When you enter the Full Name, the name is automatically displayed as last name, first name in the File As field. If you'd rather file names by first name, nicknames, or some other system, choose a different format from the File As drop-down list.

Because many of your contacts may have separate home and business addresses and multiple phone numbers, click the drop-down arrows for Address, Phone Number, and E-mail fields to identify the kind of information (home, business, fax, etc.) that you are entering in the field.

 NOTE NOTE NOTE NOTE NOTE NOTE NOTE NOTE NOTE NOTE NOTE NOTE NOTE NOTE.NOTE

If you know that a contact can only receive plain text e-mail messages, click the Send Using Plain Text check box to ensure that all the mail you send to this person will be in plain text format.

Assigning a Web URL to a Contact

SKILL
9

If one of your contacts or their company has a site on the World Wide Web, you may want to visit the site occasionally. If you enter the Web address (URL) on the Contacts form, you can access the site directly from the form (provided, of course, that you can connect to the Internet). Enter the entire URL, exactly as it appears in your browser, in the Web Page Address text box. Outlook will underline the URL and highlight it to show that it's a hyperlink.

To visit the Web page, click the link in the Web Page Address text box and go directly to the contact's Web page.

Assigning Contacts and Categories

In this version of Outlook you can assign other contacts to a contact. This is an excellent way to track referrals and to track less obvious connections between your contacts. Once you assign a contact, the reverse connection is made for you automatically. To make the assignment, click the Contact button on the bottom Contact Form and select a contact from the list.

Each Outlook item can also be assigned to one or more *categories*. Click the Categories button, and then select the appropriate categories for this contact. If you would like to create your own categories, click the Master Category List button, type a name for the category in the New Category text box, and then click Add.

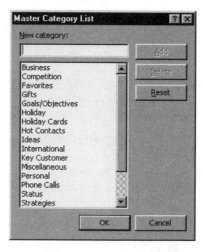

You can select existing categories and click Delete to remove them from the list. If you change your mind about adding or deleting categories and would like the original list back, click Reset and the original category list will be restored. Note, however, that you'll lose your additions as well as restore the deletions.

Categories can be applied to all Outlook items. If the Categories button isn't readily available, select the item (hold Ctrl to select multiple items in the Information Viewer) and choose Edit ➤ Categories to make the assignment.

Entering Additional Data

On the Details page of the Contacts form, you'll find fields for supporting data. Click the drop-down arrows in the Birthday and Anniversary fields to select dates using a calendar control.

The Certificates page allows you to store certificates, or digital IDs, that you can use to send encrypted mail to a contact. When you use a digital ID to send a message, only the intended recipient can decrypt the message. To use a digital ID you must first ask the recipient to send you an e-mail message that includes their digital signature. Right-click the name in the From field of the message, and then click Add to Contacts on the shortcut menu. This will copy the e-mail address and the certificate to the person's Contact form.

You can obtain a digital ID for your own use from a certifying authority such as Verisign, Inc. (http://www.verisign.com).

The Activities page replaces the Outlook 97/98 Contact form's Journal page. The Activities page shows journal entries, e-mail messages, tasks, and any other items that are related to this contact. When you switch to a contact's Activities page, Outlook searches to locate the associated items. It takes a while and happens each time you open a Contact form and view the Activities page. You may have to wait a moment for Outlook to begin searching after you click on the Activities tab:

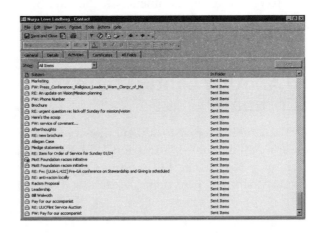

SKILL
9

The All Fields page provides access to all the Contact form fields, including fields that are automatically entered by Outlook, such as the item's creation date and time. Open the drop-down list in the Select From text box to see the lists of fields you can display.

If you imported data from another database, you may find data here that did not fit into the standard fields on the Contact form. You can also enter data here, but there are no Calendar controls or drop-down lists to assist you.

ADDING A CONTACT

1. Click the Contacts icon in the Outlook Bar and click the New Contact button on the Standard toolbar.

2. Enter data on the form, tabbing between fields.

3. Enter a new File As name if you would like to use something other than the suggested options.

4. Click the Full Name and Address buttons to enter data into individual fields.

5. Use the drop-down lists in the Address and Phone Number fields to identify the kind of data you are entering.

6. Assign the contact to other contacts or to categories, if desired.

7. Click the Details tab to enter more data about the contact, the Activities tab to view items related to this contact, and the All Fields tab to enter data in fields other than those represented on the form.

8. To return to the Contacts list, click the Save and Close button.

Adding Another Contact from the Same Company

Outlook makes it easy to add another contact from the same company without re-entering all the same information. With the original contact form open, choose Actions ➤ New Contact from Same Company. Outlook will open a new contact form with the company name, address, and main phone number already completed.

Viewing Contacts

Seven default Contacts views are available on the View menu: Address Cards, Detailed Address Cards, Phone List, By Category, By Company, By Location, and By Follow-Up Flag. Switch between views by choosing a different view from the menu. (See Skill 9.9 to create and save custom views.)

Locating a Contact

The easiest way to search through a long list of contacts is to enter a first or last name in the Find a Contact text box on the Standard toolbar—it's the empty text box next to the Address Book button. If Outlook only finds one name that matches your entry, it will open the Contact form for that person. If it finds more than one possible match, Outlook will display a list of possibilities that you can choose from.

When you don't remember the contact's first or last name, you can search for other information about the contact by clicking the Find button on the Standard toolbar to open the Find pane. Enter the data you would like Outlook to search for, make sure Search All Text in the Contact is enabled, and click the Find Now button. Even if you just remember part of the last name, Outlook will find every occurrence of those letters. In the example below, a search for schulman, part of a company name, returned all employees of the same company, Daley Shulman:

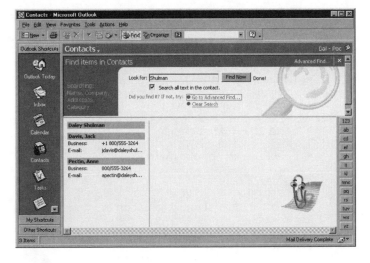

Double-click a name in the list to open the Contacts form for that individual.

VIEWING AND LOCATING CONTACTS

1. Click View ➢ Current View to select from among the available views.

2. In table views, drag column headers to rearrange columns. Click a column header to sort that column.

3. Locate a contact by entering their first or last name in the Find a Contact text box.

4. To locate a contact when you don't remember their name, click the Find button, enter the word or words you want to search for, and click Find Now.

TIP TIP TIP TIP TIP TIP TIP TIP TIP TIP TIP TIP TIP TIP TIP TIP TIP TIP TIP TIP TIP TIP TIP TIP TIP

For even more Find options, click the Find button and then click Advanced Find to open the Advanced Find dialog box.

Communicating with Your Contacts

Now that you have a well-developed contact list, it's time to start putting it to good use. Outlook has a number of things you can do with contact information. You can:

- Dial a phone number
- Write a letter in Word
- Send an e-mail message
- Schedule an appointment
- Assign a task
- Create a journal entry to document communication

Dialing a Contact

If you have a telephone connected to your PC's modem, you can place telephone calls from Outlook. Double-click the contact you want to call to open the Contact form and click the AutoDialer button. Choose a phone number from the AutoDialer drop-down list.

USING AUTODIALER TO CALL A CONTACT

1. Double-click the contact you want to call.
2. Click the AutoDialer button or click the down arrow to select the number to call.
3. Click Start Call in the New Call dialog box.
4. When the call connects, pick up the handset and click Talk.
5. When you are finished with the call, click End Call to disconnect.

TIP TIP TIP TIP TIP TIP TIP TIP TIP TIP TIP TIP TIP TIP TIP TIP TIP TIP TIP TIP TIP TIP

To record a journal entry about a call, enable the Create New Journal Entry When Starting New Call check box. When you click Start Call, a new Journal form opens and the timer starts. See Skill 9.8 for more about the Journal.

Creating a Letter to a Contact

Integration is one of the best features of Office 2000. With Outlook, you can generate regular "snail mail" letters directly from the Contacts list using the Letter Wizard.

CREATING A LETTER TO A CONTACT

SKILL
9

1. Double-click a contact to open the Contact form.
2. Choose Actions ➢ New Letter to Contact. This launches Word 2000 and starts the Letter Wizard.
3. Choose the Letter Format you would like to use, including Page Design and Letter Style. Click Next.

continued❯

4. The Recipient Info should include the contact you have open in Outlook. If it doesn't or you want to change who the letter is addressed to, click the Address Book button and select the recipient. Enter a salutation in the Salutation field. Click Next.

5. Other Elements includes more information about the address and mailing instructions. Choose options from the drop-down lists or enter your own text. Use the Address Book button to select additional addresses for courtesy copies. Click Next.

6. Enter Sender Info and Closing options. You can select the Sender Info from one of your address books (you may want to enter yourself as a contact so you can select yourself). Click Finish.

7. The Letter Wizard creates the structure of your letter. Choose if you would like to Make an Envelope, Make a Mailing Label, Rerun Letter Wizard, or Cancel the Office Assistant. Enter the body of the letter and send it to the printer.

Creating Bulk Mailings

Sometimes you want to mail, fax, or e-mail the same information to a large group of people. In Outlook 2000, this is called a *bulk mailing*, and you use the Mail Merge feature. To send bulk, choose Tools ➤ Mail Merge to open the Mail Merge Contacts dialog box.

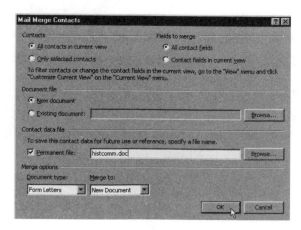

To select recipients, choose either All Contacts in Current View or Only Selected Contacts. Select the main document by browsing for an existing document or choosing New Document if you haven't created the document yet. To save the mail merge, click Permanent File and save the file under a new name. Merge Options include form letters, mailing labels, envelopes, and catalogs, and you can Merge To or export this information as a new document, to the printer as an existing document, to a fax machine, or to e-mail.

Outlook then launches Word 2000 so you can create your main document with merge fields and continue the process there (see Skill 4.2 for more about Word documents and Mail Merge).

Other Forms of Communication

Although Outlook 2000 handles the more traditional forms of communication like letters and phone calls, it was really designed to enhance newer models of business communication. Effective use of e-mail, group appointment scheduling and meeting planning, and team management are all hallmarks of the new, networked workplace. As a result, Outlook's Contacts feature is far more than an electronic address book.

Select a contact, open the Contact form, and click the New Message to Contact button on the Standard toolbar to open an e-mail form pre-addressed to the contact's e-mail mailbox. If you want to assign a task to the contact, choose Actions ➤ New Task for Contact, enter the task, and click the Assign Task button.

To invite the contact to attend a meeting, choose Actions ➤ New Meeting Request to Contact to open the Meeting Planner. Outlook 2000 opens by default to a window that lets you send a request via e-mail, but if you check the This Is an Online Meeting check box, the Planner will transform to display other options. Use the Online Meeting Planner window to invite meeting participants, to send real-time reminders, and to choose your online meeting software.

Printing Options

Outlook 2000 features several pre-established print styles that make it easy to print Outlook information. To print Contacts, first switch to the Contacts view you want to print. Address Card views print directories whereas lists, such as Phone List view, print tables of data. Once you've chosen the view you want, click File ➤ Page Setup and choose the style you want. Click the Print Preview button to get a look at what the print style will look like, and click Print if you are satisfied.

If you'd like to make some changes to the document before you print it, you can customize the print style, adjust the paper size and fonts, and change other settings in the Page Setup dialog box. You can also adjust the settings to print to the specifications of several popular types of day planners.

PRINTING CONTACT LISTS

1. Choose File ➤ Page Setup to select a report style. Choose the style you want to use.

2. To customize the style, adjust the various paper, size, and other settings, or choose the type of day planner you carry, make changes on the various tabs of the Page Setup dialog box before printing.

3. Click Print Preview to see a preview of the report.

4. Choose Print to open the Print dialog box. Change the Print Style, if desired. Choose which pages you want to print and how many copies you want. Click Collate to have each copy print completely before the next copy begins. Click OK to send the report to the printer.

You'll go through the same process to print in any Outlook module. Select a view that supports the output you desire, and then preview the output in Print Preview. Change views, if necessary, and tweak the Page Setup options to further define the preview before sending it to the printer.

Hands On

1. Open Contacts and:

   a) Add at least five contacts.

   b) Add two contacts from the same company.

   c) If you have Internet access, locate the URL of one of your contacts and enter the URL in the Web Page field. Click the link in the field to test the URL.

2. In the Contacts list, switch to a list view such as Phone List and:

   a) Rearrange the column order and sort by city.

   b) Group the items by company.

   c) Use Find to locate a contact.

   d) Create a new category and assign the category to a group of records.

3. If you have a modem and a telephone connected to it, call one of your contacts.

4. Create a letter to send to a contact using the New Letter to Contact feature.

5. Print a directory of your contacts customized to the type of planner you carry.

9.3: Using Outlook Today

If you've ever wanted a place to keep track of the day's appointments, things to do, and other important, immediate information, Outlook Today can now do that for you. Outlook Today displays everything you need to know about your day—where you have to be, when you have to be there, what you have to get done, and who you should e-mail.

Viewing the Day's Information

Outlook Today takes your appointments, tasks, and contents of your Inbox and Outbox to display your day at a glance:

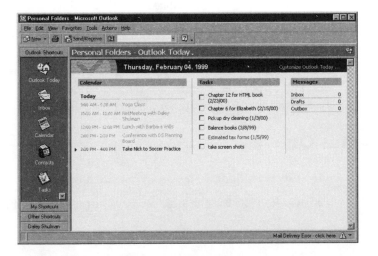

To view the details of any calendar item, individual task, or e-mail, click the link that appears when you place the mouse on the item. You can also click the gray column headers to open the Calendar, Tasks, and/or Inbox modules. Outlook will shade completed tasks or meetings to gray, allowing you to concentrate on unfinished business.

Customizing the Outlook Today View

If you want to customize your view of the Outlook Today contents, click the Outlook Today icon and then click Customize Outlook Today. You can choose to make Outlook Today your default module when Outlook starts up, you can decide how many days the Calendar portion should display, you can determine how your Tasks should be sorted, and you can select which e-mail folders should be listed. The Styles options, however, give you more sophisticated choices. Table 9.1 lists your choices and how they appear in the Outlook Today window.

TABLE 9.1: Outlook Today Style Customization Options

Style	What You Get
Standard	Calendar, tasks, and messages listed in three individual columns
Standard 2 Column	Calendar items listed in the left column, tasks and messages listed in the right
Standard 1 Column	Calendar, tasks, and messages information displayed in three horizontal rows
Summer	Similar to the Standard 2-Column view, only displayed in greens and yellows
Winter	Similar to the Standard 2-Column view, only displayed in blues and white

To apply the customizations, make your choices in the Customize Outlook Today window and click Save Changes. Outlook will reorganize your information and apply the changes. For more details on how to use Outlook's Calendar, Tasks, and E-mail modules, see Skills 9.4, 9.5, and 9.6.

Hands On

1. Open Outlook Today and view the day's events.

2. Customize the Outlook Today environment by changing to another style.

9.4: Using Outlook As a Mail Client

Although electronic mail has been around since the 1960s, it wasn't until the late 80s that it really took hold in the business world. Today, some businesses have grown so dependent on it that their entire operations would grind to a halt if their e-mail system went down. Outlook 2000 has turned e-mail into an even more valuable tool by improving message-tracking options and adding a number of other useful features.

Creating Mail

All your e-mail work can be handled using the My Shortcuts group on the Outlook Bar. When you start Outlook, this bar contains five folders:

Inbox   E-mail and fax messages you've received

Drafts   Unfinished messages

Outbox   Temporarily stores outgoing messages

Sent Items   Copies of messages you've already sent

Deleted Items   The Recycle Bin for Outlook items

Outlook creates shortcuts based on your configuration, so you may also have shortcuts for Outlook add-in products in My Shortcuts. As you start sending and receiving messages, you can add folders to My Shortcuts to keep your mail organized. (See Skill 9.7 to learn how to add folders and put shortcuts to folders on the Outlook Bar.)

Skill
9

Creating and Addressing E-mail

To create an e-mail message, open the Inbox and click the New button on the Standard toolbar. A blank Message form opens:

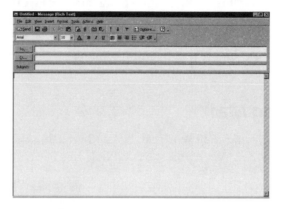

In order to be received, e-mail must be correctly addressed. To access the address book, click the To button on the Message form to open the Select Names dialog box:

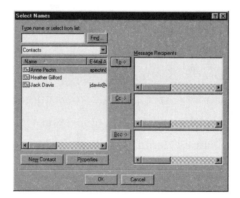

CREATING AND ADDRESSING E-MAIL

1. Open the Inbox or Outbox and click the New button on the Standard toolbar.
2. Click the To button to open the Select Names dialog box.

continued ▶

3. Select the first person's name and click the To button. Select any additional names, and place them in the appropriate field by clicking the To, Cc, or Bcc button.

4. To check the properties of a name, select the name and click Properties.

5. To add a name that is not on the list, click New Contact, choose the Entry type, select where you'd like to store the address, and click OK. Enter the data about the new address in the Mail Properties dialog box. Click OK to add the name.

6. Click OK to close the Select Names dialog box.

NOTE NOTE NOTE NOTE NOTE NOTE NOTE NOTE NOTE NOTE NOTE NOTE NOTE NOTE NOTE

If you're connected to a network, you may also have a global address book listing other users on your network. If you have more than one address book, choose the Address Book you want to use in the Show Names From list in the Select Names dialog box.

Now you're ready to enter text in the body of the message. When you're finished, choose Tools ➤ Spelling to run a spell check of the document.

Changing Mail Formats   Outlook 2000 lets you create e-mail messages in three different message formats: plain text, rich text, and HTML. Rich text supports fonts, styles, weights, and other formatting. HTML supports HTML text formats and background graphics. To set the default format for messages, choose Tools ➤ Options, and then click the Mail Format tab. Choose a format from the drop-down list.

When you create a message, you must change back to Plain Text in order to switch between rich text and HTML formats.

Setting Message-Handling Options   You can set options to determine how your message will be handled. In the message form, click the Options button to access the message-handling options shown in Table 9.2.

SKILL
9

TABLE 9.2: Message-Handling Options

Option	Description
Importance	Puts a flag on the message to alert the recipient to its importance. Click to select Normal, Low, High.
Sensitivity	Puts a flag on the message to alert the recipient to its sensitivity. Click to select Normal, Personal, Private, Confidential.
Voting options	Used to poll recipients; only available in Corporate/Workgroup configuration.
Have replies sent to	Allows you to designate an individual to collect replies to your message.
Save sent message to	Indicates which folder you want the sent message stored in.
Do not deliver before	Keeps the message from being delivered before the date you specify.
Expires after	Marks the message as unavailable after the date you specify.
Tracking options	Notifies you when messages are delivered and/or read.
Contacts	Used to link this message so it will appear on one or more contacts' Activities page.
Categories	Lets you assign this message to a category.

Flagging E-mail Messages for Follow Up

Certain messages may require action on the part of the recipient; other messages only require a quick scan on their way to the Deleted Items folder. You can flag messages sent to other Outlook users so it's obvious when and what action is expected, or flag incoming messages.

To flag a message, open the message and click the Flag for Follow Up button on the Standard toolbar. The Flag for Follow Up dialog box has two settings: Flag To and Due By. Choose a Flag To action from the list—Call, Do Not Forward, Follow Up, For Your Information, Forward, No Response Necessary, Read, Reply, Reply to All, Review—or type other text if you wish. In the Due By control, select a date for the action. The details of the flag appear in the message header. When you complete the flagged action, right-click on the message in the Information Viewer and choose Flag Complete from the shortcut menu, or open the message, open the Flag Message dialog box, and click the Completed check box. To delete a flag, right-click on the message and choose Clear Flag. The flag information disappears from the open message window.

Tracking E-mail Messages

If it's important to know whether someone reads your message, you can turn on tracking options that will let you know when they have received it or when they opened the message. You probably don't want these options set all the time or you'll double or triple the amount of mail you get, but for that important document, tracking options can't be beat.

 NOTE NOTE NOTE NOTE NOTE NOTE NOTE NOTE NOTE NOTE NOTE NOTE NOTE NOTE NOTE

Receipts are sent by the recipient's mail server. Many mail servers do not support read receipts, but most support delivery receipts.

To use Outlook's tracking feature, create a new e-mail message and click the Options button. The Message Options dialog box appears, showing you several choices for delivery and notification.

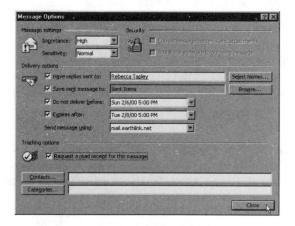

Choose to automatically store a copy of the e-mail in a separate folder or to send a copy to a third party, select an expiration date if the e-mail is time-sensitive, and set notification options using the box in the lower part of the window to request notification. Click OK and send the message as usual; a notification e-mail will be automatically sent to your Inbox when the recipient has opened the e-mail.

SKILL
9

SETTING TRACKING OPTIONS

1. Create an e-mail message and click the Options button. The Message Options dialog box opens.

2. Choose a recipient, an expiration date, and other options from this window. Check the box near the bottom requesting notification that the message has been received.

3. Send the message. You will receive notification in your Inbox when your message has been received.

Sending the Message

After you have addressed the message, entered the message body, and set options, it is ready to send. Click the Send button and it's on its way. If you're not online when you click the Send button, the message will be moved to your Outbox for sending later (see "Receiving Mail" below for more about how to send it from your Outbox). When the message is sent, a copy will be saved automatically to the Sent Items folder.

TIP TIP TIP TIP TIP TIP TIP TIP TIP TIP TIP TIP TIP TIP TIP TIP TIP TIP TIP TIP TIP TIP TIP TIP

If you want to send a copy of an Outlook item—a contact, a task, an appointment, even a note—to a colleague, you can right-click on the item in the Information Viewer and choose Forward. A mail message opens with the item attached to it. The item is sent along with the message, and the recipient just has to double-click the item to open it (of course, they must have Outlook to view the item as an Outlook item).

Personal Distribution Lists

Personal distribution lists help you manage contacts and information by sending e-mail to a group of people. You'll find distribution lists useful if you e-mail many people several times a week, or route messages within your organization.

To create a personal distribution list, choose File ➤ New ➤ Distribution List. Enter a name for the list in the New Distribution List dialog box.

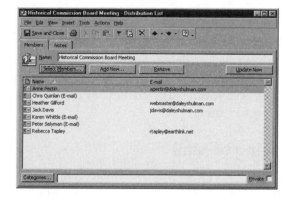

Select members for the list, and then save the list. The list will appear in your Address Book by the list name. When you send a message to the list, the message is sent to each list member.

CREATING A DISTRIBUTION LIST

1. Choose File ➢ New ➢ Distribution List or choose Distribution List from the New button's drop-down menu.
2. On the Members tab, enter a list name in the Name text box.
3. Click Select Members to choose list members from Contacts or another address book.
4. Click Save and Close to create the list.

Receiving Mail

If you're connected to a network mail server or have a full time connection to your Internet Service Provider, you receive mail directly to your Inbox. If you do not have a continuous connection, you need to connect to the Internet before you can receive (or send) mail. Outlook has combined the sending and receiving mail functions into one operation on the Tools menu, called Send/Receive. When you choose this option, Outlook connects to the mail service you select, sends the mail in your Outbox, and places any mail that is waiting for you in your Inbox.

SKILL
9

Sorting, Grouping, and Viewing Mail

Mail in the Inbox is displayed in the Information Viewer. Mail messages are presented in a table view at the top of the viewer; an optional Preview Pane appears at the bottom. (Display or hide the Preview Pane by choosing View ➤ Preview Pane). Sort your mail by clicking a column header. Double-click any mail item to open and read it.

Replying to Mail

One of the primary reasons e-mail has become so popular is that it's easy—easy to send, easy to view, and easy to respond to. When was the last time you responded to a written letter within minutes of receiving it? With e-mail, you can receive mail from across the globe, click the Reply button, write your response, click Send, and return a response within minutes. If the message you received was originally sent to more than one person, you can respond to all recipients by clicking the Reply to All button on the Standard toolbar. To send a copy of the original message to a colleague or friend, click the Forward button, enter the address, and click Send.

SENDING, RECEIVING, AND REPLYING TO MESSAGES

1. To send all messages in your Outbox and receive waiting mail, choose Tools ➤ Send/Receive, and then choose your mail account.

2. Sort the messages by clicking the column headers.

3. Choose View ➤ Current View to select how to group messages.

4. Double-click on a message to open it.

5. Click Reply to reply to a message or Reply to All to send the responses to all the names on the To, Cc, and Bcc lists.

6. Click Forward to forward the original message to someone else. Enter the address in the To field. Enter a message of your own above the original message if desired. Click Send to forward the message.

Keeping Track of Your Mail

It doesn't take long before e-mail messages get out of hand and you need to develop some system of organizing them. Outlook 2000 offers you two ways to get the junk mail out of your Inbox. The first method is as simple as dragging mail items to the Deleted Items folder.

DELETING MAIL

1. Select the message you want to delete. Click to select the first message; hold down Ctrl and click to select additional messages.
2. Point to the selected messages and drag them to Deleted Items on the Outlook Bar.
3. Open Deleted Items.
4. Select messages you want to delete for good. Point to the selected messages, right-click and choose Delete, or click the Delete button on the Standard toolbar to remove them completely.

 WARNING WARNING WARNING WARNING WARNING WARNING WARNING WARNING
Messages deleted from the Deleted Items folder cannot be recovered using Undelete tools.

The second method, Outlook 2000's Junk E-mail feature on the Actions menu, gives you options for handling unsolicited e-mail in your Inbox. First, click the Organize button on the Standard toolbar, and then click the Junk E-mail link in the Organize window.

SKILL
9

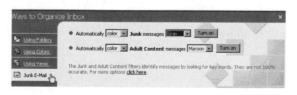

By default, Outlook will filter incoming e-mail for certain keywords to deter-mine if the messages contain junk or adult content. It first gives you simple options: you can route junk e-mail directly to the Deleted Items bin or to a Junk E-mail folder, and/or you can automatically color or move adult items depending upon your preference. For more options, click the Click Here link and add a sender's name directly to the Junk E-mail list.

Storing Mail in Folders

After you delete, highlight, or reroute all the messages you don't want, you can organize the rest into a system of logical folders. To create a new folder in the Inbox, choose File ➤ Folder ➤ New Folder, or choose Folder from the New drop-down menu. This opens the Create New Folder dialog box:

Enter a name for the new folder and make sure the Folder Contains control is set to Mail Items. In the Select Where to Place the Folder control, click the folder you want to house your new subfolder. Click OK to create the new folder. To view all Outlook folders, including your new folder, open the Folder List, either by choosing View ➤ Folder List or by clicking the Folder List button on the Standard toolbar. To temporarily display the Folder List, click the Inbox button at the top of the Information Viewer.

Click the plus symbols in front of folders to expand the folder view; the minus symbols collapse the view. To move items to other folders, select the items and right-click. Choose Move to Folder and select the folder you want from the Move Items dialog box.

Finding Messages

Being buried under a mountain of e-mail has one advantage over being buried under a similar mountain of paper mail: Outlook can search for a particular e-mail message and find it in a flash.

Click the Find button on the Standard toolbar and enter the criteria you are searching for in Look For textbox. If you want to focus your search, or if you want to search for a message by other criteria, click the Advanced Find button to open the Advanced Find dialog box:

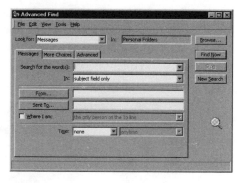

SKILL
9

Hands On

1. Create and send an e-mail message to a colleague on your office network or to a colleague who has Internet e-mail.

2. Reply to an e-mail message that you received. Flag the message for follow-up.

3. Create two new folders to store your e-mail messages:

    a) Move existing mail from your Inbox to the new folders.

    b) Use Find Items to locate a message sent by a certain individual.

    c) Delete one or more messages.

4. Search for a message using the Advanced Find options. Provide as much information in the search text boxes as you can.

9.5: Managing Tasks in Outlook

Outlook takes the To Do list to a new dimension by adding the ability to track progress, assign the task to another person (our personal favorite), set reminders for the task, and insert the task into your calendar to make sure it gets completed.

The Tasks feature is available from the Outlook Bar, the New button, and the Calendar. From the Outlook Bar, click the Tasks icon to open the task list. The default view shows the task and the due date. The icons in the first column indicate whether the task is your responsibility or has been assigned to someone else, and whether it is a recurring task. The second column indicates whether the task is completed. As in any Outlook module, choose other views from the Current View menu drop-down list. Figure 9.2 shows a Detailed List view.

			Subject	Status	Due Date	% Complete	Categories
			Click here to add a new Task.				
			Balance books	Not Star...	Mon 3/8/99	0%	
			Blueprints & specs for architect	Completed	Thu 1/6/00	100%	Business
			Chapter 12 for HTML book	Not Star...	Wed 2/23/00	0%	
	!		Chapter 6 for Elizabeth	Not Star...	Tue 2/15/00	0%	
	!	0	Edit Chapter 12	Completed	Wed 4/22/00	100%	
			Estimated tax forms	Not Star...	Tue 1/5/99	0%	Miscellaneous
			Figures for Daley Shulman	Completed	Wed 1/5/00	100%	Time & Expenses
			Pick up dry cleaning	Not Star...	Mon 1/3/00	0%	Personal
		0	Prepare outline for Publisher book	Completed	Mon 1/3/00	100%	Ideas
			take screen shots	Not Star...	None	0%	

FIGURE 9.2: The Detailed List view of the Tasks window

Creating a Task

To create a task, click in the Subject column where it says Click Here to Add a New Task, double-click a blank row in the Information Viewer, or click the New button. For a simple entry, enter the subject, date, and task. To enter more detail, double-click the entry to open the Task form. In the Task form, you can edit the task subject and due date information in addition to establishing a start date, assigning a status, setting a priority, and indicating how much of the task has been completed.

Subject   Description of the task

Due Date   Indicates when the task should be completed.

Start Date   Indicates when the task begins.

Status   Not Started, In Progress, Completed, Waiting on Someone Else, or Deferred.

Priority   Can be set at High, Medium, or Low.

Percent Complete   Used to track progress.

Reminder   Sets a date and time for a reminder about the task.

Owner   Person responsible for task completion.

Categories   Assign a category from the Master Category List.

Contacts   Assign a contact from the Address Book.

Private   Click the Private check box to prevent other users from viewing the task.

You can insert a file into the task if, for example, the task requires you to use a Word or Excel document. Click the Insert File button on the Standard toolbar to open the Insert File dialog box, then locate and select the file(s). There are three options for inserting the file. Only choose Text Only if the file contains unformatted text like a .txt or .bat file; if you insert, for example, a Word file as Text Only, the result is garbage. Choosing Shortcut inserts a link to the file. The default, Attachment, attaches a copy of the file to the task—but that's not always a good thing. Generally, you'll want to insert a shortcut so you don't end up with multiple copies of files. This will save space on your hard drive. Shortcuts will not do, however, if you are delegating the task to someone who doesn't have permissions to the drive where the file is stored. Double-click the Shortcut or Attachment icon to open the document.

SKILL
9

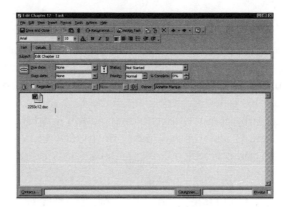

TIP TIP TIP TIP TIP TIP TIP TIP TIP TIP TIP TIP TIP TIP TIP TIP TIP TIP TIP TIP TIP TIP TIP TIP

You can insert an Outlook item by choosing Insert ➢ Item from the menu.

Creating a Recurring Task

Many of the tasks you're responsible for are cyclical tasks that are never really completed. You finish the task and it's time to do it all over again for a different week, a different month, or a different year. Outlook lets you designate recurring tasks and then reminds you when it's time to gear up for the next round.

To make a task recurring, click the Recurrence button on the Standard toolbar in the Task form window. The Task Recurrence dialog box asks you for the recurrence period—daily, weekly, monthly, or yearly. Each choice opens a list of settings to help you describe the pattern you want to establish. Set the recurrence options you want and click OK, then Save and Close to set the recurring task in motion. The task will continue to reappear on your task list with the frequency you designate until you open the Task Recurrence dialog box again and click Remove Recurrence or until the End Date you indicate is reached.

CREATING A TASK

1. Click the Task icon on the Outlook Bar to open the task list.

continued ▶

2. Click in a blank row of any list view and enter the Subject and Date or double-click a blank row to open the Task form.

3. From the Task form, enter the Start Date, Status, Priority, and Percent Complete.

4. Set the date and time you would like to be reminded of the task in the Reminder fields.

5. Enter details about the task in the open text field.

6. Insert a file into the task by clicking the Insert File button on the Standard toolbar. Insert an Outlook item by choosing Insert ➤ Item.

7. Click Save and Close to close the Task form.

Tracking Tasks

One of the more useful Task views is the Task Timeline. This shows each task on the date it needs to be completed, so you can plan your time accordingly.

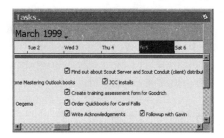

To display your tasks using the Task Timeline, choose View ➤ Current View ➤ Task Timeline. Use the horizontal scrollbar at the bottom of the Tasks window to browse future tasks—the Tasks module opens your view at the current day by default.

Delegating a Task

It's always nice when you can generate a list of tasks to be completed—by someone else. Outlook makes delegation a snap, as long as you can reach the person you want to delegate to by e-mail.

DELEGATING A TASK

1. Double-click the task you want to delegate to open it.

2. Click the Assign Task button on the Standard toolbar.

3. Click the To button and choose the address book that contains the person you want. Select a name from the Select Task Recipient list, or add a new person by clicking the New button.

4. Click the Cancel Assignment button on the Standard toolbar if you change your mind.

5. Click the Send button to send the message, or put the message in your Outbox.

Tasks that have been delegated have an icon showing a hand holding the clipboard in the Task list. If you switch to the By Person Responsible view, you'll see the tasks listed by owner. When you double-click to open a task that has been assigned to someone else, the Task page of the Task form displays the e-mail message that was used to delegate the task, rather than the typical Task page. The Details page stays the same, except that the Create Unassigned Copy button is activated. If you click it, Outlook will create a copy of the task and assign the copy back to you. However, you'll lose the ability to receive updates about the task, and the task will no longer show up under the other person's name in the By Person Responsible listing.

Updating the Status of a Task

To update the status of a completed task or a task in progress, double-click to open the task and click the Details page. The Details page is the place to record how things are going or, if the task is completed, how things went.

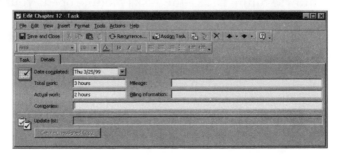

NOTE NOTE NOTE NOTE NOTE NOTE NOTE NOTE NOTE NOTE NOTE NOTE NOTE NOTE NOTE

Only the owner of a task can update the task's status. If you've delegated a task, you have to wait for the assigned person to respond.

Tracking an Assigned Task

The recipient of a delegated task can choose to accept or decline the invitation to take over the task (theoretically, at least). When you click the Accept or Decline button on the header of the e-mail message, a message is returned to the sender notifying the sender of the decision.

Once you accept a task, you can update the task's status in the Task form and send status updates by clicking the Send Status Report button on the Standard toolbar. The updates can be sent to the person who delegated the task or to anyone else in your address book.

Completing a Task

It's always great to check something off a long To Do list. Outlook provides several shortcuts to that warm feeling of accomplishment. In the Simple List view, you can literally check an item off a list. In other views, you have to mark the task as completed in some other way. If there is a Percent Completed column, change the percentage to 100%. In any view, you can right-click and choose Mark Complete from the shortcut menu.

If you prefer to open the task, changing the status to Completed or choosing Mark Complete from the Task menu will mark the task. But the biggest advantage of opening the task is that you can enter a Date Completed and other final task information on the Details page. If you need a thorough record of the task's completion, this is clearly the best choice.

SKILL
9

UPDATING THE STATUS OF A TASK

1. Double-click to open the task you want to update.
2. Click the Details tab and enter status information in the fields provided.

continued ▶

3. Click the Send Status Report button to send information about the task's status to people in your address book.

4. Complete a task by checking it off in Simple List view or by double-clicking the task to open it, clicking the Details tab, and entering a Date Completed.

Hands On

1. Create a list of 10 tasks you have to accomplish in the next month.

   a) Change the view to Detailed List.

   b) Enter details about three of the tasks on the Task form.

   c) Set one task as a recurring task.

   d) Establish a task as high priority.

   e) Complete the Details form and mark two tasks complete.

2. Identify and delegate a task to someone in your address book (preferably someone using Outlook). Ask the person to provide you with a status report.

9.6: Keeping Your Calendar

Of all the Outlook modules, the hardest for many people to make a transition to is the electronic Calendar. The Calendar requires a shift in how you handle one of the most important aspects of your work—planning and organizing your time. However, the benefits and flexibility that Outlook affords, particularly in a networked environment, make the transition worth the effort.

Viewing and Navigating the Calendar

The Calendar default view, shown in Figure 9.3, is the Day/Week/Month view that includes an hour-by-hour daily calendar, a monthly calendar (Date Navigator), and a TaskPad.

Date Navigator

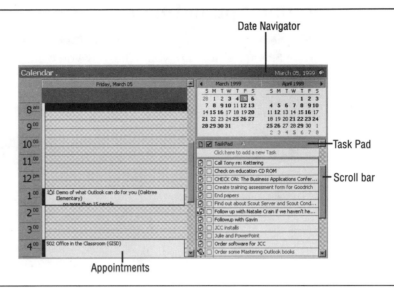

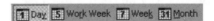

Appointments

FIGURE 9.3: Day/Week/Month view

You may be wondering, though, where the weekly view that's part of Day/Week/Month is. Four additional buttons on the toolbar are actually the prime movers in this view. These buttons, located on the Standard toolbar, control whether you're viewing today, any day, a week, or a month:

The easiest way to move to another date is to click on the date in the Date Navigator. Use the left- and right-arrow navigation buttons to move forward and backward a month. Click the Date Navigator (the header with the names of the months on it) to open a list of months. Hold the mouse button down and scroll to select the month you want to display:

SKILL
9

Scheduling Appointments

To schedule an appointment, switch to Day/Week/Month view and click the Date Navigator to bring you to the day you want to schedule. Click in the time slot that corresponds to the start time of the appointment you want to enter. Type the name of the appointment, and then drag the appointment block down to its end time:

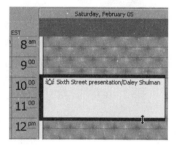

The blue line next to the appointment marks that time as busy, and the alarm clock represents a reminder that you'll receive 15 minutes before the appointment.

Setting a Reminder

Outlook's default reminder time is 15 minutes. That's great if you just have to walk down the hall, but what if you have a drive for an hour to get to the appointment? You can change the reminder time and other reminder options by double-clicking the appointment to open the Appointment form:

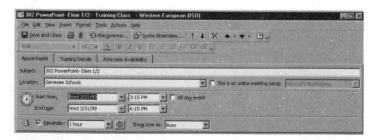

NOTE NOTE NOTE NOTE NOTE NOTE NOTE NOTE NOTE NOTE NOTE NOTE NOTE NOTE

If you want to change the default reminder time, choose Tools ➤ Options and click the Calendar tab. Change the Reminder default to a different duration.

To change the reminder for this appointment, select a duration from the Reminder drop-down list, or type a duration in the text box.

To change the sound the reminder makes when it activates, click the Sound button and enter the path to a .wav file on your hard drive. When it's time for a reminder, the sound will play and a message will open on your screen with the appointment information. You can choose to Dismiss the reminder with no additional reminder, Postpone the reminder to a new time (like an alarm clock's Snooze feature), or Open the item.

SETTING A REMINDER

1. Double-click the appointment on the calendar to open it.
2. Choose an interval for the reminder from the drop-down list; or clear the Reminder check box if you wish to remove the reminder.
3. Click Save and Close to close the Appointment form.

Planning a Recurring Meeting

Any time you have a meeting or an appointment that occurs more than once, you only have to enter it once and then let Calendar know when and how often it will recur. Calendar will enter it on the subsequent dates for you. Any changes you make to a recurring appointment can be made to the specific individual appointment or to the series of recurring appointments.

SKILL
9

Open the appointment by double-clicking it. Click the Recurrence button on the Standard toolbar to set the recurrence pattern. The Recurrence options are the same here as for recurring tasks. See Skill 9.5 for more information about recurring items.

Scheduling a Multi-Day Event

If you have an event that lasts all day, or for several days, you can set it up as an all-day event. All-day events appear at the top of your calendar for that day and show your time as Free on the Appointment form. If you plan to be unavailable for other appointments during an all-day event, click the Show Time As field and change your status to Busy or Out of the Office.

SCHEDULING A MULTI-DAY EVENT

1. Open the Appointment form for the all-day or multi-day appointment.
2. Click the All Day Event check box. The time fields disappear.
3. Enter the dates for the Start Time and the End Time of the event.
4. If you're unavailable for the day or days in question, change the Show Times As field to Busy or Out of the Office.

Planning a Meeting with Others

You can use the Outlook Calendar to plan and invite others to meetings. If you and all potential attendees are connected with Microsoft Exchange using the Corporate/Workgroup configuration, Outlook 2000 will find the first available time for everyone, send out notices to invitees, tabulate their responses, and confirm the meeting.

 Choose Actions ➤ Plan a Meeting or click the Plan a Meeting button on the Advanced toolbar when the Calendar module is active to open a Plan a Meeting form:

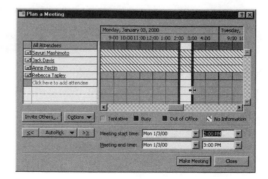

Click the Invite Others button and enter the people who are required to attend the meeting and those whose attendance is optional. Click OK. If attendees' schedules are available on your network, they show as blocked-off time on the timeline.

If you have access to your invitees' Outlook calendars and would like Outlook to select the first available time for the meeting, set the desired start time of the meeting and the first possible date in the Meeting Start time field. Enter the desired end time in the Meeting End Time field. The most critical element here is to show the duration of the meeting. (You can adjust the actual time later if need be.) Click the AutoPick button, and the meeting selection bars will move to the first available time for all attendees.

TIP TIP TIP TIP TIP TIP TIP TIP TIP TIP TIP TIP TIP TIP TIP TIP TIP TIP TIP TIP TIP TIP TIP TIP

You can drag the Meeting Selection bars to set a meeting's time and duration. The white area represents the meeting length, the green bar the start time, and the maroon bar the end time.

When you have found an acceptable time, click the Make Meeting button. Enter the details about the meeting: Subject, Location, Reminder, Description, and Categories. When all the details have been entered, click the Send button. All attendees will receive an e-mail message requesting them to notify you of their intention to attend: Accept, Reject, or Tentative.

To review the status of a meeting, open the meeting in your Calendar and click the Attendee Availability tab to view the invitees and the status of their responses. If you decide to invite others at this point, you can do so by clicking the Invite Others button. You can return to the default page by clicking the Appointment tab.

PLANNING A MEETING WITH OTHERS

SKILL
9

1. Switch to Calendar and click the Plan Meeting button on the Standard toolbar.

2. Click Invite Others and select the people you would like to have attend, either as Required, Optional, or Resources. Click OK. Calendar will display invitees' schedules (when available) in the Meeting Planner.

continued ▶

3. Enter a preferred Start and End Time for the meeting and click AutoPick to find the first available time for all invitees.

4. When you have decided on a time, click Make Meeting.

5. Enter the details about the meeting—Subject, Location, Reminders, and Categories. Enter additional information in the open text box.

6. Click Send to send messages to all invitees.

7. When messages are returned with responses, open the appointment to view the status of the responses by clicking the Attendee Availability tab.

Publishing a Calendar As a Web Page

If you embark on a business trip with three or four colleagues, it would be very useful for you all to have the same calendar listing. Outlook 2000 lets you publish a calendar as a Web page so that your colleagues, clients, and other important people can keep track of what's going on.

To save your calendar as a Web page, choose File ➤ Save As Web Page. In the Save As Web Page window, choose the span of days you wish published by choosing a Start Date and an End Date in their respective drop-down menus. You can opt to include your appointment details and whether or not to provide a background graphic, and you should enter both a Calendar Title and a File Name. Finally, if you want to preview the calendar page in your browser, check Open Saved Web Page in Browser before clicking Save.

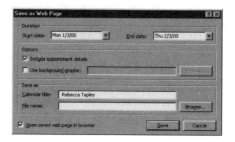

You now have an HTML page that shows your calendar; you can publish this page on a Web site as you would other HTML pages. For more information, contact your Internet Service Provider.

PUBLISHING A CALENDAR AS A WEB PAGE

1. Choose File ➣ Save As Web Page.
2. Choose a Start Date and an End Date using the calendar controls.
3. Include appointment details and/or a background graphic.
4. Give the calendar a title and filename.
5. Click Save.

Hands On

1. In the Calendar:

   a) Enter at least five appointments.

   b) Enter at least one meeting that recurs monthly.

   c) View the Calendar in three different views and use the Day, Week, and Month buttons to examine your calendar.

   d) Enter a one-week vacation using the all-day event option and indicate that you will be out of the office.

2. Plan a meeting:

   a) Invite at least one other person to your meeting.

   b) Set a reminder two hours before the meeting.

3. Save two days in your calendar as a Web page and preview the page in Internet Explorer.

SKILL
9

9.7: Creating Shortcuts

Outlook lets you add shortcuts to any Outlook module, or to any file, folder, or Web page to the Outlook Bar. To create a link to a file or folder, open the Outlook module, click the New button, and choose Outlook Bar Shortcut. You can also right-click on the Outlook Bar and choose Outlook Bar Shortcut. The Add to Outlook Bar window opens:

To create a shortcut for an existing item, such as the Tasks folder, click it once to select it and then click OK. An icon for the new item will appear in the Outlook Bar.

To add a folder elsewhere on your hard drive, open the Add to Outlook Bar window and choose File System from the Look In drop-down list. Choose the folder and double-click it to select it. An icon for the new item will also appear on the Outlook Bar.

Once the folder shortcut exists, you can use it to view files. Right-drag a file to the Outlook Bar to create the shortcut to the file.

Creating New Shortcut Groups

As mentioned, the Outlook Bar includes three default shortcut groups: Outlook Shortcuts, My Shortcuts, and Other Shortcuts. If you want to add a new, custom shortcut group, simply right-click on an empty part of the Outlook Shortcut Bar and choose Add New Group.

A blank text box appears at the bottom of the Outlook Bar where you can type in the name of the new shortcut group. Press Enter when you're finished, and the new shortcut group will appear with the others; now you can add shortcuts to the new group.

You can rename or delete a shortcut group with the same right-click menu. Point the mouse to the group name in the Outlook Bar, right-click it, and choose Rename Group or Delete Group. You can change the size of Outlook shortcuts by choosing Large Icons or Small Icons in the right-click menu.

CREATING A NEW SHORTCUT GROUP

1. Right-click on the empty part of any Outlook Shortcut Bar and choose Add New Group. A blank text box appears at the bottom of the Outlook Shortcuts pane.

2. Type the name of the new shortcut group and press Enter. The new shortcut group appears at the bottom of the Outlook Bar.

Hands On

1. Create a shortcut to a file or folder in Outlook and add it to the My Shortcuts group.

2. Create a shortcut to a file or folder elsewhere on your hard drive and add it to the Other Shortcuts group.

9.8: Using the Journal and Notes

The Journal serves as your automated, online diary. It will automatically record work you are doing or let you add entries manually. You can track time spent on projects, phone calls, documents, e-mail messages—whatever it is that you want to monitor. The Journal is located on the Outlook Bar. To open the Journal, click the Journal icon in the Outlook Bar.

Automatically Recording Journal Events

One of the useful features of the Journal is that you can have it working in the background, silently recording the work you do. You have to configure the Journal to work automatically.

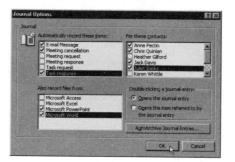

 WARNING WARNING WARNING WARNING WARNING WARNING WARNING WARNING

It's tempting to automatically record scads of Journal entries, but if you're an Office power user, doing so will greatly increase the amount of storage used by Outlook.

AUTOMATICALLY RECORDING JOURNAL ENTRIES

1. Choose Tools ➤ Options and click the Preferences tab. Click the Journal Options button.
2. Mark the items you want to record automatically.
3. Click OK.

Manually Recording an Event

Although automatically recording events is helpful, the real power of Journal is its ability to let you enter information manually to track phone calls, conversations, meetings, and any other kind of communication. To make a new journal entry, choose File ➤ New ➤ Journal Entry, or choose Journal Entry from the list on the New Item button. If you're going to be creating a number of entries, it's fastest to choose Journal in the Outlook Bar, and then click the New Journal Entry button on the toolbar.

On the Journal Entry form, shown in Figure 9.4, you can enter a Subject, Entry Type (from a list of 20 choices), Contact Name and Company, Start Time, Duration, and Notes. If you want to clock the time you spend on the phone or working on a document, click Start Timer and let it run while you work on the entry. Outlook will automatically record the time in the Duration field.

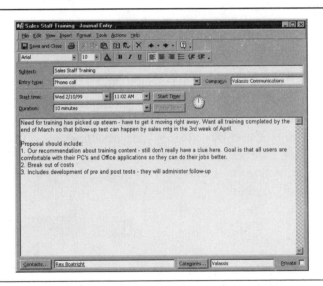

FIGURE 9.4: Enter information about an activity in the Journal Entry form.

You can insert files into journal entries, as you can with all Outlook items. Choose Insert ➤ Object and select the type of object you want to link to your Journal entry. You can't insert Outlook items in Journal entries, but you can link the entry to a contact by clicking the Contacts button in the Journal Entry form. Select the contact(s) you want to link this entry to. To see all the Journal entries linked to a contact, open the Contact form, activate the Activities page, and choose Journal from the Show drop-down list.

CREATING A MANUAL JOURNAL ENTRY

1. Choose File ➤ New ➤ Journal Entry to open a Journal Entry form.
2. Enter the Subject and Entry Type.
3. Enter a Start Time or click the Start Timer button. Either enter the Duration manually or click Pause Timer when you're finished to have Outlook enter the duration for you.
4. Enter details about the entry in the text box.
5. To link the entry to a contact, click the Contacts button and choose a contact from the Select Names dialog box. Click the Categories button to assign the entry to a category.
6. Click Save and Close to close the entry.

Locating Events in the Journal

The Journal is organized as a timeline and can be displayed in timeline or table form. The first three views available from the Current View list—By Type, By Contact, and By Category—are timeline views. The other three views—Entry List, Last Seven Days, and Phone Calls—are in table format. To locate an entry in a timeline view, click the Day button, Week button, or Month button on the Standard toolbar:

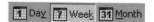

Click the plus symbol to expand the entries in the view; use the Collapse button (with the minus symbol) to hide entries. Double-click an item to open the Journal page for that item. Use the Find Items button to find entries based on criteria: for example, all the items that pertain to a particular company or subject.

LOCATING AN ENTRY IN THE JOURNAL

1. Select a view from the Current View menu.

2. If you've chosen a timeline view, click the Go To Today, Day, Week, and Month buttons to choose a particular date. Use the horizontal and vertical scroll bars to scroll through the dates. Use the Expand and Collapse buttons to hide and display entries in a timeline view.

3. If you selected a list view, use the column headers to sort the entries by date or subject.

4. Click the Find Items button on the Standard toolbar to search for an item by words, entry type, contact, categories, or other criteria. Click Find Now to initiate the search.

Creating Notes

Even in the age of the computer, most people still use a paper memo pad or sticky note to write short notes to themselves. Outlook includes an easy way to computerize notes. Choose Note from the New button on the Standard toolbar or Ctrl+Shift+N to open a Note window. Each note is automatically time- and date-stamped. Closing the Note window automatically saves the note. To view a note, click the Notes icon on the Outlook Bar to go to the Notes module:

Double-click a note to open it. Click the Note icon in the upper left corner of the note to access options for deleting, saving, and printing notes.

SKILL
9

TIP TIP TIP TIP TIP TIP TIP TIP TIP TIP TIP TIP TIP TIP TIP TIP TIP TIP TIP TIP TIP TIP TIP

You can move individual notes to the Windows desktop by dragging them onto the desktop.

CREATING A NOTE

1. Choose Note from the New button on the Standard toolbar, right-click in the Note window and choose New Note, or press Ctrl+Shift+N.

2. Type the note and click the Close button.

3. Click the Notes icon on the Outlook Bar to open the Notes window. Click once to open a note.

4. Click the Note icon in the top-left corner of a note to access Save As, Print, and other options.

Hands On

1. Set Journal options to automatically record your work on Word files and e-mail messages.

2. Make a Journal entry for a phone call to a contact in your Contacts folder. Use the timer to time the call.

3. Locate a Journal event using Find Items. Locate a Journal event using the Go to Month button and the scroll bars.

4. Create three notes and:

   a) Delete one of the notes.

   b) Drag one of the notes to the Windows desktop. Double-click the Notes icon to open the note. Close it again.

9.9: Integrating the Outlook Modules

The Outlook modules are designed to work together, to help you organize and manage your time and data most effectively. In this section, you will learn how to keep track of data and other files in Outlook and how to further customize the Outlook environment.

Managing Data and Files in Outlook

You may be surprised to discover that Outlook can be used for all your file management needs—moving, copying, opening, finding, renaming, and deleting files; creating new folders; and even printing documents. The Outlook Bar can be customized to include shortcuts to other folders, making it possible to access any document or module on your system from within Outlook. To open a list of options for customizing the Outlook Bar, right-click it.

Click the Other Group button on the Outlook Bar to see drives and folders for your computer. Click My Computer or another icon in the Outlook Bar to display its contents. Double-click files or folders in the Information Viewer to open them.

 If you want to keep a Windows Explorer-type list of folders visible, open the Folder List button on the Standard toolbar. If your screen is getting a little crowded, you could buy a bigger monitor. Or you could close the Outlook Bar (choose View ➤ Outlook Bar). It's up to you.

Moving Items to Different Folders

You can move any item to another folder with drag-and-drop. It's easiest if you can see both the current location and the destination, so having your primary mail folders on the Outlook Bar really helps. You can view your Inbox messages in the Outlook window and then drag them into folders on the Outlook Bar.

Automatically Creating a New Outlook Item from an Existing One   With Outlook's AutoCreate feature, you can use an item to quickly create an item of another type. For example, to create an Appointment item from a Mail message item, select the message, then drag and drop it on the Calendar icon or folder in the Outlook Bar. Outlook will copy information from the mail message to the appropriate fields in the appointment form, and place the text from the message in the appointment's text box. If you drag a task request to the Calendar or to Tasks, Outlook automatically notifies the sender that you accepted the task. This also works with meeting requests.

SKILL
9

TIP TIP TIP TIP TIP TIP TIP TIP TIP TIP TIP TIP TIP TIP TIP TIP TIP TIP TIP TIP TIP TIP

AutoCreate has another unique use. If you drag an Outlook item onto the desktop, you create a copy of the item that you can open from the desktop—a convenient way to remember to follow up on a task.

Archiving Items

If you use Outlook to its full potential, you'll be creating a mountain of data. Eventually, you'll want to clean out your folders to eliminate out-of-date items. Outlook gives you two ways to handle spring cleaning: *AutoArchive* and *Archive*. Before you use either archiving method, you should review and set the Archive properties for individual folders.

SETTING FOLDER ARCHIVE OPTIONS

1. Right-click on the first folder that you want to set Archive options for and choose Properties.
2. Click the AutoArchive tab.
3. Enable the Clean Out Items Older Than check box, and set a length of time.
4. Choose whether old items should be moved or deleted.
5. Click OK.
6. Repeat steps 1–5 for each folder.

AutoArchiving is the easiest option; simply tell Outlook how frequently it should check the folders.

SETTING AUTOARCHIVE OPTIONS

1. Choose Tools ➤ Options from the menu bar.
2. On the Other page, click the AutoArchive button to open the AutoArchive dialog box.
3. In the AutoArchive dialog box, set the length of time between AutoArchive operations.
4. Enable or disable prompting and the deletion of expired mail items.
5. Click OK.

You don't have to use AutoArchiving. Instead, you can archive folders and their subfolders individually as you need to. Or, you can use the Archive options you set for each folder, but start the archiving operation manually when you have time.

MANUALLY ARCHIVING FOLDERS

1. Choose File ≻ Archive to open the Archive dialog box.
2. Select Archive All Folders According to Their Archive Settings and click OK to begin archiving all folders.

–OR–

2. Choose Archive This Folder and All Subfolders.
3. Select the folder you want to archive.
4. Select a date in the Archive Files Older Than drop-down list.
5. Click OK.

Creating Custom Views

By designing your own Outlook views, you can tailor Outlook to your needs without losing the ease and functionality of Office 2000. You can create a custom view in two ways. If you already have a view open, you can alter it. When you select a different view, Outlook saves your changes. Or you can choose View ≻ Current View ≻ Define Views, and select a view to base the custom view on.

Click an existing view and then Modify or Copy to customize an existing view or create a copy to work from. Customize the preferences concerning fields shown, how the information in the view will be grouped and filtered, and formatting issues. Click OK to save the newly modified view and return to the Define Views dialog box.

MODIFYING AN EXISTING VIEW

1. Choose View ➤ Current View ➤ Define View.

2. Select a view that's similar to the one you want. Choose Copy to work with a complete duplicate, or Modify to customize an existing view without saving an original. Click Apply Settings to continue.

–OR–

2. Click New to create a view from scratch. In the Create a New View dialog box, name the view, choose its contents, and indicate whether or not you wish to share the view with others. Click Apply Settings to continue.

3. Set options in the View Settings for Fields, Group By, Sort, Filter, and Format controls.

4. Click OK to return to the Define Views dialog box.

5. Click Apply View or Close to save the view.

More on Outlook 2000

There are other ways to customize and use Outlook. Some of Outlook's features are only accessible in the Corporate/Workgroup configuration in combination with Microsoft Exchange Server. Others features are designed for use by programmers or developers. For more information on any of the topics in this list, we recommend *Mastering Outlook 2000* (Sybex 1999).

Customized Forms   You can modify the default Outlook forms to create your own forms, or create new forms from scratch. You can use Visual Basic for Applications and VBScript in Outlook 2000 to automate Outlook and create customized applications that involve other Office 2000 applications.

Sharing Calendars, Tasks, and Contacts   You can create shared Outlook mail folders on any network. However, to share schedules, task lists, or contact lists, these must be on a network with Microsoft Exchange Server, and you must have the necessary network permissions for the public folder you wish to create the shared item in.

Synchronizing Your PC with Your Office's Server   Outlook has two separate methods for handling work while you're out of the office: Remote Mail and Offline Folders. With *Remote Mail*, you can download and read the messages that have been delivered in your absence, but you can't send messages. *Offline Folders*, a second set of folders kept on your remote computer, allow you to send *and* receive mail, tasks, and other items. To use Offline Folders, you must have Dial-Up access to a Microsoft Exchange Server.

Hands On

1. If you haven't created subfolders in your Inbox, create one now. Then:

    a) Place a shortcut to the folder on the Outlook Bar.

    b) Move several Mail items to the folder.

2. Use the Outlook Bar to browse your hard drive.

3. Drag a task or appointment to the Inbox to create a mail message. Drag a mail message to the Calendar to create an appointment item.

4. Review and set the Archive properties for each of your Outlook folders. Set AutoArchive options. Manually archive all folders according to their settings.

SKILL
9

Are You Experienced?

Now you can...

- ☑ Use Outlook to track contacts, appointments, and tasks
- ☑ Send, receive, and manage your e-mail
- ☑ Schedule meetings
- ☑ Keep a journal
- ☑ Customize Outlook by creating new views

Creating Electrifying Publications with Publisher

- ➔ **Using the Publisher interface**
- ➔ **Inserting text and graphic objects**
- ➔ **Recoloring objects**
- ➔ **Changing page setup options and printing your publication**
- ➔ **Working with the Design Checker**
- ➔ **Organizing art with the Graphics Manager**
- ➔ **Creating mail merge documents and booklets**

So you've just been handed responsibility for the company newsletter. Or perhaps it's the human resources employee manual. Whatever the particular task, you have a project that requires that "extra professional" touch, and you want it to look like it came off a printing press. When working with documents that contain many graphic elements and text boxes, Publisher is the tool of choice.

Publisher is designed to handle multiple elements on a page. The focus, as you might expect, is on the overall appearance of the publication. Although you certainly can't ignore the micro aspects of your document, the real power comes from the ease with which you arrange components on the page.

Flyers, newsletters, calendars, brochures, directories, and countless other publications will glide off your printer in no time. Let's take a look at just how easy it can be.

Skill 10.1: Understanding the Publisher Interface

If you are used to working in Word or another type of word processing program, you may have to think a bit differently about how to put together a document for publication. With Publisher, you will quickly discover that it's not as simple as typing text on a page and letting it wrap at the margin. Before you place anything in a Publisher document, you need to reserve a space for it.

Working in an Object-Driven Model

Publisher works from an *object-driven* model. This simply means that everything on a page has to be in a frame. You can't just type text anywhere; you need a text box to house it.

In Publisher, graphics such as clip art and WordArt behave much the same as they do in a Word document. However, you'll find that text is treated somewhat differently in Publisher. For instance, you can move an entire block of text (in a text box) anywhere on the page with a click and drag. Tables are treated as objects, too. You can choose to edit within a cell, but you also have the ability to resize the entire table as you would a piece of clip art.

It won't take you long to get used to an object-driven model. Skill 10.2 shows you how to create text boxes using the text frame tool. The remaining skills show you other object tools so you can create extraordinary publications with ease.

Starting a Publication from Scratch

When you launch Publisher for the first time, you see the Publisher Catalog dialog box, shown in Figure 10.1. You can begin a publication in three ways: Publications by Wizard, Publications by Design, or Blank Publications.

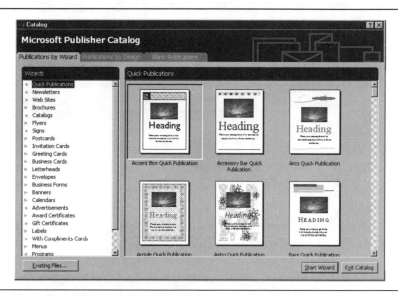

FIGURE 10.1: The Publisher Catalog dialog box

You might be tempted to start your first publication using one of the many Quick Publications Wizards, which walk you through steps to create cards, calendars, invitations, resumes, and other documents. (More on Quick Publications in Skill 10.14.) However, if you plan to edit any of the elements generated by the Wizard—and most of the time you will—you can get lost if you have no experience recognizing Publisher elements and editing them.

That's why it is helpful to start from scratch when you are just learning Publisher. Once you have built a document by placing, resizing, and formatting different objects one at a time, you can easily recognize and edit the various components produced by Wizards.

Choose the type of publication you're going to create from the Publisher Catalog. Remember, the Catalog launches automatically the first time you open Publisher. If you've disabled the Catalog start-up option (choose Tools ➤ Options ➤ General) or exited the Catalog, choose File ➤ New to open it again. To start from scratch, select the Blank Publications tab. You will see choices for business cards, banners, booklets, and other publications, as shown in Figure 10.2. Select from the list on the left or scroll through the gallery on the right to see visual representations of the list items. Click the Custom Page button to enter specific page dimensions if you don't see a style that suits your needs. Click the Custom Web Page button if you are designing for the World Wide Web.

NOTE NOTE NOTE NOTE NOTE NOTE NOTE NOTE NOTE NOTE NOTE NOTE NOTE NOTE NOTE
See Skill 12 for information on using Publisher and the other Office applications for Web publishing.

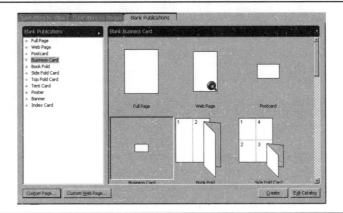

FIGURE 10.2: The Blank Publications tab of the Catalog dialog box

Once you have chosen one of the blank publication styles, click the Create button at the lower right corner of the window. Your blank page will be displayed along with the Quick Publications Wizard on the left. To allow more working space, click the button to hide this Wizard. Arrange boundaries and guides as desired, and you are ready to go!

STARTING WITH A BLANK PAGE

1. Select File ≻ New to open the Publisher Catalog. Choose the Blank Publications Tab.

2. Scroll through the list of blank document types and click on the one you wish to use.

continued

3. Click the Create button at the bottom of the Catalog window.
4. Click the Hide Wizard button to allow more work space.

Using Publisher Toolbars

Unlike the other Office applications, Publisher 2000 does not have a personalized toolbar option. Publisher displays the Standard toolbar by default when you open the program. You can always recognize the Standard toolbar because its first button is the New button. Buttons for common commands such as Print and Save also appear on this toolbar.

The Formatting toolbar is also on by default. However, you won't see it until you have created and selected an object. In Publisher 2000, the Formatting toolbar is dynamic. That is, it changes depending on what type of object is selected. If you have selected a graphic object, the Formatting toolbar displays the tools for wrapping, rotating, cropping, and flipping, as shown here. Selecting a text box causes the toolbar to display text-formatting tools: italics, alignment, and font size, to name a few.

Before you can use formatting tools, however, you first have to create an object. You use the *Object toolbar* to select the frame tools for laying out the structure of the page. You click object tools each time you add another element to a page. Using this toolbar, you will build the text and graphics that give your publication that professional look.

NOTE NOTE NOTE NOTE NOTE NOTE NOTE NOTE NOTE NOTE NOTE NOTE NOTE NOTE NOTE
While shown in a horizontal position here, the default position for the Object toolbar is vertical. You can reposition any toolbar by clicking and dragging it.

SKILL
10

Setting Boundaries and Guides

Publisher has everything you need to precisely place and align objects. You can view the nonprinting *boundaries* and *guides* when needed, and hide them when you're through. Boundaries, as shown in Figure 10.3, are the lines surrounding a document that show you where the margins are set. Guides are vertical and horizontal lines you can place on the page to assist with object alignment.

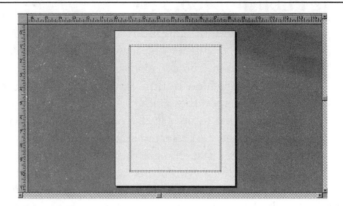

FIGURE 10.3: The Publisher interface

The red line shows page margins, which default to 1 inch all around. The blue line displays ⅛ inch inside the outer margin boundary. Use the blue line as a guide to keep from placing objects directly on the margin.

NOTE NOTE NOTE NOTE NOTE NOTE NOTE NOTE NOTE NOTE NOTE NOTE NOTE NOTE NOTE

The term *boundary* implies that the program somehow prohibits you from working outside of the designated area. This is not the case at all. Nothing prevents you from placing objects on, or even outside, Publisher's margin boundaries. Rely on your own design skills for proper object placement.

Adjust boundaries by choosing Arrange ➢ Layout Guides from the menu. In the Layout Guides dialog box, use the spin boxes or select and overtype the existing numbers to adjust left, right, top, and bottom margin boundaries. You may find it helpful to divide your page into separate areas if there is a logical separation in your publication, such as a one-page document that will be folded into thirds and mailed. In the Grid Guides section of the dialog box, change the number of rows to three. That way you can easily place mailing and return addresses in the middle of the page.

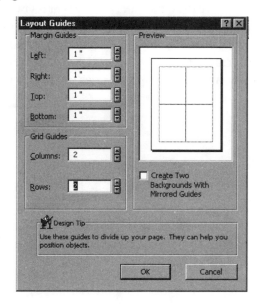

Rulers and Ruler Guides

The horizontal and vertical rulers are on by default. You can turn the rulers off by choosing View ➤ Rulers. It is likely, however, that you will need rulers frequently when creating documents with multiple objects. Click and drag either ruler to bring it onto the page of your document. Click the box at the intersection of the two rulers, as shown here, to drag both rulers at once.

SKILL
10

With the ruler on your document page, you can measure distances from clip art to boundaries and measure text boxes and other objects to ensure design consistency. Simply drag the rulers away when you're through.

If you need a randomly placed guide to align objects, *ruler guides* are easy to place, move, and remove as necessary. You can insert as many horizontal and vertical ruler guides as you need. Simply point to the edge of either ruler, hold the Shift key, and drag the green ruler guide into your document.

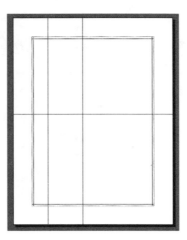

Remove a ruler guide by holding the Shift key and dragging it back to the ruler from which it came. Since boundaries and guides can be distracting at times, you may wish to hide them by choosing View ➤ Hide Boundaries and Guides from the menu bar. Display them again by clicking View ➤ Show Boundaries and Guides.

TIP TIP TIP TIP TIP TIP TIP TIP TIP TIP TIP TIP TIP TIP TIP TIP TIP TIP TIP TIP TIP TIP TIP

Pressing Ctrl+Shift+O also hides and displays nonprinting boundaries and guides.

ADJUSTING BOUNDARIES AND GUIDES

1. To adjust margin boundaries, click Arrange ➤ Layout Guides.
2. Use the spin boxes or select and overtype the existing numbers to adjust left, right, top, and bottom margin boundaries.

continued ▶

3. Use the grid guides for columns and rows to create visual sections.

4. To insert a ruler guide, point to the edge of either ruler, hold the Shift key, and drag a guide into your document.

5. Remove a ruler guide by holding the Shift key and dragging it back to the ruler.

6. Hide boundaries and guides by choosing View ➤ Hide Boundaries and Guides from the menu.

7. To display hidden guides, click View ➤ Show Boundaries and Guides.

The Scratch Area

Think of the Publisher program window as a large table where you can place blank pages along with the text and objects that you will eventually display on them. When you are working at a table with all your text and art scattered about, you might arrange a picture in a particular location, and then change your mind and place it on another page altogether. Later, you decide you really want this picture on a page at the end of the document, so you set it aside for the moment.

In Publisher, your table is the gray space surrounding the displayed page(s), called the *scratch area*. Figure 10.3 shows the scratch area, which you use to hold objects while you decide where to place them. If you're working on Page 3 and come across a piece of art you think you might need later, grab it now! Items you drag into the scratch area are saved along with your publication.

Viewing Your Publication

Since the default zoom setting for new documents is too small to easily view text, you need to enlarge text to proof it. When working with graphics, you'll want to zoom back out to determine whether the object is properly placed on the page. Zoom buttons, found toward the end of the Standard toolbar, really get a workout in Publisher. Click the plus button to move closer to your document (that is, to enlarge it); click the minus button (repeatedly, if necessary) to view from a distance.

Navigating between pages in Publisher 2000 is easier than ever. Page navigation buttons are displayed at the bottom left of the scratch area. Just click on the page you wish to view. Adjacent pages may display two at a time. Zoom in as necessary

SKILL
10

to work more closely with one page or the other. You can also access the two-page spread and zoom commands from the View menu.

Hands On

1. Start a new presentation with a blank full page:

   a) Set up layout guides as follows: left and right margins at 1.25 inches; top and bottom margins at 1 inch; columns and rows adjusted so that your page is divided into four quadrants.

   b) Add one horizontal and one vertical ruler guide.

   c) Zoom in to 66%, then zoom out to 25%.

   d) Remove the ruler guides.

   e) Adjust the layout guides to 0 rows and 0 columns.

Skill 10.2: Entering Text

 Since Publisher operates from an object-driven model, you won't just start typing on the blank page. Instead, you will use the Text frame tool to create a space to house your text.

 TIP TIP TIP TIP TIP TIP TIP TIP TIP TIP TIP TIP TIP TIP TIP TIP TIP TIP TIP TIP TIP TIP TIP

If you forget about text frames and just start typing, Publisher will create one big text frame that fills the page. To remove it and start again, select the frame and choose Edit ➤ Delete Object.

Click once on the Text frame tool to select it. Then move into your document and drag to create a frame of the approximate size and shape you need. It is important for you to recognize that object creation requires two separate actions. The first is a single click on the tool of choice; the second is a click and drag inside the document. Avoid dragging the button from the toolbar into your document since this won't allow you to create a frame.

TIP TIP TIP TIP TIP TIP TIP TIP TIP TIP TIP TIP TIP TIP TIP TIP TIP TIP TIP TIP TIP TIP TIP TIP

If you click an object tool and click on the blank page (without dragging), Publisher will create a text frame that measures 2 by 3 inches so long as Single Click Object Creation is enabled. If Single Click Object Creation is disabled, forgetting to drag creates nothing. (Publisher options are discussed at length in Skill 10.3.)

Release your mouse button when you have dragged a text frame of the size and shape you want, then begin typing. The insertion point starts at the top-left corner of the frame, effectively left-aligning your text by default.

Resizing and Repositioning a Frame

RESIZE

At some point you will decide to change the size and/or position of your text frame. Select the object you wish to resize with a single click anywhere inside the frame. Then position your mouse over one of the resize handles until you see the resize pointer. Click and drag larger or smaller.

TIP TIP TIP TIP TIP TIP TIP TIP TIP TIP TIP TIP TIP TIP TIP TIP TIP TIP TIP TIP TIP TIP TIP TIP

To resize yet maintain the original proportions of an object, hold the Shift key while resizing.

You can move an object by placing the mouse on the gray outline that frames it. When the mouse pointer changes to the moving van icon (called the *Mover*), click and drag to a new position.

CREATING, RESIZING, AND MOVING A TEXT FRAME

1. Click to select the Text frame tool on the Object toolbar.
2. Move your pointer into the document and drag a frame of any size and shape.
3. Release the mouse button and type the text that will occupy the frame.
4. Resize the frame by dragging any of the handles surrounding the text frame. If no handles are visible, select the frame with a single click inside the frame.

continued ▶

SKILL
10

5. Press the Shift key as you drag to keep the text frame's original pro-
    portions while resizing.

6. Move a text frame by pointing to the gray border surrounding the
    frame and dragging the Mover icon.

Editing Text in a Text Frame

You use two general types of text editing in Publisher: character and paragraph.
Frequently, you perform paragraph-editing functions by selecting just the text
frame. To format characters, you usually select the text itself, rather than just
the frame that houses it. Figure 10.4 illustrates the difference between selecting
a text frame and selecting text within a frame.

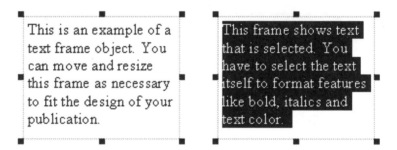

FIGURE 10.4: Selecting a text frame is very different from selecting text
within a frame.

Formatting Characters and Words

Select a text frame and click to position the insertion point next to any word or
character you wish to edit. Press the Backspace key to delete characters behind (to

the left of) the insertion point. Press Delete to erase characters to the right of the insertion point. Position the insertion point appropriately and begin typing to insert text within an existing sentence or paragraph.

TIP TIP TIP TIP TIP TIP TIP TIP TIP TIP TIP TIP TIP TIP TIP TIP TIP TIP TIP TIP TIP TIP TIP TIP TIP

If text to the right of the insertion point disappears as you type, you're probably in Overstrike mode. Press the Insert key on your keyboard to switch from Overstrike mode back to Insert mode.

Select a word, sentence, or paragraph within a text box and click the buttons on the Formatting toolbar to make them bold, italic, and/or underline. Basic text formatting works the same way as it does in Microsoft Word. Change fonts and font sizes from the toolbar drop-down lists, or choose Format ➤ Font from the menu bar. Use the toolbar buttons to increase and decrease font size by two points.

Select text and click the Text Color button on the Formatting toolbar to see available color choices. Publisher 2000 provides built-in schemes to lend consistency to your creations. If you like the default scheme, simply click on one of the color choices currently displayed to apply it to your text.

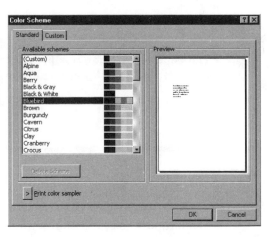

SKILL
10

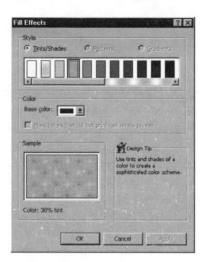

Click More Color Schemes to see additional scheme options in the Color Scheme dialog box. The More Colors choice in the dialog box takes you to the Colors dialog box, where you can blend different colors to produce the exact shade of text you're looking for. Choose Fill Effects to explore different tints of a base color.

NOTE NOTE NOTE NOTE NOTE NOTE NOTE NOTE NOTE NOTE NOTE NOTE NOTE NOTE NOTE

The Fill Effects dialog box in Publisher is very different from the one you see in PowerPoint. Background patterns and textures are more fully discussed in Skill 10.7.

FORMATTING TEXT

1. Click next to the word you wish to edit and use the Backspace or Delete key to erase characters. You can also select and delete a sentence, word, or paragraph.

2. Position the insertion point as desired and begin typing to insert new text within existing text.

continued ▶

3. Select a word, sentence, or paragraph and use the buttons on the Formatting toolbar to change font, font size, text color, and text style.

4. To preview how your text will look before you apply a new font, select the text, choose Format ➤ Font from the menu bar, and adjust font settings in the dialog box.

Paragraph Formatting

Publisher defines a paragraph as a string of characters that ends when you press Enter. In a publication, each heading, each line in a person's address, and each item in a bulleted list is seen as a separate paragraph.

Alignment   To change alignment in a text frame that contains one paragraph, you are only required to select the text frame before clicking the appropriate button. Use the alignment buttons on the Formatting toolbar to change from left-aligned to centered, right, or full justification. The Increase Indent button moves and aligns all the text in the frame one Tab space to the right. Use the Decrease Indent button to move and align the text one Tab space to the left. You will find the Increase/Decrease Indent buttons particularly helpful for offsetting bulleted lists.

To change alignment in text frames that contain multiple paragraphs, you still have to select the text itself. If you don't, you'll only see changes to the paragraph where the insertion point is located.

Bullets and Numbering   Bullets and numbering work much the same as they do in Word. Select the list of items you wish to bullet or number and click the appropriate toolbar button. The most recently used bullet or number format will be applied. If you want to choose a custom format, choose Indents and Lists from the Format menu.

In the Indents and Lists dialog box, choose the Bulleted List option in the Indent Settings control. The most recently used bullet characters will be displayed. Click the one you like and change its size, if desired. (The size of the bullet character defaults to match the size of the text it precedes.) If you increase the number in the Indent List By field, the text moves farther away from the bullet character. Change the way the list aligns within its frame by selecting a different option

SKILL
10

from the Alignment drop-down list. Use the Line Spacing button to increase or decrease the amount of space between your list items. Click the New Bullet button to see other choices for bullet characters.

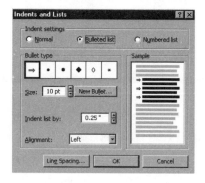

If you choose the option for a numbered list, you have three new settings to consider. First, choose a number or letter format from the list of available choices. Then choose the separator you prefer to use. Finally, adjust the Start At number if you are continuing from a previous list. You have the same options for changing the indent distance, alignment, and line spacing as you have with bulleted lists.

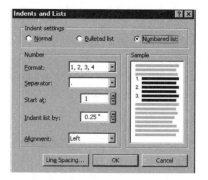

APPLYING BULLETS AND NUMBERING

1. Select the list you wish to bullet or number.
2. Click the Bulleted List (or Numbered List) button to use the most recent bullet/number settings.

continued ▶

3. For custom bullets, select the list, choose Format ➤ Indents and Lists, and select the Bulleted List option in the Indent Settings control.

4. Click the character you like and change its size. Change the number in the Indent List By field to move text farther away or closer to the bullet character. Change the list alignment by selecting a different option from the Alignment drop-down list.

5. Use the Line Spacing button to increase or decrease the amount of space between your list items.

6. Click the New Bullet button to see other choices for bullet characters.

7. For custom numbers, select the Numbered List option.

8. Select a number or letter format and a separator from the list of available choices. Adjust the Start At number if you are continuing from a previous list.

9. Change the indent distance, alignment, and/or line spacing as desired.

Drop Caps   Newsletter and magazine articles frequently begin with a *drop cap* to draw readers into the first paragraph. Publisher offers numerous options for creating this eye-catching effect.

𝒟rop Caps can create dramatic effects at the beginning of a paragraph.

Select the character you wish to format as a drop cap. Choose Format ➤ Drop Cap from the menu. Scroll through the available drop caps, click on the one you like and click OK to apply it in your publication. If you don't see a drop cap style you like, try the Custom Drop Cap tab of this dialog box to choose the number of lines above and below the drop, the font, font style, and color of the drop cap.

Change your mind later? Select the text frame with the drop cap you wish to remove. Choose Format ➤ Change Drop Cap from the menu, and click the Remove button.

Inserting Pages

To place another page into your document, choose Insert ➤ Page to open the Insert Page dialog box. Choose where to insert the page and select whether you want a new page with one large text frame, duplicated background objects, or just a blank page. If you choose the blank page option, each page you add will have the layout guides you have already set.

Importing Text from Other Sources

You'll find it easier to create complex documents by separating the design process from the writing process. You can compose and type the text for your publication in a word processing program, and then transfer that text into your Publisher document. As long as Publisher's converters are installed, you shouldn't have any problem bringing in text produced in another Windows-based program. Depending on the amount of text you want to transfer, Publisher gives you two options.

Using Copy/Paste to Bring in Text

When you are transferring a small amount of text into Publisher, Copy/Paste works just fine. Use this technique if you're selecting only *part* of another document to place in your publication.

Create an empty text frame in your Publisher document to house the text you wish to transfer. Open the text document in its native application and select the desired text. Click the Copy button or press Ctrl+C to place the selected text on the Windows Clipboard. Switch back to the Publisher window, select the empty text frame, and click the Paste button on the Standard toolbar or press Ctrl+V. If you have created a text frame that is too small to house the text you are pasting, Publisher will prompt you with a warning and options to create additional frames. Clicking Yes to these options will bring the text into connected frames. (See "Managing Text Frame Overflow" later in this skill.)

SKILL
10

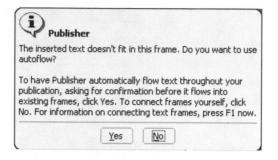

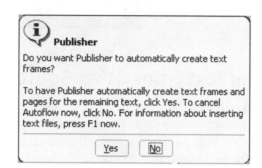

Using the Import Option

Create an empty text frame in Publisher and make sure it is selected as you choose Insert ➤ Text File from the menu. The Insert Text dialog box opens to allow you to locate and select the desired file. Click OK. Publisher will import (and convert file formats, if necessary) to the selected text frame. You will see text overflow warnings if the receiving text frame is too small for the text you are importing.

BRINGING IN TEXT FROM ANOTHER DOCUMENT

1. To use the Copy/Paste commands, create a frame in your publication to hold the text you are transferring.

2. Open the text document in its native application.

3. Select the text you want to import and click the Copy button.

continued ▶

4. Switch to Publisher and select the empty text frame.

5. Click Paste.

–OR–

1. To import a text file, create and select an empty text frame in your Publisher document.

2. Click Insert ➤ Text File.

3. Locate and select the file you wish to import. Click OK.

4. If you see overflow warnings, click Yes to have Publisher create additional frames or No to manually correct the overflow problem.

Managing Text Frame Overflow

When Publisher warns you about text frame overflow, you can ignore these warnings (click No to both) and handle the problem manually. This method allows you to better control the placement and sizing of the text frames to which the additional text flows. You can also change the current frame so that the text fits.

Publisher can automatically create more frames to hold the extra text. Generally, you do this if the amount of imported text is very large or if the publication is already laid out in such a way that the imported text will require minimal placement modification. If you choose to have Publisher create frames, read "Connecting to Another Frame" below.

Making the Text Fit the Existing Frame

When you don't want your imported text in multiple frames, you can make the existing frame larger so the text will fit. Any time you select a text frame that is too small to display its contents in total, the *Text in Overflow indicator* appears at the bottom right of the selected frame. Place your mouse over one of the object handles and drag to resize the frame to a larger size that allows all the text to be displayed. As soon as it's big enough, the Overflow indicator disappears.

If you don't want to change the frame size, try changing the font or font size to create more room in the frame. If you're double-spacing the text, consider 1.5-

SKILL
10

spacing instead. Choose Format ➤ Line Spacing and type the number of lines you want in the Between Lines field.

AutoFit Text

In Publisher, you can use Automatic Copyfitting to resize text to fit it into a designated amount of space. For example, if a title is too big to fit on one line, you can use copyfitting to reduce the font size of the text until it does fit.

Automatic Copyfitting adjusts the text often, for example, when you type or delete text, change formatting, or resize a frame. Using the Copyfitting feature does not prohibit you from making manual adjustments, however. Try a little of both when creating and formatting your next publication.

Turn on Automatic Copyfitting by choosing Format ➤ AutoFit Text. The Best Fit choice shrinks or expands text to fit in the text frame when you resize it. To reduce the point size of text until it no longer overflows, choose Shrink Text On Overflow.

To turn off Automatic Copyfitting, choose Format ➤ AutoFit Text and then click None. The font size will remain the same when you resize a text frame or insert additional text.

Connecting to Another Frame

Magazines, newspapers, and newsletters generally require layouts where articles begin on one page and continue on another. You can arrange and size the empty frames, and then bring in the text so that it automatically flows from one frame to the next frame and the next and so on.

Create, size, and place the appropriate number of text frames where you want this text to appear in your publication. Type or import text into the first frame. If you are importing and Publisher prompts you to use AutoFlow, you can click Yes as long as the frames you want to use are the *only* empty ones in your document. Publisher will give you the option to automatically create additional frames if you haven't designated enough space for the text file you are importing. Give it a try in most cases. The worst that can happen is that you will have to resize or reset the properties on the new frames. (More on frame properties in Skill 10.7.)

Text imports gone awry can be fixed with a simple click of the Undo button. Now in Publisher 2000, you have the capacity for multiple Undo (and Redo) as with the other Office applications.

As mentioned, the Text in Overflow indicator appears on the lower right corner of the text frame when there is too much text to fit inside. Choose Tools ➤ Connect Text Frames to turn on the Connect Frames toolbar. Click the Connect Text Frames button and move the mouse back into your document. The mouse icon looks like a pitcher. When you place this icon inside any empty text frame, the pitcher tips to the right. Navigate to the text frame you want to use for your continued text and click once inside the frame to "pour" overflow contents. If the second frame overflows, click the Connect Text Frames button again and pour the overflow into another empty frame.

Follow your text forward and backward through a series of linked frames using the buttons that take you to next and previous frames. To disconnect linked frames, select any of them and click the second button on the Connect Frames toolbar. You will unconnect all linked frames that follow the selected frame.

Inserting "Continued From" and "Continued To"

Help your readers follow an article through the publication with Continued notices at the top and/or bottom of linked text frames. Right-click a connected text frame and select Change Frame ➤ Text Frame Properties. Enable one or both Continued boxes.

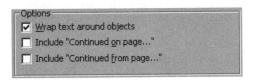

The default settings for Continued messages are Times New Roman Italic in a font size somewhat smaller than the text in the frame. To change the appearance of one of these messages, select it and format as desired. Change fonts, font size, alignment, and font color. Even reword the continued language, if you like. Rather than repeating this procedure multiple times, change the style of the Continued On and Continued From text by choosing Format ➤ Text Style. For detailed information on creating and applying styles, see Skill 3.4.

Remove Continued notices by right-clicking the linked text frame and choosing Change Frame ➤ Text Frame Properties. Disable one or both Continued boxes and repeat this procedure for each linked frame in the series.

CONNECTING TEXT FRAMES

1. Create, size, and place the approximate number of text frames you'll need to fit the text you're inserting.

2. Type or import text into the first frame. If you are importing and Publisher prompts you to use AutoFlow, click Yes to spread the text throughout the empty frames in your document. AutoFlow automatically connects frames.

–OR–

2. To manually connect text frames, click View ➤ Toolbars ➤ Text Frame Connecting to turn on the Connect Frames toolbar. Click the Connect Frames button. Your mouse pointer should become a pitcher.

3. Move the pointer into any empty frame (mouse changes to a tipped pitcher) and click.

4. Repeat the connection process on as many frames as you need to hold the text.

5. Add "Continued From" and/or "Continued To" in a selected frame by right-clicking it and choosing Change Frame ➤ Text Frame Properties. Enable one or both Continued boxes.

6. To disconnect all linked frames in a series, select the first in the series and click the Disconnect button on the Connect Frames toolbar.

Saving Your Work

The Open and Save dialog boxes in Publisher now match those found in the rest of the Office applications. When opening files, you can choose to bring them in for editing or as read only. The Save and Save As commands function as you would expect. (Skill 1 covers opening and saving files in depth.) You also have other options for storing publications.

Save Options

Click the file menu to see the choices you have for saving Publisher documents. In addition to the usual Save and Save As commands, you have the option to Save the Current Publication As a Web Site or use Pack and Go to prepare a document for use on another computer or with a commercial printing service.

Since the program only allows you to open one publication at a time, there's never a question of which document gets saved—it's always the one being displayed.

AutoConvert

Publisher 2000 allows users to convert content from existing publications into additional publications. That means you can use the articles from your newsletter to create a Web site, without importing the text into another Publisher file. Auto-Convert is a feature you can access when you create documents using Wizards. See Skill 10.14 for more information on Publisher Wizards.

Hands On

1. Create two 1 inch by 1 inch text frames on a blank page of a new or existing presentation. In the first frame:

    a) Type a paragraph of text in the first frame.

    b) Format the text for 14 point Arial bold.

    c) Make the first letter a drop cap.

2. In the same presentation created in step 1:

    a) Resize the first frame until it is small enough that the overflow indicator appears.

    b) Connect the frames so that the overflow "dumps" into the second.

3. Using the same presentation, add another page to your publication.

    a) Create a text frame on the new page.

    b) Import a text file from another application into this new frame. If the file is too large to fit, allow Publisher to create and connect additional frames.

   c)   Insert "Continued From" and "Continued To" text.

   d)   Navigate back to the first page and unconnect the first two frames.

   e)   Use AutoFit to make the text fit the first frame.

Skill 10.3: Setting Publisher Options

You can have as much or as little help from Publisher as you wish. Enable the settings that allow you to work most efficiently by choosing Tools ➤ Options from the menu bar.

Setting General Options

The General tab of the Options dialog box allows you to select the number that appears on the first page of the publication. Usually the number 1 makes sense, unless you typically create a cover page in another application (PowerPoint, for example). In this case, your Publisher documents should start page numbering with two.

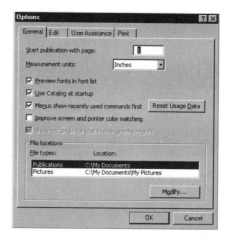

Select from the Measurement Units list to display other units of measurement on the rulers. If the Preview Fonts in Font List feature is enabled, the list of fonts on the Formatting toolbar and in the Format dialog box shows the font itself, rather than the name of the font. In the case of symbol fonts, the list displays samples from that symbol set. If you prefer to load Publisher directly to a blank page, disable the Use Catalog at Startup feature. Screen and Printer Color Matching allows you to get a better idea of how your colors will appear on the printed page. Ever wonder why your documents come off the printer in a lighter shade than they appear on screen? Try enabling this feature to see a more accurate screen view.

Modify the default locations for opening existing documents and inserting pictures by clicking the Modify button in the dialog box and selecting the folder you wish to default to. To change the settings back to system defaults, click the Reset Usage Data button.

Modifying Editing Options

The Edit tab of the Options dialog box allows you to enable or disable drag-and-drop moving and copying of text. If you tend to accidentally drag your mouse over selected text, consider turning this off. Automatic selection of the entire word means that you can't select part of a word for formatting. Enabling this feature prevents you from accidentally missing parts of your text with the Format Painter (discussed in Skill 1.6).

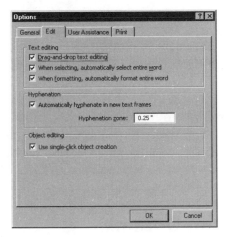

You can automatically format the entire word where the insertion point currently rests. This means you don't have to double-click before you italicize a word in a sentence. Make sure the insertion point is somewhere in the word you wish to format and click the toolbar button(s) to apply desired changes. Modifications to the hyphenation zone change how close the text can be to the frame before Publisher causes words to hyphenate. Disable this option if you prefer not to hyphenate at all. Single-click object creation allows you to click an object tool and click once (rather than dragging) in your document to create a 2–by–3-inch text frame.

SKILL
10

Enabling and Disabling User Assistance

This tab of the Options dialog box gives you some control over how certain Wizards behave. (Remember, there's more on Wizards in Skill 10.14.) The Quick Publication Wizard is on by default when you select a blank page to begin. You can hide the Wizard each time you start if it's in your way, or better yet, why not disable it here if you don't use it often?

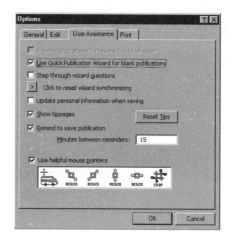

Step through Wizard Questions allows you to proceed through a series of dialog boxes to produce a publication, rather than clicking the steps from a list. Re-enable smart coloring by resetting Wizard synchronization here. Disable tippages and save reminders if you prefer not to see these messages while you work. Helpful mouse pointers include the moving truck and arrows that say "Resize." Disabling these gives you a more typical set of pointer shapes.

Setting Print Options

The print options that are available to you depend on the type of printer(s) you have installed on your system. Enable the Print Troubleshooter to assist you with problems arising after you send documents to the printer. Enabling the Print Line by Line option may help if your DeskJet printer consistently mishandles objects and upside-down text. If you are connected to a printer designated for envelope printing, you have options for automatic formatting and print feed available to you.

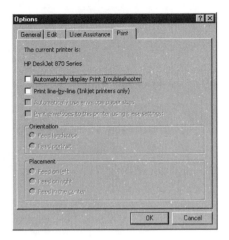

SETTING PUBLISHER OPTIONS

1. Click Tools ➤ Options.

2. Set the starting page number and measurement units on the General tab of the dialog box.

3. Enable or disable the features that allow font preview, Catalog use, dynamic menus, and screen/printer color matching. Change default file locations, if desired. Use the Reset Usage Data button to change back to default settings.

4. Click the Edit tab of the dialog box to enable or disable editing features like single-click object creation and drag-and-drop moving.

5. On the User Assistance tab, change the mouse pointer shapes and disable Publisher Help features you don't need.

6. Enable or disable the Print Troubleshooter on the Print tab of the dialog box. You can also set inkjet printers to print line by line and set envelope printing options for dedicated envelope printers.

SKILL
10

Hands On

1. Open the Options dialog box:

    a) Choose the measurement units you prefer to use.

    b) Enable and disable the other general options to fit your preferences.

    c) Select a default location for publications and pictures.

    d) Select the text editing, hyphenation, and object editing features you wish to enable.

    e) Enable the user assistance features you want to use.

    f) Enable the print options that work best with your printer.

Skill 10.4: Inserting Publisher Graphic Objects

Because so many object choices are available to you in Publisher, it can be difficult to know where to begin. You may be familiar with some of the objects you have seen in other Office applications, such as Microsoft clip art, WordArt, and tables. Certain objects (such as pictures and clip art) are easy to select and insert, while others (such as WordArt) require that you spend some time on formatting. Once you bring an object into your publication, you can recolor, rotate, flip, or otherwise edit the piece.

These Publisher frame tools in the Object toolbar work the same, in concept, as the Text frame tool discussed earlier. One click on an object tool selects it. A click and drag on your document creates a space to house the object while you format and edit it. As you would expect, you can move or resize an object at any time.

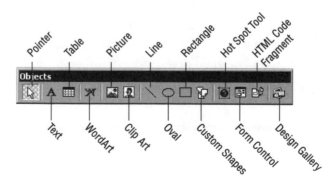

Inserting Tables

You may have heard it said that if you press Tab more than once on the same line, you should be working in a table. Use the Table frame tool to display data in columns and rows. By design, tables wrap text within each cell so that minimal reformatting is needed if you change the text. Figure 10.5 shows an example of a publication that includes a table.

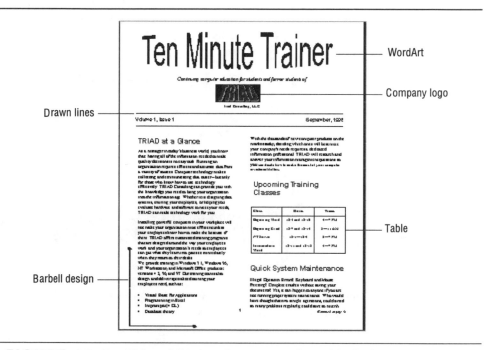

FIGURE 10.5: This publication shows several graphic design elements.

When you finish dragging the Table tool, the Create Table dialog box opens.

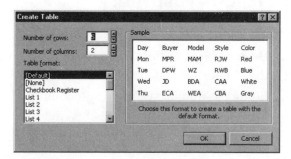

Enter the number of rows and columns for your table and choose a table format from the list on the left. Use the preview window to view the borders, shading, and special text formatting that comes with each design. Select the one that comes closest to what you had in mind; you can always modify formatting manually. When you click OK on this dialog box, Publisher places a formatted empty grid onto your page.

Enter text and/or numbers into each cell, pressing Tab to move one cell to the right. You can also use the mouse or keyboard arrows to position your insertion point in a cell. Apply or remove formatting as you would in any table (see Skill 3.3 on working in Word tables.) Select rows or columns by clicking the gray header box (your pointer changes to a hand).

Class	Dates	Times
Beginning Word	12/3 and 12/10	4—7 PM
Beginning Excel	12/7 and 12/14	8—11 AM
NT Server	12/1—12/4	2—7 PM
Intermediate Word	12/11 and 12/18	4—7 PM

Select Cells

Select multiple rows or columns by dragging the headers. Select the entire table by clicking the gray box at the upper left of the table, where row and column headers intersect. Adjust column width and row height by dragging the Adjust tool between headers.

CREATING A TABLE IN PUBLISHER

1. Click the Table tool on the Object toolbar.
2. Drag a frame to house the table. Releasing the mouse button opens the Create Table dialog box.
3. Enter the number of rows and columns for your table. Select a table format from the list.

continued ▶

4. Enter data into the cells, using Tab, arrow keys, or the mouse to move to another cell.

5. Adjust column width and row height as desired. Select rows and/or columns to add borders, shading, and other formatting as needed.

6. Resize the table by dragging a selection handle. Move the table by pointing to one of its outside borders and dragging the Mover.

7. Click away from the table when you're through editing.

Adding and Editing WordArt

Use the WordArt tool to create dramatic shapes and patterns out of text. Figure 10.5 shows two examples of WordArt: the publication title and company logo. Create letters that cascade up, ripple down, or wave like a flag. Border the letters, shade them with patterns, and rotate them for different effects.

When you work in WordArt, the Publisher tools are not available to you. You will see one toolbar with WordArt tools, but you can get back to Publisher by clicking away from the object. Double-click on an existing WordArt object to edit it. Use the WordArt tool on the Object toolbar only when you want to create a new WordArt object.

You won't see ToolTips on the buttons in the WordArt toolbar, so you may have to experiment a bit at first. Or you can choose to edit using the Format menu from within WordArt. Choosing Format ➢ Border allows you to add or edit how your letters are outlined. Selecting Format ➢ Shading allows you to fill the interior of letters with solid colors or patterns. If you want to shadow letters, choose a style and color by selecting Format ➢ Shadow. You can rotate a WordArt object or "slide" the letters horizontally by choosing Format ➢ Rotation and Effects.

TIP TIP TIP TIP TIP TIP TIP TIP TIP TIP TIP TIP TIP TIP TIP TIP TIP TIP TIP TIP TIP TIP

Publisher 2000 uses a different version of WordArt than the other Office tools. To open the more robust WordArt through Microsoft Draw, select Insert ➢ Object. From the Insert dialog box, click Microsoft Draw 98 Drawing, then click OK. Use the WordArt button on the Microsoft Drawing toolbar to create a new WordArt object. Skill 11.3 describes editing this type of WordArt in detail.

SKILL
10

Using Pictures and Clip Art

You will find frame tools for pictures and clip art on Publisher's Object toolbar. Publisher treats clip art and pictures much the same. Pictures usually look more like photographs while clip art has the flavor of a cartoon drawing. While you can insert clip art into a picture frame or a picture into a clip art frame, it's more efficient to start with the appropriate type of frame, because it will save a step later.

When you drag a space using the Picture tool, a blank frame appears in your document. Insert a picture by double-clicking the empty frame (or select the frame and choose Insert ➤ Picture ➤ From File) to open the Insert File dialog box. Navigate to the drive and folder where the picture is stored, select it, and click Insert. Double-click this object if you want to return to the Insert Picture dialog box and select a different picture to replace it.

The Clip Gallery tool behaves slightly differently. After you drag a space using this tool, Publisher automatically takes you to the Clip Gallery where you can browse the available art. Select one of the gallery objects to insert or exit the gallery and insert a picture instead. Make sure the frame is selected; then choose Insert ➤ Picture ➤ From File to select a picture stored on your local drive, a network drive, or a floppy disk.

ADDING ART TO A PUBLICATION

1. Click the object tool of choice: Picture, WordArt, or Clip Art.
2. Drag a frame to house the art.
3. If you've chosen WordArt, enter the text you want and edit as desired using the tools on the WordArt toolbar. If you've chosen to insert a picture or clip art, then locate, select, and insert the object you want.
4. Close the Clip Gallery or click away from your WordArt object, if applicable, and then select and resize your art as necessary.

NOTE NOTE NOTE NOTE NOTE NOTE NOTE NOTE NOTE NOTE NOTE NOTE NOTE NOTE NOTE
Skill 7 and Skill 11 both contain additional information on using art from the Clip Gallery.

Inserting and Filling Shapes

Publisher gives you the ability to draw lines of various weights and colors. You can also create ovals, rectangles, and a host of custom shapes like arrows, cubes, and triangles. The most commonly used shapes—lines, ovals, and rectangles—have their own buttons on the Object toolbar. Click on the button to select the shape you like and drag the size you want in your document.

  NOTE NOTE NOTE NOTE NOTE NOTE NOTE NOTE NOTE NOTE NOTE NOTE NOTE NOTE
Skill 11.3 also contains information on line art.

 Sometimes you'll want to color the inside of an object. This is called *filling*. Select the frame that contains the shape and click the Fill button to select a color for its interior. The Border button allows you to select a plain black line to outline the shape. Click More Styles to select an alternate weight and color for the border in the Border dialog box. If you want a line that is wider than 10 points, type the size in the field at the bottom left of the dialog box.

The Custom Shapes tool allows you to create hearts, stars, lightening bolts, triangles, and more. Once you have created a shape, Publisher lets you resize the object's height and width. The arrow shown below has been resized two ways: the width of the base has been narrowed and the height of the tip has been shortened:

To resize one dimension, place your pointer on the gray diamond and drag the Adjust tool. You still have the ability to resize the entire object using the regular handles.

Web Tools

The Object toolbar contains three Web tools: Hot Spot, Form Control, and HTML Fragment. These and other powerful Web-building features are discussed at length in Skill 12.

Using the Design Gallery

The Design Gallery contains roughly 20 categories of objects—such as access bars, linear accents, calendars, and logos—that you can add to your publication. You can even store objects that you create, such as a company logo, on a special tab of the Design Gallery dialog box. Figure 10.6 shows the Objects by Category tab of the Design Gallery.

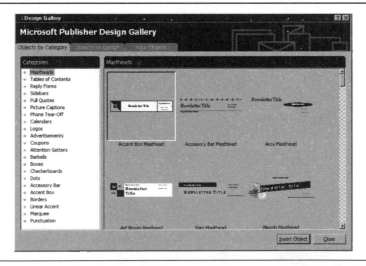

FIGURE 10.6: The Design Gallery contains many categories of objects ready to be inserted into your publication.

If you prefer, you can select a Design Gallery object based on a *design set*. Click the Objects by Design tab, shown in Figure 10.7, and select from the list on the left. You will see different types of objects with certain design elements in common. Using objects from the same set gives a consistent look and feel to your publication.

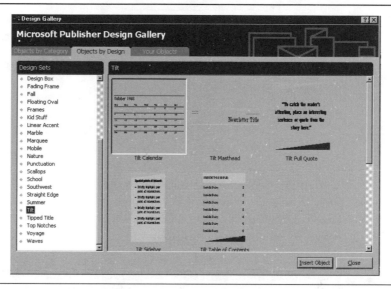

FIGURE 10.7: The Objects by Design tab with the Tilt set selected

You can store objects from your current publication on the Your Objects tab of the Design Gallery. This is particularly helpful if you have edited or recolored objects and want to have them readily available for use in other publications.

When you create a publication, its design set on the Your Objects tab is empty. You establish a design set for your publication by creating categories and adding objects to those categories. Select the object you want to add and open the Design Gallery using the last button on the Object toolbar. Choose the Your Objects tab and click the Options button in the lower left corner. Click Add Selection to Design Gallery on the menu to open the Add Object dialog box.

SKILL
10

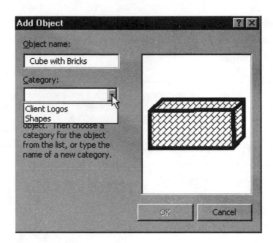

Under Object Name, type a name for the object; under Category enter a new category or select a category that you have already created. Click OK and then Close to return to your document. Changes that you make to the Design Gallery are saved when you save your publication.

 TIP TIP TIP TIP TIP TIP TIP TIP TIP TIP TIP TIP TIP TIP TIP TIP TIP TIP TIP TIP TIP TIP

You can also add a selected object to the Design Gallery by choosing Insert ➢ Add Selection to Design Gallery.

Add, delete, and rename categories in your design set by clicking Edit Categories from the Options pop-up menu on the Your Objects tab of the Design Gallery. In the Edit Categories dialog box, click the Add button and type a name for a new category to add it to your design set. Select a category you want to remove and click the Delete button.

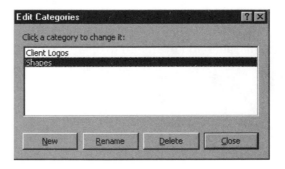

Choose a category you want to edit and click the Rename button. In the Rename Category dialog box, type the new category name and click OK.

Delete an object from your design set by selecting it and choosing Delete This Object from the shortcut menu options. Once again, these changes to the Design Gallery are saved when you save your publication.

The categories and objects you add are specific to the publication you added them from. However, if you want to insert an object from a design set you (or someone else) created in another publication, click Options on the Your Objects tab of the Design Gallery and choose Browse from the menu. Select the publication that has the object you want and click OK. The Your Objects tab now displays the design set for the publication you just selected. Choose the object you want and click the Insert Object button at the bottom right of the dialog box.

NOTE NOTE NOTE NOTE NOTE NOTE NOTE NOTE NOTE NOTE NOTE NOTE NOTE NOTE NOTE

You can only rename and delete categories from the design set in the active publication. You cannot rename or delete categories from another publication's design set. You also cannot rename or delete Publisher's built-in object categories.

ADDING YOUR OWN OBJECTS TO THE DESIGN GALLERY

1. Select the object you wish to add to the Design Gallery.

2. Open the Design Gallery by clicking the last button on the Object toolbar. Select the Your Objects tab.

3. Click the Options button at the bottom left and choose Add Selection to Design Gallery.

continued ▶

SKILL
▼10

4. Type a name for your object, and then type a new category name or choose one from the list. Click OK to close the dialog box.

5. Delete an object or edit categories by choosing those commands from the Options list on the Your Objects tab of the Design Gallery.

6. To rename an object you've added to the Design Gallery, right-click on it (inside the Design Gallery) and select Rename This Object from the shortcut menu. Type the new name and click OK.

Hands On

1. Start a new publication from scratch or open an existing publication.

2. Insert several different types of Publisher objects including (but not limited to):

   a) WordArt

   b) Clip art

   c) A custom shape

   d) A sidebar from the Design Gallery

   e) A table with two columns and three rows of information

3. Practice formatting your graphic objects:

   a) Format the WordArt so that the letters have an attractive border.

   b) Change the angle of your WordArt by rotating it.

   c) Replace the clip art with another choice from the gallery.

   d) Format your custom shape with a patterned background.

   e) Change the design set and select another type of sidebar.

   f) Add another column to your table; type data in the new cells.

   g) Add an outline border to your table.

   h) Adjust row height and column width in the table.

4. Add a custom object to the Design Gallery.

Skill 10.5: Working with Multiple Objects

Suppose you have a picture that illustrates a particular section of your employee manual. If you change the placement of the section, you would want the picture to move with it, right? What about using two pieces of clip art that need to overlap slightly. Wouldn't you like to choose which piece is on top? One final scenario: you're placing three objects at the left margin of your newsletter cover. You most certainly want them to line up, right?

Grouping Objects

If a particular graphic will always appear next to a certain piece of text, it makes sense to *group* the two objects. Two or more objects with fixed positions (relative to each other) should be grouped, because grouped objects can be moved and resized as one unit. As shown below, a title should be grouped with the object it describes so the two never become separated. Drag one and you drag the other as well.

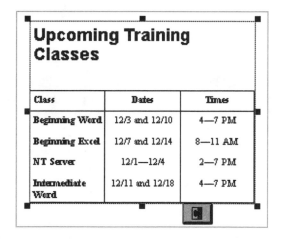

  To group objects, select the first with a click. Hold Shift and click on each additional object you want to group. Click the Group Objects icon at the bottom of the frame surrounding the selected objects. These objects are now "hooked" together so you can move and resize them as a group. Click the Ungroup Objects icon to ungroup the objects. Now you can move and/or resize them separately—just click the one you want.

SKILL
10

Layering Objects

You can easily place one object on top of another. Here is an example of a text box displayed on top of a piece of clip art. The objects are layered—clip art on the bottom, text on the top.

 TIP TIP TIP TIP TIP TIP TIP TIP TIP TIP TIP TIP TIP TIP TIP TIP TIP TIP TIP TIP TIP TIP TIP TIP
If you're planning to both group and layer two or more objects, layer them first. Once objects are grouped, you can't select them individually for layering.

 Insert and arrange the two objects you wish to layer. If you can't see the object that's currently on the bottom, select the one on the top and click the Send to Back button. If you can see at least part of the object that is underneath, select it and click the Bring to Front button.

You can create original-looking graphics by layering two or more objects from the gallery. Label photographs and diagrams with text boxes and drawn lines layered on top. These are just two examples of how to use object layering, and you're sure to discover many more.

GROUPING AND LAYERING OBJECTS

1. Select the objects you want to group by clicking on the first and using Shift+click on the other(s).

2. Click the Group Objects icon that appears below the selected objects, and then resize or move as desired.

3. To layer ungrouped objects, select the object you want to place behind the others and click the Send to Back button on the Standard toolbar.

4. Place an object on top of another by selecting it and clicking the Bring to Front button.

5. Once objects are layered correctly, you can group them so they move and resize as one unit.

Lining Up Objects

You can align selected objects to each other or to a margin. The Snap To feature lets you easily align objects to a ruler guide as well. Select all objects to be aligned and choose Arrange ➤ Align Objects to open the dialog box. (You can also right-click selected objects and choose Align from the shortcut menu.)

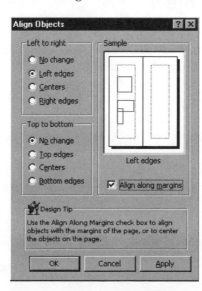

The titles of the control groups in this dialog box refer to the object frames themselves, so use the Left to Right controls to align objects vertically. Use the Top to Bottom controls to line up your objects horizontally across a page.

TIP TIP TIP TIP TIP TIP TIP TIP TIP TIP TIP TIP TIP TIP TIP TIP TIP TIP TIP TIP TIP

Enable the Align along Margins feature and then choose Left to Right Centers to center selected objects between the left and right margins.

Snap To

Snap To lets you precisely align objects with ease. This feature places an invisible, magnetic grid on your page. Objects are pulled to the lines of this grid as well as nearby boundaries and ruler guides. You can also have objects snap to other objects.

Snap To controls are under the Tools menu. Turn on Snap to Guides and each time you drag an object near a boundary, it will "jump" to the edge of the boundary. Snap to Ruler Marks works the same way; objects will snap to nearby ruler guides. If the boundaries and guides are hidden, objects will still Snap To.

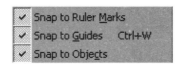

Rotating Objects

Change the angle at which an objecct is displayed by rotating that object any number of degrees. Click the Rotate tool on the Standard toolbar to open the dialog box. The rotate buttons in this dialog box will change the display angle by 5 degrees per click. For larger rotations, simpy type in the degree of angle you want and click OK.

Click Show Toolbar to see the Measurements toolbar. you can change the size, spacing, display angle, or position of a selected object using the spin boxes shown here.

For 90-degree rotations, use the buttons on the Formatting toolbar or choose Arrange ➤ Rotate or Flip ➤ Rotate Right (or Left).

TIP TIP TIP TIP TIP TIP TIP TIP TIP TIP TIP TIP TIP TIP TIP TIP TIP TIP TIP TIP TIP

If you prefer working directly in Publisher, you can rotate any object by pressing Alt and dragging an object handle.

Flipping Objects

Now Publisher lets you easily turn a graphic upside-down or face it opposite the way you inserted it. Select the object and click the Flip Horizontal or Flip Vertical button on the Formatting toolbar. You can also choose Arrange ➤ Rotate or Flip ➤ Flip Horizontal (or Vertical).

> **WARNING WARNING WARNING WARNING WARNING WARNING WARNING WARNING**
> **The Flip buttons and Rotate buttons look very similar. If you want to flip, make sure you click the button without the arrow on it.**

ROTATING AND FLIPPING OBJECTS

1. Select the object you want to rotate or flip.
2. Use the Flip/Rotate buttons on the Formatting toolbar to flip horizontally or vertically, or to rotate 90 degrees.
3. For custom rotation, click the Rotate tool on the Standard toolbar, or hold Alt and drag an object handle.

Hands On

1. Insert a picture or clip art into a new or existing publication and create a text box to serve as a caption for the picture.

    a) Group the picture and its caption.

    b) Resize the group.

    c) Move the group.

    d) Ungroup the picture and caption.

    e) Resize the picture so that it's slightly larger, then group the picture with the caption again.

2. In the same publication, insert another piece of clip art (or picture).

    a) Create one or two text boxes to serve as labels for the picture.

    b) Layer the text box in front of the picture.

    c) Bring the picture to the front, and then send it back again.

    d) Group the picture and label(s).

3. Use the Alignment dialog box to center the two object groups horizontally on the page.

    a) Remove the horizontal centering.

    b) Insert a vertical ruler guide.

    c) Enable Snap To and align the objects to the ruler guide.

4. Insert a custom shape and rotate it 90 degrees.

Skill 10.6: Recoloring and Cropping Objects

Frequently you will find a piece of clip art that looks great except for its color. Or maybe you only want to use a small section of that art. Choose and insert the piece anyway because Publisher gives you several options for changing object color(s) and/or cropping away the excess with just a few clicks of the mouse.

Recoloring

You can change all the colors in a picture to different shades of one color and leave the black lines untouched. Or you may prefer to have the black lines change with the new color as well.

To change all the colors in a picture to one color, shade, or tint, select the picture and choose Format ➢ Recolor Picture. You can also right-click the object and choose Change Object ➢ Recolor from the shortcut menu. In the Recolor Object dialog box, select a color from the drop-down list. Selecting a color enables choices for whether to recolor the entire picture or leave the black lines as is.

If you choose Fill Effects from the Color drop-down list, you have options for formatting tints and shades as well as gradients and patterns. *Tints* are a base color mixed with white; *shades* are a base color mixed with black. Tints and shades can be part of a custom color scheme.

TIP TIP TIP TIP TIP TIP TIP TIP TIP TIP TIP TIP TIP TIP TIP TIP TIP TIP TIP TIP TIP TIP TIP TIP

To create a watermark, choose View ➢ Go to Background. Insert and then recolor a picture using a lighter tint or shade of the base color. Then choose View ➢ Go to Foreground. The picture you placed in the background will appear on every page of your publication. Recoloring it with a lighter tint makes it appropriate for use as a watermark because it doesn't overpower the rest of the document.

Patterns are simple repeating designs and *gradients* use tints and shades to create vertical, horizontal, and other shading patterns. Figure 10.8 shows the difference between a pattern and a gradient. If you are planning to use a commercial printing service, it's probably best not to use patterns in your publication. Patterns can slow down the imaging time, thus increasing your costs.

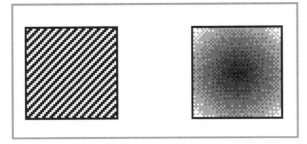

FIGURE 10.8: The object on the left is filled with a pattern, while the one on the right is filled with a gradient.

Recoloring an object using two or more colors requires help from another Office application, PowerPoint. For more information about recoloring objects in PowerPoint, refer to Skill 7.

Cropping

You can use just part of a picture or other graphic by selecting it and dragging the *Crop* tool over one of the resize handles. When you crop a graphic in Publisher,

SKILL
10

you are getting rid of the parts you *don't* want. It may appear, at first, as if you are simply resizing. But look closer. As you drag the frame border, instead of making the entire picture smaller, it removes the areas of the picture you drag over, leaving only the areas that remain inside the frame. Drag the Crop tool over as many of the resize handles as you need to use until your art is perfectly positioned. Click the Crop tool again to turn it off, or you can click anywhere else in your publication to do the same.

Hands On

1. Insert a piece of clip art into a new publication or select clip art from an existing publication.

    a)   Recolor the clip art so that it uses one color and black lines.

    b)   Undo the recoloring you did in step 1a, then recolor the clip art using a different design scheme.

    c)   Crop the art to remove some part of the picture or background.

    d)   Resize the cropped art so that it slightly larger.

Skill 10.7: Modifying Frame Properties

If you want the frame itself to print, you have to add a border to it. You can add color to the white space behind an object using a fill. You can also display text in multiple columns, if you want, by changing frame properties.

Adjusting Text Frames

Right-click any text frame and point to Change Frame on the shortcut menu. Choose Fill Color to see a multitude of possibilities for background colors, with the current scheme's colors shown first. Choose More Schemes from the Fill Color submenu to choose another scheme of colors, or More Colors to see an entire palette. Fill Effects offers you options for tints, shades, patterns, and gradients.

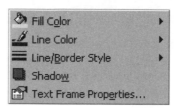

The Line Color choice on the shortcut menu is unavailable if you have not previously applied a border to the frame. Use the Line/Border Style choice to apply a border of your chosen point size and color. The next time you wish to edit this object's border, you can do so under Line Color. Shadow Effects, shown in Figure 10.9, creates a gray shadow on the right and bottom borders of the text frame. Shadows look great with or without a border.

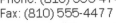

Bratcher Motor Sports

318 South Miller Road
Flint, Michigan 48502
Phone: (810) 555-4747
Fax: (810) 555-4477

FIGURE 10.9: Frame with a border and shadow

Choosing Text Frame Properties from this shortcut menu (right-click and select Change Frame) opens the Text Frame Properties dialog box, where you can adjust margins and change column settings. Change the distance from the text to the frame using the Margins spin boxes. Format text for two or more columns using the spin box on the Columns control. The Spacing control adjusts space between columns.

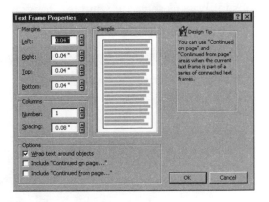

SKILL 10

Enable the Wrap Text around Objects feature if you plan to place objects in the middle of text. The template shown here includes a text frame formatted for two columns with Text Wrapping enabled. The object and its caption are in two separate frames that have been grouped.

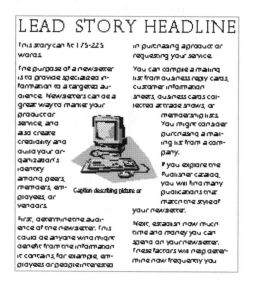

Modifying Graphic Frames

Select the object whose frame properties you want to modify. Right-click and choose Change Frame, or click the Format menu. Format borders and fill just as you would for a text frame. The Picture Frame Properties dialog box offers options for how closely you want text to wrap around the art. The margin controls in this dialog box control the distance from the picture to the frame.

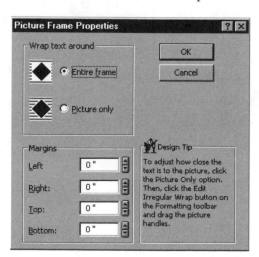

NOTE NOTE NOTE NOTE NOTE NOTE NOTE NOTE NOTE NOTE NOTE NOTE NOTE NOTE NOTE NOTE

You won't be able to modify frame properties for line art objects or custom shapes. The feature is disabled on the menu.

To control how closely the text wraps to the picture, choose the Picture Only option in the dialog box and click OK. Then click the button to Edit Irregular Wrap (on the Formatting toolbar). Drag the picture's handles closer or farther from the text as desired.

MODIFYING FRAME PROPERTIES

1. Right-click the object and choose Change Frame ➤ Picture Frame Properties (or Text Frame Properties) from the shortcut menu.

2. For pictures, choose how you want text to wrap around the frame. Adjust the margins to control how far you want the picture from the frame.

3. For text frames, adjust margins to control the distance from text to frame, and then choose the number of columns you want within the frame as well as the spacing between columns.

4. Enable or disable text frame options for wrapping and inserting "Continued From" and "Continued To" language.

5. Change frame borders and shadow and fill properties by right-clicking the frame, pointing to Change Frame, and then choosing the appropriate item from the shortcut menu.

Hands On

1. Create a new text box (or select an existing text box) and format it with a blue 2-point border.

   a) Add a drop shadow to the text frame.

   b) Fill the text box light gray.

SKILL
10

c) Format the frame so that the text inside it appears in two columns.

d) Enable text wrapping.

e) Create a new clip art or WordArt object and drag it into the text box.

f) Change the frame properties of the graphic to Picture Only and edit three of the wrap points. (Hint: you may have to zoom in to do this.)

Skill 10.8: Modifying Page Setup Options

If you are printing on paper that is a different size than your publication, you may need to modify the settings under Page Setup. To open the Page Setup dialog box, choose File ➤ Page Setup. At the bottom-left corner of the dialog box are settings for Portrait and Landscape. Choose the correct setting for your publication.

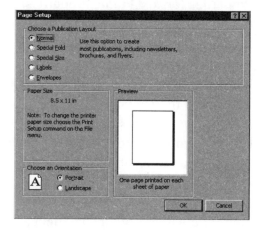

From the Publication Layout controls, choose Normal if you want one printed page on each sheet of paper (choose this if you are duplexing on a manual feed printer as well.) The Special Fold option is for printing folded documents like cards or small booklets with two pages on a sheet. The Special Size option supports banners, index cards, and poster printing. If you choose Special Fold or Special Size, be sure to choose the fold or size from the drop-down list below the control group. Options for Envelopes and Labels also require that you make a choice from the drop-down list.

Adjusting Margins

Publisher doesn't use page margins in the normal sense of the word. Instead you get boundary lines that show a 1-inch margin by default. The boundary lines don't act like margins in Word because you can place objects on or outside them without having to adjust them. You can set margins for frames. Frame margins act more like the traditional margins you may be used to. They determine how far text or art appears from the edge of the frame.

Creating Headers and Footers

Publisher treats headers and footers differently than you may have learned in Office. Text and objects that appear on every page in a Publisher document are placed on a *background* layer. Think of the background layer as your "stationery." When you're writing a letter, the print appears on top of the stationery. It's the same way with the background layer of a Publisher document. Everything else you place on a page rests on top of it.

To place objects (like headers and footers) on the background layer, choose View ➤ Go to Background. If you start with a blank page and go to the background, the workspace doesn't look much different than it did when you started a minute ago. However, you can tell you are working on the background layer if you click the View menu again and see Go to Foreground as a choice.

Any objects you may have already placed in the foreground become invisible as you work on the background. Create a header by placing and formatting text and/or object frames outside of the top margin boundary. Footers go just outside of the bottom boundary. Choose View ➤ Go to Foreground to return to your regular document. You should still be able to see your background text and objects.

To hide a header and/or footer on the first page of your document, navigate to the first page of your publication. Hide all background objects using View ➤ Ignore Background. If there are other background objects besides the header or footer that you don't want to hide, drag a new text frame to cover just the header and/or footer. When you print, you won't see the empty text frame.

TIP TIP TIP TIP TIP TIP TIP TIP TIP TIP TIP TIP TIP TIP TIP TIP TIP TIP TIP TIP TIP TIP
When you're working with a book fold publication, you may not see numbered page navigators in the status area of the document window. Choose View ➤ Go to Page to navigate without them.

You can mirror header and footer setup. Booklets are a great example of when you might want to do this. Go to the background and create the header or footer as you normally would, but make sure you set it up to appear on every *right* page of your publication. Choose Arrange ➢ Layout Guides. Enable the Create Two Backgrounds with Mirrored Guides feature and click OK. Switch back to the fore-ground and continue working.

TIP TIP TIP TIP TIP TIP TIP TIP TIP TIP TIP TIP TIP TIP TIP TIP TIP TIP TIP TIP TIP TIP TIP TIP

If the mirrored header/footer doesn't work for you the first time, disable the option for mirrored backgrounds, click OK, reopen the dialog box, and enable it again. Click OK.

CREATING HEADERS AND FOOTERS

1. Choose View ➢ Go to Background from the menu.
2. Place and format text and objects as you normally would, except place headers just outside the top margin boundary and footers just outside the bottom margin boundary.
3. Choose View ➢ Go to Foreground to resume working on the publica-tion. Headers and footers should be visible on every page.
4. Remove headers and footers from the first page of your document by navigating to page 1 and clicking View ➢ Ignore Background. This hides all background objects on page 1 of the publication. If you just want to hide headers and/or footers but not other background objects, drag an empty frame to cover the part you wish to hide.

CREATING MIRRORED HEADERS AND FOOTERS

1. For booklet printing with mirrored headers and footers, choose View ➢ Go to Background and create the frame(s) as you want them to appear on every *right* page of the publication.

continued ▶

2. Choose Arrange ➤ Layout Guides. Enable Create Two Backgrounds with Mirrored Guides. Click OK.

3. Choose View ➤ Go to Foreground to switch back to the foreground and continue working.

Hands On

1. Start a new publication with a blank 8½-by-11 page.

   a) Change its layout to an 8½-by-11 book fold document. (Allow Publisher to insert additional pages if prompted.)

   b) Edit margin boundaries to ½-inch all around.

   c) Create a mirrored footer that does *not* appear on page 1 of your publication.

Skill 10.9: Printing Your Publications

Before you get too far into the creation process, you should give serious thought to how you want to print your publication. Will you use your own printer or a commercial printing service? What type of paper will you print on? What color paper? Will you duplex? Staple? Fold? Collate?

You should set up your publication for the type of printing you want *before* you place objects on the page. Otherwise you may be forced to make design changes just before the final printing.

Desktop Printing

If you are printing from a desktop printer, choose File ➤ Print Setup for printer options. Select the size and location of the paper you will be using. (In Tray is the most common location, however, some printers have a sheet feeder as well.) Click the Properties button to set properties specific to your printer. Look for features like reverse order printing and collating. High-end printers support duplexing, booklet and banner printing, and stapling; you will find these options, if they exist for your printer, under Printer Properties.

SKILL
10

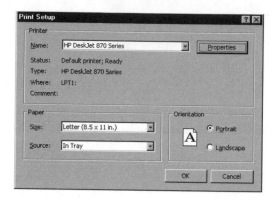

Choose File ➤ Print to set options in the Print dialog box. Choose which printer to use for this print job. Choose whether to print all pages, the current page, or specific pages. Choose the number of copies to print and click OK. The advanced printing options allow you to print at a lower resolution (it's a good idea to do this on drafts) and to choose whether to let your printer substitute fonts. You can also choose to print crop marks and bleed marks. *Bleeds* are text and images that go beyond the trim edge of your publication. If you want to print bleed marks, you have to select a paper size 1 inch larger than your document.

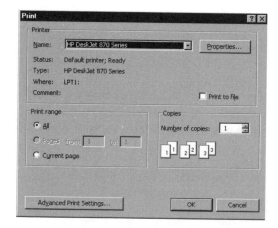

Working with a Commercial Printing Service

If you plan to print your final publication at a printing service, you should set up your publication to do this right from the start. First decide which type of printing service you will use: black-and-white printing, process-color printing, or spot-color printing.

NOTE NOTE NOTE NOTE NOTE NOTE NOTE NOTE NOTE NOTE NOTE NOTE NOTE NOTE

If you're taking your publication in Publisher format to your printing service, choose File ➢ Pack and Go to save all the files your printing service will need. Skill 10.13 discusses the Pack and Go Wizard at length.

Black-and-White Printing

In black-and-white printing, the printer uses only one color of ink (usually black, but most commercial printers will allow you to choose a different color if you want). Black-and-white printing uses grayscale to distinguish light and dark areas of your publication. Text and graphics can still produce dramatic effects in black and white. If you absolutely must have color, and budget is a concern, consider printing on colored paper.

To set up for black-and-white printing, choose Tools ➢ Commercial Printing Tools ➢ Color Printing to open the Color Printing dialog box shown in Figure 10.10.

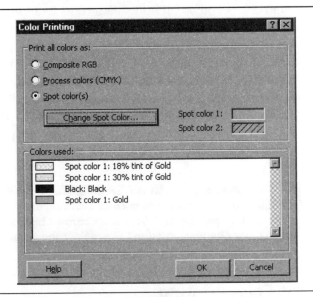

FIGURE 10.10: The Color Printing dialog box

Choose Spot Colors from the available options and then click Change Spot Color. In the Choose Spot Color dialog box, click Black and White Only. Click OK twice.

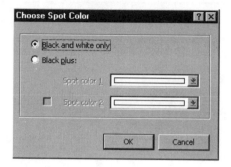

Process-Color Printing

Use process-color printing when your publication contains high-quality color photos or if you need to print a wide range of colors. As you might expect, process color printing costs more than other types because of the number of different colors you use. If budget is a consideration, you might want to look at the other two commercial printing options. To set up for process-color printing, choose Tools ➤ Commercial Printing Tools ➤ Color Printing to open the Color Printing dialog box shown in Figure 10.10. Click Process Colors (CMYK) from the list of options. Selecting the Cyan Magenta Yellow Black (CMYK) color model for a commercially printed publication is important because not all colors you see on your monitor, which displays in Red Green Blue (RGB), can be printed using CMYK. Choosing CMYK helps ensure that your printing service can match the colors on your screen.

NOTE NOTE NOTE NOTE NOTE NOTE NOTE NOTE NOTE NOTE NOTE NOTE NOTE NOTE NOTE
After setting up for process-color printing, be sure to review the publication for color changes. Some RGB colors cannot be matched to a CMYK color. If you see color changes you don't like, select the object and recolor it.

Spot-Color Printing

Spot-color printing allows you to use color for lines and accents in your publication. Your publication prints primarily in black, but you can choose up to two spot colors. Tints of the spot colors can be used throughout the publication as well. Spot-color printing is a nice budget compromise between complete black-and-white and the more expensive process-color printing.

Choose Tools➤ Commercial Printing Services ➤ Color Printing. Select Spot Colors and click Change Spot Color. Select one or two spot colors and click OK.

NOTE NOTE NOTE NOTE NOTE NOTE NOTE NOTE NOTE NOTE NOTE NOTE NOTE NOTE

If you choose black plus one spot color, all colors except black are converted to tints of the spot color.

Switching to Another Type of Printing

Change your mind about which type of printing to use? Choose Tools ➤ Commercial Printing Tools ➤ Color Printing. Choose Composite RGB to switch back to desktop printing. Choose Process Colors or Spot Colors or, if you want to switch to black and white, click Spot Colors and then Change Spot Color, and select the Black and White Only option.

SETTING UP FOR COMMERCIAL PRINTING

1. Choose Tools ➤ Commercial Printing Tools ➤ Color Printing to open the Color Printing dialog box.

2. For black-and-white printing, click the Spot Colors option and then click Change Spot Color. In the Choose Spot Color dialog box, click Black and White Only. Click OK twice.

–OR–

2. For process-color printing, click Process Colors (CMYK) from the list of options in the Color Printing dialog box. You may need to recolor graphics in your publication if you don't like the way process coloring alters them.

–OR–

continued ▶

SKILL
10

2. For spot-color printing, select Spot Colors from the options in the Color Printing dialog box. Click Change Spot Color, and then select one or two spot colors. Click OK.

3. To change to another type of printing, open the Color Printing dialog box. Choose Composite RGB to switch back to desktop printing. Choose Process Colors or Spot Colors to switch to those commercial options. If you want to switch to black-and-white printing, select the Spot Colors option, and then click Change Spot Color. Select the Black and White Only option.

Pantone Color Matching

When you work with a commercial printer, colors on your computer screen may not exactly match the colors that get printed in your publication. The colors in your Publisher file only tell your printing service *where* the color goes, not *what* the exact color will be.

Printing services support a number of different color-matching systems. It is best to ask your printer which colors and paper types would work best, before you design your publication. Most likely they will give you some numbered color swatches and suggestions for paper types. You can choose Publisher colors from process-color-matching systems that your printing service supports, and then specify colors from the swatches for use in your publication. Publisher provides the Pantone Matching System, which you can use to specify colors for a commercial printing service. Before you can use this color matching system, you have to decide whether to use spot-color printing or process-color printing.

Regardless of which type of printing you choose, navigate to the Color Printing dialog box shown in Figure 10.10. Choose the Spot Color Option, then click Change Spot Color. Select More Colors from the Spot Color 1 drop-down list and click All Colors. Under Color model, select Pantone from the list. You'll see a copyright notice and the Pantone Colors dialog box. Click OK to the notice to use the tools in the dialog box.

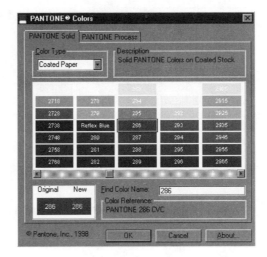

For spot-color printing, make sure you are on the Pantone Solid tab. If you're opting for process-color printing, use the Pantone Process tab. Under Color Type, choose coated or uncoated to match the type of paper your publication will be printed on. If you know the number for the color you want, type it in the Find Color Name box and press enter, or scroll to the color you want. Click OK four times to close all the dialog boxes.

When you design process-color publications (like brochures or sales materials), you may need to include spot color objects (like a company logo). In this case, you need to convert each object's Pantone solid color to a process color that matches. Select the spot-color object, then choose Format ➢ Fill Color ➢ More Colors. Choose All Colors, if it is not already selected. Under Color Model, choose Pantone. Make sure you select the Pantone Solid tab of the dialog box and choose Convert to Process under Color Type. Select the color and click OK twice to close both dialog boxes.

Font Embedding

Any time you plan to print your publication from a computer other than the one you used to create it, you should consider font embedding. Embedded fonts show up in printed material just as they appeared on screen.

Choose Tools ➢ Commercial Printing Tools ➢ Fonts to open the Fonts dialog box.

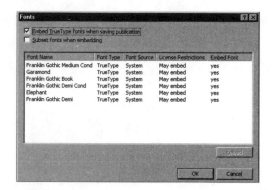

If you choose Embed True Type Fonts when saving, your fonts will appear as expected on most any computer and you will have the ability to edit using your own fonts whether the other machine has them installed or not. Choosing this first option causes your Publisher file to be larger because it saves the font sets along with it. The Subset option also embeds fonts, but only saves the actual characters you've used in your publication. If your commercial printing service needs to edit, they will be limited to those characters you have already included.

Hands On

1. Set up an existing publication for commercial black-and-white printing.

   a) Edit the print setup to one spot color.

   b) Embed fonts in your publication.

   c) Change the print setup to fit your desktop printer, or a network printer to which you have access.

Skill 10.10: Working with the Design Checker

In lengthy publications, it's easy to overlook errors such as text that hides in the overflow area or objects that overlap where they shouldn't. Publisher's Design Checker can help prevent you from overlooking problem areas such as these. Choose Tools ➤ Design Checker to open the Design Checker dialog box.

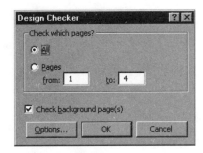

Choose whether to check all pages in your publication or a certain page range. Enable background checking if you have placed objects like watermarks or headers on the background. Publisher will check for potential design problems in several areas, although you can disable certain types of design checking under Options.

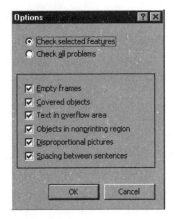

You can quickly tell Publisher to check for all problems by choosing that option at the top of the dialog box. However, you may want to disable Covered Objects if you have intentionally overlapped objects in your publication. Disable Disproportional Pictures if you have deliberately resized a piece of art to change its original dimensions. Click OK twice to close both dialog boxes and start the Design Checker. When Publisher notices a problem, it selects that frame in your document, displays a dialog box that describes the problem, and gives you options for how to handle it.

SKILL
10

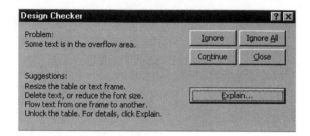

You can ignore the problem if it's something you want to leave "as is" or if you prefer to go back and manually change it later. You can click Ignore All to have Publisher skip other problems like this. You can fix it (Publisher even suggests how), and you don't have to close the dialog box to make a fix. Simply click and edit in your document, and then click Continue in the dialog box to finish design checking. If Publisher spots a disproportional object problem, it gives you a Change button that will change the selected object back to its original proportions while keeping the same approximate size.

CHECKING A PUBLICATION FOR POSSIBLE DESIGN ERRORS

1. Choose Tools ➤ Design Checker.
2. Select the option to check all pages in your publication or enter a page range. Enable background checking if you need it.
3. Click Options to deselect the design areas you want Publisher to overlook.
4. From the Options dialog box, click OK twice to start the Design Checker.
5. When Publisher stops at a potential error, work outside the dialog box to correct it, and then click Continue. You could also choose to Ignore the error or Ignore All errors like it.
6. Click OK when the Design Checker displays the "finished" message.

Hands On

1. Open an existing publication and run the Design Checker.

   a) Set options so that you're only checking for the types of design errors you wish to review.

   b) Correct or ignore errors as Publisher finds them.

Skill 10.11: Using Personal Information in Publications

Publisher can store up to four different sets of personal information. Each set contains fields such as name, address, job title, e-mail address, and logo. You can enter one set of data that reflects your business contact information and another for home information. If you are designing a publication for another organization, you can store that organization's information as well. Figure 10.11 shows the Personal Information dialog box that you open by choosing Edit ➤ Personal Information.

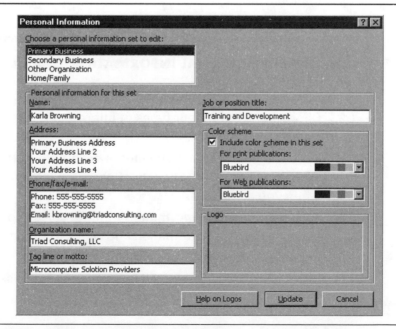

FIGURE 10.11: The Personal Information dialog box can store up to four sets of information for use in your publications.

First choose a personal information set from the list of four at the top of the dialog box. Then type information in each field, as you want it to appear in your publication. (Don't worry about fonts and sizes here, plan to handle formatting when you insert this information into your publication.) Enter data for as many personal information sets as you wish (up to four). Click Update to save it.

NOTE NOTE NOTE NOTE NOTE NOTE NOTE NOTE NOTE NOTE NOTE NOTE NOTE NOTE

Select a color scheme that is consistent with the publications you create for each personal information set. Inserting a personal information component will apply the selected color scheme to the current publication. If you update personal information by changing the scheme, then the new scheme is applied to the current publication.

To add your personal information to a page, open that page and choose Insert ➤ Personal Information. Choose which field you want from the submenu, and Publisher inserts your data in its own text frame, which you can arrange and format as you wish. To insert additional fields (components) of data, choose Insert ➤ Personal Information and select another field. You can include a field as many times as you wish throughout the publication. If you edit the information in a personal information set, all fields of that type will be updated in the current publication.

CREATE AND INSERT PERSONAL INFORMATION IN A PUBLICATION

1. Choose Edit ➤ Personal Information from the menu.
2. Choose one of the four types of information sets from the list at the top of the dialog box.
3. Type the information you want in each field of the information set. You can enter up to four sets of personal information. Click Update when you are finished.
4. To insert personal information into the current publication, choose Insert ➤ Personal Information and select a component.
5. Repeat step 3 to insert additional components.
6. Move, resize, and format the text box(es) as necessary.

Hands On

1. Open an existing publication or create a new one.

    a) Enter data for two different personal information sets.

    b) Insert at least three fields of information somewhere in the active publication.

    c) Open your personal information set and edit one of the fields you have used in the publication. View the document to see that this information was updated when you edited it.

    d) Re-edit the personal information set so that it reflects the actual data you'll be using most often.

Skill 10.12: Organizing Art with the Graphics Manager

When you add art into any Office 2000 application, you have the option to insert a *link* rather than *embed* the picture itself. This makes for much smaller file sizes in your Publisher documents. In the event you need to see details about links or edit them, you will need to use the Graphics Manager. You can also use the Graphics Manager to change an embedded object to a linked object.

Choose Tools ➤ Commercial Printing Services ➤ Graphics Manager to see a list of all the pictures or clip art in the active document.

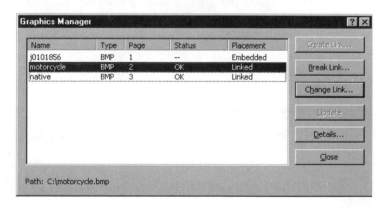

SKILL
10

Select the name of the linked picture you want to work with. Click Details to see information about the file such as its path, date last modified, and size.

To edit the link so that it points to a different picture, click Change Link. (You can do this from the Details screen or the Graphics Manager). Change to the drive or folder where the new picture is stored, select it, and click Link to File.

In the event that Publisher can't follow a link to the original file (maybe the original file was renamed, or it was on removable media like a CD that is no longer in the drive), the Update button becomes available for you to re-establish the link.

To break a link and embed the actual graphic, you have two options: full resolution embedding and low resolution embedding. You can probably get by with low resolution until you print your final draft. If you choose low resolution for a number of graphics, your file will be slightly smaller. It also saves printer toner (or ink) when you print initial drafts of the publication.

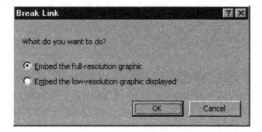

To create a link for an object that is currently embedded, open the Graphics Manager and select the file. Choose Create Link and select one of the link options. If the embedded picture is already stored in a file you can browse to, choose the Browse to Locate option. If the embedded picture doesn't have an associated file, you can make one by selecting the second option and clicking OK. Choose a folder and filename for the picture and click Save. Now you can use the picture in other publications, as well.

CREATING AND EDITING LINKS WITH THE GRAPHICS MANAGER

1. Choose Tools ➤ Commercial Printing Services ➤ Graphics Manager.
2. Create a link to a file that is currently embedded by selecting it and clicking **Create Link**.

continued ▶

3. Select one of the link options. Use Browse to Locate if the embedded picture is already stored in a file you can locate. Use the Create option if you need to make a linked file for the graphic object. Click OK to close the dialog boxes.

4. To change a link so that it points to a different graphic, select the file you wish to edit and click Change Link.

5. Navigate to the drive or folder where the new picture is stored, select it, and click Link to File.

6. To change a linked file to an embedded one, select it and click the Break Link button at the right of the dialog box.

7. Choose full or low resolution embedding and click OK twice to close both dialog boxes.

Hands On

1. Open or create a publication that contains at least one embedded picture. Open the Graphics Manager and view the details of each graphic in the publication.

2. Convert an embedded object to a linked object:

   a) Edit the link so that it points to a different picture.

   b) Re-edit the link to restore it to the previous picture.

   c) Change the linked graphic back to an embedded one.

3. Insert and embed a graphic from some type of removable media, like a floppy or CD-ROM:

   a) Change the embedded object to a linked object, using the Create option.

   b) Save and close the publication.

   c) Reopen the publication and review the links again in the Graphics Manager.

SKILL
▼ 10

Skill 10.13: Using Wizards and Shared Designs to Create Publications

How would you like to put together a design including color scheme, art, banners, sidebars, and text frames, all in a few minutes? Wizards and shared designs allow you to do just that! New and improved in Office 2000, Publisher's Wizards and designs are easier to use than ever with more document types and new design themes for electrifying publications in minutes!

The Quick Publication Wizard

For publications of a nonspecific type (i.e., it's not a newsletter, flyer, brochure, calendar, etc.), the Quick Publications Wizard can get you rolling in a hurry. From the Microsoft Publisher Catalog (File ➤ New gets you there), choose Quick Publications from the list on the left. Browse the templates on the right, select the one you like, and click the Start Wizard button at the bottom of the screen. When you start the Wizard, you will see your document on the right and the Wizard on the left, as shown in Figure 10.12.

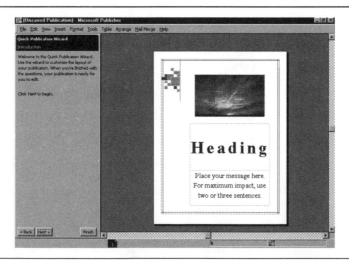

FIGURE 10.12: The Introduction step of the Quick Publications Wizard

Publisher gives you a one-page document (to which you can add other pages as needed) and a series of steps to complete the design and layout of your publication.

This Wizard (and all others) starts with an Introduction step. Click Next to proceed. At the Color Scheme step, select from the list of schemes and click Next to move to the Layout step. Select from the list of layouts to determine the position of Publisher placeholders or choose No Layout if you want to add your own design elements.

Click Next to see the Personal Information step and add elements you want to include in your publication, or click Update to change the data in a personal information set. Be sure to select which of the four personal information sets you want to use before inserting or editing personal information components. You can click the Back button at any point in the Wizard to return to a previous step. When you're through, click Finish to have Publisher create the publication based on the choices you made in the Wizard.

Any time you wish to return to the Wizard's original settings, navigate to the Design step by clicking it from the list on the left and click the Reset Design button at the bottom of that page. You'll have options to delete text and/or graphics you've added since starting the Wizard. You can also reset Page and Layout options. Hide the Wizard at any time by clicking the Hide Wizard button at the bottom left of the screen.

In general, you can edit or replace the contents of graphic object frames with a double-click. Replace sample placeholder text by clicking on the appropriate text frame and overtyping it with your own message. Any pages, objects, and text frames you insert will have the settings you entered in the Wizard.

SKILL
10

STARTING A DOCUMENT WITH THE QUICK PUBLICATION WIZARD

1. Open the Publisher Catalog. The Catalog opens automatically when you launch Publisher, unless you have disabled this option. Choosing File ➢ New also opens the Catalog.

2. Choose Quick Publications from the list on the left of the Catalog.

3. Select a template from the choices on the right and click the Start Wizard button below the Templates window.

4. The Wizard's steps are displayed on the left and your document is shown on the right. Click Next to go past the Introduction step and select the color scheme you want to use for this publication.

5. Click Next to move to the Layout step of the Wizard. Make your choice from the list and click Next.

6. Choose which personal information set you want to use for this publication. Click Update if you need to edit any data in a personal information set.

7. Click Back if you need to make changes at a previous Wizard step. Click Finish to have Publisher create your document.

8. Change the Design, Layout, Color Scheme, or Personal Information options by clicking one of those choices from the list on the left.

9. Select and edit frames in the publication where necessary.

10. Return to the Wizard's original settings at any time by clicking the Reset button in the Design step.

Using Other Wizards

The Microsoft Publisher Catalog contains dozens of Wizards to help you create many different types of documents. The Catalog opens automatically when you launch Publisher (unless you have disabled that option). To see the catalog from within Publisher, click File ➢ New. Make sure you have selected the Publications by Wizard tab.

The Catalog Wizard

Don't confuse the Catalog Wizard with the Publisher Catalog; the Catalog Wizard is an item *in* the Catalog. This Wizard helps you create a publication that lists, for instance, products and services your company sells. When you start this Wizard, you are given eight pages with frames ready for product descriptions, pictures, headings, and general information.

The Introduction, Color Scheme, and Personal Information steps work the same as with the Quick Publications Wizard. However, you'll be prompted at the third step to choose whether to include a placeholder for the customer's address. When you choose to include a customer's address, Publisher puts the text frame on the last page of the catalog, which is already formatted for mailing.

TIP TIP TIP TIP TIP TIP TIP TIP TIP TIP TIP TIP TIP TIP TIP TIP TIP TIP TIP TIP TIP TIP TIP

You can use Publisher's mail merge options to create address labels for mailing your catalog.

With catalogs, once you finish the Wizard, you have options to set up inside page content so you can quickly redesign how items and descriptions are displayed. Use the page navigators at the bottom left of the workspace to select a set of inside pages. Click the Inside Page Content step from the list on the left and select from the list of layout options below it..

Insert new pages by clicking that option from the list on the left, then clicking the Insert Page button. If you're inserting inside pages, you'll be given options for how you want the new pages to be laid out. Select from the drop-down list of layout options for the right and left pages, or click More Options to see the standard Insert Page dialog box.

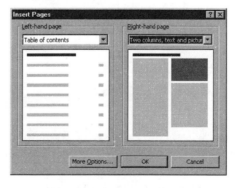

The Web Site Wizard

When you choose to create a Web site using the Publisher Wizard, you must first select a design, just as you would with any other Wizard. The first three steps to creating a Web site are similar to what you have seen in other Wizards, and the Web-specific steps are just as easy to use. Add sound, texture, or a customer order form with a few clicks. Preview animation using the Web Page Preview choice under the File menu. For more about Web publishing with Publisher 2000, see Skill 12.

The Pack and Go Wizard

Publisher file sizes tend to be much larger than regular word-processed documents. Even if you link pictures, you may find that object formatting alone can cause your file to grow past floppy diskette size in a hurry. If you need to take your file to another computer or to a commercial printer, or if you're concerned about storage space, make use of the Pack and Go Wizard.

Pack and Go only works if you have already saved the file in its regular (large) file format. Start the Wizard by clicking File ➤ Pack and Go Wizard.

The first step of Pack and Go tells you what the Wizard will do for you. Click Next to move beyond this introductory screen. Choose a location to put the packed file (the default is A:, but you can browse to select another location).

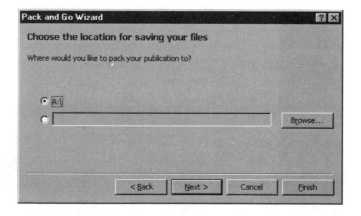

Choose whether to Embed TrueType fonts, Include Linked Graphics, and Create Links for Embedded Graphics. It's a good idea to select at least the first two if you're moving to a computer that might not have the same installed components as the system on which you created the publication. Click Next.

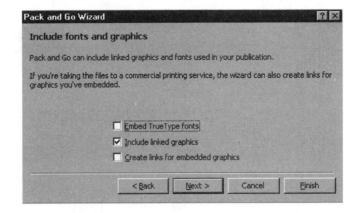

The last step of the Wizard tells you what will happen to your file and how to unpack it when you need it again. Click Finish. The Wizard prompts you for additional disks if you're packing a large publication to floppy.

If you're packing for a commercial printing service, the Wizard steps are mostly the same, but Publisher automatically creates links for embedded objects and prints proof sets as part of the process.

To open your packed publication, use the Windows Explorer to navigate to the drive or folder where it is stored and double-click unpack.exe. You will be prompted for an unpack location and warned about the possibility of overwriting files with the same name.

Using Shared Designs to Create a Publication

Let's say you have already created company letterhead using Publisher's Arcs design. Now it's time to create a company Web site. Or maybe you're trying to match design elements from the sales presentation you developed in PowerPoint. For consistency's sake, you *should* use some of the same design elements in all related publications and presentations. That's where Publisher's Shared Designs can be helpful. Figure 10.13 shows the Publications by Design tab of the Catalog.

SKILL
10

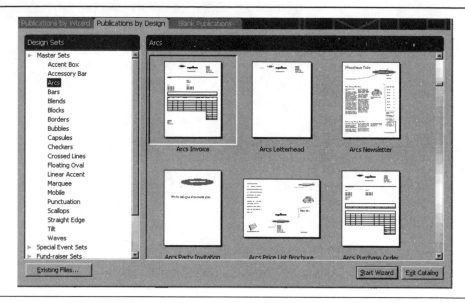

FIGURE 10.13: The Publications by Design tab of the Catalog shows many types of documents using the same design sets.

Open the Publisher Catalog (choose File ➢ New) and click the Publications by Design tab of the dialog box. The list on the left shows Publisher's design sets, many of which are shared across Office applications. Select one of the designs on the left to see the various types of publications that use that design. Select a document type from the right and click Start Wizard to begin making layout choices for that publication. Proceed through the other steps as you would in any Wizard.

Hands On

1. Create an informational flyer using the Quick Publication Wizard.

    a) Use the Blends design with a Cavern color scheme.

    b) Insert an appropriate picture in the graphics placeholder.

    c) Include and edit a response form tear-off.

    d) If you like, include a placeholder for customer address and fields for personal information.

    e) Edit the text in the text frame placeholders to fit your own purposes.

2. Use Pack and Go to save this publication on your local drive or to a floppy.

Skill 10.14: Creating Mail Merge Documents

If you have created a publication with plans to mass mail it to a long list of customers and other contacts, consider using Publisher's Mail Merge features. The Catalog Wizard and other Wizards allow you to include a placeholder for customer address. You can populate that placeholder with fields from an address list kept in Publisher or another Office application.

In general, the steps for Mail Merge are the same for Publisher as they are for Word. You open a data source (that's the file that has your names and addresses in it) and you insert the fields you need into a main merge document (that's the catalog or brochure you want to mail). You can also merge to mailing labels or envelopes, rather than printing the address right on the publication you plan to mail.

 NOTE NOTE NOTE NOTE NOTE NOTE NOTE NOTE NOTE NOTE NOTE NOTE NOTE NOTE NOTE

For additional detailed information of all Mail Merge features, see Skill 4.

Using Outlook and other Data Sources for Merge

 Now in Publisher 2000 you can use an Outlook contact list as a data source for a mail merge. In your Publisher document, select the text frame that will ultimately contain your mailing information. Choose Mail Merge ➤ Open Data Source to open the following dialog box.

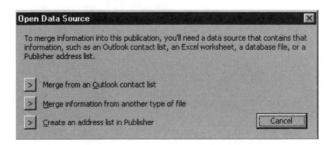

You have two data source options other than the new option for using Outlook. Choose the second option if your address list is in Excel, Word, or Access. Click the third option if you don't have an electronic address list and want to create it now.

NOTE NOTE NOTE NOTE NOTE NOTE NOTE NOTE NOTE NOTE NOTE NOTE NOTE NOTE

Once you create an address list in Publisher or any other Office application, you can use it again and again to generate mail merge documents, envelopes, and labels.

To use the new Outlook option, click Merge from an Outlook contact list. If your Outlook configuration contains multiple profiles, you will be prompted with a dialog box to choose a profile.

Select a profile from the drop-down list and click OK. Next you will be prompted to choose which Outlook fields you want to use in your merge.

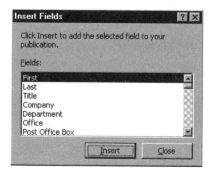

WARNING WARNING WARNING WARNING WARNING WARNING WARNING WARNING

If you forgot to select a text frame before starting the merge process, Publisher won't allow you to proceed with inserting fields. Click behind the dialog box to select (or create) a frame, and then try again.

Select the first field you need and click the Insert button. Select and insert the second field and so on until you have finished. Then click Close.

NOTE NOTE NOTE NOTE NOTE NOTE NOTE NOTE NOTE NOTE NOTE NOTE NOTE NOTE
Don't forget to type spaces and other punctuation between your merge codes in the main document. Publisher allows you to type in your document with the Insert Fields dialog box open.

Once the correct fields are inserted, choose Mail Merge ➢ Merge. Preview your merged documents using the navigation buttons in the Preview Data dialog box. If you close the Preview Data dialog box, you can retrieve it again choosing Mail Merge ➢ Show Merge Results. Sort and/or filter as you would in a Word merge, using the Mail Merge menu option.

USING MAIL MERGE IN PUBLISHER

1. Create and select the text frame that will hold your address information.
2. Click Mail Merge ➢ Open Data Source.
3. Choose the data source location if the file already exists or choose the Create option to make one from scratch. If the file is in Outlook, you may be prompted to choose a profile.
4. Select and insert the fields you need from the data source. Make sure you type spaces and punctuation in the text frame as you insert fields. Close the dialog box, when you're done.
5. Choose Mail Merge ➢ Merge from the menu bar.
6. Use the navigation buttons in the Preview Data dialog box to check each address. If you have closed the preview, you can get it back by choosing Mail Merge ➢ Show Merge Results.
7. Sort and/or filter as desired using those options under the Mail Merge menu.

SKILL
10

Printing Merged Publications

When it's time to print a document you have mail merged, proceed with caution. Choose File ➤ Print Merge to set up options for printing in the Print Merge dialog box.

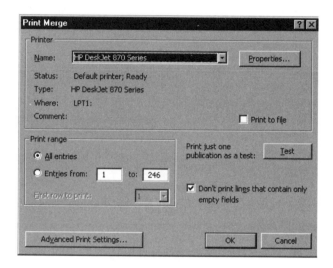

Always print a test copy of the merged document using the Test button in the dialog box. This can help you spot errors with the document or with the merge before you have to throw away a hundred catalogs. Rather than printing a large number of entries at once, consider printing entries a few at a time. You don't want to come back to the printer in an hour to find that you've printed 246 brochures using an ink cartridge that needed to be changed. Enable the Don't Print Lines that Contain Only Empty Fields feature so addresses won't have empty spaces in them where data fields are empty.

WARNING WARNING WARNING WARNING WARNING WARNING WARNING WARNING

Problems can arise using Outlook as a data source. If Personal Address Book isn't included as a service in the Outlook profile you select for your merge, Publisher won't even open it as a data source. See Skill 9 for more information about Outlook address books.

WARNING WARNING WARNING WARNING WARNING WARNING WARNING WARNING

Publisher prompts you for a sheet name when opening an Excel data source. You won't get an option to use a named range, like you do in Word. Further, Publisher asks if you want to use Row 1 as the field names. If you say No, expecting Publisher to prompt you for another range, you may wind up in trouble. Rather than letting you choose a different row when you decline to use Row 1, Publisher automatically uses Column A values as field names. Not helpful in every situation!

Hands On

1. Create or open a presentation you wish to mail to others.

   a) Attach to an existing data source, or create one on the fly.

   b) Select an empty text frame and insert the appropriate address fields from your data source. Format the text fields as desired.

   c) Merge your data with the publication, and then preview several records as a cursory check for errors.

   d) Print a test copy and fix any errors you may have discovered.

   e) Print the rest of the copies if you want.

Skill 10.15: Creating and Printing Booklets

With Publisher's improved Wizards and designs, creating booklets is as easy as putting together any other document. With booklets, however, you will need to address of a couple additional issues. Consider how your booklet will eventually be put together. Will you staple, fold, or bind it? Will you print on both sides of the page? The answers to these questions determine how you should set up the publication to begin with.

Many of Publisher's Wizards automatically set up the page appropriately for booklet printing. For instance, the Programs Wizard assumes you will print a four-page document on one 8½-by-11 page, folded booklet style. (You can always insert additional pages; you just get them four at a time.) But what if you planned to print the program on 11-by-17 paper, making an 8½-by-11 folded booklet? Simply change to the correct paper size in the Page Setup dialog box (discussed at length in Skill 10.8) and choose the appropriate fold option.

SKILL 10

Bound publications need an extra wide left margin, and if you're duplexing a bound publication, you should set up mirrored margin guides. Choose Arrange ➢ Layout Guides to open the Layout Guides dialog box and enable this feature.

Printing Booklets

In general, you'll want to print booklet publications from the dialog box (choose File ➢ Print) rather than using the Print button on the toolbar. Just as in other Office applications, the toolbar button prints one copy of your entire document. This would only work for booklets if you had a printer that supported automatic duplexing. If you don't, then you have to feed pages through the printer twice: once for odd-numbered pages and once for the evens.

WARNING WARNING WARNING WARNING WARNING WARNING WARNING WARNING

Printers vary widely in the types of document feeding they support. It is always best to check your printer manual if you're not sure which features it has and how they work.

In the Print dialog Box, if you choose Current Page, Publisher asks whether this is a new booklet, or part of a booklet already printed.

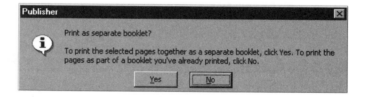

Choose Yes or No based on whether you're printing from scratch one page at a time, or whether you are just reprinting part of the document.

When you want to print an entire booklet on a printer that doesn't support automatic duplexing, you have to click the Options button in the Print dialog box to set up for booklet printing. That way you will get a prompt to re-feed pages through the printer to complete the back side. Publisher knows how to correctly paginate, so once you fold, the pages should be in the right order.

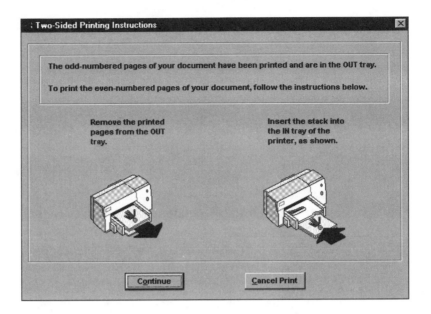

PRINTING BOOKLETS

1. Choose File ➢ Page Setup to make sure the correct fold and paper size options are selected.

2. If you're planning to bind your booklet, choose Arrange ➢ Layout Guides to enable mirrored margin boundaries.

3. Choose File ➢ Print and select whether to print the current page or the whole booklet.

4. If your printer doesn't support automatic duplexing, click Options in the Print dialog box to set up for booklet printing (if your printer supports it). Click OK to close this dialog box.

5. Click Print.

6. Flip the pages in the printer when prompted and click Print again.

SKILL
10

Hands On

1. Create or open a publication with four pages.

   a) Choose a design and color scheme you like.

   b) Change the Page Setup options so that the publication becomes a book fold document with a width of 5½ inches and a height of 8½ inches. Set page orientation appropriately.

   c) Move and resize object frames so that they fit appropriately on the new layout.

   d) Save and print your booklet. (You may wish to save under a different name if you converted an existing publication to book fold.)

2. Use the Catalog Wizard to create a book fold publication.

   a) Select a design and color scheme you find appealing.

   b) Adjust your inside pages to fit your preferences.

   c) Format text and text frames appropriately to fit your needs.

   d) Save and print your catalog.

Are You Experienced?

Now you can...

- ☑ **Create and edit text in text frames**
- ☑ **Connect text frames and manage overflow**
- ☑ **Create and edit objects using each of Publisher's object tools**
- ☑ **Crop and recolor objects**
- ☑ **Format text and picture frames**
- ☑ **Catch design errors with the Design Checker**
- ☑ **Organize art with the Graphics Manager**
- ☑ **Use Wizards and Shared Designs as shortcuts to creating publications**
- ☑ **Prepare documents for mass mailing with Mail Merge**

Working with Objects and Graphics

- ➔ Linking and embedding objects
- ➔ Inserting clips and pictures
- ➔ Using the Drawing tools
- ➔ Creating WordArt

11.1: Converting, Linking, and Embedding

An *object* is data that can be embedded or linked in another application. Object Linking and Embedding, or *OLE*, is a protocol that allows applications to communicate with each other to create or update objects. Word documents, Excel worksheets and charts, Access tables, and PowerPoint slides are all examples of objects you can convert, embed, or link in other Office 2000 documents. As you'll see below, you can also embed or link graphics, sounds, video, and virtually anything else you can select and copy to the Clipboard.

Converting, Embedding, and Linking in Word

The easiest way to convert, embed, or link data in an Office 2000 application uses a modification of copy-and-paste operations. Open the *source application* (also called the *native application*) that contains the text, picture, or other object you want to embed or link in the *destination application*. Select and copy the object to the Clipboard. You can close the source application if you wish; in some programs, you'll be asked if you want to retain the contents of the Clipboard. Choose Yes. Then open the destination document and place the insertion point where you want to paste the selection. Choose Edit ➤ Paste Special to open the Paste Special dialog box, shown in Figure 11.1, where a range from an Excel worksheet is being pasted into a Word document.

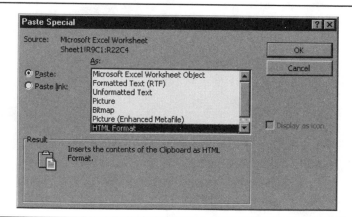

FIGURE 11.1: The Paste Special dialog box

You choose to convert, embed, or link the selection in the destination application, depending on how you want to use the selection after it arrives. *Converting* the selection changes it from its native format to a format used in the destination document. For example, an Excel chart pasted in Word can be converted to a graphic or text. From the time of conversion, you'll use Word's tools to work with the converted selection. If you *embed* the chart object, a *copy* of the object that retains its native format is saved within the destination document. If you double-click on the object to edit it, the Excel toolbars will open.

With a *link*, each time you open the destination document, the application will reload the chart object from its native application file. If you double-click to edit the linked object, the source document will open; you can't change the linked object, only its source. If a linked file is moved, opening the destination document results in an error message and the destination document will load without the picture. This means you can only successfully open the document on a computer that contains both the native application and the source document. Linking has two advantages: it saves disk space, but, more importantly, linking is *dynamic*. If the object's source changes, the change is reflected in all linked documents.

The source for the object is displayed at the top of the dialog box (see Figure 11.1). The As box allows you to select how the information should be pasted:

- Microsoft Excel Worksheet Object creates an embedded Excel object in the Word document that you can edit using regular Excel tools.

- Formatted Text (RTF), the default, converts the worksheet to a table.

- Unformatted Text converts the selection to Word tabular columns.

- Picture and Bitmap both convert the worksheet into a graphic that you can work with in Word using all the Word graphic tools.

- Picture (Enhanced Metafile) converts the selection into a Windows Metafile graphic.

- HTML inserts the contents of the Clipboard as HTML-formatted text.

- Unformatted Unicode Text inserts the worksheet without any formatting.

If you choose the Microsoft Excel Worksheet Object option, you can click the Display As Icon check box to insert an icon rather than text. If you prefer to change the type of Excel Worksheet Object icon, click the Change Icon button in the Paste Special window. You can choose from Excel's icon library or import your own using the Browse button, and you can customize the caption as well.

To link, rather than embed, the selection, choose the Paste Link option. You can link any of the converted file types listed except for Enhanced Metafile. The Enhanced Metafile option is replaced with Word Hyperlink. Choosing Word Hyperlink creates a hyperlink in the Word document; clicking the hyperlink takes the user to the source Excel worksheet. You can access the Paste As Hyperlink option directly from the Edit menu.

CONVERTING, EMBEDDING, AND LINKING

1. Open the file that contains the data to be converted, embedded, or linked.
2. Select the data and copy the selection to the Clipboard.
3. Open the destination document.
4. Place the insertion point where you want to paste the selection.
5. Choose Edit ➤ Paste Special.
6. Select a type from the As control. Choose Paste or Paste Link.
7. Select the Display As Icon option if you are choosing a Microsoft Word document object.
8. Click OK to paste the selection in the destination document.

NOTE NOTE NOTE NOTE NOTE NOTE NOTE NOTE NOTE NOTE NOTE NOTE NOTE NOTE NOTE NOTE

From the computer's point of view, OLE is a complex operation. Give the destination document a moment to accept and place the new object.

Click once on the pasted object to select it. Use the object's handles to size it, or click Delete to delete it. The real magic of OLE occurs when you double-click the object. After you click, wait a moment. If the object was embedded, the toolbars from the object's native application will open in the destination application. The embedded object is a copy. Changing the object doesn't change the original worksheet, and changes in the source worksheet have no effect on the object. With a linked object, double-click and you'll be transported to the source document to edit the object.

OLE in Excel, PowerPoint, Access, and Outlook

Convert, embed, or link data in Excel as you do in Word. Copy the data in the source document, then switch to Excel and click on the destination location. Choose Edit ➤ Paste Special to adjust the settings in the dialog box. PowerPoint creates slide and presentation objects, which can be embedded in Word and Excel documents. PowerPoint also accepts embedded objects from Word and Excel.

OLE requires a source application that can create an OLE object (an *OLE server*) and a destination application that can accept OLE objects (an *OLE client*). Access and Outlook are OLE clients, but not OLE servers, so they cannot create OLE objects. You can paste Access tables, fields, or records and Outlook items in Excel or Word, but the result will be an Excel worksheet or a Word table, not an object. Selections pasted from Access and Outlook can't be linked. As OLE clients, Access and Outlook accept objects from other applications. You can embed part of a document from Word or a worksheet from Excel in an Access form or report or Outlook item. You can also choose Insert ➤ Object (or, in Access, use the Unbound or Bound Object Frame buttons in the Toolbox) to embed a new or existing object in an Access form or Outlook item.

You can use an Excel worksheet to create an Access table, but you don't use copy and paste. Access uses importing to create a new table from an Excel worksheet or to create a link to a worksheet. Activate the database that will contain the new table. Choose File ➤ Get External Data ➤ Import (or Link Tables). Select Microsoft Excel (*.xls) from the Files of Type control. Select the Excel workbook from the file list, and then follow the steps of the Import Wizard to create a table from the file. From Excel, you can choose Data ➤ Convert to Access to convert a worksheet to a table if you have installed the AccessLinks add-in for Excel. Use Outlook's Import and Export Wizard (choose File ➤ Import and Export) to swap data with Excel and Access.

Automatic and Manual Updating

When you create a link with Paste Special, *automatic link updating* is enabled. The object is updated each time the destination document is opened; if the source changes while the destination document is open, the link will reflect the change. You can choose to update links manually rather than automatically, giving you control over when a file is updated. To change to *manual link updating*, select the linked object and then choose Edit ➤ OLE/DDE Links to open the Links dialog box. In the Update Method option at the bottom of the dialog box, choose Manual.

When you are ready to update links in the destination document, open the Links dialog box again and click the Update Now button. If you use manual linking, you should adopt a consistent method for updating so you don't pass off last month's information as the latest data.

OLE with Files

If you want to embed or link an entire file instead of a selection, it is often easier to insert the object. Choose Insert ➤ Object ➤ Create from File to open the Create from File page of the Object dialog box, shown in Figure 11.2.

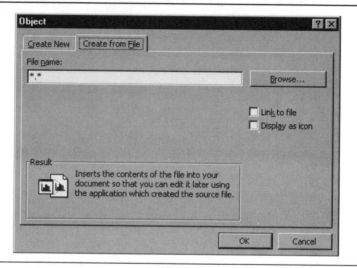

FIGURE 11.2: Create from File page of the Object dialog box

Select and open the file you want to embed or link and set the other options as you did in the Paste Special dialog box. Click OK to insert the object in the destination document. Some files are inserted as icons, whether or not you choose Display As Icon. Sound files, for example, place an icon in the destination document. Double-clicking the icon plays the sound file.

EMBEDDING OR LINKING A FILE

1. Open the destination document and place the insertion point where the object is to be inserted.
2. Choose Insert ➢ Object from the menu bar. Click the Create from File tab.
3. Select the file you want to embed or link.
4. Click OK to embed the file, or choose Link to File, and then click OK to link the file.

Creating New Objects

You can use the Object dialog box to create a new object. For example, you might want to have an Excel worksheet in a Word document. You don't have to open Excel and create the worksheet; you can create an Excel worksheet object in Word. Because new objects don't exist as separate source files, they cannot be linked, only embedded.

Office 2000 includes other programs—such as Microsoft Graph—that are OLE servers. You probably have other non-Office applications on your computer that also create objects. Choosing Insert ➢ Object from the menu bar opens the Object dialog box. The scroll list in the Create New page displays the objects that can be created using applications installed on your computer, as shown in Figure 11.3.

Select an Object Type and then click OK. The appropriate OLE server will open within the current document. Create the object, then click in the destination document (outside the object) to close the OLE server.

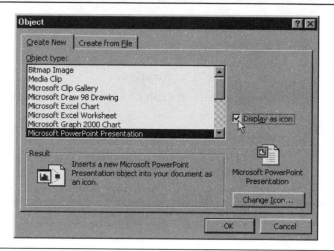

FIGURE 11.3: Creating a new object

CREATING A NEW OBJECT

1. Position the insertion point in the document and choose Insert ➤ Object from the menu bar.
2. Click the Create New tab. Select an Object Type from the scroll list.
3. Click OK to insert the newly created object.

The Object Type list is amended as new applications are installed. Applications may remain on the list, even if they have been removed from the computer. If you select an application that has been moved or removed, the destination application will provide an error message.

Hands On

1. Create or open an Excel worksheet. Select and copy a range of cells and place them in a Word document:

   a) As a converted table using Paste

   b) As a picture using Paste Special

   c) As an embedded Excel object using Paste Special

   d) As a linked Excel worksheet object

   e) As a linked picture

   Double-click either of the linked objects, and make changes to the Excel worksheet. Return to the Word document and notice the differences between the converted, embedded, and linked objects.

2. In Access:

   a) Use Get External Data to import an Excel worksheet as a table.

   b) Use Get External Data to link to an Excel worksheet.

   c) Select records in a table and copy them to Word or Excel.

3. In Outlook, use the Import and Export Wizard to export Contacts to an Excel worksheet or an Access database.

4. Create a new Excel chart object in Word or PowerPoint.

5. Link a slide from a PowerPoint presentation as a graphic in a Word document. Update the slide in PowerPoint, and notice the changes in the Word document.

6. Place a sound or video file in PowerPoint, Word, or Excel using Insert ➤ Object ➤ Create from File. Play the media file.

11.2: Inserting Clips and Graphics

You can insert graphics, sound, and video in every Office application, but each gives you menu or toolbar access to the types of media objects you'd likely place in the application. For example, PowerPoint and Publisher offer Movies and Sounds as a choice on the Insert menu. In any Office 2000 program, begin by selecting Insert from the menu bar. If the type of media you want to insert is listed on the Insert menu, select it. If not, choose Object and select the media type from the list in the Insert Object dialog box.

Adding Clips

The Microsoft Clip Gallery, included with Office 2000, has a broad selection of media clips. When you add other media files to your system, you can add them to the gallery for easy selection. You can access the Clip Gallery from Word, Excel, and PowerPoint. Click the appropriate file-type tab, then select the media file you wish to insert, as shown in Figure 11.4.

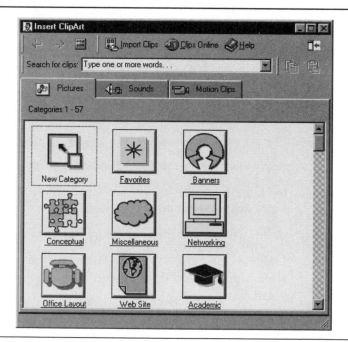

FIGURE 11.4: The Microsoft Clip Gallery

Even though the Insert menu choice says *Clip Art*, you can insert any of the files in the Gallery. In Word and Excel, it's faster to choose Insert ➣ Picture ➣ Clip Art, and then choose a sound or video clip, than to insert a sound or video object in the Insert Object dialog box.

INSERTING CLIPS FROM THE CLIP GALLERY

1. Position the insertion point where you want to insert the clip.
2. Choose Insert ➤ Picture ➤ Clip Art to open the Clip Gallery.
3. Click the file-type tab. With video and sound clips, click the Play button to preview the file.
4. Double-click the sound, video, clip art, or picture to add it to the document.

See "Grouping and Ungrouping Objects" in Skill 11.3 for information on editing clip art graphics.

Importing Clips

If your company has a logo or other clip art you want to use in Word, Excel, PowerPoint, and other Office applications, you can use the Import Clips feature in the Clip Gallery window to store them in an easily accessible place.

To import clips from other locations, click the Import Clips button to open the Add Clip to Clip Gallery dialog box shown in Figure 11.5. Find the file you want to import, then choose one of the three import options. You can import a copy of the new clip art by checking Copy into Clip Gallery or you can move the original by checking Move into Clip Gallery. Choose Let Clip Gallery Find This Clip in Its Current Folder or Volume to add a shortcut to the gallery rather than copying or moving the file to the Clip Gallery.

You can also import new clips directly from the Web by clicking the Clips Online button in the Insert Clip Art dialog box. Office will launch your browser and take you to Microsoft's online Clip Art Gallery. Search a Web site for additional clip art to be imported to the Clip Gallery.

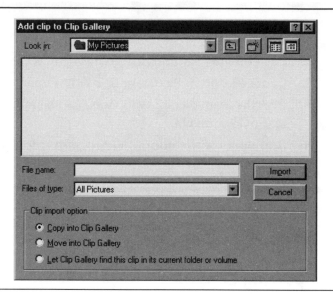

FIGURE 11.5: The Add Clip to Clip Gallery dialog box

Moving and Resizing Clips

Use the mouse to drag a selected clip to move it. Drag the clip's handle to resize the clip. You can resize a video clip as you can any other object by dragging a sizing handle. However, badly resized video is blurry, difficult to see, and sometimes skips during playback. PowerPoint includes a resizing feature designed for video that sizes it at its best size for viewing. If you need to resize a video clip for an onscreen document in Word or Excel, consider placing the clip in PowerPoint and resizing it, then moving the clip to Excel or Word.

Inserting Other Pictures

If the picture you want to insert isn't in the Clip Gallery, choose Insert ➤ Picture ➤ From File from the menu bar to open the Insert Picture dialog box, shown below. Locate and select the file to insert the selected picture in your document.

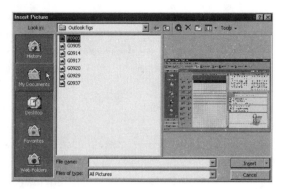

Modifying Pictures

After you've placed a picture from a file or the Clip Gallery, you can adjust the picture using the Picture toolbar. Right-click the picture and choose Show Picture Toolbar from the shortcut menu. Table 11.1 describes the buttons on the Picture toolbar.

TABLE 11.1: Picture Toolbar Buttons

Button	Name	Use
	Insert Picture from File	Insert another picture
	Image Control	Choose from Automatic, Grayscale, Black & White, or Watermark
	More Contrast	Increase color intensity
	Less Contrast	Decrease color intensity
	More Brightness	Add white to lighten the colors
	Less Brightness	Add black to darken the colors
	Crop	Trim sides of the image
	Line Style	Format the border that surrounds the picture

TABLE 11.1: Picture Toolbar Buttons *(continued)*

Button	Name	Use
	Recolor Object	Change individual colors in the object; only available in PowerPoint (see Skill 7)
	Format Picture	One-stop shopping for picture properties
	Set Transparent Color	Use like an eyedropper to make areas of the picture transparent (used extensively for Web graphics)
	Reset Picture	Return the picture to its original format

The Crop, Recolor Object, and Set Transparent Color buttons are used with areas of the picture. All other buttons affect the entire picture.

Inserting Scanned Graphics

If your computer is hooked to a TWAIN compliant scanner or digital camera, you can scan images into Excel, Word, Publisher, and PowerPoint. Choose Insert ➤ Picture ➤ From Scanner or Camera, and then choose Web Quality or Print Quality. To use the scanner's default settings, click Insert. Click Custom Insert if you're using a camera, want to change scanner options, or if the Insert button is disabled because your scanner does not support automatic scanning.

After the image has scanned, it will be placed in the document. Use the tools on the Picture toolbar to edit the picture.

INSERTING A SCANNED IMAGE

1. Choose Insert ➤ Picture ➤ From Scanner or Camera.
2. Choose Web Quality or Print Quality.
3. Click Insert or Custom Insert.
4. When the scanned image is placed in the document, use the Picture toolbar to edit the picture.

Hands On

1. In Word, PowerPoint, *and* Excel:

    a) Insert clip art from the Clip Gallery.

    b) Size and position the clip.

    c) Insert a video or sound clip.

    d) Play the clip.

2. In Word, PowerPoint, *or* Excel:

    a) Download a picture from the Microsoft online Clip Gallery.

    b) Insert the downloaded picture into a document.

    c) Use the tools on the Picture toolbar to retouch the picture.

3. In Word:

    a) Insert clip art from the Clip Gallery.

    b) Open the Picture toolbar and use the Set Transparent Color tool to make part of the clip (like the background) transparent.

4. In PowerPoint, insert a scanned image on a slide.

11.3: Doing It Yourself with Draw

Microsoft Draw is a built-in Office application that lets you create line art and other objects, such as WordArt. To design your own graphics, choose Insert ➢ Picture ➢ New Drawing or Insert ➢ Object and choose a Microsoft Draw object in the dialog box. The new object is placed in a separate layer in front of the document. While working with the object, you'll have access to all the available drawing tools, including the Drawing toolbar. When you complete your drawing, simply click outside the object's frame to return to the document layer.

To access the Drawing toolbar without creating a new object, right-click on any toolbar and select Drawing, choose View ➢ Toolbars and select Drawing, or in Word and Excel click the Drawing button on the Standard toolbar.

NOTE NOTE NOTE NOTE NOTE NOTE NOTE NOTE NOTE NOTE NOTE NOTE NOTE NOTE

There is no Drawing toolbar in Access; appropriate drawing tools are found in the Toolbox. However, you can create drawings in other applications and copy/paste them in Access.

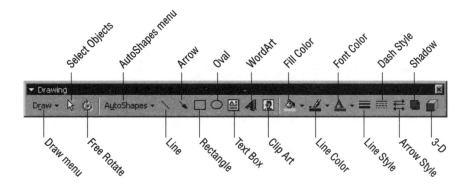

The Drawing toolbar includes two broad categories of menus and buttons. The first set, beginning with AutoShapes and ending with WordArt, is used to create drawing objects. The buttons to the right of WordArt are used to format existing objects.

Inserting AutoShapes

Clicking the AutoShapes drop-down opens a list of AutoShape categories:

Choose a category, and a menu of AutoShapes opens. Select an AutoShape, and then click or drag to insert the shape in the document. If you intend to add a lot of

AutoShapes (for example, when creating a flow chart), you can drag the bar at the top of the menu and place the menu in the document as a freestanding toolbar.

TIP TIP TIP TIP TIP TIP TIP TIP TIP TIP TIP TIP TIP TIP TIP TIP TIP TIP TIP TIP TIP TIP TIP

Callout AutoShapes are used for annotating other objects or elements, so when you place a callout, the insertion point will automatically appear. To place text in any other AutoShape, right-click on the AutoShape and choose Add Text.

Inserting Line Art Objects

To draw a line or arrow, click the Line button or the Arrow button. Move the crosshair pointer to one end of the line you want to draw. Hold the mouse button and drag to draw the line. Release the button to create the line and turn the Line or Arrow tool off. (With the Arrow tool, the arrow head appears at the end of the line where you released the mouse button.) If you want a line that is absolutely horizontal or vertical in relation to the page, hold the Shift key while dragging the line. The Line and other object buttons work like the Format Painter button: When you have more than one object to draw, begin by double-clicking on its button. The button will stay depressed, allowing you to draw more objects, until you click any button.

With the Rectangle and Oval buttons, drag from one corner of the object to the opposite corner, then release the mouse button. Hold the Shift key while dragging to create circular ovals or square rectangles.

TIP TIP TIP TIP TIP TIP TIP TIP TIP TIP TIP TIP TIP TIP TIP TIP TIP TIP TIP TIP TIP TIP TIP

If you need a series of identical objects, create one object, and then use copy and paste.

Use the Text Box tool to create text that floats on a layer above standard document text. Draw the text box as you would a rectangle. When you release the mouse button, an insertion point appears in the text box. Select and format the text using the Formatting toolbar.

ADDING DRAWING OBJECTS

1. If the Drawing toolbar is not open, right-click on any toolbar and select Drawing from the list, or click the Drawing button on the Standard toolbar.

2. Choose an AutoShape category and shape from the AutoShapes menu, or click on any of the drawing tools in the first cluster of buttons to change the pointer to crosshairs for drawing lines and shapes. Double-click the tool to draw more than one object.

3. Drag the crosshairs from a starting point to the point where you want the line or shape to end. Hold the Shift key while dragging to create straight lines, round ovals, or square rectangles.

4. Release the mouse button to end the line or shape and turn off the Drawing tool.

Adding WordArt

WordArt is used to create a graphic object from text. You'll use WordArt to create logos, emphasize titles, and add excitement to a document.

 To create WordArt, place the insertion point where you want the graphic, and click the WordArt button on the Drawing toolbar to open the WordArt Gallery, shown in Figure 11.6.

In the Gallery, select a WordArt style and click OK. (You can select a different style at any time.) When the Edit WordArt Text dialog box opens, enter the text you wish to create WordArt from. Use the Font and Size drop-downs and Bold and Italics buttons to format the text. Click OK to place the WordArt object in your document and open the WordArt toolbar. The toolbar buttons are described in Table 11.2.

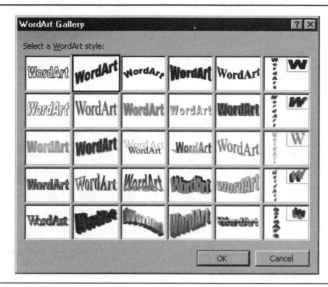

FIGURE 11.6: WordArt Gallery

INSERT TABLE 11.2: WordArt Toolbar Buttons

Button	Name	Use
	WordArt	Creates a new WordArt object.
Edit Text...	Edit Text	Opens the Edit WordArt Text dialog box to edit text.
	WordArt Gallery	Opens the WordArt Gallery.
	Format WordArt	Opens the Format WordArt dialog box so you can format colors, position, and wrap properties.
Abc	WordArt Shape	Opens a Shape menu so you can select the basic shape the text should be poured into.
	Free Rotate	Changes the object handles to rotation handles so you can rotate the text. Click again to turn off.
Aa	Same Letter Heights	Makes all letters the same height, irrespective of case.

INSERT TABLE 11.2: WordArt Toolbar Buttons *(continued)*

Button	Name	Use
	Vertical Text	Changes the WordArt orientation from horizontal to vertical. Click again to reverse.
	Alignment	Opens an alignment menu with standard options and unique WordArt options.
	Character Spacing	Opens an adjustment menu so you can change space between characters.

Use the WordArt toolbar buttons or the Drawing toolbar buttons (see "Formatting Objects" later in this skill) to enhance the Word object.

CREATING WORDART

1. Place the insertion point where you want the WordArt to appear.
2. Click the WordArt button on the Drawing toolbar.
3. Select a style from the WordArt Gallery and click OK.
4. Type the text that you want to convert to WordArt in the Edit WordArt Text dialog box. Change fonts, font sizes, and styles as desired, then click OK.
5. Use the WordArt toolbar buttons to format the WordArt object.

Formatting Objects

Use the Drawing toolbar's formatting buttons to format selected objects, including WordArt. To select a single object, just click on it.

To select multiple objects, either hold Shift while clicking on each object, or use the Select Objects tool and drag a rectangle around the objects you want to select.

Clicking the Fill Color button opens a menu of colors. If you just want an object without any "filling," choose No Fill. No fill is *not* the same as the colorless sample on the bottom row of the palette—that's the color white.

Change the line color of the selected object by clicking the Line Color button to open a color menu.

 The Font Color button changes the text color in a selected object like a text box or callout. With all three color buttons, if there is no object selected, the color you choose is the new default color and will be applied to objects you create in the future.

 The Line Style button opens a line style menu. Selecting More Lines from the menu opens a Format AutoShape dialog box, where you can set other line widths and object attributes.

 The Dash Style menu includes solid lines, dotted lines, dashed lines, and other combinations thereof.

 In the Arrow Style menu, select the style that should appear at the ends of the selected line from arrowheads and terminators of various types. If the combination of line endings you desire isn't in the menu, choose More Arrow to open the Format dialog box and set a beginning and ending style for the line.

Special Shadow and 3-D Effects

Shadow and 3-D effects are designed to give the selected drawing object more depth. You must choose one or the other; if you apply a 3-D effect to a shadowed object, the shadow is removed, and vice versa.

 From the Shadow menu, you can choose a shadow style for the selected object. To format the shadow, choose Shadow ➤ Shadow Settings to open the Shadow Settings toolbar. The toolbar includes buttons to nudge the shadow up, down, left, or right, and a Shadow Color menu.

 You can add a 3-D effect to any object. With the options on the 3-D Settings toolbar, you can change the extrusion (depth) of the object as well as rotation, perspective angle, lighting direction, surface texture, and color. When you change the color of a 3-D effect, the change affects only the effect, not the object itself.

Arranging Objects

The Draw menu on the Drawing toolbar includes other options for manipulating objects. Drawing objects are placed in separate *layers* on top of the text in a document. To move objects from layer to layer, choose Draw ➤ Order to open the Order menu.

 Bring to Front and Send to Back move the selected object(s) in relation to text and other graphic objects. If you draw an oval and place a rectangle over the right half of it, the rectangle covers part of the oval. If you want the entire oval to show, covering part of the rectangle, either send the rectangle to the back or bring the oval to the front.

If you're working with more than two layers, use the Bring Forward and Send Backward buttons to move the selected objects one layer at a time.

In Word, you can send objects behind or in front of the text layer. Use Send behind Text to create a single page watermark. (Place the watermark in a header or footer to have it appear on every page of a document.)

ORDERING OBJECTS

1. Select the object that you want to bring forward or move back.

2. Choose Bring to Front, Send to Back, Bring Forward, or Send Backward to switch the position of one graphic relative to another.

3. In Word, choose Draw ➤ Order from the Drawing toolbar, then click the Bring in Front of Text or Send behind Text button on the Drawing toolbar to position text in relation to a graphic.

You can adjust individual objects in a drawing using the Nudge, Align and Distribute, and Rotate or Flip options on the Draw menu. If you're doing detailed work, consider turning on a grid (choose Draw ➤ Grid) to help you properly align various objects in the drawing.

Grouping and Ungrouping Objects

When your drawing is complete, you can *group* all the drawing objects so that they are treated as a single object.

Select all the objects, then choose Draw ➤ Group from the Drawing toolbar. The handles on the multiple selected objects will be replaced with one set of handles that can be used to size or move the entire object.

If an object contains more than one element, you can *ungroup* it into separate objects, each of which can be individually moved, sized, formatted, or deleted. This is the easiest way to format clip art images. Ungroup the image, then change fills and line colors, or delete portions of the image. When you have finished editing, select all the objects and group them again so you can move or size the entire image.

TIP TIP TIP TIP TIP TIP TIP TIP TIP TIP TIP TIP TIP TIP TIP TIP TIP TIP TIP TIP TIP TIP TIP

Microsoft Graph 2000 helps you create charts from your data without the use of Excel. If you have access to Excel, you can copy and paste a chart into Word. However, if you do not have Excel, you can use Graph to create a wide variety of charts, including pie charts, bar charts, and other specialty charts. To access Microsoft Graph 2000, choose Insert ➤ Picture ➤ Chart.

Hands On

1. In Word, PowerPoint, or Excel:

    a) Use the Drawing tools to draw a simple picture that includes AutoShapes and lines.

    b) Use the formatting tools on the Drawing toolbar to format individual objects in the drawing.

    c) Select and group all the drawing objects.

    d) Create and format WordArt.

2. In Word:

    a) Place an AutoShape.

    b) Apply 3-D effects to the AutoShape.

    c) Use the 3-D Settings toolbar to format the 3-D effects.

3. In PowerPoint:

    a) Insert clip art from the Clip Gallery.

    b) Ungroup the clip.

    c) Move, resize, and recolor individual elements in the clip.

    d) Regroup the changed clip.

4. In Excel, use the arrow and text box tools to point out and annotate important features in a chart or worksheet.

Are You Experienced?

Now you can...

- ☑ Link and embed objects in Office documents
- ☑ Insert and modify clips and pictures
- ☑ Use the Drawing tools to create illustrations
- ☑ Create WordArt

Internet Publishing with Office 2000

- ➔ Creating HTML in Word
- ➔ Saving PowerPoint presentations for the Internet
- ➔ Saving Excel spreadsheets as HTML documents
- ➔ Creating Outlook calendars for the Web
- ➔ Using Publisher to create Web pages
- ➔ Creating Data Access Pages with Access

Office 95 and even Office 97 used a *document-centric* approach to working with files, focusing in on cross-application compatibility between all the different types of Office files. The *Web-centric* approach dominates Office 2000 in much the same way, but with an eye towards doing business on the Internet. Every application can export files for immediate use in e-mail, on the Web, and on the Internet. In this skill, you'll learn how to create Web-ready documents in Word, Power-Point, Excel, Outlook, Access, and Publisher.

12.1: Creating Word Documents As HTML

In Office 97, you could create a Word document and save it as an *HTML* (Hypertext Markup Language) document for publication on the Web, but the results were marginal at best. In Office 2000, HTML is a companion format and as a result, you can use Word to create Web pages that are fully HTML compliant. With a number of additional Web tools at your disposal, Word could very well become your Web page design tool of choice.

Using Word's Web Tools

To begin a Word document for the Web from scratch, choose File ➤ New and select Web Page from the New dialog box. You now have access to all of Word's editing and formatting features to help you create your Web page. In addition, you can add themes that consist of backgrounds, colors, fonts, and navigational buttons. Choose Format ➤ Theme to add a theme to a page.

Frames pages are another useful feature available in Word 2000. Frames allow you to display more than one page at a time. They are typically used to provide a stable navigational page while users move around the other pages of a Web site. To add frames to your pages, choose Format ➤ Frames and choose either Tables of Contents in Frame or New Frames Page. Table of Contents pages look for text formatted as Heading styles and use these to provide navigational links for your users to other pages.

Creating Hyperlinks in Word

Hyperlinks are links to another location in the current document, a file, or a page on the World Wide Web. When users click on a hyperlink, they are transported to the source for the link. To create a hyperlink in Word, begin by selecting text that will lead to the link: for example, Click Here to Visit Our Internet Site.

With the text selected, choose Insert ➤ Hyperlink, or click the Insert Hyperlink button on the Standard toolbar to open the Insert Hyperlink dialog box.

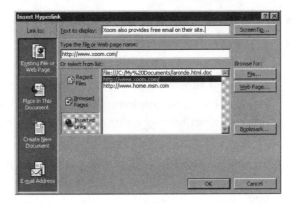

For links to files, enter the full path to the file or select something from the three lists of recent links, accessed by the Recent Files, Browsed Pages, or Inserted Links buttons. Similarly, click the Browse for File button if you need to find the file or check the path information—choose a file, Web page, or bookmark. After you've entered the filename and path, click OK.

For links to Web pages, enter the *URL* (Uniform Resource Locator), or click the Browse for Web Page button to open the Link to File dialog box. To find the URL for a Web page, click the Search the Web button on the Web toolbar. Word will launch your default browser, and you'll be prompted to establish an Internet connection. After you connect, use your browser to go to the site you want to link. Click back on the Word document in the Windows Taskbar and the site address appears in the Web Page Name text box. When you close the hyperlink dialog box, the selected text in your Word document will be underlined and the font will be blue to indicate a hyperlink.

To test the hyperlink, point to the hyperlink text. The mouse pointer will change to a pointing finger; click to activate the hyperlink. If the link is to a file on a local or network drive, the file's application will launch and the file will be displayed. If the link is to an Internet site, your default browser will launch, and you'll be prompted to connect to the Internet. After connection, the linked page will appear in the browser. When you close the browser, you'll return to the hyperlinked text in Word. The hyperlink will be displayed in a different color, to show that you've already used the link.

CREATING A HYPERLINK TO A WEB PAGE OR FILE

1. Enter and select text that will serve as the hyperlink.

2. Choose Insert ≻ Hyperlink or click the Insert Hyperlink button on the Standard toolbar to open the Insert Hyperlink dialog box.

3. Choose a file, Web page, bookmark, or other existing document for the link by using the Insert Hyperlink dialog box options. After entering or selecting the filename and path, click OK to establish the link.

–OR–

3. To link to a page on the Web, enter the URL for the file. To locate the page, click the Browse for Web Page button, then click the Search the Web button to open the Link to File dialog box. Your default browser will load and open a search engine at http://www.microsoft.com.

4. Use the search engine, Favorites list, bookmarks, or another search engine to go to the Web page you wish to link to.

5. Switch back to Word.

6. Click OK to create the link.

Creating Web Forms

When you create a Web page, two additional toolbars, Web and Web Tools, will open with your new document. These toolbars contain Web-related features and shortcuts you'll need to help you create your Web pages. The Web toolbar is the same toolbar displayed in Internet Explorer to help you navigate through the Web.

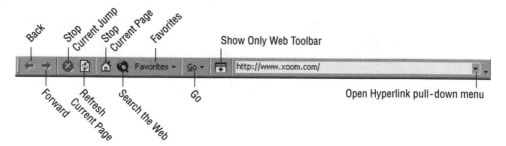

The Web Tools toolbar contains fast links to advanced features like the Script Editor, along with shortcuts for inserting form controls, movies, sounds, and other non-text items:

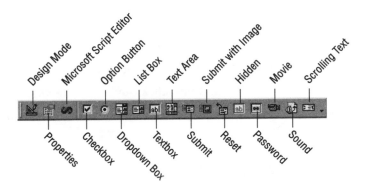

Click the Design mode button on the Web Tools toolbar to create a Web form and add form controls such as check boxes, option buttons, and drop-down, list, and text boxes. When you click a form control button and then click to insert that control on your page, Word automatically places Top of Form and Bottom of Form markers on your page.

Right-click on a form control and choose Properties to enter values and set other properties for the control. Choose View Code from the shortcut menu to review the HTML code for the page. You can also add multimedia elements such as sound and video by clicking the toolbar button and identifying the location of the appropriate file. When you have finished entering text and placing controls in the form, click the Design Mode button to exit Design Mode.

Saving a Web Page in Word

When you save a Word document as a Web page, Word automatically creates the files and folders you need to house frames pages, graphics, and other files to support the Web page. To make it easier to locate all of the associated files, it's helpful to create a folder first in which to save the Web document. You can choose to save your Web page to a Web folder, to an FTP site for transfer to the Web, or to a local or network drive for Web publication at a later date. Check with your Web administrator or your ISP to see which method you should use to publish your Web pages.

SAVING A WEB PAGE IN WORD

1. Choose File ➢ Save As Web Page.
2. Open the folder (or create a new folder) where you want to save your Web page.
3. Enter a title for the Web page, if desired.
4. Enter a filename and click Save.

Browsing through Files

To preview a Web page in your default browser, choose File ➢ Web Page Preview. Use the Web toolbar in Word, or in any Office program, to browse documents that contain hyperlinks or linked pages on the Web. Choose View ➢ Toolbars ➢ Web to open the toolbar. After you've activated a hyperlink, use the Web toolbar's Back button to return to the hyperlink.

The toolbar keeps a history of the last 10 documents or pages accessed with hyperlinks or the toolbar. To return to one of these documents or pages, click the drop-down history list and select the document or URL, as shown in Figure 12.1. To connect to your standard start page on the Internet, click the Search the Web button.

FIGURE 12.1: Browsing a document in Word

Hands On

1. In a new or existing Word document:

    a) Add a hyperlink to a Web page to the document.

    b) Test the hyperlink.

c) Open the Web and Web Tools toolbars.

    d) Switch to Design view and create a simple Web form using two types of form controls. Edit the values using the Form Control properties (right-click and choose Properties).

    e) View the form in your browser.

    f) Save the document a Web page with a new title.

12.2: Saving PowerPoint Presentations for the Internet

PowerPoint presentations are seeing increased use on the Internet. PowerPoint 2000 includes tools to help you package your presentation by creating multiple linked pages for Internet use. If you know that you'll be publishing a presentation on the Internet or an intranet, select the Web Presentation option in the Presentation Style step of the AutoContent Wizard.

If the presentation has already been created, make sure it's saved, and then choose File ➢ Save As Web Page. Change the filename if you wish, and then click Publish to open the Publish As Web Page dialog box, shown in Figure 12.2.

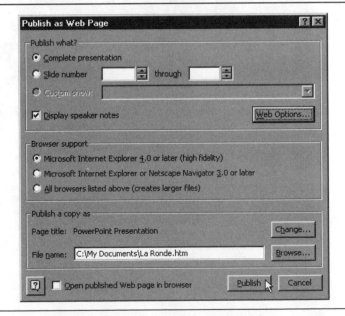

FIGURE 12.2: The Publish As Web Page dialog box

Use the options at the top of the dialog box to determine which slides you want to include; set Browser Support options in the middle section. (Unless you're publishing to a company intranet where you know everyone will be using the same browser, select All Browsers Listed Above.) The Web Options button is for advanced features such as enabling PNG support and target monitor size, and it's also where you set general options such as how the Web navigation controls appear.

Customize the page title using the Change button if you want the Web page title to differ from the PowerPoint document title. Finally, when you are finished, check Open Published Page in Web Browser if you want to see the final results, and then click Publish. PowerPoint will convert the presentation to Web pages and open it in your default browser.

To make changes to the presentation, return to PowerPoint. To preview the changes, choose File ➢ Web Page Preview.

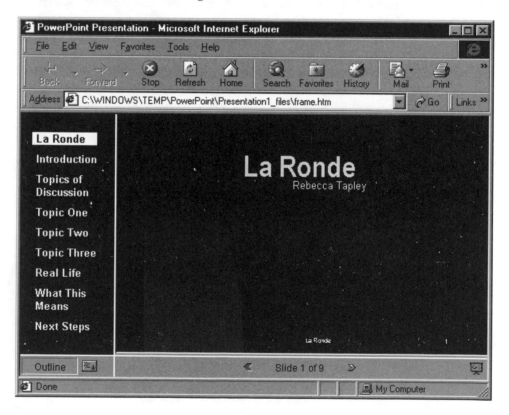

SAVING A PRESENTATION FOR THE INTERNET

1. Choose File ➤ Save As Web Page from the menu bar.
2. Enter a filename and location for the presentation.
3. To change the name of the title page, click Change Title.
4. Click Publish to choose which slides to print, establish browser support, and customize the Web page title. Check the Open Published Page in Web Browser box to preview the Web page and click Publish.

 You can distinguish the Web version of your presentation from the regular PowerPoint version by the Web icon that appears in the Open dialog box. To make changes to the Web presentation in PowerPoint, simply double-click or select this icon in the Open dialog box as you would the PowerPoint version. Make any edits or changes as necessary and resave.

Hands On

1. Open an existing presentation. Save the presentation as a Web page. Set the Publishing and Web options. View the presentation in your default browser.

2. Make changes to the presentation. Preview the changes in the browser. Save the presentation again.

12.3: Saving Excel Worksheets As Web Documents

Excel 2000 also includes a streamlined Web publishing process. To save ranges or charts in the open workbook to HTML, choose File ➤ Save As Web Page to launch the Save As dialog box. From this point forward, the process is very similar to the one for Word (see Skill 12.1)—Figure 12.3 shows Excel's Save As dialog box with the Web publishing features displayed.

FIGURE 12.3: The Save As dialog box in Excel

When you click Publish to publish an Excel document as a Web page, you are presented with slightly different options:

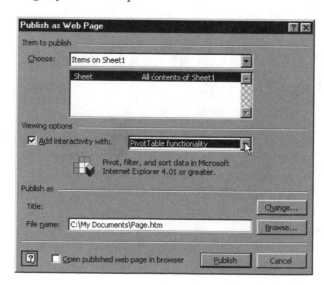

Excel lets you add an interactive Office Web Component to a Web page—just check the Add Interactivity option. This lets Office 2000 users sort and filter or rearrange the published data with their Web browser. There are three different components to create interactive PivotTable reports, charts, and worksheets. None of the changes a user makes is saved to the original worksheet; however, users can export the changes back to an Excel worksheet (click the Export to Excel button on the component's toolbar).

SKILL
12

Check the Open Published Page in Web Browser option to look at the book or sheet and click Publish to create the page.

SAVING EXCEL DATA AS HTML

1. Choose File ➤ Save As Web Page to open Excel's Save As dialog box. Click Publish.

2. In the Publish As Web Page dialog box, add interactivity and decide on other options, and then click Publish.

3. Choose File ➤ Web Page Preview to view the book or page in the default browser.

Hands On

1. Open an existing worksheet. Save it as a Web page with interactive spread-sheet functionality. View the page in your browser.

2. Open a workbook that contains an Excel PivotTable report. Publish the worksheet with PivotTable functionality. View the page in your browser.

3. Publish either workbook without interactivity. View the page in your browser.

12.4: Publishing Outlook Information on the Web

Outlook is the ideal way to schedule, plan, and coordinate events for one or more people. In the 2000 release, you can also save and upload Outlook information to the Web for wider circulation. To publish your calendar, open the Calendar and choose File ➤ Save As Web Page, and establish your preferences in the Save As Web Page dialog box.

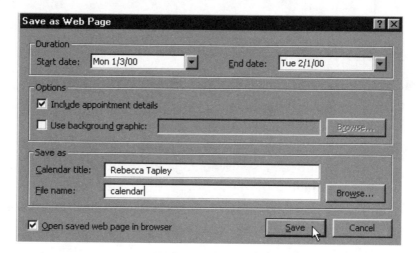

Choose the range of pages from your calendar to include in the Web page by selecting starting and ending dates. You can choose whether to include appointment book details and a background graphic if you want to add a special look. You can enter a title for the calendar and you must identify a location to save the file—if you have access to Web folders, you'll probably want to save it there for immediate publication. By default, the option in the lower left corner is checked—this shows you a preview of your calendar page in Internet Explorer 5. Click Save, and Explorer launches to show your preview.

SAVING CALENDAR INFORMATION AS A WEB PAGE

1. Choose File ➢ Save As Web Page to open Outlook's Save As Web Page dialog box.

2. Select a range of calendar pages by setting starting and ending dates. Include appointment details if you want. Give the calendar a title and filename.

3. Check the option in the lower left corner to preview the calendar Web page in Internet Explorer 5 and click Save. The browser will open and show you how your calendar will look on the Web.

SKILL
12

Hands On

1. Open an existing calendar. Save a range of three or four pages as a Web publication and preview it in Internet Explorer 5.

12.5: Creating Web Pages with Publisher

Publisher 2000 is unlike PowerPoint and Excel because it does have a Web Publishing Wizard to help you create Web pages and entire Web sites. The easiest way to work with a Wizard in Publisher is to turn on the Step through Wizard Questions option (choose Tools ➢ Options ➢ User Assistance), and then create a new doucment from a Wizard (if you are greeted with a catalog at startup, click Exit Catalog to change the User Assistance options). To create a Web site, select Web Sites in the left column on the Publications by Wizard page of the New dialog box (shown in Figure 12.4) and click Start Wizard. The Wizard appears in a frame on the left side of the Publisher window. Read the Introduction page and click Next to get started.

The First stop is Color Scheme. Publisher offers you many preset palettes to choose from; click one and preview it in the window on the right. If you prefer a custom palette you design yourself, choose Custom at the top of the list. Click Next when you've decided.

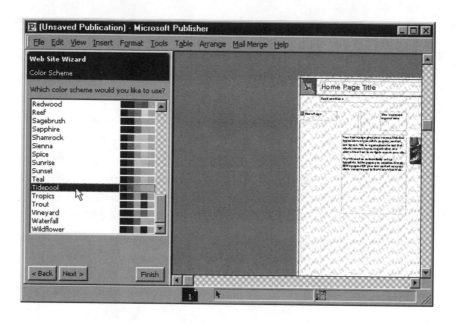

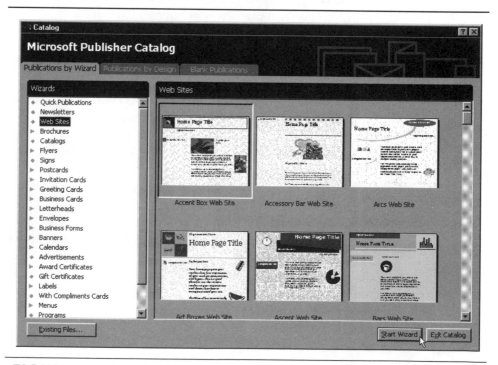

FIGURE 12.4: Launching the Web Page Wizard in Publisher

The Additional Pages page lets you choose more Web pages to round out your Web site. When you choose an additional page from the preset list, Publisher updates your view and displays the default for that page in the right window. Click Next to continue.

The Forms page lets you select one or more forms to add to your Web pages, for responses, placing orders, or other functions. Check the form you want to add, and Publisher tells you which page contains the form you chose.

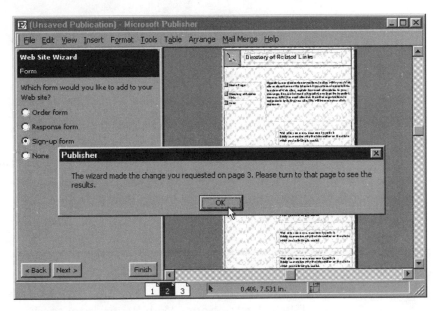

Click OK and then Next to continue.

You can select a vertical and horizontal navigation bar, or just a vertical navigation bar, on the Navigation Bar page—and then whether or not to put a texture in the background on the Texture page. Keep in mind that you can use the Back button to revise your changes at any time.

Click Next to continue, and then Finish. Publisher asks if you want to save your changes; click Yes and the regular Publisher desktop will open.

You can also add some advanced features to your Web page by choosing File ➤ Web Properties. The Web Properties dialog box lets you add searchable keywords to describe your Web site to search engines, so people looking for information on the Web will have a better chance of locating your site.

Also, click the Page tab to specify the file extension your ISP requires, add a background sound file (*Loop* refers to the number of times you want it to play before it stops), and decide whether or not you want to add a hyperlink to this page on your Standard toolbar.

CREATING A WEB PAGE IN PUBLISHER WITH THE WEB PAGE WIZARD

1. Click File ≻ New, choose Web Pages from the Wizard list and click Start Wizard.

2. Choose a color scheme or click Custom if you're going to build your own palette, and click Next.

3. Choose any additional pages for the Web site on Additional Pages. Click Next to continue.

4. Add a response, ordering, or other kind of form on the Forms page. Click Next.

5. Choose your navigation bar scheme on the Navigation Bar page. Click Next.

continued ▶

6. Decide whether or not you want a texture on the background of your pages and click Finish to exit the Wizard. Save your changes.

7   Add advanced user options by choosing File ➤ Web Properties. Click OK to apply them.

Hands On

1. Create a Web page using an existing color palette, a directory page, an ordering form, both a vertical and a horizontal navigation bar, a background sound, and a background texture using the Wizard.

12.6: Viewing Access Pages on the Web

In Skill 8.7, you learned how to share snapshots of Access reports with others. Data Access Pages bring your information to life and allow your information to be edited as well as viewed over the Internet!

Understanding Data Access Pages

Access provides four ways to create Data Access Pages: AutoPages, the Page Wizard, editing an existing Web page, and Design view. Many of the techniques are the same as or similar to those used in the creation of standard Access forms. To review what forms are and how they are created, refer to Skills 8.2 and 8.6.

WARNING WARNING WARNING WARNING WARNING WARNING WARNING WARNING

Data Access Pages will only work with Internet Explorer 5, so if your target audience uses a different browser, they are out of luck. Also, anyone viewing Data Access Pages should own Office 2000. If you don't know about the software on your users' machines, consider using report snapshots instead—Microsoft distributes the Snapshot Viewer software for free!

Creating AutoPages

To create an AutoPage, click the Pages button on the left-hand navigation bar of the database window, and then click the New button to open the New Data Access Page dialog box.

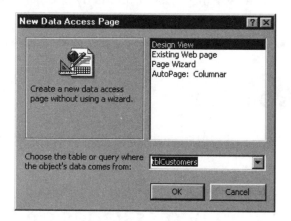

Select the AutoPage: Columnar type, then select the table to base the page on from the list. When you click OK, Access creates and displays your new Data Access Page.

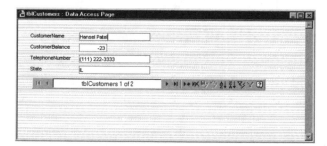

Like the columnar AutoForm, this page displays records one at a time. Users move back and forth through your data using the navigation bar. However, if your users need to view or edit more than one record at a time, you should use one of the other page creation options.

CREATING AUTOPAGES

1. Click the Pages button on the left-hand navigation bar of the database window, then click the New button to open the New Data Access Page dialog box.
2. Choose AutoPage: Columnar from the list.
3. Select a table from the drop-down list.
4. Click OK to create the AutoPage.

Using the Page Wizard

The Page Wizard lets you choose the fields you want on the page— including fields from more than one table—and designate how the data should be grouped, sorted, and formatted. To start the Page Wizard, click the Pages button on the left-hand navigation bar of the database window, and then click the New button to open the New Data Access Page dialog box. Choose Page Wizard and click OK to start the Wizard. You don't have to choose a table at this point—you'll have a chance to do that in the first step of the Wizard. In the Wizard, you select, group, and sort the fields on the page, and possibly apply a theme. When you click Finish, Access creates the Data Access Page and opens it in Page view.

Themes

Themes are combinations of graphics, formats, and color settings for all the parts of your Data Access Pages. All of the themes' constituent pieces are coordinated, so you only need to decide which theme gives your page the appropriate look and feel.

If you choose to apply a theme in the last step of the Wizard, a Theme dialog box opens when the Wizard closes. You can change themes any time from Design view by choosing Format ➤ Theme.

CREATING DATA ACCESS PAGES WITH THE PAGE WIZARD

1. Click the Pages button on the left-hand navigation bar of the database window, and then click the New button to open the New Data Access Page dialog box.

2. Choose Page Wizard from the list and click OK to start the Wizard.

3. Choose the table or query on which to base the report. Click the right arrow to move individual fields to the Selected Fields box, or the double arrow to move all the fields. When you have selected all the fields you want from the first table/query, select the next object from the list, if desired.

4. Click Next when you have finished selecting fields.

5. Choose the levels you want to group by, if any. Use the Priority buttons to reverse the order of the grouping levels. Click Next.

continued ▶

6.   Choose the fields you would like to sort by, and indicate whether you'd like the records in ascending or descending order. Click Next.
7.   Enter a title for the page, choose whether you'd like to open the page in Page view or Design view, and choose whether or not you'd like to apply a theme. Click Finish.
8.   If you chose to apply a theme, choose the mix of graphics that you like, then click OK.

Entering and Editing in Data Access Pages

Working with data on pages is quite similar to working with columnar AutoForms. You should still drag to select all the text in a field before entering new data. Use the navigation buttons to move between existing records and the Delete Record button to delete the selected record.

Printing Data Access Pages

Access allows you to print Data Access Pages just as you see them on the screen. However, you should be aware of a few things. If you click on the Print toolbar button, you will print a page for every record in your database: one hundred records will print one hundred pages. Be sure to set the Selected Record(s) option in the Print dialog box if you want to limit the records printed to a specific range.

Sorting Records

It is very easy to sort records while entering, editing, or viewing data in a Data Access Page.

SORTING RECORDS

1.   Position the cursor in the field by which you want to sort.
2.   Click either of the Sort buttons on the toolbar to rearrange the data based upon the order of the selected field.

Filtering Records

Applying a filter to a Data Access Page temporarily hides records that don't match the text or value currently in the field you have selected. Filtering in Access pages works almost exactly like Filtering by Selection in Access forms. For more information about using this feature, refer to Skill 8.2.

WARNING WARNING WARNING WARNING WARNING WARNING WARNING WARNING

Unlike Access forms, a filter in a Data Access Page does not match based upon only part of a field. Even if you only select part of the data in a field, the filter is applied based upon the entire value.

Creating from an Existing Web Page

The possibilities for Web page design are seemingly limitless when you use a good high-end Web page editor like FrontPage 2000. A good way to get great-looking Data Access Pages, then, would be to start off creating pages in one of these editors. Once you have everything looking the way that you like, you can then import your work into Access and add whatever data you deem appropriate.

To open an existing page in Access, select Pages in the Database window, and then click the New button. Choose Existing Web Page in the New Data Access Page dialog box. Select the HTML file you would like to work with and click Open.

CREATING DATA ACCESS PAGES FROM AN EXISTING WEB PAGE

1. Select Pages in the Database window and then click the New button to open the New Data Access Page dialog box.
2. Choose Existing Web Page.
3. Select the file containing the Web page that you would like to work with and click Open.

Modifying Data Access Page Design

Often, the results produced by AutoPage and the Page Wizard will not be suffi-
cient for your needs. Access offers a Design view for Data Access Pages just as it
does for tables, queries, forms, and reports. If you open one of your pages in
Design view, it should look approximately like this:

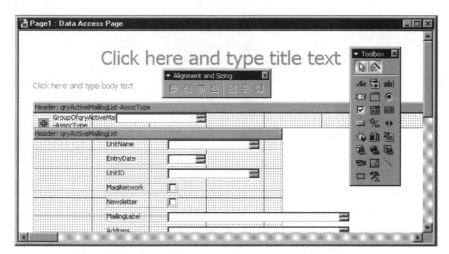

Notice that the contents of the Toolbox are significantly different from what you
have seen up to this point. The Formatting toolbar, on the other hand, should appear
reassuringly familiar.

Working with Data

You add data fields to pages in approximately the same way that you add them
to forms—via the Field List.

This field list looks more complicated than the one that you're used to, but it really isn't that different once you understand what you're looking at. The Database tab at the top contains a list of all the fields that are available for your use. The Page tab shows all the fields that you're actually using. The clear hierarchy shows you not only what fields are available and in use, but also where they are coming from. By drilling down into this structure, you can find out whether you are pulling information from a table or a query. In the case of a table on the Database tab, you can even find out the names of all its related tables. To use any of these on your Data Access Page, simply drag them from the Database tab onto the desired location.

If the table containing the field(s) you are adding has no existing relationships with any of the tables that the page is based upon, you will see the New Relationship dialog box. Simply choose the fields in the drop-down lists on the left (which represent the table being added) that are related to the fields you choose on the right (which represent the existing table). You can choose to build a relationship with a different table on the page by clicking the drop-down list at the top of the dialog box.

New Relationship

Choose a table to relate 'tblOrders' to: | tblCustomers |

How do you want to relate 'tblOrders' to this table?

This field in 'tblOrders'...   Relates to this field in 'tblCustomers'.

| TelephoneNumber | ⇨ | TelephoneNumber |

| | ⇨ | |

| | ⇨ | |

| | ⇨ | |

⊙ Many records in 'tblOrders' match one record in 'tblCustomers'.

○ One record in 'tblOrders' matches many records in 'tblCustomers'.

| OK | | Cancel |

Working with Text

Adding a title to your Data Access Page is extremely easy. You will notice a text box containing the words, "Click here and type title text." To add a title, simply click on it and type the text of your title. To add additional text to your page, click the text box marked, "Click here and type body text" and then type your additional text.

Formatting Text   Formatting text on Data Access Pages is very similar to formatting text on standard Access forms and reports. The chief difference is in the way that pages align text. Text alignment on Data Access Pages is done from the Alignment and Sizing toolbar, which can be made visible by choosing Format ➢ Alignment and Sizing.

Standard HTML doesn't offer the absolute positioning needed to support the kinds of alignment that you are used to working with in forms and reports. If the first Align button you click doesn't produce exactly the effect that you were expecting, don't be alarmed. Simply reposition your control accordingly and try again.

Grouping and Sorting

In order to make your Data Access Pages as easy to comprehend as possible, it is important that you look for every opportunity to logically group the data that they contain. Besides this, sorting the data on your pages is the next best way to increase the speed with which users can find the information for which they are looking.

Grouping   Data Access Pages support four kinds of sections that you can use to group your records together:

> **Caption**   Used mainly to hold text boxes describing the contents of the columns of data in the sections below. When used, this is visible above the group header when its next-higher group level is expanded.
>
> **Group header**   This is the main focus of your pages. The lowest level group header acts like the detail section of a report, so you must have at least one in order to show your records, even if you aren't doing any grouping!
>
> **Group footer**   If you have at least two group headers on your page (meaning that you have at least one level of grouping), you can use this section to present calculated totals. When used, this is visible above the navigation bar.
>
> **Navigation bar**   Used to navigate through the records at a given level of grouping.

To go about actually using these sections to group your data, simply select the control(s) upon which you would like to base a level of grouping. Click the Promote button on the main toolbar and Access will create a group header and navigation bar for you. Repeat the process until you have created as many levels of grouping as you desire.

If you'd like to add a caption or footer to any of your groups, click the Sorting and Grouping button to open this dialog box:

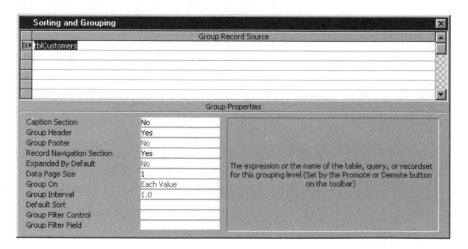

After you select the appropriate grouping level at the top of the Sorting and Grouping dialog, you can give yourself a caption section by changing the Caption Section property to Yes. To give yourself a footer section, change the Group Footer property to Yes.

Sorting   To change the default sort order for a group, enter the name(s) of the fields that you would like to sort by in the Default Sort property. If there is more than one, separate them with commas. If you would like any of the columns to sort in descending (rather than ascending) order, simply follow the name of the field with the letters DESC. For instance:

```
FirstName, LastName DESC, Telephone
```

would sort a group of your data by ascending telephones within descending last names within ascending first names.

GROUPING AND SORTING

1.   Open the page in Design view.
2.   Select the control(s) upon which you wish to group your data.
3.   Click the Promote button on the Standard toolbar.
4.   Click the Sorting and Grouping button on the Sorting and Grouping toolbar.
5.   Select the appropriate grouping level at the top of the Sorting and Grouping dialog box.
6.   If you'd like a caption, change the Caption Section property to Yes.
7.   If you'd like a footer, change the Group Footer property to Yes.
8.   Enter the name(s) of any field(s) you would like to sort by in the Default Sort property.

Calculating Totals

Data Access Pages allow you to present calculated totals at the single-record, group, and grand levels. These totals are typically displayed in group footer sections.

Calculating Single-Record Totals   To calculate totals for a single record, begin by opening your page in Design view. From the Toolbox, drag and drop a Bound HTML control wherever you would like to see a calculated total on your page.

Open the Bound HTML control's properties and find the ControlSource property. Enter an alias and a valid expression in this property to get the calculation you would like. For example:

```
AverageSickDays: (DaysSick / DaysInThisMonth)
```

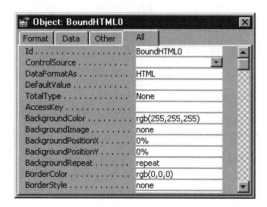

Calculating Group Totals   To provide totals calculations for an entire group of data, use the Bound HTML control's TotalType property. You should recognize the options in the drop-down list here from your previous experience creating summary queries. If you can't remember exactly how these work, please refer back to Skill 8.8.

CALCULATING TOTALS

1. Open the page in Design view.
2. Add a Bound HTML control for each total you would like to calculate.
3. Set each Bound HTML control's ControlSource property to an alias and an appropriate expression.
4. If you are totaling a group, select the appropriate aggregate function in the Bound HTML control's TotalType property.

Calculating Grand Totals   A total that is calculated for a single field on a page-level basis is referred to as a grand total. You can calculate a grand total much as you would calculate a total for any other group on your page.

First, add a Bound HTML control to your page and set its ControlSource property equal to an alias and the name of the control containing the data for which you would like to calculate a total. Then, with the Bound HTML control still selected, click the Promote button on the Standard toolbar and select the appropriate aggregate function in the TotalType property.

CALCULATING GRAND TOTALS

1. Open the page in Design view.
2. Add a Bound HTML control wherever you would like the grand total to appear on the page.
3. Set the Bound HTML control's ControlSource property to an alias and the name of the control containing the data for which you would like to calculate a total.
4. With the Bound HTML control still selected, click the Promote button on the main toolbar.
5. Select the appropriate aggregate function in the TotalType property.

Viewing Data Access Pages

Data Access Pages represent a new and exciting way to interact with your data even within the confines of Access 2000. When you put these pages on the Internet or your corporate intranet, however, they really begin to realize their full potential. As you are designing your pages, you should be constantly checking to ensure that they look and operate as you would expect when viewed in Internet Explorer.

Viewing Your Pages Locally

Access provides a convenient way for you to quickly switch between viewing your pages in Design view and examining them in your Web browser. Simply open your page in Design view and, to see what it looks like in Internet Explorer, choose File ➢ Web Page Preview from the menu bar.

Any changes you make to the design of your page after this point will not be automatically transferred to the page in your Web browser. So, if you want to see your edits in Internet Explorer, you'll have to close it for a moment and repeat the steps outlined above.

VIEWING YOUR PAGES LOCALLY

1. Open your page in Design view.
2. Choose File ➢ Web Page Preview.

Putting Your Pages on the Web

When your Data Access Pages are ready to be published to the Web, talk with your Web Administrator to determine the best method for transferring the files to a Web server. It may be as simple as saving them to a designated web folder, or you may have to use FTP to transfer the files. Your Web Administrator can help you do this.

Hands On

1. Create a Data Access Page using AutoPage.

2. Create a Data Access Page using the Page Wizard.

3. Create a Data Access Page from an existing Web page.

4. Modify the page in Exercise 1 to:

    a) Sort its records in reverse

    b) Group its records differently

    c) Calculate totals at the record, group, and grand level

Are You Experienced?

Now you can...

☑ **Save Word documents as HTML**

☑ **Add hyperlinks to documents or Web pages**

☑ **Save and display PowerPoint presentations in an Internet browser**

☑ **Save Excel spreadsheets as HTML documents**

☑ **Publish pages of your Outlook calendar on the Web**

☑ **Use Publisher's Wizard to create a multi-page Web site**

☑ **Create and view Data Access Pages on the Web**

Creating and Using Macros in Office 2000

→ Creating macros

→ Running macros

→ Viewing and editing macros

→ Customizing command bars

A *macro* is a set of instructions that a program executes on command. The instructions can be simple keystrokes or complex menu selections. If you have tasks you regularly complete that include the same series of steps, creating a macro to automate the task saves time and effort. If you're creating documents for others, adding a few macros can make the documents more user-friendly. In this skill, you'll learn how to create and use macros in Word, PowerPoint, and Excel.

13.1 Recording a Simple Macro

Most macros complete repetitive tasks that involve several steps. You record (create) the series of steps you want to repeat. The next time you need to carry out the operation, you can run (play back) the macro to repeat the steps. Before recording a macro, you should practice the steps you want to record, because once you begin recording, all your actions are recorded, mistakes included. Then determine what conditions your macro will operate under and set up those conditions. Will you always use the macro in a specific document? If so, open the document. Will the macro be used to change or format selected text or numbers? Then have the text or numbers selected before you begin recording the macro, just as you will when you play the macro back at a later time.

When you have practiced the steps and set up the same conditions the macro will run under, select Tools ➢ Macro ➢ Record New Macro to open the Record New Macro dialog box. The Excel Record Macro dialog box is shown in Figure 13.1.

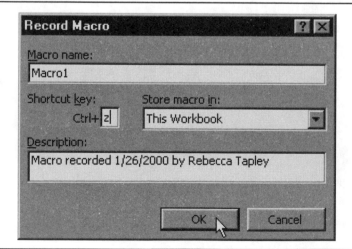

FIGURE 13.1: The Excel Record Macro dialog box

The suggested name is Macro1. (Microsoft didn't waste a lot of imagination here.) Enter a more descriptive name for the macro like PrintFigures. Macro names can be up to 255 characters long; can contain numbers, letters, and underscores (but not spaces or other punctuation); and must begin with a letter. Enter a new description. If other users will have access to the macro, include your name for reference. The Record Macro dialog box from Word is shown in Figure 13.2.

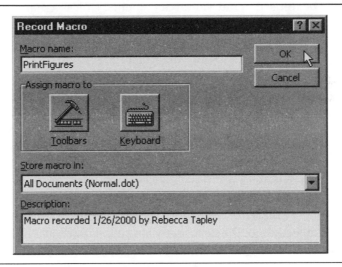

FIGURE 13.2: The Word Record Macro dialog box

Storing a Macro

In the Store Macro In drop-down, select which document you want the macro stored in. PowerPoint macros are stored with the presentation. In Word and Excel, a macro's storage location determines how you'll be able to access it on playback:

- If you select the current document, then the macro will only be available in the current document. If you want the same macro somewhere else, you'll have to copy or recreate it. In Excel, you can also store the macro in a new workbook then add other functionality to the workbook. Macros that are stored in a document are *local macros*.

- Storing a macro in `Normal.dot`, the default template, or the Personal Macro workbook in Excel creates a *global macro*, available to all documents created in the program.

From the description, you'd think that you should save every macro as a global macro, but all the global macros will be loaded each time you launch Excel or Word. They'll take up space in memory, and any macro names you use here can't be re-used in individual documents. Unless a macro is going to receive wide usage, it's best to store it in the current document.

In Excel, you can assign a shortcut keystroke combination to macros, and Word lets you assign a shortcut or place the macro on the toolbar. While you can assign macros to shortcut keys, you should use extreme caution when making assignments. Most of the Ctrl+ combinations and many of the Ctrl+Shift combinations are already in use. It's safer to assign frequently used macros to a toolbar. You don't have to make this decision when you record the macro; you can always add a macro to a toolbar later (see "Adding Macros to a Toolbar").

Once you've set the options in the dialog box, click the OK button to begin macro recording. The message "Recording" is displayed at the left end of the status bar to show that you are recording a macro.

The Stop Recording toolbar opens. The macro recorder records the actions you take, but not the delay between actions, so take your time. If you want the macro to enter text, enter the text now. Type carefully—if you make and correct a mistake, the mistake and correction will be included when you replay the macro until you edit the mistake (see "Editing Macros"). Make menu selections as you normally would to include them in the macro.

When you are finished entering all the steps in the macro, click the Stop button on the Stop Recording toolbar. The toolbar will close automatically. You don't need to save the macro now. Local macros are saved when you save the document. Excel saves global macros automatically.

Word prompts you to save changes to `Normal.dot` when you end your Word session if the Prompt to Save Normal Template option (choose Tools ➤ Options ➤ Save) is enabled. If the option is not enabled, global macros are saved automatically.

Formatting Options in Macros

If you want to format text in a macro, choose the formatting options from a formatting dialog box rather than choosing the font, font style, size, and alignment by clicking toolbar buttons. If you use the buttons, the playback results will be unpredictable because the toolbar buttons are toggle buttons. If, for example, selected text is already italicized, clicking the Italics button will turn Italics off. Whenever possible, don't use format toggle buttons in macros unless you can guarantee that the text you select when you play back will be formatted exactly as the text was when you recorded the macro.

Excel Cell References in Macros

All macro cell references are absolute by default. If you click in a cell during macro recording, the macro will select that exact cell each time you play it back. This wouldn't be terribly useful. For example, you might want to format cells, and then move to the cell below the selection. When you record the macro, the cell below the selection is J22. But each time you play the macro, you don't want Excel to select J22; you want to select the cell below the cells you just formatted.

To instruct Excel to use relative cell references, click the Use Relative References button on the Macro toolbar. The macro will record references relative to the current cell until you click the button again to turn relative references off. Then you can record other actions using absolute references.

CREATING A MACRO

1. Create the same conditions that will be in effect when you play the macro.
2. Choose Tools ➣ Record Macro ➣ Record New Macro to open the Record Macro dialog box.
3. Enter a Macro Name and Description.
4. Choose a storage location from the drop-down list.
5. Click OK to begin recording the macro.
6. Perform the steps that you want included in the macro. If you want to include relative cell references in Excel, click the Use Relative References button on the Macro toolbar. Click again to turn relative references off if you need to include absolute references.
7. Click the Stop button on the Stop Recording toolbar when you have finished recording the steps of the macro.

Opening a File with Macros

A *macro virus* is a computer virus written as a macro. When you open a document that contains a virus, the virus copies itself into the Normal template. From that point forward, every document you save using the Normal template will be infected, which means that every file you give to someone else on a disk or via the Internet will also contain the virus.

WARNING WARNING WARNING WARNING WARNING WARNING WARNING WARNING

Office 2000 does not include virus detection software (although you should install some unless you *never* receive files from another computer by disk, network, or Internet connection).

Office 2000 Macro Protection   Word, Excel, Outlook, and PowerPoint notify you if any macros exist in a document you are trying to open. (Outlook doesn't have a macro recorder, but you can type macros in the Visual Basic Editor for Outlook.) You can decide whether you want to open the document with macros enabled or to disable them. Disabling the macros gives you an opportunity to look at them in the Visual Basic Editor without endangering your computer. If you decide you want to enable the macros, just close and then reopen the file.

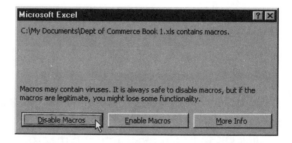

If you know that the document contains macros that you or a co-worker put there, choose Enable. If, on the other hand, you received the workbook, unsolicited, from someone whose Internet name is HackU, you should consider disabling the macros or not opening the file.

Updating Macros from Previous Versions

Some earlier versions of Excel used a macro programming language called XLM. Visual Basic for Applications (VBA) replaced XLM as the programming language beginning with Excel version 5.0. Excel 2000 supports both macro programming languages: if you have workbooks that contain XLM macros, Excel 2000 will let you play them. However, you cannot record XLM macros in Excel 2000. All Excel 2000 macros are recorded in VBA.

Word also had its own macro language in earlier versions called Word Basic. When you open a Word document from a prior version that contains macros, Word 2000 automatically converts the macros.

Running Macros

It's always a good idea to save anything you have open before you run a new macro. If you make a mistake during recording, the playback results may not be what you expected. (If there was an error, you can record the macro again using the same name. You might also have to click Undo a few times to back out of any problems the macro created.) To run a macro, choose Tools ➤ Macro ➤ Macros to open the Macro dialog box, shown in Figure 13.3. Select the macro below the scroll list of macro names in the Macro Name/Reference control, and then click the Run button. The macro will execute one step at a time. You can't enter text or choose menu options while the macro is executing. When the macro is done playing, the application will return control to you.

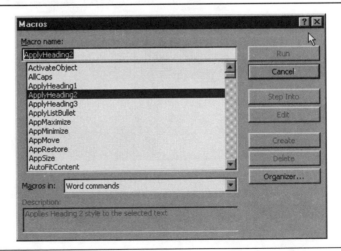

FIGURE 13.3: The Macro dialog box

RUNNING A MACRO

1. Choose Tools ➤ Macro ➤ Macros.
2. Select the macro from list of available macros and click Run.

Examining and Editing Macros

Office 2000 macros are stored in Visual Basic *modules* and edited in the Visual Basic Editor. (Access 2000 is the exception; Access macros are stored as part of the database, but can be converted to Visual Basic and stored in a module.) To examine or edit a macro, choose Tools ➤ Macros ➤ Macros to open the Macros dialog box, select the macro you want to examine, then click the Edit button to open the Visual Basic Editor, shown in Figure 13.4.

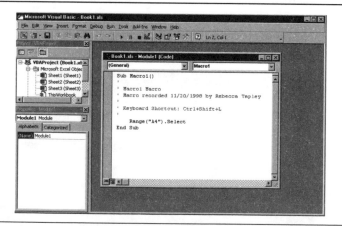

FIGURE 13.4: The Visual Basic Editor

The Visual Basic window may contain a number of windows. In Figure 13.4, a Properties window and a Project window are open on the left and a Code window on the right. You can scroll through the Visual Basic Code window to see the information recorded in a macro. The macro name and description appear at the top of the macro. Programming code follows. If you know VBA programming language, you can create macros and other procedures directly by typing Visual Basic code into a module's Code window. If you want to learn about Visual Basic, recording macros and studying the resulting code is a good way to begin. Even if you don't understand Visual Basic, you can do some simple editing here.

You could edit the Excel macro shown in Figure 13.4 by entering a different cell reference, creating another macro. When you are finished editing a macro, save and close the Visual Basic Window.

SKILL
13

EDITING A MACRO

1. Choose Tools ➢ Macro ➢ Macros to open the Macros dialog box.
2. Select the macro, and click the Edit button.
3. Make the changes you desire.
4. Save the macro and close the Visual Basic window.

Adding Macros to a Toolbar

To add an existing macro to a toolbar, right-click any toolbar and choose Customize or choose View ➢ Toolbars ➢ Customize to open the Customize dialog box. Click the Commands tab to open the Commands page, shown in Figure 13.5.

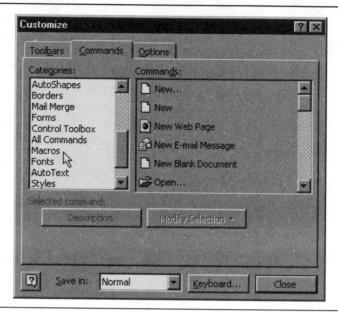

FIGURE 13.5: Customize dialog box

Select Macros from the Categories list. In Word and PowerPoint, the list of available macros appears in the right pane.

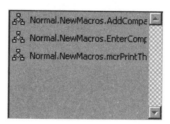

In Excel, two options will appear in the Commands List: Custom Menu Item and Custom Button. If you want to add the macro anywhere on the menu bar, choose Custom Menu Item. If you'd prefer a button (with a picture, text, or both), choose Custom Button.

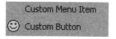

To add a menu item, drag the macro (Custom Menu Item in Excel) from the Command List to the menu bar. If you want to place the custom menu item on an existing drop-down menu, move to the menu, hover a moment, and the menu will open. Drop the menu item where you want it to appear on the menu.

To add a toolbar button, drag the macro (Custom Button in Excel) and drop it on the appropriate toolbar. If you drop it on an existing button, the other buttons will move over to make room for the new button. (Be careful here—buttons will move to the right, so you can't see them on the screen unless you scroll the toolbar.)

While the Customize dialog box is open, you can modify all the command bars. Drag menu items or buttons to new locations to rearrange them, or drop them in the document window to delete them. To add something other than a macro, scroll the Categories and Commands lists until you find the command you want. Drag the command onto a menu or toolbar. If you mess things up completely, you can always select and reset the menu bar and the toolbars on the Toolbars page of the Customize dialog box.

To create an entirely new toolbar, click the New button on the Toolbar page. Drag any buttons you wish onto the toolbar from the Commands list. To copy a button from an existing toolbar, hold Ctrl while dragging the button.

Changing Command Settings

After you've placed your button or menu item, right-click on the item to open the shortcut menu. In Word and PowerPoint, the button or menu item is attached to the macro you dragged to the command bar. In Excel, you must assign the macro. Choose Assign Macro from the bottom of the menu, and the familiar Macro dialog box opens. Select the macro you want to assign from the list, and then click OK.

Changing Command Bar Item Options   The default toolbar button picture is the yellow smiley face. With the Customize dialog box open, right-click on a button and choose Change Button Image to open a menu of icons you can assign to a command item.

If you prefer, you can label the button or menu item by changing the contents of the Name box on the shortcut menu. The ampersand (&) is used on menu items and appears before the letter that a user can press to choose the menu item. The letter will be underlined on the menu bar like the F in File and E in Edit.

SKILL
13

You can also create your own button images. While you are still in the Customize mode, select the button, right-click to get the shortcut menu, and then choose Edit Button Image to open the Button Editor.

When you are finished adding menu items, assigning macros, and sprucing up your button images, close the Customize dialog box. Now, you can play the macro by clicking a toolbar button or making a menu selection. To remove a button or menu item, reopen the Customize dialog box and drag the item off the menu or toolbar.

ADDING A MACRO TO A MENU OR COMMAND BUTTON

1. If the macro is not global, open the document that contains the macro.

2. Right-click on any toolbar and choose Customize. Click the Commands tab.

3. Choose Macros from the Categories list.

4. In Word or PowerPoint, drag the macro onto a toolbar or menu, then close the Customize dialog box.

–OR–

continued ▶

4. In Excel, drag Custom Menu Item or Custom Button from the Commands List to the toolbar or menu and drop it in the desired location.

5. Right-click on the new item and select Assign Macro from the shortcut menu.

6. Choose the macro from the Macro dialog box.

7. Click OK to assign the macro to the button, then close the Customize dialog box.

SKILL
13

Deleting Macros

You can delete a macro in two ways. If you have recorded a macro and are not pleased with the way it executes, you can record the macro again, using the same name. You will be asked if you want to overwrite (delete) the existing macro. You can also choose Tools ➤ Macro ➤ Macros, select the macro from the macro list, and click the Delete button to delete the macro from the template. If you delete a macro that has a command bar item, you also need to remove the macro's button from the toolbar.

You can copy macro modules from one workbook to another, add pauses for user input or the insertion of specific information, and otherwise customize macros. When you have mastered the information in this skill and want to learn more, choose Help ➤ Contents and Index from the menu bar and enter **macro** in the Index to find more information.

Hands On

1. In Word or Excel, record a global macro that checks the spelling in the active document and then sends the document to the printer. Name the macro SpellPrint. Add it to the Standard toolbar and test it.

2. In Word or Excel, record a global macro that:

    a) Opens the Page Setup dialog box.

    b) Inserts a header with your name and the current date.

    c) Sets all four margins at 1 inch.

Name the macro StandardPageSetup. Execute the macro to see that it works the way you designed it.

3. In PowerPoint, create a macro that prints the current outline.

4. In any Excel workbook, create individual macros to complete the tasks below. Create your own macro names. When all macros are recorded, create a new toolbar and add all the macros to the toolbar.

   a) Create a macro to format a range of cells for currency, no decimal places, Arial 12-point, dark blue.

   b) Record a macro that creates a header that includes "All rights reserved, *your company name* (or *your name*)," and the current date.

   c) Record a macro to change the paper orientation to landscape.

5. In Word, create a macro that turns table gridlines off. Add the macro to a toolbar button.

Are You Experienced?

Now you can...

☑ **Create a macro to automate a frequently performed task**

☑ **Play back a macro**

☑ **Assign macros or other functions to the toolbars in Office 2000**

Index

Note to the Reader: Page numbers in **bold** indicate the principal discussion of a topic or the definition of a term. Page numbers in *italic* indicate illustrations.

Numbers and Symbols

A

B

C

D

F

U

Y

ESSENTIAL SKILLS

for the
ESSENTIAL TOPICS

WINDOWS 98
NO EXPERIENCE REQUIRED

ISBN 0-7821-2128-4
$24.99; 544 pages

OFFICE 2000
NO EXPERIENCE REQUIRED

ISBN 0-7821-2293-0
$24.99; 704 pages

THE INTERNET
NO EXPERIENCE REQUIRED

ISBN: 0-7821-2385-6
$19.99; 496 pages

LOTUS NOTES 5
NO EXPERIENCE REQUIRED

ISBN: 0-7821-2184-5
$24.99; 560 pages

WORD 2000
NO EXPERIENCE REQUIRED

ISBN 0-7821-2400-3
$19.99; 452 pages

OUTLOOK 2000
NO EXPERIENCE REQUIRED

ISBN 0-7821-2483-6
$19.99; 400 pages

ACCESS 2000
NO EXPERIENCE REQUIRED

ISBN 0-7821-2485-2
$24.99; 608 pages

EXCEL 2000
NO EXPERIENCE REQUIRED

ISBN 0-7821-2374-0
$19.99; 432 pages

FRONTPAGE 2000
NO EXPERIENCE REQUIRED

ISBN 0-7821-2482-8
$19.99; 400 pages

SYBEX
www.sybex.com